INSTRUCTOR'S MANUAL
WITH TEST BANK FOR EGAN'S

The Skilled Helper

Helper

SEVENTH EDITION

David E. Reagan   Janet E. Reagan

BROOKS/COLE

™

THOMSON LEARNING

Australia • Canada • Mexico • Singapore • Spain • United Kingdom • United States

BROOKS/COLE

THOMSON LEARNING

Contents

Chapter   **Page**

1	Introduction to Helping	1
2	Overview of the Helping Model	38
3	The Helping Relationship: Values in Action	73
4	Introduction to Communications and the Skill of Visibly Tuning in to Clients	114
5	Active Listening: The Foundations of Understanding	136
6	Sharing Empathic Highlights: Communicating and Checking Understanding	169
7	The Art of Probing and Summarizing	202
8	Step I-A: Helping Clients Tell Their Stories "What Are my Concerns?"	227
9	Reluctant and Resistant Clients	260
10	Step I-B: I. The Nature of Challenging	285
11	Step I-B: II. Specific Challenging Skills	314
12	Step I-B: III. The Wisdom of Challenging	340
13	Step I-C: Leverage: Helping Clients to Work on the Right Things	359
14	Introduction to Stage II: Helping Clients Identify, Choose and Shape Goals…	383
15	Step II-A: "What Do I Need and Want?" Possibilities for a Better Future	413
16	Step II-B: "What Do I Really Want?" Moving From Possibilities to Choices	447
17	Step II-C: Commitment: "What Am I Willing To Pay for What I Want?"	475
18	Step II-A: Action Strategies: "How Many Ways Are There to Get What I Need and Want?"	502
19	Step III-B: Best Fit Strategies: "What Strategies Are Best for Me?"	524
20	Step III-C: Helping Clients Make Plans: "What Kind of Plan Will Help Me Get What I Need and Want?"	545
21	"How Will I Make It All Happen?" Helping Clients Get What They Want and Need	576
	TESTBANKS	612

Chapter One:

Introduction to Helping

	Pages
Chapter Outline	**2 - 3**
Detailed Lecture Notes	**4 - 15**
Lecture Enhancers	**16-18**
Class Activities	**19-20**
Videos	**21**
Websites	**22**
Transparencies	**23-37**

CHAPTER ONE OUTLINE

LAYING THE GROUNDWORK

1. FORMAL AND INFORMAL HELPERS - A VERY BRIEF HISTORY.

2. WHAT HELPING IS ABOUT:

   a. Clients with Problem Situations and Unused Resources and Opportunities.

       (1). Problem Situations

       (2). Missed Opportunities and Unused Potential

3. POSITIVE PSYCHOLOGY AND HELPING.

4. THE TWO PRINCIPAL GOALS OF HELPING:

   a. Helping Clients Manage Problem Situations and Develop Opportunities:

       (1). The Importance of Results.

       (2). A Results-Focused Case (The Case of Martha).

   b. Helping Clients Learn and Use the Helping Model in Everyday Life.

5. DOES HELPING HELP?

       a. What Evidence Is There for the Effectiveness of Helping?

       b. What Do Clients Think?

       c. What About Efficacy Studies and Treatment Manuals?

       d. Are There Good Helpers and Bad Helpers?

       e. What Are We To Conclude?

6. WHAT THIS BOOK IS - AND WHAT IT IS NOT:

       a. A Practical Model of Helping.

       b. Not the Whole Curriculum.

7. MOVING FROM THE SMART TO WISE - MANAGING THE SHADOW SIDE OF HELPING:

       a. The Downside: The Messiness of Helping.

       b. The Upside: Common Sense and Wisdom in the Helping Professions.

Detailed Lecture Notes

(Please note: The designation OH in the detailed lecture notes indicates an overhead transparency is available. Please locate the overhead transparencies in the final section of each chapter in this Instructors' Manual.)

Chapter 1:
INTRODUCTION TO HELPING

Section One: FORMAL AND INFORMAL HELPERS - A VERY BRIEF HISTORY

1. Throughout history there has been a deeply embedded conviction that, under the proper conditions, some people are capable of helping others come to grips with problems in living.

    A. Helping is done differently in different cultures, but is a cross-cultural phenomenon.

    B. Today we have formal helping professions: **(OH-1)**

            1. Counselors   2. Psychiatrists
            3. Psychologists   4. Social Workers
            5. Ministers

    C. We also have informal helpers who often deal with people in times of crisis:

            1. Organizational Consultants   2. Dentists
            3. Doctors   4. Lawyers
            5. Nurses   6. Probation Officers
            7. Teachers   8. Managers
            9. Supervisors   10. Police Officers

    D. Most help on a daily basis comes from the informal helpers.

    E. A study has shown that more than a quarter of Americans have at one time or another felt they were headed for serious psychological help.

(1). Most of these individuals sought help from informal social supports such as friends and relatives. (Swindle, Heller, Pescosolido, & Kikuzawa, 2000)

F. In the end, of course, all of us must learn how to help ourselves cope with problems and crises in life.

(1). Training in both solving one's problems and helping others solve theirs should be as common as training in reading, writing, and math. Unfortunately, this is not the case.

Section Two: WHAT HELPING IS ABOUT: (OH-2)

1. To determine what helping is about, it is useful to consider (1) why people seek - or are sent to get - help in the first place and (2) what the principal goals of the helping process are.

A. Problem Situations: A Common Starting Point for Helping.

(1). Clients come for help because of problems they are not handling well or they feel they are not living fully: therefore, we refer to clients' problems as "problem situations" and not just as "problems". Problem situations and unused opportunities constitute the starting point of the helping process.

(2). Problem Situations: The complex and messy problems in living that clients don't know how to handle or they feel they do not have the resources needed to cope with the problems. Problem situations are often poorly defined.

(3). Problem Situations arise in our interactions with ourselves, with others, and the social settings, organizations, and institutions of life (e.g., self doubt, serious illness, failing marriages, uncertainty and job loss in the "new economy").

(4). The Case of Martha S.: Age 58, loss of son, job loss, husband's death, financial concerns, and no close family. Support from many quarters: new found solidarity with her family, church support group, minister, and informal chats with psychologist who provided direction for the church support.

(5). Important to note that none of Martha's help "solved" the problems of loss she had experienced. The goal of helping is not to "solve" problems but to help the person with "problem situations" learn to manage the problem situations more effectively or even transcend them by taking advantage of new possibilities in life.

(6). Jones, Rasmussen, and Moffit (1997) see problem solving as an opportunity for learning. The problem situation is a stimulus to learning.

(a). Jones, Rasmussen, and Moffit, although they focus on educational systems, the kind of "engaged learning" they discuss can take place in the helper-client relationship.

(b). What is learned in the give-and-take of helping sessions is first applied to the current "problem situation" and then can be applied to both sorting out other problems in relationships and to preventing problems from arising in the first place.

B. Missed Opportunities and Unused Potential: A Second Starting Point for Helping.

(1). Some clients come not because of major problems but because they believe they are not living as fully as they would like to be.

(2). Therefore, clients' missed opportunities and unused potential constitute a second starting point for helping.

(3). People feel trapped in dead-end jobs, bland marriages, or guilty because they are failing to live up to their own values, ideals, and potential.

(4). In this case, it is a question not of what is going wrong but of what could be better. It has often been suggested that most of us use only a small fraction of our potential.

(5). The case of Carol: Job burnout, berating herself for not being dedicated enough.

(a). The counselor helped her explore what she did enjoy (e.g., asked to help other mental health centers that were experiencing problems) and helped her look at solutions (e.g., enrolling in an organizational development program to be a human-service organizations consultant.)

(b). With Carol, the counselor helped her manage her problems (burn out, guilt) by helping her explore and develop an opportunity (a new career).

Section Three: POSITIVE PSYCHOLOGY AND HELPING: (OH-3)

1. Helping clients identify and develop unused potential and opportunities can be called a "positive psychology" goal.

2. Seligman and Csikszentmihalyi (2000) call for a better balance of perspectives in the helping professions. In their minds, too much attention is focused on pathology and too little on what they call "positive psychology":

"Our message is to remind our field that psychology is not just the study of pathology, weakness, and damage; it is also the study of strength and virtue. Treatment is not just fixing what is broken; it is nurturing what is best" (p. 7)

Positive Psychology includes such upbeat topics as: **(OH-4)**

1. subjective well-being, happiness, hope, and optimism;
2. the capacity for love, forgiveness, nurturance, altruism
3. courage, perseverance, moderation
4. a civic sense
5. spirituality, wisdom

3. Seligman and Csikszentmihalyi suggest counselors would better serve their clients if they would weave the spirit of the preceding topics into their interactions with them.

4. Seeing problem management as life enhancing learning and treating all encounters with clients as opportunity-development sessions are part of the positive psychology approach.

Section Four: THE TWO PRINCIPAL GOALS OF HELPING: (OH-5)

1. The goals of helping should be based on the needs of clients.

2. Positive psychology offers us an overall foundation or quality-of-life goal for all clients - subjective well-being (SWB) or happiness (Diener, 2000; Myers, 2000, Robbins & Kliewer, 2000).

3. Clients come to helpers because they are unhappy with one or more aspects of their lives.

4. Diener points out that scientific knowledge of SWB is both possible and desirable, but that the psychological community does not appear to take it seriously.

5. The two basic counselling goals: one relating to clients' managing specific problems in living more effectively or developing unused opportunities; the other goal relating to their general ability to manage problems and develop problems in everyday life. Both goals are related to increasing clients' happiness.

A. **GOAL ONE: Help clients manage their problems in living more effectively and develop unused or underused resources and opportunities more fully.**

(1). Helpers are successful to the degree which their clients are in a better position to manage specific problem situations and developed unused resources and opportunities more effectively. It is important to note that the success of the helper is based on the degree to which the client is better positioned to take action: in the end, clients can choose to live more effectively or not.

(2). Related to Goal One is that helping is about results, outcomes, accomplishments, and impact. Over the years this has become such a strong orientation that what has developed is "solution-focused" therapy (O'Hanlon & Weiner-Davis, 1989; Manthei, 1998; Rowan, O'Hanlon & O'Hanlon, 1999).

(3). Helping is an "-ing" word: it includes a series of activities in which helpers and clients engage. However, they only have value to the degree that they lead to valued outcomes in client's lives (e.g., unreasonable fears disappear or diminish, self-confidence replaces self-doubt, a woman and man breathe new life into their marriage.)

(4). The case of Andrea (Driscoll, 1984, p. 64) From being mistreated to outcomes of a sense of worth and self-confidence, more assertive, reduction of resentment and of being a passive victim. The helper interaction led to valued outcomes not just "good sessions" with the counselor.

(5). The focus on outcomes is also greatly influenced by the economics of third-party payees who demand meaningful treatment plans and the delivery of problem-managing outcomes (Meier & Letsch, 2000).

B. **GOAL TWO: Help clients become better at helping themselves in their everyday lives.**

(1). Clients are often poor problem solvers or whatever problem-solving ability they have tends to disappear in times of crisis.

(2). Individuals in our society are not educated to manage problem living and are equally poor in identifying and developing opportunities and unused resources.

(3). Although this book is about a process helpers can use to help clients, more fundamentally, it is about a problem management and opportunity development process that clients can use to help themselves - to become better decision makers, and more responsible "agents of change" in their own lives.

Section Five: DOES HELPING HELP? (OH-6)

1. Does Helping Help? has been an ongoing debate ever since Eysenck (1952) questioned the usefulness of psychotherapy.

2. The ongoing debate has questioned the legitimacy of helping professions themselves, even claiming that helping is a fraudulent process, a manipulative and

malicious enterprise (see, for example Cowen, 1982; Eysenck, 1984, 1994; Masson, 1988). Masson went so far as to assert that in the United States, helping is a multibillion-dollar business that does no more than profit from people's misery. He also maintained that devaluing people is part and parcel of all therapy and that the helper's values and needs are inevitably imposed on the client.

3. These claim's are extreme, yet they should not be dismissed out of hand. What they say may be true of some forms of helping and some helpers.

4. On the other hand, we have yet come up with an unqualified yes to the questions: Does Helping Help? The debates regarding: Does Helping Help? rages on. Any good psychology search engine will provide numerous web locations that will provide an in depth discussion. Select your search engine and enter such terms as the effectiveness of psychotherapy, psychotherapy outcomes, customer satisfaction with psychotherapy, treatment efficacy studies, and manualized treatments. One such web location is www.talkingcure.com and is the home page for the Institute for the Study of Therapeutic Change.

5. The evidence for the effectiveness of helping:

   a. There is a long history of outcome research. Hill and Corbett (1993) and Whiston and Sexton (1993) provide reviews that cover 50-year periods.

   b. There is a great deal of evidence showing that different kinds of helping, including counselling (Lambert & Cattani-Thompson, 1996), does help many people in many different situations.

   c. One sign of the maturing of the helping profession is the fact that the Surgeon General of the United States has issued the first-ever report on mental health (see Satcher, 2000 for an executive overview). In the report there are four major findings:

   (1). Mental health is fundamental to physical or overall health.

   (2). Mental disorders are real health conditions.

   (3). The efficacy of mental health treatments are well documented.

   (4). A range of treatments exists for most mental disorders.

   d. Meta-analysis - a kind of study of studies and a reinterpretation of their findings - has been a powerful tool in demonstrating that helping helps (see Smith, Glass, Miller, 1980; Lipsy & Wilson, 1993).

   e. Still, doubt exists. Many outcome studies are done in the artificial setting of the lab under lablike conditions. Real helping does not take place in a lab (see

Henggeler, Schoenwald, & Pickrel, 1995; Weisz, Donenberg, Han, & Weiss, 1995). Additionally, meta-analysis, the major tool used in efficacy studies, has come under criticism (Matt & Navarro, 1997).

6. What do clients think about the helping they have received?

a. Consumer Reports (1994; 1995) published results that included:

(1). clients believed that they had benefited very substantially from psychotherapy;

(2). psychotherapy alone did not differ in effectiveness plus medication;

(3). no specific form of helping did better than any other for any particular kind of problem;

(4). psychiatrists, psychologists, and social workers did not differ in their effectiveness as helpers;

(5). long term treatment produced appreciably better results than did short term treatment;

(6). clients whose choice of helper or length of therapy was limited by insurance or managed-care systems did not benefit as much as clients without those restrictions.

b. The Consumer Reports Study provided good support, but the Consumer Report Study has received a great deal of criticism on both theoretical and methodological grounds (Brock, Green, & Reich, 1998).

c. Additionally, it has been demonstrated that client satisfaction does not always mean that problems are managed and opportunities developed (Pekarik & Wolff, 1996; Pekarik & Guidry, 1999). Clients might be satisfied because they like their counselors or because they feel less stressed. It does not necessarily mean they are managing problem situations or developing opportunities any better.

7. What about efficacy studies and treatment manuals? Efficacy studies focus on the usefulness of a specific methodology for a particular kind of problem - for example, a cognitive therapy for panic disorders. These studies been have carried out under carefully controlled conditions (see Luborsky, 1993; Seligman, 1995). Over the years these studies have led to "empirically supported" (ESTs) or "empirically validated treatments" (EVTs) (Nathan, 1998; Waeher, Kalodner, Wampold, & Lichtenberg, 2000).

a. Treatments that have proved to be robust have been "manualized." That is, a manual on how to deliver the treatment for a particular kind of client is written for practitioners. Manuals have been written for anxiety, phobias, depression, personality disorders, PTSD, and substance abuse to name a few.

b. There is a great deal of controversy over manualized treatments. Some findings (Najavits, Weiss, Shaw, & Dierberger, 2000) indicated a very positive view of manuals, extensive use, and few concerns. Other studies (see Soldz & McCullough, 2000; Waddington, 1997) report that manuals ignore the role of the therapist as model of adult living, the place of art and clinical judgment is demeaned or ignored, and manual treatments are often highly specialized, cumbersome, time consuming, expensive, and not user friendly.

c. Another concern of manuals is that they focus on problems and not on the development of opportunities that should be one of the principal forms of helping. Still, if you intend to become a professional helper, keep you eye on developments in manualized treatments. They are not going to go away (Foxhall, 2000).

8. Are there good helpers and bad helpers? Yes. There is some evidence that therapy sometimes not only does not help but also actually makes things worse (see Mohr, 1995, and Strupp, Hadley, & Gomes-Schwartz, 1977, for reviews of the negative-outcome literature).

9. Research shows that some of the factors associated with negative outcomes in helping are associated with clients, others with helpers. Sometimes clients who have severe interpersonal problems and severe symptomatology, who are poorly motivated, or who expect helping to be painless become more dysfunctional through therapy.

10. Helpers who underestimate the severity of clients' problems, experience interpersonal difficulties with clients, use poor techniques, overuse any given technique, or disagree with clients over helping methodology can make things worse rather than better.

11. Luborsky and his associates (1986) note the following:

a. There are considerable differences between therapists in their average success rates.

b. There is considerable variability in outcome within the caseload of individual therapists.

c. Variations in success rates typically have more to do with the therapist than with the type of treatment.

12. Although helping can and often does work, there is plenty of evidence that ineffective helping also abounds. Yet, common sense tells us that some forms of helping actually help in the hands of good helpers.

13. It is important that we all:

a. appreciate the complexity of the helping process

b. acquaint ourselves with the issues involved in evaluating the outcomes of helping

c. appreciate that, poorly done, helping can actually harm others

d. make ourselves reasonably cautious as a helper, and

e. motivate ourselves to become a high-level helper, learning and using practical models, methods, skills, and guidelines for helping.

14. Therefore, become competent, don't over promise, remain professionally self-critical, keep your eyes on results - that is, problem managing and opportunity-developing outcomes for clients, and do not confuse difficult cases with impossible cases.

Unit Six: Is Helping For Everyone? (OH-8)

1. Just because helping, for the most part, does work doesn't mean it is for everyone. Most people muddle through without professional help.

2. Just because a person might benefit from counselling doesn't mean that he or she "needs" counselling. Many clients can "get better" in a variety of ways.

3. Working with clients who don't want to deal with their issues is a waste of time and money. It doesn't hurt to try, but a helper most know when to quit.

4. Be cognizant that helping is an expensive proposition, whether paid for by the individual or if covered by tax dollars or insurance premiums. Get to the point in your helping. Do not assume you have a client for life.

Unit Seven: What This Book Is - And What It Is Not: (OH-9)

1. There is danger in a book being viewed as the single source of knowledge for an entire field. *The Skilled Helper* is not and cannot be "all that you've ever wanted to know about helping."

2. *The Skilled Helper* is designed to enable helpers to engage in activities that will help their clients manage their lives more effectively. It is also a model helpers can teach their clients so that clients can manage their lives better on their own.

3. *The Skilled Helper* is not a total curriculum. A complete curriculum would include the following plus more:

    a. applied developmental psychology

    b. cognitive psychology

    c. principles of human behavior

    d. applied personality theory

    e. abnormal psychology

    f. principles of social psychology

    g. an understanding diversity of age, race, ethnicity, religion, sexual orientation, culture, social standing, and economic standing

    h. an understanding of the needs of special populations such as persons with physical disabilities, substance abusers, and the homeless.

    i. an understanding of the dynamics of the helping professions themselves as they are currently practiced in our society.

4. It is important to note that although paraprofessionals and informal helpers do not go through such a rigorous and comprehensive curriculum studies have demonstrated that paraprofessional helpers can be just as effective as professional helpers and in some cases even more helpful (Durlak, 1979; Hattie, Sharpley, & Rogers, 1984).

Unit Eight: Managing The Shadow Side Of Helping (OH-10)

1. The model of helping outlined in the text is rational, linear, and systematic. The world is often irrational, nonlinear, and chaotic? Effective helpers understand the limitations not only of helping models but also of helpers, the helping profession, clients,

and the environments that the affect the helping process. These limitations are often identified as the "shadow side" of life:

All those things that adversely affect the helping relationship, process, outcomes, and impact in substantive ways but that are not identified and explored by helper or client or even the profession itself make up the "shadow side" of the helping.

2. Helping models are flawed, helpers are sometimes selfish, lazy, and even predatory, and they are prone to burnout. Clients are sometimes selfish, lazy, and predatory even in the helping relationship. It is important to be cognizant of the following realities:

a. Some helpers are not very committed even though they are in a profession that demands high commitment.

b. Clients often play games with themselves, their helpers, and the helping process.

c. Clients have their blind spots that keep them mired down in their problems, and helpers also have theirs.

d. Managing the shadow side is an exercise in integrity, social intelligence, and competence, not in cynicism.

3. Helping models demand common sense and wisdom. **(OH-11)** Part of the positive-psychology approach to helping involves a focus on such things as wisdom, sagacity, street smarts, practical intelligence, and common sense in helping (Baltes & Staudinger, 2000; and Sternberg, Wagner, & Horvath, 1995).

4. What characterizes wisdom? Here are some possibilities (see Sternberg, 1990, 1998): **OH-12, 13**

a. self-knowledge, maturity

b. knowledge of life's obligations and goals

c. an understanding of cultural conditions

d. the guts to admit mistakes and the sense to learn from them

e. an insight into human interactions

f. the ability to understand the meaning of events

g. tolerance of ambiguity and the ability to work with it

h. "meta-thinking" or the ability to think about thinking

i. the ability to take the long view of problems

j. the refusal to let experience create blind spots

k. an understanding of the spiritual dimensions in life

5. Wisdom is about excellence in living. As such, it focuses on knowing "how" (the procedural dimension) rather than merely knowing "what" (the factual dimension). **OH-14**

6. It is important to understand that the shadow side of helping can provide benefits. The shadow side of helping is a kind of "noise" in the system. For example, in the helping profession noise in the guise of the debate around what makes helping both effective and efficient can ultimately benefit the clients.

7. *The Skilled Helper* is unabashedly upbeat. However, helpers must ignore the less palatable dimensions of the helping professions, including the less palatable dimensions of themselves. The shadow side of helping will be brought up throughout the book to remind us of the importance of dealing with both sides of the helping model.

8. Wise helpers are idealistic without being naïve; they see the journey "from smart to wise" as a never ending one.

You should be able to find the full text of the following items in your library or by using your web-based library access tool of choice (e.g., PsycINFO, EBCoHOst).

Item One: Hope

Hope as a Common Factor Across Psychotherapy Approaches: A Lesson from the Dodo's Verdict.

Snyder, C.R., & Taylor, J.D. (2000). Hope as a common factor across psychotherapy approaches: A lesson from the dodo's verdict. In Snyder, C.R. (Ed.); et al. (2000) Handbook of hope: Theory, measures, and applications. (pp. 89 - 108). San Diego, Ca, US: Academic Press, Inc.

Synopsis: This chapter by Snyder and Taylor nicely explores the issue of which mechanisms underlie the efficacy of various approaches to psychological interventions. The authors focus on the role of hope and through use of meta-analytic studies and conclude: "Overall, using examples of therapeutic approaches from cognitive-behavioral to psychoanalytic to Gestalt, we have argued that specific psychotherapeutic intervention techniques bolster pathways thinking, an important component of hope."

Item Two: Optimism

Accentuating the Positive - A Positive Path of Study: The Popularity of Optimism Research has sold some Scholars on Focusing Less on Misery, More on Joy.

Monmaney, T. (2000) Accentuating the Positive - A Positive Path of Study: The Popularity of Optimism Research Has Sold Some Scholars on Focusing Less on Misery, More on Joy. Vancouver Sun, January 8, 2000, Final Edition, p. A9.

Synopsis: The author cites dozens of recent studies "that optimists do better than pessimists in work, school, sports, suffer less depression, achieve more goals, respond better to stress, wage more effective battles against disease and live longer." The author then proceeds to explain that: "The popularity of optimism research has convinced some scholars that psychology should focus less on misery and more on why things go right."

After a discussion of optimism, the author concludes with: "This view has its critics. A false sense of security can be dangerous when it comes to taking physical risks, says Neil Weinstein, a psychologist at Rutgers University. Epidemics of sexually transmitted diseases, for example, are fueled in part by people who make overly optimistic assumptions abut their sexual partners, he said, 'You can think of many instances in which people's underestimation of risk can get them into serious trouble.'"

Item Three:

A Psychometric Validation of Treatment Effects

Kolden, G. G., et al., (2000) The Therapeutic Realizations Scale-Revised (TRS-R): Psychometric characteristics and relationship to treatment process and outcome. Journal of Clinical Psychology. Sep. Vol 56(9): 1207-1220.

Synopsis: This is an excellent article to show your students how a psychometric instrument can be used to study "session-level effects." The article reports on a study of ninety-five psychotherapy patients (ages 18 to 34) to show the value of the TRS-R in the treatment process and outcome from the perspective of the patient and therapist. The TRS-R is reported to be a "reliable and valid multidimensional index of session-level treatment effects."

Item Four: Templeton Positive Psychology Prize Largest in Psychology

APA News Release
Date: May 2, 1999

"NEW PROGRAM SEEKS TO PROMOTE A SCIENCE OF HUMAN STRENGTHS

Templeton Positive Psychology Prize Largest in Psychology

WASHINGTON — The American Psychological Association (APA), with underwriting support from the John Templeton Foundation (JTF), has created a new program designed to promote the advancement of the new science of positive psychology. The Templeton Positive Psychology Prize will be awarded annually and will include the largest monetary prize ever given in the field of psychology. The Templeton Positive Psychology Prize (TPPP) is intended to encourage first-rate mid-career scientists to devote their best efforts to positive psychology topics such as goal-focused living, self-control, future-mindedness, optimism, persistence, work-ethic, thrift, courage and moral identity. "The program will recognize and encourage the best, brightest and most visionary amongst the rising generation of young researchers who share a vision for transforming their discipline toward a science of the best things in life," said program director Martin E. P. Seligman, Ph.D., professor of psychology at the University of Pennsylvania and the immediate past President of APA.

Up to four awards will be given annually. The First Place Award totals $100,000 which is divided as a prize of $30,000 to be used any way the recipient chooses, and a grant of $70,000 to support research in the positive psychology field. The Second Place Award totals $50,000, which includes a prize of $15,000 and a grant of $35,000; the Third Place Award totals $30,000, which includes a prize of $10,000 and a grant of $20,000; and the Fourth Place Award totals $20,000, which includes a prize of $7,500 and a grant of $12,500."

For current information check the APA Home Page . Search . Site Map.

Class Activities

In addition to the exercises in the Workbook that accompanies this text, you may find the following in-class activities to be of value:

Activity # 1: Why Are You Here: To Help or Be Helped?

Quite often students enroll in a counselling course to look for help with their own life issues. I find it helpful to have an icebreaker activity to determine why students are in the class. The activity is simple and can take as little as fifteen minutes or as much as a full hour.

Have each student take a piece of paper and spend five minutes listing all of the reasons he or she is taking the course. Ask your students to be as creative as possible and to list as many reasons as they can think of in the five minutes. Next, have the students go through their lists and identify which of their reasons are professional/career related and which are related to personal issues. Have the students place a "C" next to all professional/career related items and a "P" next to all personal issues.

Have the students pair off or work in triads to share their reasons for wanting to take the course. You may opt to have the student groups report out to the entire class and you or a student volunteer can record reasons for being in the class on the board. It will be quite revealing to find out how many students are here for predominately professional/career reasons versus how many are here for personal issues. You may also want to collect the student responses and take them back to your office for a quick perusal to see why students are taking your class. You may opt to start your next class period by ensuring students know the direction you plan to take the course and which of their professional/career and personal issues will not be addressed in the class. Activity #2 that follows is a nice continuation of this activity.

Activity #2: Setting Limits on Self-Disclosure

You may find it helpful to have an activity of setting limits on self-disclosure. It is not unusual for students in a counselling course who have had horrific experiences in their lives to want to share these experiences with the class (e.g., incest, rape, drug addiction, non-sexual physical abuse, divorce, etc.). You may want to set some limits on self-disclosure early in the term.

I have found it helpful to have the class agree to the types of self-disclosure and the amount of disclosure they are willing to accept as a class. It is effective to have the class form groups of three or four students and set some rules for self-disclosure. Have

Websites

1. www.talkingcure.com
    This is the homepage for the Institute for the Study of Therapeutic Change. This is an excellent site for discussions on the effectiveness of counselling. Make certain you get to "Baloney Watch": go to the website, click on News and Reviews, and then click on "Baloney Watch".

2. www.apa.org
    The homepage of the American Psychological Association.

3. www.cpa.ca
    The homepage of the Canadian Psychological Association.

4. www.counseling.org
    The homepage of the American Counseling Association.

5. www.counselingNetwork.com/
    The homepage for the World Counseling Network.

6. www.nbcc.org
    The homepage for the National Board for Certified Counselors

7. www.mhhe.com/catalogs/0070556113.mhtml
    A website dedicated to the social psychology of helping and altruism

8. www.Lemoyne.edu/OTRP/otrpresources/helping-online.html
    A website that provides a student guide to careers in the helping professions.

9. www.uni-konstanz.de/ag-moral/helpers.htm
    A website that asks the question: Are helpers always moral?

Overhead Transparencies

Starting on the next page are copies of recommended overhead transparencies. Please feel free to convert the following pages to overheads as this will enhance the lecture portion of your class presentation.

Formal Helping Professions:

1. Counselors   2. Psychiatrists
3. Psychologists   4. Social Workers
    5. Ministers

Informal Helpers:

1. Organizational Consultants
2. Dentists
3. Doctors
4. Lawyers
5. Nurses
6. Probation Officers
7. Teachers
8. Managers
9. Supervisors
10. Police Officers

OH 1

WHAT HELPING IS ABOUT:

A. Problem Situations:

A Common Starting Point for Helping.

B. Missed Opportunities and Unused Potential:

A Second Starting Point for Helping.

OH 2

POSITIVE PSYCHOLOGY AND HELPING:

"Our message is to remind our field that psychology is not just the study of pathology, weakness, and damage; it is also the study of strength and virtue. Treatment is not just fixing what is broken; it is nurturing what is best"

Seligman and Csikszentmihalyi (2000, p.7)

OH 3

Positive Psychology includes such upbeat topics as:

1. subjective well-being, happiness, hope, and optimism;

2. the capacity for love, forgiveness, nurturance, altruism

3. courage, perseverance, moderation

4. a civic sense

5. spirituality, wisdom

OH 4

THE TWO PRINCIPAL GOALS OF HELPING:

GOAL ONE:
Help clients manage their problems in living more effectively and develop unused or underused resources and opportunities more fully.

GOAL TWO:
Help clients become better at helping themselves in their everyday lives.

DOES HELPING HELP?

Masson went so far as to assert that in the United States, helping is a multibillion-dollar business that does no more than profit from people's misery. He also maintained that devaluing people is part and parcel of all therapy and that the helper's values and needs are inevitably imposed on the client.

OH 6

Surgeon General of the United States issued the first-ever report on mental health.

In the report there are four major findings:

(1). Mental health is fundamental to physical or overall health.

(2). Mental disorders are real health conditions.

(3). The efficacy of mental health treatments are well documented.

(4). A range of treatments exists for most mental disorders.

(See Satcher, 2000 for an Executive Overview).

OH 7

Is Helping For Everyone?

1. Just because helping, for the most part, does work doesn't mean it is for everyone. Most people muddle through without professional help.

2. Just because a person might benefit from counselling doesn't mean that he or she "needs" counselling. Many clients can "get better" in a variety of ways.

3. Working with clients who don't want to deal with their issues is a waste of time and money. It doesn't hurt to try, but a helper most know when to quit.

4. Be cognizant that helping is an expensive proposition, whether paid for by the individual or if covered by tax dollars or insurance premiums. Get to the point in your helping. Do not assume you have a client for life.

OH 8

What This Book Is - And What It Is Not:

1. There is danger in a book being viewed as the single source of knowledge for an entire field. *The Skilled Helper* is not and cannot be "all that you've ever wanted to know about helping."

2. *The Skilled Helper* is designed to enable helpers to engage in activities that will help their clients manage their lives more effectively. It is also a model helpers can teach their clients so that clients can manage their lives better on their own.

3. *The Skilled Helper* is not a total curriculum.

OH 9

The Shadow Side Of Helping

All those things that adversely affect the helping relationship, process, outcomes, and impact in substantive ways but that are not identified and explored by helper or client or even the profession itself make up the
"shadow side" of the helping.

Helping models are flawed, helpers are sometimes selfish, lazy, and even predatory, and they are prone to burnout. Clients are sometimes selfish, lazy, and predatory even in the helping relationship.

OH 10

Helping Models Demand Common Sense and Wisdom.

Part of the positive-psychology approach to helping involves a focus on such things as wisdom, sagacity, street smarts, practical intelligence, and common sense in helping

(Baltes & Staudinger, 2000; and Sternberg, Wagner, & Horvath, 1995).

OH 11

What Characterizes Wisdom?

a. self-knowledge, maturity

b. knowledge of life's obligations and goals

c. an understanding of cultural conditions

d. the guts to admit mistakes and the sense to learn from them

e. an insight into human interactions

f. the ability to understand the meaning of events

g. tolerance of ambiguity and the ability to work with it

OH 12

What Characterizes Wisdom? (continued)

h. "meta-thinking" or the ability to think about thinking

i. the ability to take the long view of problems

j. the refusal to let experience create blind spots

k. an understanding of the spiritual dimensions in life

OH 13

WISDOM

Wisdom is about excellence in living. As such, it focuses on knowing "how" (the procedural dimension) rather than merely knowing "what" (the factual dimension).

Wise helpers are idealistic without being naïve; they see the journey "from smart to wise" as a never ending one.

OH 14

Chapter Two:

Overview of the Helping Model

	Pages
Chapter Outline	**39**
Detailed Lecture Notes	**40-56**
Lecture Enhancers	**57-58**
Class Activities	**59-60**
Videos	**61**
Websites	**62**
Transparencies	**63-72**

OVERVIEW OF THE HELPING MODEL

RATIONAL PROBLEM SOLVING AND ITS LIMITATIONS

THE SKILLED-HELPER MODEL

THE STAGES AND STEPS OF THE HELPING MODEL

STAGE I: "WHAT'S GOING ON?"

➢ Clarification of the Key Issues Calling for Change
➢ The Three "Steps" of Stage I

STAGE II: "WHAT DOES SUCCESS LOOK LIKE?"

➢ Helping Clients Determine Solutions: Goals, Accomplishments, Impact
➢ The Three "Steps" of Stage II

STAGE III: "HOW DO I GET WHAT I NEED AND WANT?"

➢ Helping Clients Develop Strategies for Accomplishing Goals
➢ The Three "Steps" of Stage III

THE ACTION ARROW ☐ "HOW DO I GET RESULTS?" ☐ HELPING CLIENTS IMPLEMENT PLANS

"HOW ARE WE DOING?" ☐ ONGOING EVALUATION OF THE HELPING PROCESS

FLEXIBILITY IN THE USE OF THE MODEL

BRIEF THERAPY AND A "HOLOGRAM" APPROACH TO HELPING

USING THE MODEL AS A "BROWSER": THE SEARCH FOR BEST PRACTICE

UNDERSTANDING AND DEALING WITH THE SHADOW SIDE OF HELPING MODELS

(Please note: The designation OH in the detailed lecture notes indicates an overhead transparency is available. Please locate the overhead transparencies in the final section of each chapter in this Instructors' Manual.)

Chapter 2:
OVERVIEW OF THE HELPING MODEL

Section One: RATIONAL PROBLEM SOLVING AND ITS LIMITATIONS

1. The problem-solving process is often described as a more or less straightforward natural and rational process of decision making. Yankelovich (1992) offered a seven-step process. Applied to helping, it looks something like this: **(OH-1)**

   i)   **Initial awareness**, clients become aware of an issue or a set of issues.

   ii)   **Urgency**, a sense of urgency develops, especially as the underlying problem situation.

   iii) **Initial search for remedies**, clients begin to look for remedies and the parties may try out one more of these remedies without evaluating their cost or consequences.

   iv)   **Estimation of costs.** The costs of pursuing different remedies begin to become apparent. At this point clients often back away from dealing with the problem situation directly because there is no cost-free or painless way of dealing with it.

   v)   **Deliberation**, since the problem situation does not go away, it is impossible to retreat completely. And so a more serious weighing of choices takes place. Often, a kind of dialogue goes on in the client's mind between steps iv) and v).

   vi)   **Rational decision**, an intellectual decision is made to accept some choice and pursue a certain course of action.

vii) **Rational-emotional decision**. A merely intellectual decision is often not enough to drive action. So the heart joins the head, as it were, in the decision. Decisions driven by emotion and convictions are more likely to be translated into action.

2. Four things should be noted in the problem-management opportunity-development process.

> First, these steps, however logically sequenced on paper, are often jumbled and intermingled in real-life problem-management situations.

> Second, this natural process can be derailed at almost any point along the way. For instance, uncontrolled emotions spill out and make a bad situation worse. Or the costs of managing the problem seem too high and so the process itself is put on the back burner.

> Third, decision making in difficult situations is seldom as rational as this process suggests. Indeed, some see decision making as a journey as complex as life itself (Scott, 2000).

> Fourth, this natural process often lacks a method for turning decisions into solution-focused action.

3. The problem-management and opportunity-development process outlined in this chapter and developed in the rest of the book borrows from this natural process, complements it with other steps and techniques, suggests ways of helping clients turn decisions into action, focuses on solutions, that is, life-enhancing outcomes, provides ways of challenging backsliding, and, at its best, speeds up the entire process.

Section Two: THE SKILLED-HELPER MODEL

A PROBLEM-MANAGEMENT/OPPORTUNITY-DEVELOPMENT APPROACH TO HELPING

1. Common sense suggests that problem-solving models, techniques, and skills are important for all of us, since all of us must grapple daily with problems in living of greater or lesser severity. Yet review the curricula of our primary, secondary, and tertiary schools, and you will find little about problem solving that focuses on problems in living. Some say that formal courses in problem-solving skills are not found in our schools because such skills are picked up through experience. To a

certain extent, that's true. A problem-solving mentality should be second nature to us. The world may be the laboratory for problem solving, but the skills needed to optimize learning in this lab should be taught. They are too important to be left to chance.

2. Helping professions. In the 1980s it was estimated that there were between 250-400 different approaches to helping (see Herink, 1980; Karasu, 1986). Some of the approaches discussed then have, of course, fallen by the wayside, but many more have been added since. All are proposed with equal seriousness and all of which to lead to success. In the face of all this diversity, helpers, especially beginning helpers, need a basic, practical, working model of helping.

3. Since all approaches must eventually help clients manage problems and develop unused resources, the model of choice in these pages:

   a. is a flexible, humanistic, broadly based problem-management and opportunity-development model

   b. is straightforward without ignoring the complexities of clients' lives or of the helping process itself.

   c. provides an excellent foundation for any "brand" of helping you eventually choose.

   d. recognizes that a problem-management model in counseling and therapy has the advantage of the vast amount of research that has been done on the problem-solving process itself. The model, techniques, and skills outlined in this book tap that research base.

Section Three: THE STAGES AND STEPS OF THEHELPING MODEL (OH-2)

1. All worthwhile helping frameworks, models, or processes ultimately help clients ask and answer for themselves four fundamental questions:
   (1). **What's Going On?** What are the problems, issues, concerns, or **undeveloped** opportunities I should be working on? This is the *present state*.
   (2). **What Do I Need or Want?** What do I want my life to look like? What changes would make me happier? This is the *preferred state*.
   (3). **What Do I Have To Do To Get What I Need Or Want?** What plan will get me where I want to go? The plan outlines the *remedial actions* to be taken.
   (4). **How Do I Get Results**? How do I turn planning and goal setting into *solutions, results, outcomes*, or *accomplishments?* How do I get going and stay going?

2. These four questions, turned into four logical "stages" in Figure 2-1, provide the basic framework for the helping process. In practice the four stages overlap and interact with one another as clients struggle to manage problems and develop opportunities.

3. An extended example is used to bring this process to life and illustrates ways in which one client was helped to ask and answer the four fundamental questions outlined above. The client, Carlos, is voluntary, verbal, and, for the most part, cooperative. In actual practice, cases do not always flow as easily as this one. The simplification of the case, however, will help you see the main features of the helping process in action.

Section 4: STAGE I: "WHAT'S GOING ON?"

A. CLARIFICATION OF THE KEY ISSUES CALLING FOR CHANGE

1. The present state spells out the range of difficulties the client is facing. What are the problems, issues, concerns, and undeveloped opportunities with which Carlos needs to grapple?

2. The Case of Carlos, in his mid-twenties, working for a consulting firm for about a year, well-educated, bright, though practical rather than academic intelligence is his strong suit, quite personable when he wants to, but he doesn't always want to. Feedback from his colleagues that "you're your own worst enemy. You're headed for a fall and don't even know it." While he certainly doesn't think that he needs help, he is unsettled enough to be willing to talk with someone.

The Three "Steps" of Stage I (OH-3)

Each "stage" is divided into three "steps." Like the stages themselves, the steps are not steps in a mechanistic, "now do this" sense. The steps, like the stages, are interactive. In Stage I they are activities that help clients develop answers to two questions: What's going on in my life? What should I work on?

Step I-A: Help clients tell their *stories*. Though helping is ultimately about solutions, some review of the problem or unused opportunity is called for.

1. Carlos's counselor, helps him tell his story. Through their dialogue, she helps him review what is happening in the workplace. Elena knows that if she can help Carlos get an undistorted picture of himself, his problems, and his unused opportunities, he will have a better chance of doing something about them. Her overall goal is to help Carlos manage the interpersonal dimensions of his work life better. His interpersonal style is both problem and opportunity.

2. Carlos feels that he is being discriminated against at work and he doesn't feel that he's on the fast track and he thinks that he should be. People at work don't understand and appreciate him and he feels distant from his family. He and his girl friend are currently at odds.

Step I-B: Help clients break through *blind spots* **that prevent them from seeing themselves, their problem situations, and their unused opportunities as they really are**. Counselors add great value when they can help their clients identify significant blind spots related to their problems and unused opportunities. Effectively challenged, blind spots yield to new perspectives that help clients think more realistic about problems, opportunities, and solutions.

1. Carlos tends to blame others for his problems. He does not realize how self-centered he is. He gets angry when others stand in his way or don't cater to his needs and wants. Yet he is quite insensitive to anybody else's needs. His arrogant style rubs both colleagues and customers the wrong way.

2. Without being brutal, Elena helps him see himself as others see him.

Step I-C: Help clients choose the *right* **problems and/or opportunities to work on.** If clients have a range of issues, help them gain *leverage* by working things that will make a difference. If a client wants to work only on trivial things or does not want to work at all, then it might be better to defer counseling.

1. Carlos becomes more cooperative as it becomes clear to him that Elena has both his interests and those of the firm in mind.

2. He comes to realize that he had better work on his interpersonal communication style and his relationships with both colleagues and clients.

3. He also needs to do something about the "victim" mentality he has developed.

4. He quickly sees that becoming a better communicator and relationship builder will help him in every social setting in life.

Section Five: STAGE II: "WHAT DOES SUCCESS LOOK LIKE?"

A. Helping Clients Determine Outcomes: Goals, Accomplishments, Impact

1. In Stage II the counselors help clients explore and choose possibilities for a better future ☐ a future in which key problem situations are managed and key opportunities developed. "What do you want this future to look like?" asks the helper. The client's answer constitute his or her "change agenda."

2. Stage II focuses on outcomes by asking such questions as: What do I want? What do I need, whether I currently want it or not? What would my business life look like if it were more tolerable or ☐ even better ☐ more engaging and fulfilling?

3. Unfortunately, some approaches to problem solving or management skip Stage II. They move from the "What's wrong?" stage (Stage I) to a "What do I do about it?" stage (Stage III). Helping clients discover what they want has a profound impact on the entire helping process.

B: The Three Steps of Stage II (OH-4)

Stage II also has three steps □ that is, three ways of helping clients answer as creatively as possible the question "What do I need and want?"

Step II-A: Help clients use their imaginations to spell out *possibilities for a better future*. This often helps clients move beyond the problem-and-misery mind-set they bring with them and develop a sense of hope. Brainstorming possibilities for a better future can also help clients understand their problem situations better □ "Now that I am beginning to know what I want, I can see my problems and unused opportunities more clearly."

1. Elena helps Carlos brainstorm goals that would help him repair some damaged relationships with both colleagues and clients and help him do something about his victim mentality.

2. Carlos declares that he needs to become a "better communicator." Elena, pointing out that "becoming a better communicator" is a rather vague aspiration, asks him, "What do some of the good communicators you know look like?"

3. Carlos comes up with a range of possibilities.

4. All of these become possibilities for a better communication style.

5. She also gets him to explore further possibilities by asking him what a "repaired relationship" would look like both from his perspective and from the perspective of customers and colleagues he might have alienated.

Step II-B: Help clients choose *realistic and challenging goals* **that are real solutions to the key problems and unused opportunities identified in Stage I**. Possibilities need to be turned into goals because helping is about solutions and outcomes.

1. A client's goals constitute his or her *agenda for change*.

2. Goals need to be clear, related to the problems and unused opportunities the client has chosen to work on, substantive, realistic, prudent, sustainable, flexible, consistent with the client's values, and set in a reasonable time frame.

3. Effective counselors help clients "shape" their agendas to meet these requirements.

4. It becomes clear that changes in his interpersonal communication style would help him manage some problems and develop some opportunities at the same time. But he needs more than skills. He needs to change his self-centered and poor-me attitude.

5. Becoming a better communicator with upbeat interpersonal relationship values and attitudes is a substantial package. It includes Carlos's becoming good at the give-and-take of dialogue and the skills that make it work. These skills include visibly tuning in to others, active listening, thoughtfully processing what he hears, demonstrating understanding of the key points others are making, getting his own points across clearly, drawing others into the conversation, and the like. It also includes embracing the values that make conversations serve relationships □ mutual respect, social sensitivity, emotional control, and collaboration.

Step II-C: Help clients find the *incentives* that will help them *commit* themselves to their change agendas. The question clients must ask themselves is: "What am I willing to pay for what I need and want?"

1. Without strong commitment, change agendas end up as no more than some "nice ideas." Counselors provide an important service when they help clients test their commitment to the better future embedded in the goals they choose.

2. Elena helps him review the incentives he has for engaging in such work. His current interpersonal communication style will probably get him fired and prevent him from being successful in the future.

3. Developing the values that should permeate dialogue is even harder work. It means undoing bad habits developed over years. Undoing bad habits is difficult even when a client is committed to doing so.

4. Elena does not dwell on Carlos's bad habits. Rather she believes that embracing good habits like showing interest in others and checking his understanding of what they have to say will drive out his bad habits. Since communication is at the heart of everything he does, better communication skills and values will serve him well in every dimension of life.

Section Six: STAGE III: "HOW DO I GET WHAT I NEED AND WANT?"

1. Helping Clients Develop Strategies for Accomplishing Goals

Stage III defines the actions that clients need to be take in order to translate goals into problem-managing accomplishments. Stage II answer the question: "How do I get there." It is about identifying and choosing action strategies and plans.

2. The Three "Steps" of Stage III (OH-5)

Stage III, too, has three steps that, in practice, intermingle with one another and with the steps of the other stages.

Step III-A: Possible actions. Help clients see that there are many different ways of achieving their goals. Stimulating clients to think of different ways of achieving their goals is usually an excellent investment of time. That said, clients should not leap into action. Hasty and disorganized action is often self-defeating.

1. Elena helps Carlos explore different ways of becoming the "competent communicator" he wants to be.

2. In order to develop the skills he needs he can read books, take courses at local colleges, attend courses for professionals, get a tutor or coach, or come up with his own approach to developing the skills and attitudes he needs.

3. Elena helps Carlos brainstorm the possibilities and points out where he can get more information, but then let's him do his homework.

Step III-B: Choosing best-fit strategies. Step III-B helps clients choose the action strategies that best fit their talents, resources, style, temperament, environment, and timetable.

1. With Elena's help Carlos chooses to attend an interpersonal-communication program for working professionals. While more expensive than university-based programs, there is greater flexibility. This fits better with Carlos's rather hectic travel schedule.

2. Elena helps Carlos see that life is his lab. That is, every conversation is part of the program because every conversation is an opportunity to practice the skills he will be learning and demonstrating the attitudes that foster relationship building.

3. Carlos decides to get a peer coach □ a colleague that has both an excellent communication style and excellent relationships with both colleagues and clients. He says to his colleague: "Be honest with me. Tell me the way it is."

Step III-C: Crafting a plan. Help clients organize the actions they need to take to accomplish their goals. Plans are simply maps clients use to get where they want to go. A plan can be quite simple. Indeed, overly sophisticated plans are often self-defeating.

1. Carlos's plan is straightforward.

2. He will begin the interpersonal-communication course within two weeks.

3. He will use every conversation with colleagues and clients as his lab. At the end of each working day he will review the conversations he has had in terms of both skillfulness and values.

4. He creates a checklist for himself that includes such questions as "How effectively did I listen? How clearly did I get my points across? How

5. respectful and collaborative was I? How did I handle sensitive conversations such as those with colleagues and clients who had been turned off by my interpersonal style?"

6. Time and schedules willing, he will meet with his peer coach once a week and with Elena once a month.

Section Seven: STAGE IV: THE ACTION ARROW "HOW DO I GET RESULTS?" (OH-6)

Helping Clients Implement Their Plans

All three stages of the helping model sit on the "action arrow," indicating that clients need to act in their own behalf right from the beginning of the helping process. Stages I, II, and III are about planning for change, not constructive change itself. Planning is not action. Each stage and step of the process can promote problem-managing and opportunity-developing action right from the beginning. Carlos, like most clients, runs into a number of obstacles as he tries to implement his plan.

1. First of all, his travel schedule keeps conflicting with even the flexible communication-skills program in which he has enrolled. He decides to use a tutor from the program to bring him up to speed whenever he cannot fit a session into his travel schedule.

2. He also finds that he is not very consistent in using the skills he is learning in the "lab of life." So in one of his discussions with Elena, he reviews the ups and downs of his program, and discusses his discouragement how slowly some of his disenchanted colleagues are warming up to him. He uses the discussion to reset the program.

3. He agrees to see her for a half hour every other week. This provides him with an incentive to keep to the program. He wants to give her a good report.

4. He resets his schedule so he can get together with his peer coach.

5. His sessions with both Elena and his peer coach help and he does make progress.

6. Figure 2-2 presents the full model in all its stages and steps and their relationship to the action arrow. It includes two-way arrows between both stages and steps to suggest the kind of flexibility needed to make the process work.

Section Eight: "HOW ARE WE DOING?"

ONGOING EVALUATION OF THE HELPING PROCESS

In psychological research there has been a long history of what are called N=1 designs both to evaluate practice and conduct research. (Blampied, 2000; Hilliard, 1993; Lundervold & Belwood, 2000; Persons, 1991; Valsiner, 1986). What's the difference if we know that helping in general "works" if we do not know that it is working in this case.

1. In many helping models, evaluation is presented as the last step in the model. However, if evaluation occurs only at the end, it is too late. As Mash and Hunsley (1993) noted, early detection of what is going wrong in the helping process is needed to prevent failure. They claimed that an early-detection framework should be theory-based, ongoing, practical, and sensitive to whatever new perspectives might emerge from the helping process.

2. Elena works with Carlos in using the helping model as the evaluation framework. Carlos comes to appreciate Elena's skill in using the model.

3. Once Carlos takes ongoing evaluation seriously, he begins to make progress. The ultimate feedback comes from goal accomplishment.

   a) In what ways and to what degree is he becoming a more competent communicator?

   b) How effectively are relationships with clients and colleagues being repaired?

   c) To what degree is he shedding his self-centered approach to relationships that contribute to his "others are out to get me" attitude?

Section Nine: FLEXIBILITY IN THE USE OF THE MODEL (OH-7)

There are many reasons why you need to use the helping model flexibly. The main one is this: helping is for the client. Clients' needs take precedence over any model. That said, a number of points about flexibility need to be made.

1. Clients start and proceed differently. Any stage or step of the helping process can be the entry point. For instance,

   a) Client A might start with something that he tried to do to solve a problem but that did not work. The starting point is a failed strategy.

   b) Client B might start with what she believes she wants but does not have. Stage II is her entry point.

   c) Client C might start with the roots of his problem situation. Stage I is the entry point.

   d) Client D might announce that she really has no problems but is still vaguely dissatisfied with her life. The implication here is that she has not been seizing the kind of opportunities that could make her happy. Opportunity rather than problem is the starting point.

2. Clients engage in each stage and step of the model differently.

   a) Some clients spill out their stories all at once.

   b) Others "leak" bits and pieces of their story throughout the helping process.

   c) Still others tell only those parts that put them in a good light.

   d) Most clients talk about problems rather than opportunities.

   e) Since clients do not always present all their problems at once in neat packages, it is impossible to work through Stage I completely before moving on to Stages II, III, and IV. It is not even advisable to do so.

   f) Some clients don't even understand their problems until they begin talking about what they want but don't have.

   g) Some clients need to engage in some kind of remedial action before they can adequately define the problem situation. That is, action sometimes precedes understanding. If some supposedly problem-solving action is not successful, then the counselor helps the client learn from it and return to the tasks of clarifying the problem or opportunity and then setting some realistic goals.

   h) The case of Woody, a sophomore in college, came to the student counseling services with a variety of interpersonal and somatic complaints. After exploring this with the counselor he had gone out with a few women, but the chemistry never seemed right. Then he did meet someone he liked quite a bit but was ultimately rejected for being too preoccupied with himself. He and the counselor took another look at his social life. This time, however, he had some experiences to probe. Woody put into practice Weick's (1979) dictum that chaotic action is sometimes preferable to orderly inactivity. Once he acted, he learned a few things about himself. Some of these learnings proved to be painful, but he now had a better chance of examining his interpersonal style much more concretely.

3. Since the stages and steps of the model intermingle, helpers will often find themselves moving back and forth in the model. Often two or more steps or even two stages of the process merge into one another. For instance:

   a). Clients can name parts of a problem situation, set goals, and develop strategies to achieve them in the same session. New and more substantial concerns arise while goals are being set, and the process moves back to an earlier, exploratory stage. Helping is seldom a linear event.

   b). Your challenge is to make sense of clients' entry points and guide them through whatever stage or step that will help move toward problem-managing and opportunity-developing action.

   c). In addition to flexibility, focus and direction in helping are also essential. Letting clients wander around in the morass of problem situations under the guise of flexibility leads nowhere.

   d). The structure of the helping model the underlying "system" that keeps helping from being a set of random events. It is like a map that helps you know, at any given moment, "where you are" with clients and what kinds of interventions would be most useful.

   e). The stages and steps of the model are orientation devices. At its best, it is a *shared* map that helps clients participate more fully in the helping process. They, too, need to know where they are going.

Section Ten: BRIEF THERAPY AND A "HOLOGRAM" APPROACH TO HELPING (OH-8)

A. How long does therapy take? How long is a piece of string? I have known people who were in therapy most of their lives. Others need only once session to reset some area of their lives. Over the past decade there has been growing interest in "brief therapies" or what Nick and Janet Cummings (2000) call "time-sensitive" psychotherapies.

1. There is a growing body of evidence that time-sensitive psychotherapies are effective with a large number of patients, perhaps as many as 85% of all those seen in the usual practice (Austad, 1996; Budman & Steenbarger, 1997; Cummings, Pallak, & Cummings, 1996; Hoyt, 1993), but it is not advocated that all psychotherapy be brief psychotherapy.

2. Miller (1996), an outspoken critic of short-term therapy, begrudgingly concedes that there is a place for time-sensitive psychotherapies and that psychotherapists of the future must be trained in both short-term and long-term interventions to know when to use one or the other (p. 44).

3. They advocate "clinically determined" therapy rather than therapy determined by the economic needs of either clinicians or managed-care enterprises.

4. Effective and efficient helping (Cummings, Budman, & Thomas (1998) rather than the length of helping should remain center stage.

5. Although the whole helping process can take days, weeks, months, or even years, it can also take place, literally, within minutes.

6. The case of Lara, a social worker in a tough urban neighborhood, gets a call from a local minister who says that a teenager who fears for his life because of neighborhood gang activity needs to see someone. She sees the boy, listens to his concerns, feels his anxiety.

   a.) Lara realizes that his anxiety stems from a recent shooting that had nothing to do with him directly.

   b.) She talks with him to get some idea what his daily comings and goings are like. It is soon clear that he is not the kind of person who courts trouble (Stage I).
   c.) She then talks him through the kinds of prudent things he needs to do to avoid trouble "in a neighborhood like ours" and in their dialogue points out that he is doing most of those things (Stage II).

   d.) She gently challenges his false perception that the recent shooting somehow involved him directly. All of this helps allay his fears. But he discovers there are a couple of things he needs to do differently like having "good" friends and not letting himself be a lone target on the streets (Stage III).

e.) She also points out that he is more likely to be hit by lightning than a stray bullet. The boy calms down as he begins to realize that in many ways his life is in his own hands.

7. Lara listens to the boy's immediate concerns and elicits from him a picture of what his daily life in the community looks like (Stage I). Realizing that he needs some relief from his anxiety (Stage II), she "talks him down." Through their dialogue the boy learns some things he can do to assure his safety (Stage III). She also helps his dispel a couple of blind spots, that is, that he is an immediate target of gang activity and that he is in imminent danger of being hit by a stray bullet.

8. Even if you have only have only one meeting with a client, it would be a mistake to assume that only Stage-I things could happen.

9. Preston, Varzos, and Liebert (1995) have written a manual for clients who are in or are considering going into brief therapy.

B. Helping can be "lean and mean" and still be fully human.

1. A colleague of mine experimented, quite successfully, with shortening the counseling "hour." He arrived at the point where he would begin a session by saying, "We have five minutes together. Let's see what we can get done." He was very respectful, and it was amazing how much he and his clients could get done in a short time.

2. The helping industry is focusing more and more on results-oriented brief psychotherapy. But even if that were not the case, helpers would still owe their clients value for money. Helping that achieves only partial results may, at times, be the best that we can do.

C. Helpers would do well to develop a "whole-process" mentality about helping.

1. Any part of any stage or step can be invoked at any time in any session if it proves beneficial for the client.

2. Think of the helping process as a hologram. The helping model is more like a hologram than a tool kit □ it works best when the whole is found in each of its parts.

3. The hologram is at the center of effective brief therapy.

Section Eleven: USING THE MODEL AS A "BROWSER": THE SEARCH FOR BEST PRACTICE (OH-9)

The claim in this book is this: Problem management and opportunity development is one of the principal processes □ perhaps the principal process □ underlying all successful counseling and psychotherapy. What is the novice to do in face of the bewildering array of models and methods available to them? Even though there is only a handful of "major brands" of psychotherapy (see Capauzzi & Gross, 1999; Corey, 1996; Gilliland & James, 1997; Prochaska & Norcross, 2000; Sharf, 1996, 1999; Wachtel & Messer, 1997), choices need to be made.

A. **Eclecticism.** Many experienced helpers, even when they choose one specific school or approach to helping, often borrow methods and techniques from other approaches. This borrowing and stitching is called "eclecticism" (Jensen, Bergin, & Greaves, 1990; Lazarus, Beutler, & Norcross, 1992; Prochaska & Norcross, 2000). In one study, some 40% of helpers said that eclecticism was their primary approach to helping (Milan, Montgomery, & Rogers, 1994). There must be some integrating framework to give coherence to the entire process; that is, to be effective, eclecticism must be systematic.

B. **Problem-management as underlying process**. When any school, model, or eclectic mixture is successful, it is so precisely because it helps clients:

1. Identify and explore problem situations and unused opportunities,

2. Determine what they need and want.

3. Discover ways of getting what they need and want

4. Translate what they learn into problem-managing action.

C. **The "browser" approach**. The helping model in this book can also be used as a tool □ a "browser," to use an internet term □ for mining, organizing, and evaluating concepts and techniques that work for clients, no matter what their origin.

1. **Mining.** Helpers can use the problem-management model to mine any given school or approach, "digging out" whatever is useful without having to accept everything that is offered. The stages and steps of the model serve as tools for identifying methods and techniques that will serve the needs of clients.

2. **Organizing.** Since the problem-management model is organized by stages and steps, it can be used to organize the methods and techniques that have been mined from the rich literature on helping. For instance, a number of contemporary therapies have elaborated excellent techniques for helping clients identify blind spots and develop new perspectives on the problem

situations they face.

3. **Evaluating.** Since the problem-management model is pragmatic and focuses on outcomes of helping, it can be used to evaluate the vast number of helping techniques that are constantly being devised. The model enables helpers to ask in what way a technique or method contributes to the "bottom line," that is, to outcomes that serve the needs of clients.

Section Twelve: UNDERSTANDING AND DEALING WITH THE SHADOW SIDE OF HELPING MODELS (OH-10)

Besides the broad shadow-side themes mentioned in Chapter 1, there are a number of shadow-side pitfalls in the use of any helping model.

A. **No model.** Some helpers "wing it."

1. They have no consistent, integrated model that has a track record of benefiting clients.

2. If helpers-to-be leave professional training programs knowing a great deal about different approaches but lacking an integrated approach for themselves, then they need to develop one quickly.

B. **Fads.** The helping professions are not immune to fads.

1. A fad need not be something new; it can be the "rediscovery" of a truth or a technique that has not found its proper place in the helping tool kit.
2. Note them and integrate them into a comprehensive approach to your clients. Don't ignore them, but take the claims with a grain of salt and test the approach.

C. **Rigid applications of helping models**.

1. Some helpers buy into a model early on and then ignore subsequent challenges or alterations to the model. The "purity" of the model becomes more important than the needs of clients.

2. Other helpers, especially beginners, apply a useful helping model too rigidly. They drag clients in a linear way through the model even though that is not what clients need. All of this adds up to excessive control.

3. Effective models effectively used are liberating rather than controlling

D. **Virtuosity.** A third form of ineptness is virtuosity.

1. Some helpers tend to specialize in certain techniques and skills □ exploring the past, assessment, goal setting, probing, challenging, and the like.

2. Helpers who specialize not only run the risk of ignoring client needs but also often are not very effective even in their chosen specialties. For example, the counselor whose specialty is challenging clients is often an ineffective challenger.

3. Challenge must be based on understanding.

The antidote to all this is simple. Helpers need to become radically client-centered. Client-centered helping means that the needs of the client, not the models and methods of the helper, constitute the starting point and guide for helping. Therefore, flexibility is essential. In the end, helping is about solutions, results, outcomes, and impact rather than process. The values that drive client-centered helping are reviewed in Chapter 3.

You should be able to find the full text of the following items in your library or by using your web-based library access tool of choice (e.g., PsycInfo).

Item One: Positive Psychotherapy
Positive psychotherapy: Effectiveness of an interdisciplinary approach.

Tritt,-Karin; Loew,-Thomas-H.; Meyer,-Martin; Werner,-Birgit; Peseschkian,-Nossrat;   European-Journal-of-Psychiatry. 1999 Oct-Dec; Vol 13(4): 231-242, 1999

Synopsis: Positive Psychotherapy (PPT) is a short-term psychotherapy with a focus on transcultural issues of psychology. It is currently used in more than fourteen countries. In one longitudinal study,   use of PPT with patients captured an important reduction of symptoms as well as improved feelings and behavior when compared to a control group where no significant changes were observed. These results are an indication of the lasting effect of the value of PPT.

Item Two: The Importance of Hope

The meaning of Easter: Hope & Strength: Psychologists learn how people with a high level of hope are much happier in life

Alan Bavley; Knight Ridder Newspapers, Calgary Herald, April 22, 2000, Final Edition, p.O10 / FRONT

Synopsis: According to University of Kansas psychologist Rick Snyder, hope is the best indicator of success in life whether it is athletic accomplishment, achievement in school, or career success. "It's a powerful force in our lives," Snyder said, "and I sort of stumbled onto it." Snyder who has conducted years of research on the topic of hopefulness in studies involving more than 10,000 people, has found hope to be the constant in individuals who feel most positive about their accomplishments and optimistic about their futures.

Hope is an one of the best indicators of success rather it be excelling athletic competition or overcoming an eating disorder. Snyder's work compliments the positive psychology work being done by many other psychological researchers.

Item Three:Tap into the power of negative thinking

Erica Goode, Edmonton Journal, August 20, 2000, Final

Synopsis: Dr. Barbara Held, a clinical psychologist at Bowdoin College in Brunswick, Maine, has a different take than those who are always accuentating the positive. Held's concerns are echoed in the work of James Pennebaker, a professor of psychology at the University of Texas at Austin, whose focus is on "constructive negativity." The concern of an increasing number of psychologists is that those who don't live up to the standards of always being "positive" and looking at the bright side of the bad things that happen in life can become depressed because they cannot meet the unrealistic and unreasonable goal of being positive all the time. There may be merit to experiencing the full range of emotions and not always trying to be positive.

Class Activities

In addition to the exercises in the Workbook that accompanies this text, you may find the following in-class activities to be of value:

Activity #1: The Art of Being Positive

In this activity your goal is to have students portray positive events in an artistic fashion. Provide groups of three or four students with poster paper and colored marking pens and ask them to capture on paper and with colour symbols that represent positive images in our world (e.g., the smiley face, the shining sun) and then have the students explain why the images represent happiness and positive feelings. Follow-up with a discussion of the power of positive images and how positive images can remind us of the importance of being positive.

Activity #2: The Shadow Side of the Bright Side

In this activity have students discuss in groups of three or four how always trying to be positive can mask important feelings such as anger, depression and uncertainty. Have the students list at least five situations where making feelings can only make the client's situation worse and not better.

As a continuation of the activity, have the students think of ways that not feeling positive may make a person feel worse because they are not living up to the standards of a positive world.

Activity #3: Lemonade

Have students work individually first and then in pairs to share the results and then move to a class discussion asking the pairs to report out examples from their work. Step one is to have each student list at least three issues in their life that are not going as well as he or she would like at this time. Next, have the individual student think of at least two things that could change his or her attitude about what they have just listed as being negative. When the students work in pairs have them share their issues and the things that could change their attitudes about the negative issue in their lives. Have the pairs support and challenge each other by asking for clarification or adding to the list of things that could improve the situation. Next, have the students report to the full class as you or a student record responses on the board or flipchart paper. At the conclusion of the activity do a group scan to see how many of the solutions to feeling negative are material in nature and how many are within an individual's control and how many are not within an individual's control. The discussion should wrap up with key points around internal versus external sources of happiness.

Videos

Discovering Psychology, Part 22: Psychotherapy (1990, 30 min., ANN/CPB). Use footage from actual therapy sessions students can view cognitive, behavioral, humanistic, psychodynamic, and biomedical treatments for mental health cases.

Meanings of Madness: The Medicine Men (25 min, PENN). A discussion of medical approaches to mental illness and how medical approaches impact treatment.

Three Approaches to Psychotherapy, 6 parts/30-45 minutes each. (Psychological Films, Inc.) The work of Rogers, Meichenbaum, Beck and Perls are covered.

Rational Emotive Therapy, 30 min (Research Press). Rational Emotive Therapy is discussed by Albert Ellis

Don't Make Me Laugh (FAN, 45 min., VHS, #QA-233) Comedian Spike Milligan shares techniques from cognitive behavioral therapy to manage depression.

Fatal Attraction (1987, Paramount Home Video, 120 min). An excellent video to generate discussion about the positive and negative aspects of making decisions and living with the consequences.

Websites

1. www.psychwatch.com/counsel_journals.htm
   Links to over thirty-five counselling journals.

2. www.humankinetics.com
   The sport psychologist website.

3. www.plenum.com/title.cgi?2011
   The American Journal of Community Psychology

4. http://web.spectra.net/cgi-bin/haworth/
   The Journal of Divorce and Remarriage

5. http://selfworth.com/therapy.html
   Self Improvement Online

6. http://www.positiveparenting.com/index.html

7. www.keirsey.com
   A free test that is similar to the Myers-Briggs Inventory.

Overhead Transparencies

Starting on the next page are copies of recommended overhead transparencies. Please feel free to convert the following pages to overheads as this will enhance the lecture portion of your class presentation.

The Problem Solving Process:

     i) Initial awareness

     ii) Urgency

     iii) Initial search for remedies.

     iv) Estimation of costs.

     v) Deliberation

     vi) Rational decision.

     vii)Rational-emotional decision.

OH 1

THE THREE STEPS OF STAGE TWO

1. Help clients use their imaginations to spell out *possibilities for a better future*.

2. Help clients choose *realistic and challenging goals* that are real solutions to the key problems and unused opportunities identified in Stage One.

3. Help clients find the *incentives* that will help them *commit* themselves to their change agendas.

OH 4

THE THREE STEPS OF STAGE THREE
"HOW DO I GET WHAT I NEED AND WANT?"

1. Possible actions.

2. Choosing best-fit strategies.

3. Crafting a plan.

OH 5

STAGE IV: THE ACTION STAGE FOUR:
THE ACTION ARROW
"HOW DO I GET RESULTS?"

1. Help Clients Implement Their Plans

2. Overcome Obstacles

3. Reset the Plan

4. Take Action

5. Monitor progress

6. Flexibility

OH 6

FLEXIBILITY IN THE USE OF THE MODEL

1. Clients start and proceed differently.

2. Clients engage in each stage and step of the model differently.

3. Helpers will often find themselves moving back and forth in the model.

OH 7

BRIEF THERAPY AND A "HOLOGRAM" APPROACH TO HELPING

1.   How long does therapy take?

2.   Helping can be "lean and mean" and still be fully human.

3. Develop a "whole-process" mentality about helping.

OH 8

THE SEARCH FOR BEST PRACTICE

1. Eclecticism.

2. Problem-management as underlying process.

3. The "browser" approach.

   a.) Mining

   b). Organizing

   c). Evaluating

OH 9

Chapter Three:

The Helping Relationship: Values in Action

	Pages
Chapter Outline	74
Detailed Lecture Notes	75-95
Lecture Enhancers	96-97
Class Activities	98-99
Videos	100
Websites	101
Transparencies	102-113

CHAPTER THREE OUTLINE

Chapter 3
THE HELPING RELATIONSHIP:
VALUES IN ACTION

THE HELPING RELATIONSHIP

THE WORKING ALLIANCE

VALUES IN ACTION

- ➢ Putting Values into the Broader Context of Culture
- ➢ The Importance and Practicality of Values in Helping

RESPECT AS THE FOUNDATION VALUE

EMPATHY AS THE ORIENTATION VALUE

- ➢ The Nature of Empathy
- ➢ Empathy —Understanding Clients As They Are: Diversity and Multiculturalism
- ➢ Guidelines Related to Diversity and Multiculturalism

GENUINENESS AS A PROFESSIONAL VALUE

CLIENT EMPOWERMENT AS THE OUTCOME VALUE

- Helping as a Social-Influence Process
- Norms for Empowerment and Self-Responsibility

A WORKING CHARTER: THE CLIENT-HELPER CONTRACT

SHADOW-SIDE REALITIES IN HELPING RELATIONSHIPS

Detailed Lecture Notes

(Please note: The designation OH in the detailed lecture notes indicates an overhead transparency is available. Please locate the overhead transparencies in the final section of each chapter in this Instructors' Manual.)

Section One: THE HELPING RELATIONSHIP (OH-1)

Although theoreticians, researchers, and practitioners alike, not to mention clients, agree that the relationship between client and helper is important, there are significant differences as to how this relationship is to be characterized and played out in the helping process (Gaston, Goldfried, Greenberg, Horvath, Raue, & Watson, 1995; Hill, 1994; Sexton & Whiston, 1994; Weinberger, 1995). Some stress the *relationship* itself (see Bailey, Wood, & Nava, 1992; Kahn, 1990; Kelly, 1994; Patterson, 1985), others highlight the *work* that is done through the relationship (Reandeau & Wampold, 1991), and still others focus on the *outcomes* to be achieved through the relationship (Horvath & Symonds, 1991).

A. The relationship itself.

1. Patterson (1985) made the relationship itself central to helping. At that time he claimed that counseling or psychotherapy does not merely involve an interpersonal relationship; rather, it *is* an interpersonal relationship.

2. Kelly (1994, 1997), in offering a humanistic model of counseling integration, argued that all counseling is distinctively human and fundamentally relational. Some traditional schools of psychotherapy indirectly emphasize the centrality of the helping relationship.

3. For instance, in psychoanalytic or psychodynamic approaches, "transference" —the complex and often unconscious interpersonal dynamics between helper and client that are rooted in the client's and even the helper's past —is central (Gelso, Hill, Mohr, Rochlen, & Zack, 1999; Gelso, Kivlighan, Wise, Jones, & Friedman, 1997; Hill & Nutt-Williams, 2000). Resolving these often murky dynamics is seen as intrinsic to successful therapeutic outcomes.

4. Schneider (1999), in discussing the treatment manuals mentioned in Chapter 1, claims that clients deserve the kind of relationship with their helpers through which human meaning, purpose, and values can be explored.

5. Carl Rogers (1951, 1957), one of the great pioneers in the field of counseling, emphasized the quality of the relationship in representing the humanistic-experiential approach to helping (see Kelly, 1994, 1997). Rogers claimed that the unconditional positive regard, accurate empathy, and genuineness offered by the helper and perceived by the client were both necessary and often sufficient for therapeutic progress. Through this highly empathic relationship counselors, in his eyes, helped clients understand themselves, liberate their resources, and manage their lives more effectively. Rogers's work spawned the widely discussed client-centered approach to helping (Rogers, 1965). Unlike psychodynamic approaches, however, the empathic helping relationship was considered a facilitative condition, not a "problem" in itself to be explored and resolved.

B. The relationship as a means to an end.

1. Others see the helping relationship as very important but still as a means to an end. In this view, a good relationship is practical because it enables client and counselor to do the work called for by whatever helping process is being used.

2. The relationship is instrumental in achieving the goals of the helping process. Practitioners using cognitive and behavioral approaches to helping, although sensitive to relationship issues (Arnkoff, 1995), tend toward the means-to-end view.

3. Overstressing the relationship is a mistake because it obscures the ultimate goal of helping: clients' managing this particular problem better. This goal won't be achieved if the relationship is poor, but if too much focus is placed on the relationship itself, both client and helper can be distracted from the real work to be done.

C. The relationship and outcomes.

1. Finally, some emphasize outcomes over both means and relationship. Practitioners from solution-focused approaches to helping fall in this category (de Shazer, 1985, 1994; Manthei, 1998; O'Hanlon & Weiner-Davis, 1989; Rowan, O'Hanlon, & O'Hanlon, 1999).

2. Solution-focused practitioners tend to focus, not on the relationships as end or means —though, if pushed, would see the relationships as a means —but on what clients need to do right away to begin to remedy the problem situations they face. In their eyes, spending a great deal of time exploring the exact character of the problem and its roots is a waste of time. Helping tends to be time limited. Therefore, "Let's get working on this right away" is part of the pragmatics of helping.

Section Two: THE RELATIONSHIP AS A WORKING ALLIANCE (OH-2)

The term working alliance, first coined by Greenson (1967) and now used by advocates of different schools of helping, can be used to bring together the best of the relationship-in-itself, relationship-as-means, and solution-focused approaches. Bordin (1979) defined the working alliance as the collaboration between the client and the helper based on their agreement on the goals and tasks of counseling. Although there is, predictably, considerable disagreement among practitioners as to what the critical dimensions of the working alliance are, how it operates, and what results it is to produce (see Hill & Nutt-Williams, 2000; Horvath, 2000; Weinberger, 1995), it is relatively simple to outline what it means in the context of the problem-management and opportunity-development process.

A. The collaborative nature of helping.

1. In the working alliance, helpers and clients are collaborators. Helping is not something that helpers do to clients; rather, it is a process that helpers and clients work through together. Helpers do not "cure" their patients.

2. Both have work to do in the problem-management and opportunity-development stages and steps, and both have responsibilities related to outcomes.

3. Outcomes depend on the competence and motivation of the helper, on the competence and motivation of the client, and on the quality of their interactions. Helping is a two-person team effort in which helpers need to do their part and clients theirs.

4. If either party refuses to play or plays incompetently, then the entire enterprise can fail.

B. The relationship as a forum for relearning.

1. Even though helpers don't cure their clients, the relationship itself can be therapeutic.

2. In the working alliance, the relationship itself is often a forum or a vehicle for social-emotional relearning (Mallinckrodt, 1996).

3. Effective helpers model attitudes and behavior that help clients challenge and change their own attitudes and behavior.

4. Furthermore, protected by the safety of the helping relationship, clients can experiment with different behaviors during the sessions themselves. The shy person can speak up, the reclusive person can open up, the aggressive person can back off, the overly sensitive person can ask to be challenged, and so forth.

5. These learnings can then be transferred to other social settings.

6. Needed changes in both attitudes and behavior often take place within the sessions themselves through the relationship.

C. Relationship flexibility.

1.   Different clients have different needs, and those needs are best met through different kinds of relationships and different modulations within the same relationship.

2. Effective helpers use a mix of styles, skills, and techniques tailored to the kind of relationship that is right for each client (Lazarus, 1993; Mahrer, 1993). And they remain themselves while they do so.

3. We should neither underestimate or overestimate the importance of the helping relationship. It certainly does contribute to outcomes, but in the end it is one among a number of key variables (Albano, 2000)

Section Three: VALUES IN ACTION (OH-3)

One of the best ways to characterize a helping relationship is through the values that should permeate and drive it. The relationship is the vehicle through which values come alive. Values, expressed concretely through working-alliance behaviors, play a critical role in the helping process (Bergin, 1991; Beutler & Bergan, 1991; Kerr & Erb, 1991; Norcross & Wogan, 1987; Vachon & Agresti, 1992). Since it has become increasingly clear that helpers' values influence clients' values over the course of the helping process, it is essential to build a value orientation into the process itself.

A. Putting Values into the Broader Context of Personal Culture

1. Values are central to culture, but culture is a wider reality. Shared beliefs and assumptions interact with shared values and produce shared norms that drive shared patterns of behavior.

2. This basic culture framework applied to an individual. It goes something like this:

    a). Over the course of life individuals develop *assumptions and beliefs* about themselves, other people, and the world around them. For instance, Isaiah, a client suffering from post traumatic stress disorder stemming from gang activity in his neighborhood and a brutal attack on his person, has come to believe that the world is a heartless place.

    b). *Values*, what people prize, are picked up or inculcated along the path of life. Isaiah, because of a number of ups and downs in his life, has come to value or prize personal security.

    c). Assumptions and beliefs, interacting with values, generate *norms*, the "dos and don'ts" we carry around inside ourselves. For Isaiah one of these is, "Don't trust people. You'll get hurt."

d). These norms drive *patterns of behavior* and these patterns of behavior constitute, as it were, the *bottom line* of personal or individual culture —"the way I live my life." For Isaiah this means not taking chances with people. He's a loner.

3. Effective helpers come to understand the personal cultures of clients and the impact these individual cultures have both in everyday life and in helping sessions. Of course, since no individual is an island, personal cultures do not develop in a vacuum.

4. The beliefs, values, and norms people develop are greatly influenced by their environments.

5. Culture is usually not applied to individuals but rather to societies, institutions, companies, professions, groups, and families. In this case, *shared* assumptions and beliefs, interaction with *shared* values, produces *shared* norms, that drive *shared* patterns of behavior.

6. Individuals within any given culture can and often do differ widely in their personal cultures. Even though individuals are deeply influenced by both biological and cultural inheritance, over the life span, influenced by both their social environment and their inner lives, they pick and choose their interests, values, and activities, thus creating their own personal cultures (Massimini & Delle Fave, 2000).

7. The helper's personal culture interacts with the client's for better or for worse.

B. The Pragmatics of Values

1. Values are a set of practical criteria for making decisions. As such, they are drivers of behavior.

2. Working values enable the helper to make decisions on how to proceed.

3. Helpers without a set of working values are adrift. Helpers who don't have an explicit set of values have an implicit or "default" set which may or may not serve the helping process.

4. You need to be proactive in your search for the beliefs, values, and norms that will govern your interactions with your clients.

5. Tradition is an important part of value formation, and we all learn from the rich tradition of the helping professions.

6. Four major values from the tradition of the helping professions

   ➢ **Respect** is the *foundation* value;

   ➢ **Empathy** is the value that *orients* helpers in every interaction with their clients.

   ➢ **Genuineness** is the what-you-see-is-what-you-get *professional* value.

   ➢ **Client empowerment** is the value that *drives* outcomes.

Section Four: RESPECT AS THE FOUNDATION VALUE (OH-4)

Respect for clients is the foundation on which all helping interventions are built. The word comes from a Latin root that includes the idea of "seeing" or "viewing." Indeed, respect is a particular way of viewing oneself and others. There norms that flow from the interaction between a belief in the dignity of the person and the value of respect.

A. Do no harm. This is the first rule of the physician and the first rule of the helper. Helping is not a neutral process —it is for better or for worse. It is important to emphasize a nonmanipulative and nonexploitative approach to clients. Studies show that some instructors exploit trainees both sexually and in other ways and that some helpers do the same with their clients. Such behavior obviously breaches the code of ethics espoused by all the helping professions.

B. Become competent and committed. Get good at whatever model of helping you use. Get good at the basic problem-management and opportunity-development framework outlined in this book and the skills that make it work because there is no place for the "caring incompetent" in the helping professions.

C. Make it clear that you are "for" the client. Your manner should indicate that you are "for" the client, that you care for him or her in a down-to-earth, nonsentimental way. Respect is both gracious and tough-minded. Being for the client is not the same as taking the client's side or acting as the client's advocate. "Being for" means taking clients' points of view seriously even when they need to be challenged. Respect often involves helping clients place demands on themselves. "Tough love" in no way excludes appropriate warmth toward clients.

D. Assume the client's goodwill. Work on the assumption that clients want to work at living more effectively, at least until that assumption is proved false. The reluctance and resistance of some clients, particularly involuntary clients, is not necessarily evidence of ill will. Respect means entering the world of the clients to understand their reluctance and a willingness to help clients work through it.

E. Do not rush to judgment. You are there to help them identify, explore, and review and challenge the consequences of the values they have adopted. First try to understand the client's point of view and let him know that she/he understands —even if she/he realizes that this point of view needs to be reviewed and challenged later.

F. Keep the client's agenda in focus. Helpers should pursue their clients' agendas, not their own.

Section Five: EMPATHY AS A PRIMARY ORIENTATION VALUE (OH-5)

Empathy, though a rich concept in the helping professions, has been a confusing one (see Bohart & Greenberg, 1997 and Duan & Hill, 1996 for overviews). Some have seen it as a *personality trait*, a disposition to feel what other people feel or to understand others "from the inside," as it were. Others have seen empathy, not as a personality trait, but as a situation-specific *state* of feeling for and understanding of another person's experiences. Still others, building on the state approach, have focused on empathy as a *process* with stages. For instance, Barrett-Lennard (1981) identified three phases — empathic resonance, expressed empathy, and received empathy, while Carl Rogers (1975) talked about sensing a client's inner world and communicating that sensing. Finally, Egan (1998) in the sixth edition of this book focused on empathy as an *interpersonal communication skill*. Skilled helpers work hard at understanding their clients and then communicate this understanding to help clients understand themselves, their problem situations, their unused resources and opportunities, and their feelings more fully in order to manage them more effectively.

1. **Empathy: A rich term**. A number of authors look at empathy from a value point of view and talk about the behaviors that flow from it. Sometimes their language is almost lyrical.

   a). Kohut (1978) said, "Empathy, the accepting, confirming, and understanding human echo evoked by the self, is a psychological nutrient without which human life, as we know and cherish it, could not be sustained" (705).

   b). Covey (1989), said that empathy provides those with whom we are interacting with "psychological air" that helps them breathe more freely in their relationships.

c). Goleman (1995, 1998) puts empathy at the heart of emotional intelligence. It is the individual's "social radar" through which he or she senses others' feelings and perspectives and takes an active interest in their concerns.

d). Rogers (1980) talked passionately about basic empathic listening — being with and understanding the other —even calling it "an unappreciated way of being" (p. 137). He used the word unappreciated because in his view few people in the general population developed this "deep listening" ability and even so-called expert helpers did not give it the attention it deserved. Here is his description of basic empathic listening:

> "It means entering the private perceptual world of the other and becoming thoroughly at home in it. It involves being sensitive, moment by moment, to the changing felt meanings which flow in this other person, to the fear or rage or tenderness or confusion or whatever that he or she is experiencing. It means temporarily living in the other's life, moving about in it delicately without making judgments." (p. 142)

2. **Empathy: A key helping value**. As Goleman (1995, 1998) notes, there is nothing passive about empathy. Empathy as a value is a radical commitment on the part of helpers to understand clients as fully as possible in three different ways.

   a). Empathy is a commitment to work at understanding each client from *his or her point of view* together with the feelings surrounding this point of view and to communicate this understanding whenever it is deemed helpful.

   b). Empathy is a commitment to understand individuals in and through the *context* of their lives. The social settings, both large and small, in which they have developed and currently "live and move and have their being" provide routes to understanding.

   c). Empathy is also a commitment to understand the *dissonance* between the client's point of view and reality.

B. Empathy —Understanding Clients As They Are: Diversity and Multiculturalism (OH-6)

There has been an explosion of literature on diversity and multiculturalism over the past few years (Axelson, 1999; Bernstein, 1994; Cuellar & Paniagua, 2000; Das, 1995; Hermans & Kempen, 1998; Hogan-Garcia, 1999; Ivey & Ivey, 1999; Ivey, Ivey, & Simek-Morgan, 1997; Lee, 1997; Okun & Okun, 1999; Patterson, 1996; Pedersen, 1994, 1997; Ponterotto & , 2000; Richards & Bergin, 2000; Sue, 1999; Sue, Carter, Casas, & Fouad, 1998; Sue, Ivey, and Pedersen, 1996; Sue & Sue, 1999; Weinrach & Thomas, 1996 to name but a very few). There is both an upside and a downside to this avalanche. One upside is that helpers are forced to take another look at the blind spots they may have about diversity and culture and to take another look at the world in which we live. One downside is that multiculturalism has become in many ways a fad, if not an industry.

1. The Case of Sue, a Midwestern American, married to Lee, an immigrant from Singapore. They are having problems. Helping Sue and Lee, individuals from different cultures, achieve the "right balance" depends on understanding what the "right balance" means in any given culture.

2. Understanding clients' different approaches to developing and sustaining relationships is important. Guisinger and Blatt (1994) put this in a broader multicultural perspective.

    > Western psychologies have traditionally given greater importance to self-development than to interpersonal relatedness, stressing the development of autonomy, independence, and identity as central factors in the mature personality. In contrast, women, many minority groups, and non-Western societies have generally placed greater emphasis on issues of relatedness. (p. 104)

3. This is an important social problem that has implications for the helping professions. The relationship of counseling to social movements is confusing and difficult.

C. Understand diversity. While clients have in common their humanity, they differ from one another in a whole host of ways —accent, age, attractiveness, color, developmental stage, abilities, disabilities, economic status, education, ethnicity, fitness, gender, group culture, health, national origin, occupation, personal culture, personality variables, politics, problem type, religion, sexual orientation, social status, to name some of the major categories.

1. We differ from one another in hundreds of ways. And who is to say which differences are key?

2. Helpers can, over time, come to understand a great deal about the characteristics of the populations with whom they work —for instance, they can and should understand the different development tasks and challenges that take place over the life span.

D. Challenge whatever blinds spots you may have. Since helpers often differ from their clients in many ways, there is often the challenge to avoid diversity-related blind spots that can lead to inept interactions and interventions during the helping process.

1. Counselors would do well to become aware of their own cultural values and biases.

2. They should also make every effort to understand the world views of their clients.

3. Helpers with diversity blind spots are handicapped. Helpers should, as a matter of course, become aware of the key ways in which they differ from their clients and take special care to be sensitive to those differences.

E. Tailor your interventions in a diversity-sensitive way. Both this self-knowledge and this practical understanding of diversity need to be translated into appropriate interventions.

1. With clients who come from a culture that has a different perception of self-disclosure or with any client who finds self-disclosure difficult, it might make more sense, after an initial discussion of the problem situation in broad terms, to move to what the client wants instead of what he or she currently has (that is, Stage II) rather than to the more intimate details of the problem situation.

2. Once the helping relationship is on firmer ground, the client can move to the work he or she sees as more intimate or demanding. Although the helping model outlined here is a "human universal," helpers need to apply its stages and steps with sensitivity.

F. Work with individuals. The diversity principle is clear:

1. The more helpers understand the broad characteristics, needs, and behaviors of the populations with whom they work —African Americans, Caucasian Americans, diabetics, the elderly, the drug addict, the homeless, you name it —the better positioned they are to adapt these broad parameters and the counseling process itself to the individuals with whom they work.

2. But, whereas diversity focuses on differences both between and within groups — cultures and subcultures, if you will —helpers interact with clients as individuals.

3. Patel (1996) pointed out: "Psychotherapy can never be about celebrating racial diversity because it is not about groups; it is about individuals and their infinite complexity" (p. A 14). Your clients are individuals, not cultures, subcultures, or groups.

4. Individuals often have group characteristics, but they do not come as members of a homogeneous group because there are no homogeneous groups.

5. There are as many differences, and sometimes more, within groups as between groups (see Weinrach & Thomas, 1996, pp. 473-474).

6. Valuing diversity is not the same as espousing a splintered, antagonistic society in which one's group membership is more important than one's humanity. On the other hand, valuing individuality is not the same as espousing a "society of one" —radical individualism being the ultimate form of diversity. Moving to a "society of one" makes counseling and other forms of human interaction impossible.

G. Guidelines for Integrating Diversity and Multiculturalism Into Counseling

1. Ultimately, you have to come to grips with diversity and pull together your own set of guidelines such as the one suggested by Weinrach and Thomas (1996, pp. 475-476).

    a). Place the needs of the client above all other considerations.

    b). Identify and focus on whatever frame of reference, self-definition, or belief system is central to any given client, with consideration for, but not limited to, issues of diversity.

    c). Select counseling interventions on the basis of the client's agenda. Do not impose a social or political agenda on the counseling relationship.

    c). Make sure that your own values do not adversely affect a client's best interests.

    d). Avoid cultural stereotyping. Do not overgeneralize. Recognize that within-group differences are often more extensive than between-group differences.

    e). Do not define diversity narrowly. This client's concern about being unattractive deserves the helper's engagement just as much as that client's concern about racial intolerance.

    f). Provide opportunities for practitioners to be trained in the working knowledge and skills associated with diversity-sensitive counseling.

    g). Subject the assumptions, models, and techniques of diversity-sensitive counseling to the same scrutiny as other aspects of the counseling profession.

h). Create an environment that supports professional tolerance.

2. When it comes to clients, the very best helpers have always been learners.

3. The principles of cultural understanding apply to everyone. If helping is to be a collaborative event, then mutual understanding must be part of the game.

Section Six: GENUINENESS AS A PROFESSIONAL VALUE (OH-7)

Like respect, helper genuineness refers to both a set of attitudes and a set of counselor behaviors. Some writers call genuineness "congruence." Genuine people are at home with themselves and therefore can comfortably be themselves in all their interactions.

A. Do not overemphasize the helping role. Genuine helpers do not take refuge in the role of counselor. Ideally, relating at deeper levels to others and helping are part of their lifestyle, not roles they put on or take off at will.

1. Gibb (1968, 1978) suggested ways of being "role-free." He said that helpers should learn how to:

> ➢ express directly to another whatever they are presently experiencing,
> ➢ communicate without distorting their own messages,
> ➢ listen to others without distorting the messages they hear,
> ➢ reveal their true motivation in the process of communicating their messages,
> ➢ be spontaneous and free in their communications with others rather than use habitual and planned strategies,
> ➢ respond immediately to another's need or state instead of waiting for the "right" time or giving themselves enough time to come up with the "right" response,
> ➢ manifest their vulnerabilities and, in general, the "stuff" of their inner lives,
> ➢ live in and communicate about the here and now,
> ➢ strive for interdependence rather than dependence or counter dependence in their relationships with their clients,
> ➢ learn how to enjoy psychological closeness,
> ➢ be concrete in their communications, and
> ➢ be willing to commit themselves to others.

2. Gibb did not mean that helpers should be "free spirits," inflicting themselves on others. Indeed, "free spirit" helpers can even be dangerous.

3.   Being role-free is not license. Freedom from role means that counselors should not use the role or facade of counselor to protect themselves, to substitute for competence, or to fool the client in other ways.

B. Be spontaneous. Many of the behaviors suggested by Gibb are ways of being spontaneous.

1.   Effective helpers, while being tactful as part of their respect for others, do not constantly weigh what they say to clients.

2.   They do not put a number of filters between their inner lives and what they express to others.

3.   Being genuine does not mean verbalizing every thought to the client.

C. Avoid defensiveness. Genuine helpers are nondefensive.

1.   They know their own strengths and deficits and are presumably trying to live mature, meaningful lives. When clients express negative attitudes toward them, they examine the behavior that might cause the client to think negatively, try to understand the clients' points of view, and continue to work with them.

2.   Consider the example:
Counselors A and B are both defensive, though in different ways. It is more likely that the client will react to their defensiveness than that she will move forward. Counselor C centers on the experience of the client, with a view to "resetting the system" and helping her explore her responsibility for making the helping process work.

3. Since genuine helpers are at home with themselves, they can allow themselves to examine negative criticism honestly. Counselor C, for instance, would be the most likely of the three to ask himself or herself whether he or she is contributing to the apparent stalemate.

D. Be open. Genuine helpers are capable of deeper levels of self-disclosure even within the helping relationship. They do not see self-disclosure as an end in itself, but they feel free to reveal themselves, even in deeper ways, when and if it is appropriate. Being open also means that the helper has no hidden agendas: "What you see is what you get."

Section Seven: CLIENT EMPOWERMENT AS AN OUTCOME VALUE (OH-8)

The second goal of helping, outlined in Chapter 1, deals with empowerment —that is, helping clients identify, develop, and use resources that will make them more effective agents of change both within the helping sessions themselves and in their everyday lives

(Strong, Yoder, & Corcoran, 1995). The opposite of empowerment is dependency (Abramson, Cloud, Kesse, & Keese, 1994; Bornstein & Bowen, 1995), deference (Rennie, 1994), and oppression (McWhirter, 1996). Since helpers are often experienced by clients as relatively powerful people and since even the most egalitarian and client-centered of helpers do influence clients, it is necessary to come to terms with social influence in the helping process.

A. Helping as a Social-Influence Process

People influence one another every day in every social setting of life.

1. Smith and Mackle (2000) consider it one of eight basic principles needed to understand human behavior. William Crano (2000) suggests that "social influence research has been, and remains, the defining hallmark of social psychology" (p. 68). However, social influence is a form of power and power too often leads to manipulation and oppression.

2. Helping as a social-influence process has received a fair amount of attention in the helping literature (Dorn, 1986; Heppner & Claiborn, 1989; Heppner & Frazier, 1992; Houser, Feldman, Williams, & Fierstien, 1998; Hoyt, 1996; McCarthy & Frieze, 1999; McNeill & Stolenberg, 1989; Strong, 1968, 1991; Tracey, 1991).

3. Helpers can influence clients without robbing them of self-responsibility. Even better, they can exercise their trade in such a way that clients are, to use a bit of current business jargon, "empowered" rather than oppressed both in the helping sessions themselves and in the social settings of everyday life.

4. With empowerment comes increased self-responsibility.

5. Hare-Mustin and Marecek (1986) noted, there is a tension between the right of clients to determine their own way of managing their lives and the therapist's obligation to help them live more effectively.

B. Norms for Empowerment and Self-Responsibility

Helpers don't self-righteously "empower" clients. Freire (1970) warned helpers against making helping itself just one more form of oppression for those who are already oppressed. Effective counselors help clients discover, develop, and use the untapped power within themselves. Here, then, is a range of empowerment-based norms, some adapted from the work of Farrelly and Brandsma (1974).

1. Start with the premise that clients can change if they choose.

a). Clients have more resources for managing problems in living and developing opportunities than they —or sometimes their helpers —assume.

b). The helper's basic attitude should be that clients have the resources both to participate collaboratively in the helping process and to manage their lives more effectively. These resources may be blocked in a variety of ways or simply unused.

c). The counselor's job is to help clients identify, free, and cultivate these resources.

d). The counselor also helps clients assess their resources realistically so that their aspirations do not outstrip their resources.

2. **Do not see clients as victims**. Even when clients have been victimized by institutions or individuals, don't see them as helpless victims. Don't be fooled by appearances.

3. **Share the helping process with clients**.

a) Clients have a right to know what they are getting into (Heinssen, 1994; Heinssen, Levendusky, & Hunter, 1995; Hunter, 1995; Manthei & Miller, 2000).

b) Clients should be told as much about the model as they can assimilate.

4. **Help clients see counseling sessions as work sessions**.

a) Helping is about client-enhancing change. This is work pure and simple.

b) This search for and implementation of solutions can be arduous, even agonizing, but it can also be deeply satisfying, even exhilarating.

c) Helping clients develop the "work ethic" that makes them partners in the helping process can be one of the helper's most formidable challenges.

d) Some helpers go so far as to cancel counseling sessions until the client is "ready to work." Helping clients discover incentives to work is, of course, less dramatic and hard work in itself.

5. **Become a consultant to clients**.

a) Consultants in the business world adopt a variety of roles. They listen, observe, collect data, report observations, teach, train, coach, provide support, challenge, advise, offer suggestions, and even become advocates for certain positions.

b) Consulting, is a social-influence process, but it is a collaborative one that does not rob managers of the responsibilities that belong to them.

c) The best clients, like the best managers, learn how to use their consultants to add value in managing problems and developing opportunities.

6. Accept helping as a natural, two-way influence process.

a) Tyler, Pargament, and Gatz (1983) focused on the give-and-take that should characterize the helping process. In their view, either client or helper can approach the other to originate the helping process. The two have equal status in defining the terms of the relationship, in originating actions within it, and in evaluating both outcomes and the relationship itself. In the best case, positive change occurs in both parties.

b) Helping is a two-way street. For instance, Wei-Lian has to correct Timothy, his counselor, a number of times when Timothy tries to share his understanding of what Wei-Lian has said. When Timothy finally realizes what he is doing, he says to Wei-Lian, "When I talk with you, I need to be more of a learner. I'm coming to realize that Chinese culture is quite different from mine. I need your help."

7. Focus on learning instead of helping.

a). Effective counseling helps clients get on a learning track.

b). Howell (1982) said that "learning is incorporated into living to the extent that viable options are increased" (p. 14).

c). Learning takes place when options that add value to life are opened up, seized, and acted on.

d). If the collaboration between helpers and clients is successful, clients learn in very practical ways. They have more "degrees of freedom" in their lives as they open up options and take advantage of them.

8. Do not see clients as overly fragile.

a) Neither pampering nor brutalizing clients serves their best interests.

b) Many clients are less fragile than helpers make them out to be. Helpers who constantly see clients as fragile may well be acting in a self-protective way.

c) Driscoll (1984) noted that too many helpers shy away from doing much more than listening early in the helping process.

d) The natural deference many clients display early in the helping process (Rennie, 1994) —including their fear of criticizing the therapist, understanding the therapist's frame of reference, meeting the perceived expectations of the therapist, and showing indebtedness to the therapist —can send the wrong message to helpers.

e) Clients early on may be fearful of making some kind of irretrievable error. This does not mean that they are fragile. Reasonable caution on your part is appropriate, but you can easily become overly cautious.

f) Driscoll suggested that helpers intervene more right from the beginning —for instance, by reasonably challenging the way clients think and act and by getting them to begin to outline what they want and are willing to work for.

Section Eight: A WORKING CHARTER: THE CLIENT-HELPER CONTRACT

If helping is to be a collaborative venture, then both parties must understand what their responsibilities are. Perhaps the term working charter is better than contract. It avoids the legal implications of the latter term and connotes a cooperative venture.

A.   To achieve these objectives, the working charter should include: **(OH-9)**

1. The nature and goals of the helping process,

2. An overview of the helping model together with the techniques to be used and a sense of the flexibility built into the process.

3. How this process will help clients achieve their goals.

4. Relevant information about yourself and your background. **(OH-10)**

5. How the relationship is to be structured and the kinds of responsibilities both you and the client will have.

6. The values that will drive the helping process.

7. Procedural issues, such things as where sessions will be held and how long they will last. Procedural limitations should also be discussed —for instance, how free the client is to contact the helper between sessions.

8. Manthei and Miller (2000) have written a practical book for clients on the elements of a working charter. Charters also work with the seriously mentally ill (Heinssen, Levendusky, & Hunter, 1995).

B. The working charter need not be too detailed, nor should it be rigid. Helpers need to provide structure for the relationship and the work to be done without frightening or overwhelming the client. A working charter can:

1. Help client and helper develop realistic mutual expectations.

2. Give clients a flavor of the mechanics of the helping process.

3. Diminish initial client anxiety and reluctance.

4. Provide a sense of direction.

5. Enhance clients' freedom of choice.

Section Nine: SHADOW-SIDE REALITIES IN THE HELPING RELATIONSHIP (OH-11)

There are common flaws in the working alliance that remain in the shadows either because they are not dealt with effectively by the helping professions themselves or because individual helpers are inept at addressing them with clients.

A. Ethical flaws. There is a vast literature on ethical responsibilities in the helping professions (see Bersoff, 1995; Canter, Bennett, Jones, & Nagy, 1994; Claiborn, Berberoglu, Nerison, & Somberg, 1994; Corey, Corey, & Callanan, 1997; Cottone & Claus, 2000; Fisher & Younggren, 1997; Keith-Spiegel, 1994; Lowman, 1998). Helpers-to-be are urged to make this part of their professional development program.

B. Human tendencies in both helpers and clients. Neither helpers nor clients are usually heroic figures.

1. They are human beings with all-too-human tendencies. They must be able to manage closeness in therapy in a way that furthers the helping process (Schwartz, 1993).

2. They must deal with both positive and negative feelings toward clients lest they end up doing silly things.

3. They may have to fight the tendency to be less challenging with attractive clients or not to listen carefully to unattractive clients.

4. Clients, too, have their tendencies. Some have unrealistic expectations of counseling (Tinsley, Bowman, & Barich, 1993), while others trip over their own distorted views of their helpers. In such cases helpers have to manage both expectations and the relationship.

5. Unskilled helpers can get caught up in both their own and their clients' games. The working alliance breaks down.

6. Skilled helpers, on the other hand, understand the shadow side of both themselves and their clients and manage them. Tools that helpers need to challenge themselves and their clients are discussed in the Chapters 10, 11, and 12.

C. Trouble in the relationship itself.

1. The helping relationship might be flawed from the beginning. That is, the fit or chemistry between helper and client might not be right.

2. Even if the relationship starts off on the right foot, it can deteriorate (Arnkoff, 2000; Omer, 2000). In fact, some deterioration is normal. Kivlighan and Shaugnessy (2000) talk about the "tear-and-repair" phenomenon.

3. Some helping relationships get caught up in what Binder and Strupp (1997) called "negative process." They suggested that the ability of therapists to establish and maintain a good alliance has been overestimated.

4. Hostile interchanges between helpers and clients are common in all treatment models. When impasses and ruptures in the relationship take place, ineffective helpers get bogged down.

5. Many helpers and clients lack both the skill and the will for repair (Watson & Greenberg, 2000).

6. Factors associated with relationship breakdowns include "a client history of interpersonal problems, a lack of agreement between therapists and clients about the tasks and goals of therapy, interference in the therapy by others, transference, possible therapist mistakes, and therapist personal issues" (Hill, Nutt-Williams, Heaton, Thompson, & Rhodes, 1996, p. 207).

7. If impasses and ruptures are not addressed, premature termination often takes place. Such helpers fail to create the right chemistry.

D. Vague and violated values.

1. Helpers do not always have a clear idea of what their values are.

2. Their espoused values do not always coincide with their actions.

3. Values too often remain "good ideas" and are not translated into specific

norms that drive helping behavior.

E. Failure to share the helping process.

1. Some counselors are reluctant to let the client know what the process is all about.

2. Still others seem to think that knowledge of helping processes is secret or sacred or dangerous and should not be communicated to the client.

3.   There is no evidence to support such beliefs (Dauser, Hedstrom, & Croteau, 1995; Somberg, Stone, & Claiborn, 1993; Sullivan, Martin, & Handelsman, 1993; Winborn, 1977).

F. Flawed contracts. There is an extensive shadow side to both explicit and implicit contracts.

1. Even when a contract is written, the contracting parties interpret some of its provisions differently.

2. Over time they forget what they contracted to and differences become more pronounced.

3. These differences are seldom discussed.

4. In counseling, the helper-client contract has been, traditionally, implicit, even though the need for more explicit structure has been discussed for years (Proctor & Rosen, 1983). Because of this, the expectations of clients may differ from the expectations of their helpers (Benbenishty & Schul, 1987).

5. Implicit contracts are not enough, but they still abound (Handelsman & Galvin, 1988; Weinrach, 1989; Woody, 1991).

G.   Warring professionals. There are not just debates but also conflicts close to internecine wars in the helping professions.

1. For instance, the debate on the "correct" approach to diversity and multiculturalism brings out some of the best and some of the worst in the helping community.

2. Accusations, however subtle or blatant, of cultural imperialism on the one side and "political correctness" on the other fly back and forth.

3. The debate on whether or how the helping professions should take political stands or engage in social engineering generates, as has been noted, more heat than light.

4. No significant article is published about any significant dimension of counseling without a barrage of often testy replies.

5. The search for the truth gives way at times to the need to be right. It is not always clear how all of this serves the needs of clients.

6. The helping professions should continually reinvent themselves by looking at helping through the eyes of clients.

Lecture Enhancers

Item One: Empathic Listening

Empathic listening: Reports on the experience of being heard.

Myers,-Sharon, U New Brunswick, Faculty of Education, Fredericton, NB, Canada
Journal-of-Humanistic-Psychology. 2000 Spr; Vol 40(2): 148-173

Synopsis: This qualitative study looked at the experiences of five female clients who participated in counselling sessions with two different therapists. The clients reported being heard when the therapist created a safe environment for self-exploration and were actively involved in the dialogue (e.g., clarifying, remembering details, and paraphrasing). This empathetic listening helped the clients to discuss painful content with greater ease when the therapeutic process included empathetic listening. This positive experience was in stark contrast to therapeutic relationships where the client did not believe they were being heard. Empathetic listening does make a difference.

Item Two: Competence Transfer

Competence transfer in solution-focused therapy: Harnessing a natural resource.

Lamarre,-Josee; Gregoire,-Andre Journal-of-Systemic-Therapies. 1999 Spr; Vol 18(1): 43-57

Synopsis: The authors build on the work of M.H. Erickson's utilization strategy and use the term competence transfer to capture the concept of using the client's resources, strengths, and talents to the client's maximum benefit in resolving the client's problem areas. (Note: This fits nicely into Egan's leverage step.)

Item Three: Limits on Visible Speech and Gestures

Some limits on encoding visible speech and gestures using a dichotic shadowing task.

Thomspon,-Laura-A.; Guzman,-Felipe-A. Journals-of-Gerontology:-Series-B:-Psychological-Sciences-and-Social-Sciences. 1999 Nov; Vol 54B(6): P347-P349

Synopsis: This study looked at age difference in an individual's ability to use compensatory mechanisms to encode visual language in extremely attention-demanding listening conditions. The results of the study revealed that older adults were not able to use a compensatory encoding method under attention-demanding listening conditions. The study does suggest differences in how we communicate with individuals in the senior category.

Class Activities

In addition to the exercises in the Workbook that accompanies this text, you may find the following in-class activities to be of value:

Activity #1: Age Sensitive

In this activity your goal is to have students experience what it is like to have impaired vision and hearing. This is generally thought of as an age related issue, but individuals of all ages can suffer from visual and auditory limitations.

For this activity bring to class several pairs of dark sunglasses and ear plugs. Have several student volunteers put on the sunglasses and insert the earplugs and then have another student attempt to communicate with the student with the sunglasses and the earplugs. Have other students observe what happens with the communication between the two (e.g., voices get louder, a level of frustration can develop). It is ideal if all students can experience both roles in this activity. Finish the activity by students reporting out what they see and what can be learned from this activity and carried forward to the helping relationship.

Activity #2: Empathy vs. Non-Empathy

In this activity students can have an educational and a fun time experiencing empathy and non-empathy. Ask students to pair off and then engage in a helping session where the helper shows no empathy toward the client. No empathy is characterized by such actions as giving and advice and not responding to the emotional needs of the client. Next, have the students pair off with another student and this time have the students use all the good empathetic skills discussed in the book (e.g., paraphrasing, appropriate body language, etc.)

Have the students take five minutes individually to list how they felt when they were treated with empathy and when they were not treated with empathy. After five minutes of individual time, have the students report out their feelings and record on the board or on a flip chart the two different experiences: one column for empathy and one column for non-empathy. Ask students to remember this activity the next time they are not feeling too empathetic in a helping relationship.

Activity #3: I Can Do It!

Ask students to think of an issue in their life right now where they are not feeling competent. (Please stress the limits on self-disclosure and remind the students that what they think of will be shared with the rest of the class.) Next, ask students to think of a situation in their lives where they didn't think they could master a task, but eventually they were able to succeed. Finally, ask the students to list the steps it took to finally become accomplished at the particular task (e.g., practice, encouragement from others, watching how others complete the task, etc.).

In pairs, have the students share their work and look for what are common steps to becoming competent at a particular skill or task. Have the pairs report their findings to the class. Have the class make the connection between this activity and the helping relationship.

Videos

Basic Interviewing Skills for Psychologists (1991, 51 min., IM). A good review of the do's and don't of the helping profession.

Prisoners of Childhood: Exploring the Inner Child (1992, 52 min., IM). Actors work with a therapist to highlight the lost feelings they bring with them from their childhood.

Erik Erikson: A Life's Work (38 min., IM) Erikson's life stage development theory is presented.

Growing Old in a New Age (1993, 13 parts, 60 min each, ANN/CPB). This video series covers the full range of aging topics from sexuality to death.

The Elementary Mind (1992, 30 min., IM) Gelman and Sternberg dicuss Piaget's views of memory, cognition, and intelligence. The video also includes experiments related to age development.

Friendship (1989, 30 min., IM) The concept of gender difference in friendship development is discussed.

Websites

1. www.selfgrowth.com/therapy.html
   Self-improvement Online

2. www.deafness.minigco.com/library/bltopic.htm
   Deaf Awareness Issues

3. www.algy.com/anxiety
   Resources for Anxiety and Panic

4. www.piaget.org/
   Piaget's Theory

5. www.personal.psu.edu/faculty/n/x/nxd10/adolesce.htm#top
   Adolescent Development

6. www.geron.org
   A Guide to on-line resources related to aging.

7. www.alzweb.org
   Alzheimer's Disease and Research

Overhead Transparencies

Starting on the next page are copies of recommended overhead transparencies. Please feel free to convert the following pages to overheads as this will enhance the lecture portion of your class presentation.

THE HELPING RELATIONSHIP

A. The relationship itself.

B. The relationship as a means to an end.

C. The relationship and outcomes

OH 1

A WORKING ALLIANCE

1. The collaborative nature of helping.

2. The relationship as a form for relearning

3. Relationship flexibility

OH 2

VALUES IN ACTION

1. **Respect** is the *foundation* value

2. **Empathy** is the value that *orients* helpers in every interaction with their clients.

3. **Genuineness** is the what-you-see-is-what-you-get *professional* value.

4. **Client empowerment** is the value that *drives* outcomes.

OH 3

RESPECT AS THE FOUNDATION VALUE

A. Do no harm.

B. Become competent and committed.

C. Make it clear that you are "for" the client.

D. Assume the client's goodwill.

E. Do not rush to judgment.

F. Keep the client's agenda in focus.

OH 4

EMPATHY AS A PRIMARY ORIENTATION VALUE

A. The Nature of Empathy.

Rodgers (1980) "It means entering the private perceptual world of the other and becoming thoroughly at home in it. It involves being sensitive, moment by moment, to the changing felt meanings which flow in this other person, to the fear or rage or tenderness or confusion or whatever that he or she is experiencing. It means temporarily living in the other's life, moving about in it delicately without making judgments."

OH 5A

UNDERSTANDING CLIENTS AS THEY ARE

1. Understand diversity.

2. Challenge whatever blind spots you may have.

3. Tailor your interventions in a diversity-sensitive way.

4. Work with individuals.

5. Guidelines for Integrating Diversity and Multiculturalism into Counseling

OH 5B

GENUINENESS AS A PROFESSIONAL VALUE

1. Do not overemphasize the helping role.

2. Be spontaneous.

3. Avoid defensiveness.

4. Be open.

OH 6

CLIENT EMPOWERMENT AS AN OUTCOME VALUE

A. Helping as a Social-Influence Process

B. Norms for Empowerment and Self-Responsibility

1. Start with the premise that clients can change if they choose.
2. Do not see clients as victims.
3. Share the helping process with clients.
4. Help clients see counseling sessions as work sessions.
5. Become a consultant to clients.
6. Accept helping as a natural, two-way influence process.
7. Focus on learning instead of helping.
8. Do not see clients as overly fragile.

OH 7

A WORKING CHARTER: THE CLIENT-HELPER CONTRACT

1. The nature and goals of the helping process.

2. An overview of the helping model and techniques.

3. How this process will help clients achieve their goals.

4. Relevant information about yourself and your background.

OH 8A

A WORKING CHARTER:
THE CLIENT-HELPER
CONTRACT
Cont'd.

5. How the relationship is to be structured and the kinds of responsibilities both you and the client will have.

6. The values that will drive the helping process.

7. Procedural issues and limitations.

8. Manthei and Miller (2000) (Heinssen, Levendusky, & Hunter, 1995).

OH 8B

SHADOW-SIDE REALITIES IN THE HELPING RELATIONSHIP

A. Ethical flaws.

B. Human tendencies in both helpers and clients.

C. Trouble in the relationship itself.

D. Vague and violated values.

E. Failure to share the helping process.

F. Flawed contracts.

G. Warring professionals.

OH 9

Chapter Four:

Introduction to Communications and the Skill of Visibly Tuning in to Clients

	Pages
Chapter Outline	**115**
Detailed Lecture Notes	**116**
Lecture Enhancers	**124-125**
Class Activities	**126-127**
Videos	**128**
Websites	**129**
Transparencies	**130-135**

CHAPTER FOUR OUTLINE

Chapter 4

INTRODUCTION TO COMMUNICATION AND THE SKILL OF VISIBLY TUNING IN TO CLIENTS

THE IMPORTANCE OF DIALOGUE IN HELPING

VISIBLY TUNING IN TO CLIENTS: THE IMPORTANCE OF EMPATHIC PRESENCE

➢   Nonverbal Behavior As a Channel of Communication
➢   Helpers' Nonverbal Behavior
➢   The Microskills of Visibly Tuning In

THE SHADOW SIDE OF INTERPERSONAL COMMUNICATION SKILLS

Detailed Lecture Notes

(Please note: The designation OH in the detailed lecture notes indicates an overhead transparency is available. Please locate the overhead transparencies in the final section of each chapter in this Instructors' Manual.)

Section One: THE IMPORTANCE OF DIALOGUE IN HELPING (OH-4.1)

A. Conversations between helpers and their clients should be a therapeutic or helping dialogue. There are four requirements for true dialogue (Egan, 2001):

1. **Turn taking**. Dialogue is interactive. Monologues on the part of either client or helper don't add value. Turn taking opens up the possibility for mutual learning. Helpers learn about their clients and base their interventions on what they come to understand through the give-and-take of the dialogue. Clients come to understand themselves and their concerns more fully and learn how to face up to the challenge their problems and opportunities present.

2. **Connecting**. What each person says in the conversation should be connected in some way to what the other person has said.

3. **Mutual influencing**. The parties in a dialogue should each be open to being influenced by what the other person has to say. This echoes the social-influence dimension of counseling discussed in Chapter 3.

4. **Co-creating outcomes**. Good dialogue leads to outcomes that benefit both parties. Counseling is about results, accomplishments, outcomes. The counselor's job to act as a catalyst for the kind of problem-managing dialogue that helps clients find their own answers. In true dialogue, neither party should know exactly what the outcome will be. Only clients can change themselves, but, because of the helping dialogue, these changes will have the mark of effective helpers on them.

B.   Dialogue is beginning to be discussed in mental health (Corrigan, Lickey, Schmook, Virgil, & Juricek, 1999) and other human service settings such as medicine (Hellstroem, 1998). Dialogue is essential because helping is a collaborative endeavor (Roberts, 1998).

1. It is through dialogue that helpers act as catalysts for change.

2. It is through dialogue that clients give expression to their responsibility and accountability for change in their lives.

3. Bugas and Silberschatz (2000) even see clients as "coaches" for their helpers. Clients should "prompt, instruct, and educate" their helpers to key aspects of themselves and their plans to accomplish treatment goals.

C.   While individual communication skills are a necessary part of communication competence, dialogue is the integrating mechanism. Individual skills for effective dialogue are as follows:

1. Attending or, visibly tuning in

2. Active listening

3. Empathy in the form of sharing empathic highlights

4. Probing and summarizing

**Section Two: VISIBLY TUNING IN TO CLIENTS:
THE IMPORTANCE OF EMPATHIC PRESENCE**

At some of the more dramatic moments of life, simply being with another person is extremely important. Your empathic presence is comforting. Most people appreciate it when others pay attention to them. By the same token, being ignored is often painful. Given how sensitive most of us are to others' attention or inattention, it is paradoxical how insensitive we can be at times about paying attention to others. Helping and other deep interpersonal transactions demand a certain robustness or intensity of presence. Attending, that is, visibly tuning in to others, contributes to this presence.

A. Nonverbal Behavior as a Channel of Communication (OH-4.2)

Over the years both researchers and practitioners have come to appreciate the importance of nonverbal behavior in counseling (Andersen, 1999; Ekman, 1992, 1993; Ekman & Friesen, 1975; Grace, Kivlighan, Jr., & Kunce, 1995; Hickson & Stacks, 1993; Highlen & Hill, 1984; Knapp & Hall, 1992; McCroskey, 1993; Mehrabian, 1972, 1981; Norton, 1983; Richmond & McCroskey, 2000; Russell, 1995; Siegman & Feldstein, 1987).

1. Highlen and Hill suggested that nonverbal behaviors:

a) Regulate conversations.

b) Communicate emotions.

c) Modify verbal messages.

d) Provide important messages about the helping relationship.

e) Give insights into self-perceptions.

f) Provide clues that clients (or counselors) are not saying what they are thinking.

2. The face and body are extremely communicative.

   a). We know from experience that even when people are together in silence, the atmosphere can be filled with messages.

   b). Sometimes the facial expressions, bodily motions, voice quality, and physiological responses of clients communicate more than their words do.

3. The following factors (OH-4.3)

4. The part of both helpers and clients, play an important role in the therapeutic dialogue:

   1. **bodily behavior**, such as posture, body movements, and gestures;

   2. **eye behavior**, such as eye contact, staring, eye movement;

   3. **facial expressions**, such as smiles, frowns, raised eyebrows, and twisted lips;

   4. **voice-related behavior**, such as tone of voice, pitch, volume, intensity, inflection, spacing of words, emphases, pauses, silences, and fluency.

   5. **observable autonomic physiological responses**, such as quickened breathing, blushing, paleness, and pupil dilation.

   6. **physical characteristics**, such as fitness, height, weight, and complexion;

   7. **space**, how close or far a person chooses to be during a conversation;

8. **general appearance**, such as grooming and dress.

4. People constantly "speak" to one another through their nonverbal behavior. Effective helpers learn this "language" and how to use it effectively in their interactions with their clients. They also learn how to "read" relevant messages embedded in the nonverbal behavior of their clients.

B. Helpers' Nonverbal Behavior

1. Before you begin interpreting the nonverbal behavior of your clients (discussed in Chapter 5), take a look at yourself.

    a. At times your nonverbal behavior is as important as or even more important than, your words and influences clients for better or for worse.

    b. Clients read in your nonverbal behavior cues that indicate the quality of your presence to them.

    c. Clients may misinterpret your nonverbal behavior.

    d. Part of listening, then, is being sensitive to clients' reactions to your nonverbal behavior.

2. Effective helpers are mindful of the stream of nonverbal messages they send to clients. Reading your own bodily reactions is an important first step.

3. You can also use your body to censor instinctive or impulsive messages that you feel are inappropriate. Not dumping your annoyance or anger on your clients through nonverbal behavior is not the same as denying it. Becoming aware of it is the first step in dealing with it.

4. You can "punctuate" what you say with the nonverbal messages.

5. Don't become preoccupied with your body and the qualities of your voice as a source of communication. Rather, learn to use your body instinctively as a means of communication.

6. Your nonverbal behavior should enhance rather than stand in the way of your working alliance with your clients.

7. Although the skills of being visibly tuned in can be learned, they will be phony if they are not driven by the attitudes and values such as respect and empathy discussed in Chapter 3. Your mind set — what's in your heart — is as important as your visible presence. If you are not actively interested in the

welfare of your client or if you resent working with a client, subtle or not-so-subtle nonverbal clues will color your behavior.

C. The Microskills of Visibly Tuning in to Clients (OH-4.4)

A. There are certain key nonverbal microskills you can use to visibly tune in to clients. These microskills can be summarized in the acronym SOLER. Since communication skills are particularly sensitive to cultural differences, care should be taken in adapting what follows to different cultures. What follows, however is only a framework.

> **S: Face the client *Squarely***; that is, adopt a posture that indicates involvement. In North American culture, facing another person squarely is often considered a basic posture of involvement. The point is that your bodily orientation should convey the message that you are involved with the client. Your body sends out messages whether you like it or not. Make them congruent with what you are trying to do.

> **O: Adopt an *Open* posture**. Crossed arms and crossed legs can be signs of lessened involvement with or availability to others. In North American culture, an open posture is generally seen as a nondefensive posture. If you are empathic and open-minded, let your posture mirror what is in your heart.

> **L: Remember that it is possible at times to *Lean* toward the other**. In North American culture, a slight inclination toward a person is often seen as saying, "I'm with you, I'm interested in you and in what you have to say." Leaning back (the severest form of which is a slouch) can be a way of saying, "I'm not entirely with you" or "I'm bored." Leaning too far forward, however, or doing so too soon, may frighten a client. It can be seen as a way of placing a demand on the other for some kind of closeness or intimacy. In a wider sense, the word lean can refer to a kind of bodily flexibility or responsiveness that enhances your communication with a client. And bodily flexibility can mirror mental flexibility.

> **E: Maintain good *Eye* contact**. In North American culture, fairly steady eye contact is not unnatural for people deep in conversation. Maintaining good eye contact with a client is another way of saying, "I'm with you; I'm interested; I want to hear what you have to say." Obviously, this principle is not violated if you occasionally look away. But if you catch yourself looking away frequently, your behavior may

give you a hint about some kind of reluctance to be with this person or to get involved with him or her. Or it may say something about your own discomfort. In other cultures, however, too much eye contact, especially with someone in a position of authority is out of order. Much can be learned about the cultural meaning of eye contact from Asian students and clients.

R: Try to be relatively *Relaxed* or natural in these behaviors. Being relaxed means two things. First, it means not fidgeting nervously or engaging in distracting facial expressions. The client may wonder what's making you nervous. Second, it means becoming comfortable with using your body as a vehicle of personal contact and expression. Your being natural in the use of these skills helps put the client at ease.

B. A counselor trained in the *Skilled Helper* model was teaching counseling to visually impaired students in the Royal National College for the Blind. Most of her clients were visually impaired. However, she wrote this about SOLER:

1. In counseling students who are blind or visually impaired, eye contact has little or no relevance. However, attention on voice direction is extremely important, and people with a visual impairment will tell you how insulted they feel when sighted people are talking to them while looking somewhere else.

2. I teach SOLER as part of listening and attending skills and can adapt each letter of the acronym [to my visually impaired students] with the exception of the E.... After much thought, I would like to change your acronym to SOLAR, the A being for "Aim," that is, aim your head and body in the direction of your client so that when they hear your voice, be it linguistically or paralinguistically, they know that you are attending directly to what they are saying (private communication).

C. This underscores the fact that people are more sensitive to how you orient yourself to them nonverbally than you might imagine. Anything that distracts from your "being there" can harm the dialogue. Box 4-1 summarizes, in question form, the main points related to being visibly tuned in to clients. Turn to the *Exercises in Helping Skills* for opportunities to "practice" the skill of visibly tuning in.

Section Three: THE SHADOW SIDE OF COMMUNICATION SKILLS

A. Interpersonal communication competence is critical for effective everyday living yet. It is the principal enabling skill for just about everything we do.

121

1. "Given the importance of effective human relationships in just about every area of life, how important is it for your kids to develop a solid set of interpersonal communication skills? On a scale from 1-100, how high would you rate the importance?"

2. "Given the importance of these skills, where do your kids pick them up? How does society make sure that they acquire them? In what forums do they learn them?"

3. Although most parents rate the importance of these sets of skills very highly, we live in a society that leaves their development to chance. Nothing is done systematically to make sure that our kids learn these skills. And, by the way, there is no assurance that they will pick them up on the run.

4. Children learn a bit from their parents, they might get a dash in school, perhaps a sitçom on TV helps. But, in the main, they are more often exposed to poor communicators than good ones.

A. Ideally, helpers-to-be would arrive at training programs already equipped with a solid set of interpersonal communication skills. Training would help them adapt these skills to the counseling process.

    1. Since trainees don't ordinarily arrive so equipped, they need time to come up to speed in communication competence.

    2. Some helper-training programs focus almost exclusively on interpersonal communication skills. As a result, trainees know how to communicate but not necessarily how to help.

    3. Most adults feel that they are "pretty good" at these skills. What they actually mean is they see themselves as good as others.

BOX 4-1
Questions on Visibly Tuning In

1. What are my attitudes toward this client?

2. How would I rate the quality of my presence to this client?

3. To what degree does my nonverbal behavior indicate a willingness to work with the client?

4. What attitudes am I expressing in my nonverbal behavior?

5. What attitudes am I expressing in my verbal behavior?

6. To what degree does the client experience me as effectively present and working with him or her?

7. To what degree does my nonverbal behavior reinforce my internal attitudes?

8. In what ways am I distracted from giving my full attention to this client? What am I doing to handle these distractions? How might I be more effectively present to this person?

Lecture Enhancers

You should be able to find the full text of the following items in your library or by using your web-based library access tool of choice (e.g., PsycInfo).

Item One: Cultural Issue In Counselling

Counseling the culturally different: Theory and practice (3rd ed.).
Sue,-Derald-Wing; Sue,-David , New York, NY, USA: John Wiley and Sons, Inc. (1999).

Synopsis: This book nicely captures the issues of the dominant values of the larger society playing a major role in the counselling of individuals from a different culture. The authors provide many real-life examples to make the point that not only are traditional communication skills important in the helping relationship, but that culturally sensitive communication skills are just as important.

Item Two: The Challenging Client

Dealing with challenges in psychotherapy and counseling.

Brems,-Christiane, Wadsworth Publishing Co. (2000).

Synopsis: The author stresses the challenges of working with clients in critical situations. The book confirms that the common practices of humanity, thoroughness, preparedness, and sensitivity, along with good solid communication skills are the key to turning challenging helping situations into manageable helping situations. The book provides a wide philosophical orientation which provides the reader with a wide array of helping strategies for helpers engaging challenging clients.

Item Three: Notice the difference.

Nelson,Victor, Journal-of-Family-Psychotherapy. 1998; Vol 9(1): 81-84

Synopsis: Solution focused therapies (SFT) provides a wide array of resources for helpers. In this article the authors discuss the value of "Notice the Difference" technique as an effective SFT intervention. When using this technique the helper assists the client in noticing the difference in situations and then attempts to help the client realize what brought about the difference and how that same process may be of value in other situations. The helper's goal is to provide the client with the skill to notice positive change, realize what brought about the change, and empower the client to transfer that same change process to other situations that the client encounters and desires to change.

Class Activities

In addition to the exercises in the Workbook that accompanies this text, you may find the following in-class activities to be of value:

Activity #1: Not Being Heard

In this activity students are encouraged to think of times that they felt they were not listened to. Ask students, in groups of three or four to list times that they felt they were not being listened to and what was it that made them not feel heard. Have the students make three lists: what behaviors or actions on the part of the other person made them feel not heard, how they felt when they were not being heard, and what actions they took as result of not being heard.

Have the groups report their findings to the class. Focus on behaviors, actions, and reactions.

Activity #2: Making Change

Bring a hand full of change to class with a number of 3x5 cards with numbers ranging from 1 to 30 on the card. Have students pair off with one student provided a handful of coins and the other student several of the 3x5 cards. Have the student with the 3x5 cards select a card and then attempt to communicate, non-verbally, to the other student to use the coins to display the number on the card. Ask other class members to be observers and to note the frustration level the two students attempting to communicate non-verbally experience. Also ask the observers to carefully note how the communication is finally made and how they communication becomes easier with time.

Activity #3: When Acting Is Not Acting

Have students form triads with one student designated the helper, one the client, and one the observer. Ask the helper to play the role of a helper with poor communication skills. Ask the observer to list as many of the poor communication skills he or she can detect. Next, have the client list how he or she felt having a helper with

126

poor helping skills attempt to help them. Lastly, have the helper talk about how it felt to use poor communication skills.

Videos

Aggression (1989, 30 min, IM). A look at predicting violence.

Eye of the Strom (1971, 29 min., CHU). A third-grade class is divided based on eye color. Then various acts of discrimination are practiced toward one of the groups based on their eye color.

Face Value (Perceptions of Beauty) (28 min., FHS) An engaging discussion of the universal principles of beauty.

Gender and Relationships (1990, 30 min., IM) The issues of attraction, liking, and love are discussed.

Faces of the Enemy (1987, 58 min., IM) A discussion of the concepts of dehumanization, propaganda, and mass persuasion are covered in this candid discussion of communication used to the detriment of many.

Twelve Angry Men (1957, 93 min., MGM/UA). An interesting look a verbal and nonverbal communication in the issues of conformity and social pressure.

Websites

1. www.sp.uconn.edu/~marshall/html/afigure5.html
Facial attractiveness and related issues

2. www.sci.monash.edu.au/psych/courses/1022_97/social5.htm
Attribution Theory

3. www.socioweb.com/~markbl/socioweb/
The Socio Web.

4. www.gwu.edu/~tip/festinge.html
Cognitive Dissonance

5. http://samiam.Colorado.edu/~mcclella/expersim/introsocial.html
Social Facilitation

6. http://sputnik.ethz.ch/~miguel/humor/funnies/Rejection_lines.html
Rejection Lines. A humorous and painful look at rejection lines used by men and women.

7. www.public.asu.edu/~kelton/
The Science of Persuasion and Compliance

Overhead Transparencies

Starting on the next page are copies of recommended overhead transparencies. Please feel free to convert the following pages to overheads as this will enhance the lecture portion of your class presentation.

THE IMPORTANCE OF DIALOGUE IN HELPING

A. Four requirements for true dialogue

1. Turn taking.
2. Connecting.
3. Mutual influencing.
4. Co-creating outcomes.

B. Helping is a collaborative endeavour.

1. Helpers act as catalysts for change.
2. Clients give expression to their responsibility and accountability.
       Clients as "coaches" for their helpers.

OH 4.1A

THE IMPORTANCE OF DIALOGUE IN HELPING
Continued

C. Individual skills for effective dialogue.

1. Attending or, visibly tuning in.
2. Active listening.
3. Empathy in the form of sharing empathic highlights
4. Probing and summarizing.

OH 4.1B

VISIBLY TUNING IN TO CLIENTS: THE IMPORTANCE OF EMPATHIC PRESENCE

A. Nonverbal Behavior as a Channel of Communication

1. Regulate conversations.

2. Communicate emotions.

3. Modify verbal messages.

4. Provide important messages about the helping relationship.

5. Give insights into self-perceptions.

6. Provide clues that clients (or counselors) are not saying what they are thinking.

OH 4.2

B.   Factors that play an important role in the therapeutic dialogue.

1. Bodily behavior.

2. Eye behavior.

3. Facial expressions.

4. Voice-related behavior.

5. Observable autonomic physiological responses.

6. Physical characteristics.

7. Space.

8. General appearance.

OH 4.3

THE MICROSKILLS OF VISIBLY TUNING TO THE CLIENT (S.O.L.E.R.)

S: Face the client *Squarely*.

O: Adopt an *Open* posture.

L: Remember that it is possible at times to *Lean* toward the other.

E: Maintain good *Eye* contact.

R: Try to be relatively *Relaxed* or natural in these behaviors.

OH 4.4

Chapter Five:

Active Listening: The Foundations of Understanding

	Pages
Chapter Outline	**137-138**
Detailed Lecture Notes	**139-152**
Lecture Enhancers	**153-154**
Class Activities	**155-156**
Videos	**157**
Websites	**158**
Transparencies	**159-168**

CHAPTER FIVE OUTLINE

ACTIVE LISTENING:
THE FOUNDATION OF UNDERSTANDING

INADEQUATE LISTENING

➤ Non-Listening
➤ Partial Listening
➤ Tape-Recorder Listening
➤ Rehearsing

EMPATHIC LISTENING

➤ Listening to Words

· Stories: Experiences, Behavior, and Affect
· Points of View: Reasons, Implications, Flexibility
· Decisions: Reasons, Implications, Flexibility
· Intentions and Proposals: Reasons, Implications, Flexibility
· Resources and Opportunities

➤ Listening to Clients' Nonverbal Messages and Modifiers

➤ Confirming or Repeating
➤ Denying or Confusing
➤ Strengthening or Emphasizing
➤ Adding Intensity
➤ Controlling or Regulating

PROCESSING WHAT YOU HEAR: THE THOUGHTFUL SEARCH FOR MEANING

➤ Identifying Key Messages and Feelings
➤ Understanding Clients Through Context
➤ Picking Up the Slant or Spin: Tough-Minded Listening and Processing
➤ Identifying What's Missing

LISTENING TO ONESELF: THE HELPER'S INTERNAL CONVERSATION

THE SHADOW SIDE OF LISTENING TO CLIENTS

➢   Forms of Distorted Listening
➢   Myths About Nonverbal Behavior

(Please note: The designation OH in the detailed lecture notes indicates an overhead transparency is available. Please locate the overhead transparencies in the final section of each chapter in this Instructors' Manual.)

Chapter 5:
ACTIVE LISTENING: THE FOUNDATION OF UNDERSTANDING

Introduction:

We tune in both mentally and visibly in order to listen to the stories, points of view, decisions of our clients, and both the intentions and proposals of our clients. Full listening means listening actively, listening accurately, and listening for meaning. Listening is a rich metaphor for the helping relationship.

The following case will be used to help you develop a better behavioral feel for both visibly tuning in and listening.

Jennie, an African American college senior, was raped by a "friend" on a date. She received some immediate counseling from the university Student Development Center and some ongoing support during the subsequent investigation. But even though she was raped, it turned out that it was impossible for her to prove her case. The entire experience — both the rape and the investigation that followed — left her shaken, unsure of herself, angry, and mistrustful of institutions she had assumed would be on her side (especially the university and the legal system). When Denise, a middle-aged and middle-class African American social worker who was a counselor for a health maintenance organization (HMO), first saw her a couple of years after the incident, Jennie was plagued by a number of somatic complaints, including headaches and gastric problems. At work, she engaged in angry outbursts whenever she felt that someone was taking advantage of her. Otherwise she had become quite passive and chronically depressed. She saw herself as a woman victimized by society and was slowly giving up on herself.

Section One: INADEQUATE LISTENING (OH-5.1)

A. Effective listening requires work. The following are forms of inactive or inadequate listening:

1. **Non-Listening.** Sometimes we go through the motions of listening, but are not really engaged. Obviously no helper sets out not to listen, but even the best can let their mind wander as the listen to the same kind of stories over and over again, forgetting that the story is unique to *this* client.

2. **Partial listening**. This is listening that skims the surface. The helper picks up bits and pieces, but not necessarily the essential points the client is making. Inadequate listening helps neither understanding nor relationships.

3. **Tape-recorder listening**. What clients look for from listening is not the helpers's ability to repeat their words. People want more than physical presence in human communication; they want the other person to be present psychologically, socially, and emotionally. Sometimes helpers fail to demonstrate that visibly tuning in and listening mean that they are totally present. The client picks up some signals that the helper is not listening very well. Your clients want **you**, a live counselor, not a tape recorder.

4. **Rehearsing**. Even when experienced helpers begin to mull over the perfect response to what their clients are saying, they stop listening. Effective helpers listen intently to clients and to the themes and core messages embedded in what they are saying. They are never at a loss in responding. They don't need to rehearse. And their responses are much more likely to help clients move forward in the problem-management process. When the client stops speaking, they often pause to reflect on what he or she just said and then speak. Pausing says, "I'm still mulling over what you've just said. I want to respond thoughtfully." They pause because they have listened.

Section Two: EMPATHIC LISTENING

The opposite of inactive or inadequate listening is empathic listening, listening driven by the value of empathy. Carl Rogers (1980) talked passionately about basic empathic listening. Rogers pointed out that this deeper understanding of clients remains sterile unless it is somehow communicated to them. Although clients can appreciate how intensely they are attended and listened to, they and their concerns still need to be understood. Empathic listening begets empathic understanding, which begets empathic responding.

A. Listening to Words (OH-5.2)

Listening to what clients are saying is not a free-form activity. Helpers need to be focused. Recognizing modes of client discourse — for instance, clients tell *stories*, share *points of view*, and deliver *decisions*, and state *intentions* or offer *proposals* — can help you organize your listening, that is, they can help you listen for the client's key points and relevant detail.

1. Listening to Clients' Stories

Most immediately, helpers listen to clients' "stories," that is, their accounts of their problem situations and unused opportunities. Stories tend to be mixtures of clients' experiences, behaviors, and emotions.

a). Clients talk about their **experiences** that is, what happens to them.

> Most clients spend a fair amount of time, sometimes too much time, talking about what happens *to* them. It is of paramount importance to listen to and understand clients' experiences. Some clients talk about experiences that are internal and out of their control. They feel that they are no longer in control of their lives or some dimension of life. Therefore, they talk extensively about these experiences. For other clients, talking constantly about experiences is a way of avoiding responsibility: Sykes (1992) in his book *A Nation of Victims* was troubled by the tendency of the United States to become a "nation of whiners unwilling to take responsibility for our actions." Whether his statement is true or not, counselors must be able to distinguish "whiners" from those who are truly being victimized.

b). Clients talk about their **behavior** — that is, what they do or refrain from doing.

> All of us do things that get us into trouble and fail to do things that will help us get out of trouble or develop opportunities. Some clients talk freely about their experiences, what happens to them, but seem more reluctant to talk about their behaviors. One reason for this is that they can't talk about behaviors without bringing up issues of personal responsibility.

c). Clients talk about their **affect** — that is, the feelings, emotions, and moods that arise from or are associated with their experiences and both internal and external behavior.

> Feelings, emotions, and moods constitute a river that continually runs through us — peaceful, meandering, turbulent, or raging — often beneficial, sometimes dangerous, seldom neutral. They are certainly an important part of clients' problem situations and undeveloped

141

opportunities (Greenberg & Paivio, 1997; Plutchik, 2001). Understanding the role of feelings, emotions, and moods in client's problem situations and their desire to identify and develop opportunities is central to the helping process. Emotions highlight learning opportunities.

References: (Norcross & Kobayashi, 1999, p. 275; the *Journal of Clinical Psychology*, *55*, March, 1999; Chamberlin, 2000; McKay & Dinkmeyer, 1994; McKay, Davis, & Fanning, 1997; Lang (1995); Machado, Beutler, & Greenberg, 1999; Salovey, Rothman, Detweiler, & Steward, 2000)

Since experiences, actions, and emotions are interrelated in the day-today lives of clients, they mix them together in telling their stories. And stories, often in the form of examples, are used to explain and illustrate points of view, decisions, intentions, and proposals. Your first job is to listen carefully to the mix clients use to talk about their concerns and what they would like to do about them.

2. Listening to Clients' Points of View

As clients tell their stories, explore possibilities for a better future, set goals, make plans, and review obstacles to accomplishing these plans, they often share their points of view.

   a) A point of view is a client's personal estimation of something.

   b) A full point of view includes the point of view itself, the reasons for it, an illustration to bring it to life, and some indication how open the client might to modifying it.

   c) Points of view reveal clients' beliefs, values, attitudes, and convictions.

   d) Clients may share their points of view about everything under the sun.

   e) The ones that are relevant to their problem situations or undeveloped opportunities need to be listened to and understood.

   f) Points of view have power.

3. Listening to Clients' Decisions

From time to time, we all tell others about decisions we are making or that we've made.

   a) Decisions usually have implications for the decision maker and for others.

b) Commands, instructions, and even hints are, in a way, decisions about other people's behavior.

c) Sharing a decision fully means spelling out the decision itself, the reasons for the decision, the implications for self and others, and some indication as to whether the decision or any part of it is open to review.

d) Decisions can be tricky. Often enough, *how* they are delivered says a great deal about the decision itself.

4. Listening to Clients' Intentions and Proposals

a) Clients state intentions, offer proposals, or make a case for certain courses of action.

b) The case includes what she/he wants to, the reasons for doing, and the implications for herself/himself and others.

c) When clients talk about their concerns, they mix all these forms of discourse together.

d) Developing frameworks for listening can help you zero in on the key messages your clients are communicating and help you identify and understand the feelings, emotions, and moods that go with them.

5. "Hearing" Opportunities and Resources

a) If you listen only for problems, you will end up talking mainly about problems. And you will shortchange your clients.

b) Every client has something going for him or her.

c) Your job is to spot clients' resources and help them invest these resources in managing problem situations and opportunities.

d) If people generally use only a fraction of their potential, then there is much to be tapped.

B.   Listening to the Client's Nonverbal Messages and Modifiers (OH-5.3)

1.   Clients send messages through their nonverbal behavior. The ability of people to read these messages can contribute to their relationship well-being (Carton, Kessler, & Pape, 1999). Helpers need to learn how to read these messages without distorting or overinterpreting them.

2.   Our nonverbal behavior has a way of "leaking" messages about what we really mean. The very spontaneity of nonverbal behaviors contributes to this leakage even in the case of highly defensive clients. It is not easy for clients to fake nonverbal behavior (Wahlsten, 1991). The real messages still tend to leak out.

3.   Besides being a channel of communication in itself, such nonverbal behavior as facial expressions, bodily motions, and voice quality often modify and punctuate verbal messages in much the same way that periods, question marks, exclamation points, and underlining punctuate written language.

4.   All the kinds of nonverbal behavior can punctuate or modify verbal communication in the following ways:

   a)   **Confirming or repeating**. Nonverbal behavior can confirm or repeat what is being said verbally.

   b)   **Denying or confusing**. Nonverbal behavior can deny or confuse what is being said verbally.

   c)   **Strengthening or emphasizing**. Nonverbal behavior can strengthen or emphasize what is being said.

   d)   **Adding intensity**. Nonverbal behavior often adds emotional color or intensity to verbal messages.

   e)   **Controlling or regulating**. Nonverbal cues are often used in conversation to regulate or control what is happening.

5.   In reading nonverbal behavior — "reading" is used here instead of "interpreting" — caution is a must. We listen to clients in order to understand them, not to dissect them.

6.   Merely reading about nonverbal behavior is not enough. Identifying relevant clues in videotaped interactions can help great deal (Costanzo, 1992).

7. Effective helpers listen to the entire context of the helping interview and do not become overly fixated on details of behavior.

8. There is no need to go overboard on listening. Remember that you are a human being listening to a human being, not a vacuum cleaner indiscriminately sweeping up every scrap.

9. Quality, not quantity.

Section Three: PROCESSING WHAT YOU HEAR: THE THOUGHTFUL SEARCH FOR MEANING

Even though we do it while we listen, we process what we hear. The trick is to become a thoughtful processor.
.

A. **Identifying Key Messages and Feelings**. (OH-5.4)

1. Denise listens to what Jennie has to say early on about her past and present experiences, actions, and emotions.

2. She listens to Jennie's points of view and the decisions she had made or is in the process of making.

3. She listens to Jennie's intentions and proposals.

4. As Denise listens to Jennie speak, questions based on the listening frameworks outlined here arise in the back of her mind:

   a) "What are the main points here?"
   b) "What experiences and actions are most important?"
   c) "What themes are coming through?"
   d) "What is Jennie's point of view?"
   e) "What is most important to her?"
   f) "What does she want me to understand?"
   g) "What decisions are implied in what she's saying?"
   h) "What is she proposing to do?"

5. If helpers think that everything that their clients say is key, then nothing is key.

6. In the end, helpers make a clinical judgment as to what is key

7. Helpers have ways of checking their understanding.

145

B. Understanding Clients Through Context. (OH-5.5)

1. People are more than the sum of their verbal and nonverbal messages.

2. Listening in its deepest sense means listening to clients themselves as influenced by the contexts in which they "live, move, and have their being."

3. Earlier it was pointed out how important it is to interpret a client's nonverbal behavior in the context of the entire helping session.

4. It is also essential to understand clients' stories, points of view, and messages through the wider context of their lives.

5. Effective helpers listen through this wider context without being overwhelmed by the details of it.

6. McAuliffe and Eriksen (1999), for example, a where-when-how-what model for helping helpers think about their clients in context. There are four questions that go something like this.

   a) The first deals with background, the circumstances of the client's life. What circumstances surround the client and how do these circumstances affect the way the client understands and deals with her problems and opportunities?

   b) The second question deals with developmental stage. What age-related psychosocial tasks and challenges is the client currently facing and how does the way he goes about these tasks affect the problem situation or opportunity?

   c) The third question deals with the client's approach to coming to know and make sense of the world about him or her. How does the client go about constructing meaning, including such things as determining what is important and what is right?

   d) The last question deals with personality. How does the client's personality style and temperament affect his understanding of himself and his approach to the world?

7. You need to discover for yourself the contextual frameworks that can help you understand your clients as "people-in-systems" (Egan & Cowan, 1979)? And contextual frameworks need to be updated.

C. Hearing the Slant or Spin: Tough-Minded Listening and Processing.

1. Skilled helpers not only listen to the client's stories, points of view, decisions, intentions, and proposals but also to any slant or spin that clients might give their stories.

2. Although clients' visions of and feelings about themselves, others, and the world are real and need to be understood, their perceptions of themselves and their worlds are sometimes distorted.

3. Tough-minded listening includes detecting the gaps, distortions, and dissonance that are part of the client's experienced reality.

4. To be client-centered, helpers must first be reality-centered.

5. Helpers need not challenge clients as soon as they hear any kind of distortion. Rather, they note gaps and distortions, choose key ones, and challenge them when it is appropriate to do so (see Chapters 10-12).

D. Musing on What's Missing. Clients often leave key elements out when talking about problems and opportunities.

1. Having frameworks for listening can help you spot key things that are missing. For instance, they tell their stories but leave out key experiences, behaviors, or feelings.

2. As you listen, it's important to note what they put in and what they leave out.

3. Note that this is not a search for the "hidden stuff" that clients are leaving unsaid. We all leave out key details from time to time.

4. Use clinical judgment — a large part of which is common sense — to determine whether to ask about the missing parts or not.

Section Four: LISTENING TO ONESELF: THE HELPER'S INTERNAL CONVERSATION

The conversation helpers have with themselves during helping sessions is the "internal conversation."

1. To be an effective helper, you need to listen not only to the client but also to yourself.

2. Listening to yourself on a "second channel" can help you identify both what you might do to be of further help to the client and what might be standing in the way of your being with and listening to the client.

3. It is a positive form of self-consciousness.

4. These messages can refer to the helper, the client, or the relationship.

   a) "I'm letting the client get under my skin. I had better do something to reset the dialogue."
   b) "My mind has been wandering. I'm preoccupied with what I have to do tomorrow. I had better put that out of my mind."
   c) "Here's a client who has had a tough time of it, but her self-pity is standing in the way of her doing anything about it. My instinct is to be sympathetic. I need to talk to her about her self-pity, but I had better go slow."
   d) "It's not clear that this client is interested in changing. It's time to test the waters."

5. This internal conversation goes on all the time.

6. It can be a distraction or it can be another tool for helping. The client, too, is having his or her internal conversation.

7. One intriguing study (Hill, Thompson, Cogar, & Denman, 1993) suggested that both client and therapist are more or less aware of the other's "covert processes." This study showed that helpers, even though they knew that clients were having their own internal conversations and left things unsaid, were not very good at determining what those things were. At times there are verbal or nonverbal hints as to what the client's internal dialogue might be.

8. Helping clients move key points from their internal conversations into the helping dialogue is a key task.

Section Five: THE SHADOW SIDE OF LISTENING TO CLIENTS

Listening as described here is not as easy as it sounds. Obstacles and distractions abound. Some relate to listening generally. Others relate more specifically to listening to and interpreting the nonverbal behavior of clients.

A. Forms of Distorted Listening (OH-5.6)

The following kinds of distorted listening, as you will see from your own experience, permeate human communication. They also insinuate themselves at times into the helping dialogue. Sometimes more than one kind of distortion contaminates the helping dialogue. They are part of the shadow side because helpers never intend to engage in these kinds of listening. Rather helpers fall into them at times without even realizing that they are doing so. But they stand in the way of the kind of open-minded listening and processing needed for real dialogue.

1. **Filtered listening**. It is impossible to listen to other people in a completely unbiased way.

   a) Through socialization we develop a variety of filters through which we listen to ourselves, others, and the world around us.

   b) We need filters to provide structure for ourselves as we interact with the world.

   c) But personal, familial, sociological, and cultural filters introduce various forms of bias into our listening and do so without our being aware of it.

   d) The stronger the cultural filters, the greater the likelihood of bias.

   e) Prejudices, whether conscious or not, distort understanding.

   f) Helpers are tempted to pigeonhole clients because of gender, race, sexual orientation, nationality, social status, religious persuasion, political preferences, lifestyle, and the like.

   g) Self-knowledge on the part our part as helpers is essential and includes ferreting out the biases and prejudices that distort listening.

2. **Evaluative listening**. Most people, even when they listen attentively, listen evaluatively.

   a) As they listen, they are judging what the other person is saying as good/bad, right/wrong, acceptable/unacceptable, likable/unlikable, relevant/irrelevant, and so forth.

   b) Helpers are not exempt from this universal tendency.

   c) Clients should first be understood, then, if necessary, challenged or helped to challenge themselves.

   d) Evaluative listening, translated into advice giving, will just put clients off.

   e) There are productive forms of evaluative listening. It is practically impossible to suspend judgment completely.

f) It is possible to set one's judgment aside for the time being in the interest of understanding clients, their worlds, their stories, their points of view, and their decisions "from the inside."

3. **Stereotyped-based listening**.

   a) The very labels we learn in our training — paranoid, neurotic, sexual disorder, borderline — can militate against empathic understanding.

   b) Books on personality theories provide us with stereotypes: "He's a perfectionist."

   c) In psychotherapy diagnostic categories can take precedence over the clients being diagnosed.

   d) Helpers forget at times that their labels are interpretations rather than understandings of their clients.

   e) What you learn as you study psychology may help you to organize what you hear, but it may also distort your listening.

   f) To use terms borrowed from Gestalt psychology, make sure that your client remains "figure" — in the forefront of your attention — and that models and theories about clients remain "ground" —

   g) Knowledge that remains in the background and is used only in the interest of understanding and helping this unique client.

4. **Fact-centered rather than person-centered listening**.

   a) Some helpers ask clients many informational questions.

   b) It's entirely possible to collect facts but miss the person.

   c) The antidote is to listen to clients contextually, trying to focus on themes and key messages.

5. **Sympathetic listening.** Since most clients are experiencing some kind of misery and since some have been victimized by others or by society itself, there is a tendency on the part of helpers to feel sympathy for them.

   a) Sometimes these feelings are strong enough to distort the stories that clients are telling.

b) Expressing sympathy can reinforce self-pity in a client.

c) Self-pity has a way of driving out problem-managing action.

6. Interrupting.

When helpers interrupt their clients, they, by definition, stop listening.

Interrupters often say things that they have been rehearsing, which means that they have been only partially listening.

There are benign and malignant forms of interrupting.

If interrupting promotes the kind of dialogue that serves the problem-management process, then it is useful.

Care must be taken to factor in cultural differences in storytelling.

One possible reason counselors fall prey to these kinds of shadow-side listening is the unexamined assumption that listening with an open mind is the same as approving what the client is saying. This, of course, is not the case. Rather, listening with an open mind helps you learn and understand. Whatever the reason for shadow-side listening, the outcome can be devastating because of a truth philosophers learned long ago — a small error in the beginning can lead to huge errors down the road. If the foundation of a building is out of kilter, it is hard to notice with the naked eye. But, by the time construction reaches the ninth floor, it begins to look like the leaning tower of Pisa. Tuning in to clients and listening both actively and with an open mind are foundation counseling skills. Ignore them and dialogue is impossible.

B. Myths About Nonverbal Behavior (OH-5.7)

Richmond and McCroskey (2000) spell out the shadow side of nonverbal behavior in terms of commonly-held myths (pp. 2-3):

Nonverbal communication is nonsense. All communication involves language. Therefore, all communication is verbal. This myth is disappearing. It does not stand up under the scrutiny of common sense.

Nonverbal behavior accounts for most of the communication in human interaction. Early studies tried to "prove" this, but they were biased. Studies were aimed at dispelling myth number 1 and overstepped their boundaries.

You can read a person like a book. Some people, even some professionals, would like to think so. You can read nonverbal behavior, verbal behavior, and context and still be wrong.

If a person does not look you in the eye while talking to you, he or she is not telling the truth. Tell this to liars! The same nonverbal behavior can mean many different things.

Although nonverbal behavior differs from person to person, most nonverbal behaviors are natural to all people. Cross-cultural studies give the lie to this. But it isn't true within the same culture.

Nonverbal behavior stimulates the same meaning in different situations. Too often the context is the key. Yet some professionals buy the myth and base interpretive systems on it.

Lecture Enhancers

You should be able to find the full text of the following items in your library or by using your web-based library access tool of choice (e.g.,PsycInfo).

Item One: Being Heard

Empathetic listening: Reports on the experience of being heard.

Myers, Sharon. (2000) Empathetic listening: Reports on the experience of being heard. In Journal of Humanistic Psychology, 2000 Spr;Vol 40(2): 148-173.

Synopsis: This qualitative study compares empathic listening from the perspective of clients with histories of not being heard in therapeutic sessions to the same clients' therapeutic sessions in which empathic listening and understanding occurs. The therapeutic dialogue between the client and the therapist is greatly enhanced through empathic listening and previously undisclosed issues emerge.

Research provides that the following elements are essential to empathic listening: paraphrasing, clarifying, questioning, and remembering details. Furthermore, empathic listening is considered more than an applied therapeutic technique and instead is considered a unique opportunity for the client to truly interact with the therapist and most importantly, be heard.

Item Two: Racism

Reeves, Kenneth M. (2000). Racism and projection of the shadow. In Psychotherapy. 2000 Spr; Vol 37(1): 80-88

Synopsis: This article uses the Jungian concepts of the shadow and shadow projection in relation to racism and provides strategies for psychotherapy for both the targets and the perpetrators. The recognition of the effects of racism and empowerment of targeted individuals in therapy is emphasised in contrast to therapy for perpetrators that focuses on examination, acceptance and monitoring of his/her shadow side.

The author also stresses the need for therapists to be cognisant of the shadow as a means of establishing rapport with clients of various cultures.

Item Three: Critiques of Psychotherapy

Facing, understanding and learning from critiques of psychotherapy and counselling.

Feltham,-Colin. (1999). Facing, understanding and learning from critiques of psychotherapy and counselling. In British-Journal-of-Guidance-and-Counselling. 1999 Aug; Vol 27(3):301-311.

Synopsis: This article addresses the difficult issue that therapists must manage when faced with criticism directed at psychotherapy and counselling. The author presents the valuable aspects of valid criticism that could transfer to a proactive examination of therapy's shadow side, an exploration that may well be work to the advantage of the field in terms of social, ethical and clinical effectiveness. In addition, Feltham recommends the self-critique of therapy by those in the field, a skill that could be learned while a student of psychotherapy.

Class Activities

In addition to the exercises in the Workbook that accompanies this text, you may find the following in-class activities to be of value:

Activity #1: Are You Listening

There is something to be said about bad listening habits: we can learn from them. Students always enjoy the opportunity to demonstrate bad listening habits. It usually results in lots of good laughs and some very good "teachable moments."

Have the student for triads rotating the roles of helper, client, and observer. Have the help display as many "bad" listening skills as he or she can imagine. Have the observer record the "bad" listening skills and then have the triad talk about the experience from the point of view of the client, the helper and the observer. If time allows, have the triads report out to the class their most important and interesting conclusions about listening skills.

Activity #2: From One Extreme to the Other

In this activity have students do just the opposite and demonstrate good listening skills to the extreme or even the absurd. Back in triads, have the students model too much positive body language, too much empathy, too much facial expression, to much concern. Again, have the triads debrief by sharing how the experience felt from the point of view of the client, the helper, and the observer. Have the students change roles until all three students have had the opportunity to play all three roles.

The learning point to be made is that too much emphasis on listening skills can be detracting and detrimental to the helping relationship. The "Skilled Helper" has just the right level of listening skills to be effective with the client.

Activity #3: When I Felt Heard

In this brief activity, have students take out a piece of paper and list three times in their lives that they felt very listened to by another person. Have them list the following:

1. The person listening:

2. The situation:

3. What gave him or her the feeling of being listened to (e.g., body language, facial expressions, constructive silence, appropriate reflection)?

Next have the students share in small groups or as a class the elements of item three above, what gave them the feeling of being listened to, that worked best for them.

Finally, discuss how one could use these positive experiences to enhance the helping relationship.

Videos

Approaches to Therapy (1990, 30 min, IM). The same client is viewed in a cognitive-behavioural, psychodynamic, and humanistic therapeutic setting.

Basic Interviewing Skills for psychologists (1991, 50 min, IM). An excellent guide foe appropriate interviewing of clients.

Demonstrations Of Counselling: Rational-Emotive Theory (1970, 90 min, IM). Applications of RET by Ellis include a young boy, a divorcee, and a woman with self-expression issues.

Ethnicity and Counselling (4 parts, 1990, 267 min total, IM). The videos represent ethnicity and counselling issues for Mexican, Vietnamese, African American, and Native American clients.

Three Approaches to Counselling (1993, 80 min, IM). The approaches include humanistic counselling, psychodynamic dream work, and assertiveness training.

Rational-Emotive Therapy (Research Press, 30 min, colour, #2100). The film includes Albert Ellis discussing RET, sessions with clients, and RET related activities.

Websites

1. http://www.atee.org/htm/conferences/leipzig/h_klinzing2.html
   Improving the perceptiveness to non verbal clues.

2. http://www.coun.uvic.ca/personal/assert.html
   Assertiveness, analysis and development.

3. http://cogsci.uwaterloo.ca/Articles/Pages/Empathy.html - anchor01
   Empathy and listening skills.

4. http://www.medinfo.ufl.edu/year1/bcs96/slides/comm/comm17.html
   Steps in communicating empathy.

5. http://www.opendoors.com.au/commun.htm
   Communicating with empathy.

Overhead Transparencies

Starting on the next page are copies of recommended overhead transparencies. Please feel free to convert the following pages to overheads as this will enhance the lecture portion of your class presentation.

INADEQUATE LISTENING

1. Non-Listening.

2. Partial listening.

3. Tape-recorder listening.

4. Rehearsing.

OH 5.1

LISTENING TO WORDS

1. Listening to Clients' Stories

        a. Experiences
        b. Behavior
        c. Affect

2. Listening to Clients' Points of View

3. Listening to Clients' Decisions

4. Listening to Clients' Intentions and Proposals

5. "Hearing" Opportunities and Resources

OH 5.2

LISTENING TO THE CLIENTS' NONVERBAL MESSAGES

1. Confirming or repeating.

2. Denying or confusing.

3. Strengthening or emphasizing.

4. Adding intensity.

5. Controlling or regulating.

OH 5.3

IDENTIFYING KEY MESSAGES AND FEELINGS

a) "What are the main points here?"

b) "What experiences and actions are most important?"

c) "What themes are coming through?"

d) "What is their point of view?"

e) "What is most important to her/him?"

OH 5.4A

IDENTIFYING KEY MESSAGES
AND FEELINGS
continued

f)   "What does she/he want me to understand?"

g)   "What decisions are implied in what she's/he's saying?"

h)   "What is she/he proposing to do?"

OH 5.4B

UNDERSTANDING CLIENTS THROUGH CONTEXT

1. Background, the circumstances of the client's life.

2. The client's developmental stage.

3. The client's approach to coming to know and make sense of the world about him or her.

4. The client's personality style and temperament.

OH 5.5

FORMS OF DISTORTED LISTENING

1. Filtered listening.

2. Evaluative listening.

3. Stereotyped-based listening.

4. Fact-centered rather than person-centered listening.

5. Sympathetic listening.

6. Interrupting

OH 5.6

MYTHS ABOUT NONVERBAL BEHAVIOR

1. Nonverbal communication is nonsense. All communication involves language. Therefore, all communication is verbal.

2. Nonverbal behavior accounts for most of the communication in human interaction.

3. You can read a person like a book.

OH 5.7A

MYTHS ABOUT NONVERBAL BEHAVIOR (cont'd).

4. If a person does not look you in the eye while talking to you, he or she is not telling the truth.

5. Although nonverbal behavior differs from person to person, most nonverbal behaviors are natural to all people.

6. Nonverbal behavior stimulates the same meaning in different situations.

OH 5.7B

Chapter Six:

Sharing Empathic Highlights: Communicating and Checking Understanding

	Pages
Chapter Outline	**170**
Detailed Lecture Notes	**171-185**
Lecture Enhancers	**186-187**
Class Activities	**188-189**
Videos	**190**
Websites	**191**
Transparencies	**192-201**

CHAPTER SIX OUTLINE

SHARING EMPATHIC HIGHLIGHTS: COMMUNICATING AND CHECKING UNDERSTANDING

RESPONDING SKILLS

THE THREE DIMENSIONS OF RESPONDING SKILLS: PERCEPTIVENESS, KNOW-HOW, AND ASSERTIVENESS

SHARING EMPATHIC HIGHLIGHTS: COMMUNICATING UNDERSTANDING TO CLIENTS

THE KEY BUILDING BLOCKS OF EMPATHIC HIGHLIGHTS

➢ The Basic Formula
➢ Respond Accurately to Clients' Feelings, Emotions, and Moods
➢ Respond Accurately to the Key Experiences and Behaviors in Clients' Stories
➢ Respond with Highlights to Clients' Points of View, Decisions, and Proposals

PRINCIPLES FOR SHARING HIGHLIGHTS

TACTICS FOR COMMUNICATING HIGHLIGHTS

A CAUTION: THE IMPORTANCE OF EMPATHIC RELATIONSHIPS

THE SHADOW SIDE OF SHARING EMPATHIC HIGHLIGHTS

(Please note: The designation OH in the detailed lecture notes indicates an overhead transparency is available. Please locate the overhead transparencies in the final section of each chapter in this Instructors' Manual.)

Section One: RESPONDING SKILLS

Helpers listen to clients in order to respond to them at the service of a helping dialogue. The logic of listening includes, as we have seen, visibly tuning in to clients, listening actively, processing what is heard contextually, and identifying the key ideas, messages, or points of view the client is trying to communicate — all at the service of understanding clients. Listening, then, is a very active process that serves understanding. But helpers also respond to clients in a variety of ways. They share their understanding, they check to make sure that they've got things right, they ask questions, they probe for clarity, and they challenge clients in a variety of ways. In this chapter the focus is on sharing empathic highlights as a way of both communicating understanding to clients and checking to see if that understanding is accurate. When helpers communicate accurate understanding to clients, they help their clients understand themselves more fully.

Section Two: THE THREE DIMENSIONS OF RESPONDING SKILLS: PERCEPTIVENESS, KNOW-HOW, AND ASSERTIVENESS (OH-6.1)

The communication skills involved in responding to clients have three dimensions: perceptiveness, know-how, and assertiveness.

A. **Perceptiveness**. Your responding skills are only as good as the accuracy of the perceptions on which they are based.

   1. The kind of perceptiveness needed to be a good helper comes from basic intelligence, social intelligence, experience, reflecting on your experience, developing wisdom, and, more immediately, tuning in to clients, listening carefully to what they have to say, and objectively processing what they say.

   2. Perceptiveness comes with social-emotional maturity.

B. **Know-how**. Once you are aware of what kind of response is called for, you need to be able to deliver it. If you are aware that a client is anxious and confused because this is his first visit to a helper, it does little good if you don't know how to translate your perceptions and your understanding into words.

C. **Assertiveness**. Accurate perceptions and excellent know-how are meaningless if they remain locked up inside you. They need to become part of the therapeutic dialogue. For instance, if you see that self-doubt is a theme that weaves itself throughout a client's story about her frustrating search for a better relationship with her estranged brother but fail to share your hunch with her, you do not pass the assertiveness test. To be assertive without perceptiveness and know-how is to court disaster.

Section Three: SHARING EMPATHIC HIGHLIGHTS: COMMUNICATING UNDERSTANDING TO CLIENTS

A. "Feeling empathy" for others is not helpful if the helper's perceptions are not accurate.

1. Ickes (1993, 1997) talked about "empathic accuracy" which he defined as "the ability to accurately infer the specific content of another person's thought and feelings" (1993, p. 588).

2. According to Ickes (1997, p. 2), this ability is a component of success in many walks of life.

> Empathically accurate perceivers are those who are consistently good at "reading" other people's thoughts and feelings. All else being equal, they are likely to be the most tactful advisors, the most diplomatic officials, the most effective negotiators, the most electable politicians, the most productive salespersons, the most successful teachers, and the most insightful therapists. (1997, p. 2)

3. The assumption is that such people are not only accurate perceivers but they can also weave their perceptions into their dialogues with their constituents, customers, students, and clients.

4. Helpers do this by sharing empathic highlights with their clients.

5. The communication skill involving helpers' sharing their understanding of clients' key experiences, behaviors, and feelings has been renamed *sharing empathic highlights* — or, more simply, sharing highlights.

6. If you are truly empathic, if you listen actively.

7. If you thoughtfully process what you hear, putting what the client says in its proper context, then you do more than paraphrase or restate. There is something of you in your response.

8. A good response is a product of caring and hard work.

9. Good highlights are fully human, not mechanical.

10. If visibly tuning in and listening are the skills that enable helpers to get in touch with the world of the client, then sharing highlights is the skill that enables them both to communicate their understanding of that world and to check the accuracy of that understanding.

11. A secure starting point in helping others is listening to them carefully, struggling to understand their concerns, and sharing that understanding with them.

12. When clients are asked what they find helpful in counseling sessions, being understood gets top ratings. There is such an unfulfilled need to be understood.

Section Four: THE KEY BUILDING BLOCKS OF EMPATHIC HIGHLIGHTS

A. The Basic Formula. Basic empathic understanding can be expressed in the following stylized formula:

You feel... [here name the correct emotion expressed by the client]...

because ... [here indicate the correct experiences and behaviors that give rise to the feelings]....

1. The formula — "You feel ..... because ...." — is a beginner's tool to get used to the concept of sharing highlights.

2. It focuses on the key points of clients' stories, points of view, decisions, and proposals together with the relevant feelings, emotions, and moods associated with them.

3. The helper captures both the emotion and the reason for the feeling. And the client moves forward in terms of thinking about possible actions she could take.

4. The key elements of an empathic highlight are the experiences, behaviors, and feelings that make up that story.

B. Respond Accurately to Clients' Feelings, Emotions, and Moods. (OH-6.3)

The importance of feelings, emotions, and moods in our lives was discussed in Chapter 5. Helpers need to respond to clients' emotions in such a way as to move the helping process forward. This means identifying key emotions the client either expresses or discusses (helper perceptiveness) and weaving them into the dialogue (helper know how) even when they are sensitive or part of a messy situation (helper courage, or assertiveness). Remember the last time you got a problem resolved with a good customer service representatives?   "I know you're angry right now because the package didn't arrive and you have every right to be. After all, we did make you a promise. Here's what we can do to make it right for you...." Rather than ignoring the customer's emotions, good customer service reps face up to them as helpfully as possible.

1. **Use the right family of emotions and the right intensity**. In the basic highlight formula, "You feel..." should be followed by the correct family of emotions and the correct intensity.

   Family. The statements "You feel hurt," "You feel relieved," and "You feel enthusiastic" specify different families of emotion.

   Intensity. The statements "You feel annoyed," "You feel angry," and "You're furious" specify different degrees of intensity in the same family (anger).

The words sad, mad, bad, and glad refer to four of the main families of emotion, whereas "content," "quite happy,"and "overjoyed" refer to different intensities within the "glad" family.

2. **Distinguish between expressed and discussed feelings.** Clients both *express* emotions they are feeling during the interview and *talk about* emotions they felt at the time of some incident. Clients don't always name their feelings and emotions. However, if they express emotion, it is part of the message and needs to be identified and understood.

3. **Read and respond to feelings and emotions embedded in clients' nonverbal behavior.** Often helpers have to read their clients' emotions — both the family and the intensity — in their nonverbal behavior. Of course, you do not yet know the experiences and behaviors that give rise to these emotions.

4. **Be sensitive in naming emotions**. Naming and discussing feelings threatens some clients. In this case, it might be better to focus on experiences and behaviors and proceed only gradually to a discussion of feelings. However, being sensitive to clients' sensitive emotions should not rob counseling of its robustness. Too much tiptoeing around clients' "sensitivities" does not serve them well. Remember what was said earlier. Clients are not as fragile as we sometimes make them out to be.

5. Use different ways to share highlights about feelings and emotions. Since clients express feelings in a number of different ways, helpers can communicate an understanding of feelings in a variety of ways.

a) **By single words.** You feel good. You're depressed. You feel abandoned. You're delighted. You feel trapped. You're angry.

b) **By different kinds of phrases.** You're sitting on top of the world. You feel down in the dumps. You feel left in the lurch. Your back's up against the wall. You're really steaming. You're really on a roll.

c) **By what is implied in behavioral statements.** You feel like giving up (implied emotion: despair). You feel like hugging him (implied emotion: joy). Now that you see what he's done to you, you almost feel like throwing up (implied emotion: disgust).

d) **By what is implied in experiences that are revealed.** You feel you're being dumped on (implied feeling: victimized). You feel you're being stereotyped (implied feeling: resentment). You feel you're at the top of her list (implied feeling: elation). You feel you're going to get caught (implied feeling: apprehension). Note that the implication of each could be spelled out: You feel angry because you're being dumped on. You resent the fact that you're being stereotyped. You feel great because it seems that you're at the top of her list.

6. Neither overemphasize nor underemphasize feelings, emotions, and moods. Some counselors take an overly rational approach to helping and almost ignore clients' feelings. Others become too preoccupied with clients' emotions and moods. They pepper clients with questions about feelings and at times extort answers. To say that feelings, emotions, and moods are important is not to say that they are everything. The best defense against either extreme is to link feelings, emotions, and moods to the experiences and behaviors that give rise to them (see Anderson & Leitner, 1996).

C. Respond Accurately to the Key Experiences and Behaviors in Clients' Stories

Key experiences and behaviors give rise to clients' feelings, emotions, and moods.

1. The "because..." in the empathic-highlight formula is to be followed by an indication of the experiences and behaviors that underlie the client's feelings.

2. The stylized formula "you feel... because..." is too wooden. Experienced trainers use it only when it sounds natural. Otherwise they use ordinary language to share highlights.

D. Respond with Highlights to Clients' Points of View, Decisions, and Proposals (OH-6.4)

Sharing highlights communicates to clients that you are working hard at understanding them at the service of constructive change.

    1. Communicating Understanding of Clients' Points of View.
       Once the counselor communicates understanding of the client's point of view, he (the client) moves on.

    2. Communicating Understanding of Clients' Decisions.

       a) When clients announce key decisions or express their resolve to do something, it's important to recognize the core of what they are saying.
       b) In a positive psychology mode, the counselor focuses on past successes. They go on to discuss the kind of "rachets" he needs to stay on track.

    3. Communicating Understanding of Intentions or Proposals.

       a) The client comes up with a proposal for a course of action.

       b) The helper's response recognizes her enthusiasm and sense of determination.

       c) They go on to have a dialogue about practical tactics.

       d) Providing some examples helps the client identify the implications of her/his proposal.

**Section Five: PRINCIPLES FOR
SHARING HIGHLIGHTS (OH-6.5)**

Here are a number of principles that can guide you as you share highlights. Remember that these guidelines are principles, not formulas to be followed slavishly.

A. Use Empathic Highlights at Every Stage and Step of the Helping Process.
    Sharing highlights is useful at every stage and every step of the helping process. Communicating and checking understanding is always helpful.

1. Here are some examples of helpers sharing highlights at different stages and steps of the helping process.

> **Stage I: Problem clarification and opportunity identification.** A teenager in his third year of high school who has just found out that he is moving with his family to a different city. The counselor realizes that he has to help his client pick up the pieces and move on, but sharing his understanding helps build a foundation to do so.

> **Stage II: Evaluating goal options.** A woman who has been discussing the trade-offs between marriage and career: At one point her helper says, "There's some ambivalence here. If you marry Jim, you might not be able to have the kind of career you'd like. Or did I hear you half say that it might be possible to put both together? Sort of get the best of both worlds." The client goes on the explore the possibilities around "getting the best of both worlds." It helps her greatly in preparing for her next conversation with Jim.

> **Stage III: Choosing actions to accomplish goals.** A man has been discussing his desire to control his cholesterol level without taking a medicine whose side effects worry him. He says that it might work. The helper recognizes an important part of the client's message, but then seeks further clarification.

> **The Action Arrow: Implementation Issues**. A married couple who have been struggling to put into practice a few strategies to improve their communication with each other. They've both called their attempts a "disaster." The counselor communicates understanding of their disappointment in not implementing their plan, but, in the spirit of positive psychology, focuses on what they can learn from the failure.

2. Communicating understanding by sharing empathic highlights is a mode of human contact, a relationship builder, a conversational lubricant, a perception-checking intervention, and a mild form of social influence. It is always useful.

3. Driscoll (1984), in his common-sense way, referred to highlights as "nickel-and-dime" interventions which each contribute only a smidgen of therapeutic movement, but without which the course of therapeutic progress would be markedly slower" (p. 90).

4. Since sharing highlights provides a continual trickle of understanding, it is a way of providing support for clients throughout the helping process.

5. It is never wrong to let clients know that you are trying to understand them from their frame of reference.

6. Clients who feel they are being understood participate more effectively and more fully in the helping process.

7. Since sharing highlights helps build trust, it paves the way for stronger interventions on the part of the helper, such as challenging.

B. Respond Selectively to Core Client Messages. It is impossible to respond with highlights to everything a client says.

1. As you listen to clients, try to identify and respond to what you believe are core messages — that is, the heart of what the client is saying and expressing, especially if the client speaks at any length.

2. Sometimes this selectivity means paying particular attention to one or two messages even though the client communicates many.

3. Clients are not always obliging, so helpers must continually ask themselves as they listen, "What is key? What is most important here?" and then find ways of checking it out with the client. This helps clients sort out things that are not clear in their own minds.

4. Responding selectively sometimes means focusing on experiences or actions or feelings rather than all three.

C. Respond to the Context, Not Just the Words.

1. A good empathic response is not based just on the client's immediate words and nonverbal behavior.

2. It also takes into account the context of what is said, everything that "surrounds" and permeates a client's statement.

3. This client may be in crisis.

4. That client may be doing a more leisurely "taking stock" of where he is in life.

5. You are listening to clients in the context of their lives.

6. The context modifies everything the client says.

D. Use Highlights as a Mild Social-Influence Process.

1. Because helpers cannot respond with highlights to everything their clients say, they are always searching for core messages.

2. They are forced into a selection process that influences the course of the therapeutic dialogue.

3. Even sharing highlights can be part of the social-influence process outlined in Chapter 3.

4. Helpers believe that the messages they select for attention are core primarily because they are core for the client.

5. Helpers also believe, at some level, that certain messages should be important for the client.

6. Helpers need to be careful not to put words in a client's mouth.

E. Use Highlights to Stimulate Movement in the Helping Process.

1. Sharing highlights is an excellent tool for building the helping relationship.

2. It also needs to serve the goals of the helping process.

3. Sharing highlights is useful to the degree that it helps the client move forward.

4. What does "move forward" mean? That depends on the stage or step in focus.

   a) sharing highlights helps clients move forward in Stage I if it helps them explore a problem situation or an undeveloped opportunity more realistically.

   b) It helps clients move forward in Stage II to the degree that it helps them identify and explore possibilities for a better future, craft a change agenda, or discuss commitment to that agenda.

   c) Moving forward in Stage III means clarifying action strategies, choosing specific things to do, and setting up a plan. In the action phase, moving forward means identifying obstacles to action, overcoming them, and accomplishing goals.

5. It often happens that sharing highlights that hit the mark puts pressure on clients to move forward.

6.   Sharing highlights, even though it is a communication of understanding, is also part of the social-influence process.

F. Recover from Inaccurate Understanding.

1.   Although helpers should strive to be accurate in the understanding they communicate, all helpers can be inaccurate at times.

2.   Sharing highlights is a perception-checking tool. If the helper's response is accurate, the client often tends to confirm its accuracy in two ways.

    a) The first is some kind of verbal or nonverbal indication that the helper is right. That is, the client nods or gives some other nonverbal cue or uses some assenting word or phrase such as "that's right" or "exactly."

    b) The second and more substantive way in which clients acknowledge the accuracy of the helper's response is by moving forward in the helping process

3. The next cycle may mean further clarification of the problem or opportunity or it may mean moving on to goal setting or some kind of problem-managing action.

4. When a response is inaccurate, the client often lets the counselor know in different ways. He or she may:

    a) Stop dead,

    b) Fumble around,

    c) Go off on a different tangent,

    d) Tell the counselor "That's not exactly what I meant,"

    e) Try to get the helper back on track.

5. Helpers need to be sensitive to all these cues.

6. If you are intent on understanding your clients, they will not be put off by occasional inaccuracies on your part.

G. Use Empathic Highlights As a Way of Bridging Diversity Gaps.

1.   Highlights based on effective tuning in and listening constitute one of the most important tools you have in interacting with clients who differ from you in significant ways.

2. Sharing highlights is one way of telling clients that you are a learner, especially if the client differs from you in significant ways.

3. Scott and Borodovsky (1990) referred to empathic listening as "cultural role taking." They could have said "diversity role taking."

Section Six: TACTICS FOR COMMUNICATING HIGHLIGHTS (OH-6.6)

The principles just outlined provide strategies for sharing empathic highlights. Here are a few hints — tactics, if you will — to help you improve the quality of your responses.

A. Give yourself time to think. Beginners sometimes jump in too quickly with an empathic response when the client pauses. "Too quickly" means that they do not give themselves enough time to reflect on what the client has just said in order to identify the core message being communicated. Watch some experts on tape. They often pause and allow themselves to assimilate what the client is saying.

B. Use short responses. I find that the helping process goes best when I engage the client in a dialogue rather than give speeches or allow the client to ramble. In a dialogue the helper's responses can be relatively frequent, but lean and trim. In trying to be accurate, the beginner is often long-winded, especially if he or she waits too long to respond. Again, the question "What is the core of what this person is saying to me?" can help you make your responses short, concrete, and accurate.

C. Gear your response to the client, but remain yourself. If a client speaks animatedly, telling you how he finally got his partner to listen to his point of view about a new venture, and you reply accurately but in a flat, dull voice, your response is not fully empathic. This does not mean that you should mimic your clients, go overboard, or not be yourself. It means that part of being with the client is sharing in a reasonable way in his or her emotional tone. On the other hand, helpers should not adopt a language that is not their own just to be on the client's wavelength.

Section Seven: A CAUTION: THE IMPORTANCE OF
EMPATHIC RELATIONSHIPS

A. In day-to-day conversations, sharing empathic highlights is a tool of civility.

    1. Making an effort to get in touch with your conversational partner's frame of reference sends a message of respect.

    2. Sharing highlights plays an important part in building relationships.

    3. Given enough time, people establish empathic relationships with one another in which understanding is communicated in a variety of rich and subtle ways without necessarily being put into words.

B. People with empathic relationships often express empathy in actions. An arm around the shoulders of someone who has just suffered a defeat expresses both empathy and support.

C. Some people enter caringly into the world of their relatives, friends, and colleagues and are certainly "with" them but don't know how to communicate understanding through words.

    1. In general, the more frequent use of empathic highlights in everyday life, especially when relationships are not going as well as they might, is highly desirable.

    2. Sharing highlights plays an important role in developing empathic relationships.

    3. Box 6-1 summarizes the main points about the use of empathy as a communication skill.

Section Eight: THE SHADOW SIDE OF SHARING

EMPATHIC HIGHLIGHTS (OH-6.7)

Some helpers are poor communicators without even realizing it. Many responses that novice or inept helpers make are really poor substitutes for sharing accurate empathic highlights. Here are some possibilities that are better avoided.

A. **No response.** It can be a mistake to say nothing, though cultures differ widely in how they deal with silence (Sue, 1990).

1.   In North American culture, generally speaking, if the client says something significant, respond to it, however briefly. Otherwise the client may think that what he or she has just said doesn't merit a response.

2.   A skilled helper would realize that a person's nonacceptance of his or her body could generalize to other aspects of life (Dworkin & Kerr, 1987; Worsley, 1981) and therefore should not be treated as just a "vanity" problem.

B. Distracting questions. Some helpers, like many people in everyday life, cannot stop themselves from asking questions instead of responding with an empathic highlight.

C. Cliche-talk turns the helper into an insensitive instructor and probably sounds dismissive to the client. Cliches are hollow and are a very poor substitute for understanding.

D. Interpretations. For some helpers interpretive responses based on their theories of helping seem more important that expressing understanding. The counselor fails to respond to the client's feelings and also distorts the content of the client's communication. The response implies that what is really important is hidden from the client.

E. Advice. In everyday life giving unsolicited advice is extremely common. Advice giving at this stage is out of order and, to make things worse, the advice given has a cliche flavor to it. Furthermore, advice giving robs clients of self-responsibility.

F. Parroting. Sharing a highlight does not mean merely repeating what the client has said. Such parroting is a parody of sharing empathic highlights.

1.   Real understanding, since it passes through you, should convey some part of you. Parroting doesn't.

2.   To avoid parroting, tap into the processing you've been doing as you listened, come at what the client has said from a slightly different angle, use your own words, change the order, refer to an expressed but unnamed emotion — in a word, do whatever you can to let the client know that you are working at understanding.

G. Sympathy and agreement. Being empathic is not the same as agreeing with the client or being sympathetic.

1.   An expression of sympathy has much more in common with pity, compassion, commiseration, and condolence than with empathic understanding.

2.   Sympathy denotes agreement, whereas empathy denotes understanding and acceptance of the person of the client.

3.   At its worst, sympathy is a form of collusion with the client.

H. Faking it.

1.   Clients are sometimes confused, distracted, and in a highly emotional state. All these conditions affect the clarity of what they are saying about themselves.

2.   Helpers may fail to pick up what the client is saying because of the client's confusion or because clients are not stating their messages clearly.

3.   The helpers themselves have become distracted in one way or another.

4.   Genuine helpers admit that they are lost and then work to get back on track again.

5.   Faking it is never a substitute for competence.

FIGURE 5-1

The Movement Caused by Accurate and Inaccurate Highlights

BOX 5-1

Suggestions for Sharing Empathic Highlights

1.   Remember that empathy is a value, a way of being, that should permeate all communication skills.
2.   Tune in carefully, both physically and psychologically, and listen actively to the client's point of view.
3.   Make every effort to set your judgments and biases aside for the moment and walk in the shoes of the client.
4.   As the client speaks, listen especially for core messages.
5.   Listen to both verbal and nonverbal messages and their context.
6.   Respond with highlights fairly frequently, but briefly, to the client's core messages.
7.   Be flexible and tentative enough that the client does not feel pinned down.
8.   Use highlights to keep the client focused on important issues.
9.   Move gradually toward the exploration of sensitive topics and feelings.
10. After sharing a highlight, attend carefully to cues that either confirm or deny the accuracy of your response.
11. Determine whether your highlights are helping the client remain focused and stimulate the clarification of key issues.

12. Note signs of client stress or resistance; try to judge whether these arise because you are inaccurate or because you are too accurate in your responses.

13. Keep in mind that the communication skill of sharing empathic highlights, however important, is just one tool to help clients see themselves and their problem situations more clearly with a view to managing them more effectively.

Lecture Enhancers

You should be able to find the full text of the following items in your library or by using your web-based library access tool of choice (e.g., PsycInfo).

Item#1: Client-Centered Care
Client-centered care means that I am a valued human being.

Corring,-Deborah-J.; Cook,-Joanne-V. (1999). Client-centered care means that I am a valued human being. In Canadian-Journal-of-Occupational-Therapy. 1999 Apr; Vol 66(2): 71-82

Synopsis: When one thinks of a client-centered approach to practice, one would expect the participation of the client as the major focus of the collaborative relationship yet, ironically, no reported studies of the client's perspective of a client-centered approach could be found. This article describes a qualitative research project that explores the opinions of individuals who have experienced mental illness and the mental health service delivery system, then outlines the inadequacies of past and present practice with recommendations for change. By recognizing that clients are valued human beings, who are also the center of their practice, therapists will have grasped the true meaning of a client-centered approach.

Item Two: Ethical Conflicts
Ethical conflicts in psychology (2nd ed.)

Bersoff,-Donald-N. (1999). Ethical Conflicts in Psychology (2nd ed.). In Washington, DC, USA: American Psychological Association. xxiv, 597 pp.

Synopsis: Designed for use by students, researchers, teachers and practitioners, this book explores basic ethical issues that may arise in the multiple roles of psychologists, such as multiple relationships; privacy, privilege, and the duty-to-warn; and deception in research. This new edition takes an international approach to ethical codes by providing both American and Canadian guidelines to practice. Testifying as an expert witness, providing services on the Internet, and practicing ethically within the parameters of managed care are also detailed.

Item Three: Serious Psychiatric Disorders
Effective treatment relationships for persons with serious psychiatric disorders: The importance of attachment states of mind.

Tyrrell,-Christine-L.; Dozier,-Mary; Teague,-Gregory-B.; Fallot,-Roger-D. (1999).
Effective treatment relationships for persons with serious
psychiatric disorders: The importance of attachment states of mind. In Journal-of-
Consulting-and-Clinical-Psychology. 1999 Oct; Vol 67(5): 725-733.

Synopsis: This study examines how attachment states of mind of both 54 clients with serious psychiatric disorders and 21 case managers influence the effectiveness of therapeutic relationships and client functioning. The outcomes of this study emphasize the importance of clients and clinicians being paired in a manner that balances their interpersonal and emotional strategies.

Class Activities

In addition to the exercises in the Workbook that accompanies this text, you may find the following in-class activities to be of value:

Activity #1: Faking It!

Insincerity can easily be detected by a client. In this group activity, have the students form triads and then have them take turns in the roles of helper, client, and observer. In this case the helper discloses some personal, but not too personal, information with the client. The client is then asked to decide if the information is true or not. The helper should disclose three things about himself with two of the items being false and one of the items being true. The client is to try to determine each two items are false and which two items are true. The client may ask for the help of the observer in determining which two items are false and which two items are true.

At the conclusion of the activity, have students share as a class what concludes helped them determine which items where true and which items were false.

Activity #2: No Communication

In this activity have students do what they can to interfere with effective communication ranging from body language and talking too fast, to having their hand covering their mouth and using slang or other unintelligible language. Have the helper, the client, and the observer all report out which actions on the part of the helper interfered the most with communication and how it made them feel to communicate in such an ineffective manner.

Activity #3: When I Felt Understood

In this brief activity, have students take out a piece of paper and list three times in their lives that they felt very understood by another person. Have them list the following:

1. The person listening:

2. The situation:

3. What gave him or her the feeling of being understood (e.g., feedback, facial

expressions, constructive silence, restatement of what was said)?

Next have the students share in small groups or as a class the elements of item three above that worked best for them.

Finally, discuss how one could use these positive experiences to enhance the helping relationship.

Videos

APA Psychotherapy Series (1995, 12 Parts, APA). These training tapes include a full range of therapeutic approaches and techniques: client-centered, cognitive-behavioral, and psychoanalytic. Excellent for classroom presentations.

B.F. Skinner on Counselling (1972, 25 min, IM). Skinner discusses why a focus on emotions is not sufficient in a counselling relationship. He then discusses the advantages of behavioral change programs.

Discovering Psychology, Part 22: Psychotherapy. (1990, 30 min., ANN/CPB). Through a combination of actual footage and recreations, a full range of treatments are covered including humanistic, biomedical, behavioral and psychodynamic.

Multicultural Counselling (Parts I (44 min) and II (29 min), 1992, IM). Using a series of role plays, the video covers major issues to be sensitive to when counselling individuals from different ethnic and religious backgrounds.

Race and Psychiatry (25 min, FHS). Racism in mental health? This video discusses and presents issues that are certain to engage your students and generate excellent classroom discussion.

Websites

1. http://www.ee.ed.ac.uk/~gerard/Management/art7.html
   Communication skills.

2. http://www.ascusc.org/jcmc/vol11/issue/IMG_JCMC/ResourceUse.html
   This is information on communication, everything you could want.

Overhead Transparencies

Starting on the next page are copies of recommended overhead transparencies. Please feel free to convert the following pages to overheads as this will enhance the lecture portion of your class presentation.

THE THREE DIMENSIONS
OF RESPONDING SKILLS

1. **Perceptiveness**

2. **Know-How**

3. **Assertiveness**

OH 6.1

THE KEY BUILDING BLOCKS OF EMPATHIC HIGHLIGHTS

1. **The Basic Formula.**

   You feel...

   Because...

2. **The helper captures both the emotion and the reason for the feeling.**

OH 6.2

RESPOND ACCURATELY TO CLIENTS

1. Use the right family of emotions and the right intensity.

2. Distinguish between expressed and discussed feelings.

3. Read and respond to feelings and emotions embedded in clients' nonverbal behavior.

OH 6.3A

RESPOND ACCURATELY TO CLIENTS cont'd.

4. Be sensitive in naming emotions.

5. Use different ways to share highlights about feelings and emotions.

6. Neither overemphasize nor underemphasize feelings, emotions, and moods.

RESPOND WITH HIGHLIGHTS

1. Communicating Understanding of Clients' Points of View.

2. Communicating Understanding of Clients' Decisions.

3. Communicating Understanding ofIntentions or Proposals.

OH 6.4

PRINCIPLES FOR SHARING HIGHLIGHTS

1. Use Empathic Highlights at Every Stage and Step of the Helping Process.

2. Respond Selectively to Core Client Messages.

3. Respond to the Context, Not Just the Words.

4. Use Highlights as a Mild Social-Influence Process.

OH 6.5A

PRINCIPLES FOR SHARING HIGHLIGHTS cont'd.

5. Use Highlights to Stimulate Movement in the Helping Process.

6. Recover from Inaccurate Understanding.

7. Use Empathic Highlights As a Way of Bridging Diversity Gaps.

OH 6.5B

TACTICS FOR COMMUNICATING HIGHLIGHTS

1. Give yourself time to think.

2. Use short responses.

3. Gear your response to the client, but remain yourself.

OH 6.6

THE SHADOW SIDE OF SHARING:

Situations to be avoided:

1. No response.

2. Distracting questions.

3. Cliches

4. Interpretations

5. Advice

6. Parroting

7. Sympathy and agreement

OH 6.7

Chapter Seven:

The Art of Probing and Summarizing

	Pages
Chapter Outline	**203**
Detailed Lecture Notes	**204-214**
Lecture Enhancers	**207-208**
Class Activities	**217-218**
Videos	**219**
Websites	**220**
Transparencies	**221-226**

THE ART OF PROBING AND SUMMARIZING

VERBAL AND NONVERBAL PROMPTS

DIFFERENT FORMS OF PROBES

USING QUESTIONS EFFECTIVELY

PRINCIPLES IN THE USE OF PROBES

- ➤ Use probes to Help Clients Engage in Dialogue
- ➤ Use Probes to Help Clients Achieve Concreteness and Clarity
- ➤ Use Probes to Explore and Clarify Clients' Points of View, Decisions, and Proposals
- ➤ Use Probes to Help Clients Fill in Missing Pieces of the Picture
- ➤ Use Probes to Help Clients Get a Balanced View of Problem Situations and Opportunities
- ➤ Use Probes to Help Clients Move into More Beneficial Stages and Steps of the Helping Process
- ➤ Use Probes to Help Clients Move Forward within Some Step of the Process
- ➤ Use Probes to Help Clients Explore and Clarify Their Points of View, Decisions, and Proposals
- ➤ Use Probes to Help Clients Challenge Themselves

THE ART OF SUMMARIZING: PROVIDING FOCUS AND DIRECTION

INTEGRATING COMMUNICATION SKILLS: THE SEAMLESS USE OF VISIBLY TUNING IN, LISTENING, PROCESSING, UNDERSTANDING, SHARING HIGHLIGHTS, PROBING, AND SUMMARIZING

BECOMING PROFICIENT AT COMMUNICATION SKILLS

THE SHADOW SIDE OF COMMUNICATION SKILLS

(Please note: The designation OH in the detailed lecture notes indicates an overhead transparency is available. Please locate the overhead transparencies in the final section of each chapter in this Instructors' Manual.)

Chapter 7:
THE ART OF PROBING AND SUMMARIZING

In most of the examples used in the discussion of sharing empathic highlights, clients have demonstrated a willingness to explore themselves and their behavior relatively freely. Obviously, this is not always the case. Although it is essential that helpers respond with highlights when their clients do reveal themselves, it is also necessary at times to encourage, prompt, and help clients to explore their concerns when they fail to do so spontaneously. Therefore, the ability to use prompts and probes well is another important communication skill. If sharing highlights is the lubricant of dialogue, then probes provide often-needed nudges.

Prompts and probes are verbal and sometimes nonverbal tactics for helping clients talk more freely and concretely about any issue at any stage or step of the helping process. For instance, counselors can use probes to help clients identify and explore opportunities they have been overlooking, to clear up blind spots, to translate dreams into realistic goals, to come up with strategies for accomplishing goals, and for working through obstacles to action. Probes, judiciously used, provide focus and direction for the entire helping process. They make it more efficient. But first a few words about prompts.

Section One: VERBAL AND NONVERBAL PROMPTS (OH-7.1)

Prompts are brief verbal or nonverbal interventions designed to let clients know that you are with them to encourage clients to talk further.

    A. Nonverbal prompts:

        1. Various nonverbal behaviors on the part of counselors can have the force of probes.

2. Such things as bodily movements, gestures, nods, eye movement, and the like can be used as nonverbal prompts.

B. **Vocal and Verbal Prompts**.

1. You can use such responses as "um," "uh-huh," "sure," "yes," "I see," "ah," "okay,"and "oh" as prompts.

2. You must use them intentionally and not simply a sign that your attention is flagging, that you don't know what else to do, or are on automatic pilot.

3. Prompts should never be the main course. They are part of the therapeutic dialogue only as a condiment.

Section Two: DIFFERENT FORMS OF PROBES (OH-7.2)

Probes, used judiciously, help clients name, take notice of, explore, clarify, or further define any issue at any stage or step of the helping process. They are designed to provide clarity and to move things forward. Probes take different forms.

A. **Statements:** One form of probe is a statement indicating the need for further clarity.

B. **Requests:** Probes can take the form of direct requests for further information or more clarity. Obviously requests should not sound like commands. "Come on, just tell me what you are thinking." Tone of voice and other paralinguistic and nonverbal cues help to soften requests.

C. **Questions:** Direct questions are perhaps the most common type of probe. "How do you react when he flies off the handle?" "What keeps you from making a decision?" "Now that the indirect approach to letting him know your needs is not working, what might Plan B look like?"

D. **Single words or phrases that are in effect questions or requests:** Sometimes single words or simple phrases are, in effect, probes.

Whatever form probes take, they are often, directly or indirectly, questions of some sort.

Section Three: USING QUESTIONS EFFECTIVELY

Helpers, especially novices and inept counselors, tend to ask too many questions. When in doubt about what to say or do, they ask questions that add no value. It is as if gathering information were the goal of the helping interview. Social intelligence calls for restraint.

Questions, judiciously used, can be an important part of your interactions with clients. Here are two guidelines.

A. Do not ask too many questions.

1. When clients are asked too many questions, they feel grilled, and that does little for the helping relationship.

2. Many clients instinctively know when questions are just filler, used because the helper does not have anything better to say.

3. Helping sessions were never meant to be question-and-answer sessions that go nowhere.

B. Ask open-ended questions.

1. As a general rule, ask open-ended questions — that is, questions that require more than a simple yes or no or similar one-word answer.

2. Counselors who ask closed questions find themselves asking more and more questions. One closed question begets another.

3. If a specific piece of information is needed, then a closed question may be used.

4. In moderation, open-ended questions at every stage and step of the helping process help clients fill in what is missing.

Section Four: PRINCIPLES IN THE USE OF PROBES (OH-7.3)

A. Use Probes to Help Clients Engage as Fully as Possible in the Therapeutic Dialogue.

1. Many clients do not have all the communication skills needed to engage in the problem-managing and opportunity-developing dialogue.

2. If you have these skills, then you can use your skills to help your clients engage in the kind of turn taking, connecting, mutual influence, and co-creation of outcomes that characterizes dialogue.

3. Probes are the principal tools needed to help all clients engage in the give-and-take of the helping process.

4. Helping clients engage in dialogue is not some form of manipulation.

5. You can help clients engage in dialogue without in any way being patronizing or condescending.

6. This is a robust use of probes, often very useful in interacting with nonassertive and reluctant clients.

7. You can't force your clients to do anything, but your invitations can be strong.

8. Social intelligence will tell you how far you can go.

B. Use Probes to Help Clients Achieve Concreteness and Clarity.

1. Probes can help clients turn what is abstract and vague into something concrete and clear — something you can get your hands on and work with.

2. The goal is not to get more and more detail. Rather, it is to get the kind of detail that makes the problem or unused opportunity clear enough to see what can be done about it.

C. Use Probes to Help Clients Fill in Missing Pieces of the Picture.

1. Probes further the therapeutic dialogue by helping clients identify missing pieces of the puzzle — experiences, behaviors, and feelings that would help both clients and helpers get a better fix on the problem situation, possibilities for a better future, or drawing up a plan of action.

2. Through probes the counselor helps the client fill in a missing part of the picture.

3. The strategy is to help determine what the client wants and then help her/him see what needs to be done to get it.

D. Use Probes to Help Clients Get a Balanced View of Problem Situations and Opportunities.

1. Clients, in their eagerness to discuss an issue or make a point, often describe one side of a picture or one viewpoint.

2. Probes can be used to help them fill out the picture.

E. Use Probes to Help Clients Move Into More Beneficial Stages and Steps of the Helping Process.

1. Probes can be used to open up new areas for discussion.

2. They can be used help clients engage in dialogue about any part of the helping process — telling their stories more fully, attacking blind spots, setting goals, formulating action strategies, discussing obstacles to action, and reviewing actions taken.

3. Probes can help clients move into whatever stage or step of the helping process might be most useful for them.

4. The counselor uses probes to brainstorm possibilities.

F. Use Probes to Help Clients Move Forward within Some Step of the Helping Process. Probes can be used not only to help clients move to a different stage or step but also to move within a step.

G. Use Probes to Explore and Clarify Clients' Points of View, Decisions, and Proposals.

1. Clients often fail to clarify their points of view, decisions, intentions, and proposals.

2. The counselor is using probes to help the client explore the implications of a decision he's making.

3. The counselor's statement is a probe aimed at giving substance and order to the client's proposal. What do you want to accomplish?

H. Use probes to challenge clients and help them challenge themselves.

1. Sharing highlights can act as mild form of social-influence or challenge.

2. Effective highlights often act as probes. That is, they can be indirect requests for further information or ways of steering a client toward a different stage or step of the helping process.

3. Probes can have an edge of challenge in them.

4. Many probes are not just requests for relevant information. They often place some kind of demand on the client to respond, reflect, review, or reevaluate. Such probes are challenges of one kind or another.

5. Probes serve as a bridge between communicating understanding to clients and helping them challenge themselves.

6. Using probes as mild forms of challenge is perfectly legitimate provided you know what you are doing.

7. Probes can also be used to help clients remain focused on relevant and important issues.

8. Probes help clients stay focused.

9. Clients wander because the topic at hand is getting too uncomfortable. Probes are then gentle nudges to keep them focused on real issues.

10. Probes should not be ways of extorting from clients things they don't want to give.

11. High-quality probes increase rather than decrease the client's sense of self-responsibility.

Section Five: THE RELATIONSHIP BETWEEN SHARING

HIGHLIGHTS AND USING PROBES

The trouble with dealing with skills one at a time is that each skill is taken out of context.

A. In the give-and-take of any given helping session, however, the skills must be intermingled in a natural way. In actual sessions, skilled helpers continually tune in, listen actively, and use a mix of probes and empathy to help clients clarify and come to grips with their concerns, deal with blind spots, set goals, make plans, and get things done. There is no formula for the right mix. That depends on the client, client needs, the problem situation, possible opportunities, the stage, and the step.

B. After using a probe to which a client responds, share a highlight that expresses and checks your understanding. Be hesitant to follow one probe with another. The logic of this is straightforward. First, if a probe is effective, it will yield information that needs to be listened to and understood. Second, a shared highlight, if accurate, tends to place a demand on the client to explore further. It puts the ball back in the client's court.

C. Years ago Bob Carkhuff suggested, with his usual edge, that if helpers find themselves asking two questions in a row, they may just have asked two stupid questions.

D. You should be careful not to become either an empathic highlight "machine", grinding out one highlight after another or an "interrogator," peppering your clients continually with needless probes.

E. All responses to clients, including probes and challenges are empathic if they are based on a solid understanding of the client's core messages and point of view. All responses that build on and add to the client's remarks are implicitly empathic. Since these responses are empathic in effect, they cut down on the need for a steady stream of highlights.

Section Six: THE ART OF SUMMARIZING: PROVIDING FOCUS AND DIRECTION (OH-7.4)

The communication skills of visibly tuning in, listening, sharing highlights, and probing need to be orchestrated in such a way that they help clients focus their attention on issues that make a difference. The ability to summarize and to help clients summarize the main points of a helping interchange or session is a skill that can be used to provide both focus and challenge.

Brammer (1973) listed a number of goals that can be achieved by judicious use of summarizing — "warming up" the client, focusing scattered thoughts and feelings, bringing the discussion of a particular theme to a close, and prompting the client to explore a theme more thoroughly. There are certain times when summaries prove particularly useful: at the beginning of a new session, when the session seems to be going nowhere, and when the client gets stuck.

A. At the beginning of a new session.

1. When summaries are used at the beginning of a new session, especially when clients seem uncertain about how to begin, they prevent clients from merely repeating what has already been said before.

2. They put clients under pressure to move on.

3. It shows the client that she had listened carefully to what he had said in the last session and that she had reflected on it after the session.

4. The summary gives the client a jumping-off point for the new session.

5. It gives him an opportunity to add to or modify what was said. Finally, it places the responsibility for moving forward on the client. The implied sentiment of the summary is: "Now where do you want to go with this?"

6. Summaries put the ball in the client's court and give them an opportunity to exercise initiative.

B. During a session that is going nowhere.

A summary can be used to give focus to a session that seems to be going nowhere. One of the main reasons sessions go nowhere is that helpers allow clients to keep "going 'round the mulberry bush" — that is, saying the same things over and over again — instead of helping them either go more deeply into their stories, focus on possibilities, and goals, or discuss strategies that will help clients get what they need and want.

C. **When the client gets stuck**.

1. Summaries can be used when clients don't seem to know where to go next either in the helping session itself or in an action program out there is their real worlds.

2. Summaries have a way of keeping the ball in the client's court.

3. The helper does not always have to provide the summary. Often it is better to ask the client to pull together the major points. This helps the client own the helping process, pull together the salient points, and move on.

4. The counselor should provide clients whatever help they need to stitch the summary together.

D. **When the client needs a new perspective**.

Often when scattered elements are brought together, the client sees the "bigger picture" more clearly. The summary may provide the client with a mild jolt.

Section Seven: HOW TO BECOME PROFICIENT AT COMMUNICATION SKILLS

Understanding communication skills and how they fit into the helping process is one thing. Becoming proficient in their use is another.

A. Some trainees think that these "soft" skills should be learned easily and fail to put in the kind of hard work and practice that makes them "fluent" in them (Binder, 1990; Georges, 1988).

1. Doing the exercises on communication skills in the manual that accompanies this book and practicing these skills in training groups can help, but that isn't enough to make the skills second nature.

2. These skills must become part of your everyday communication style.

B. In the beginning it may be difficult to practice all these skills in everyday life, not because they are so difficult, but because they are relatively rare in conversations.

1. Take sharing highlights. Listen to the conversations around you. If you were to use an unobtrusive counter, pressing the plunger every time you heard someone share an empathic highlight, you might go days without pressing the plunger.

2. But you can make sharing highlights a reality in your everyday life. And those who interact with you will notice the difference.

3. On the other hand, you will hear many probes in everyday conversations. People are much more comfortable asking questions than providing understanding. However, many of these probes tend to be aimless.

4. Learning how to integrate purposeful probes with highlights demands practice in everyday life.

5. Every conversation is an opportunity.

Section Eight: THE SHADOW SIDE OF COMMUNICATION SKILLS

A. Some helpers tend to overidentify the helping process with the communication skills, that is, with the tools, that serve it.

1. Being good at communication skills is not the same as being good at helping.

2. An overemphasis on communication skills can turn helping into a great deal of talk with very little action. And few outcomes.

B. Communication skills must serve both the process and the outcomes of helping. You can be good at communication, good at relationship building, even good at social-emotional reeducation and still shortchange your clients, because they need more than that.

C. Some practitioners underestimate the need for solid communication skills.

1. There is a subtle assumption that the "technology" of their approach, such as manualized treatments, suffices.

2. They listen and respond through their theories and constructs rather than through their humanity.

3. They become technologists instead of helpers.

4. They are like some medical doctors who become more and more proficient in the use of medical technology and less and less in touch with the humanity of their patients.

BOX 6-1

Suggestions for the Use of Probes

Keep in mind the goals of probing:

1. To help clients engage as fully as possible in the therapeutic dialogue.
2. To help nonassertive or reluctant clients tell their stories and engage in other behaviors related to managing their problems and developing their opportunities.
3. To help clients identify experiences, behaviors, and feelings that give focus to their stories.
4. To open up new areas for discussion.
5. To help clients explore and clarify points of view, decisions, and proposals.
6. To help clients be as concrete and specific as possible.
7. To help clients remain focused on relevant and important issues.
8. To help clients move on to a further stage or step in the helping process
9. To provide mild challenges to client to examine the way they think, behave, and act both within helping sessions and in their daily lives as they try to manage problems and develop opportunities.
10. Make sure that probing is done in the spirit of empathy.
11. Use a mix of statements, open-ended questions, prompts, and requests, not questions alone.
12. Do not engage clients in question-and-answer sessions.
13. If a probe helps a client reveal relevant information, follow it up with an empathic highlight rather than another probe.
14. Use whatever judicious mixture of highlights and probing is needed to help clients clarify problems, identify blind spots, develop new scenarios, search for action strategies, formulate plans, and review outcomes of action.

Summarizing can lead to new perspectives. Pulling the strands of a client's story together and presenting it as a whole can help him or her get the big picture. In the following example, the client is a 52-year-old man who has been talking about a number of problems in living. He has come for help because he has been "down in the dumps" and can't seem to shake it.

> **HELPER:** Let's take a look at what we've seen so far. You're down — not just a normal slump; this time it's hanging on. You worry about your health, but you check out all right physically, so this seems to be more a symptom than a cause of your slump. There are some unresolved issues in your life. One that you seem to be stressing is the fact that your recent

change in jobs has meant that you don't see much of your old friends anymore. Since you're single, this leaves you, currently, with a rather bleak social life. Another issue — one you find painful and embarrassing — is your struggle to stay young. You don't like facing the fact that you're getting older. A third issue is the way you — to use your own word — "overinvest" yourself in work, so much so that when you finish a long-term project, suddenly your life is empty.

CLIENT (pauses): It's painful to hear it all that baldly, but that about sums it up. I've suspected I've got some screwed-up values, but I haven't wanted to stop long enough to take a look at it. Maybe the time has come. I'm hurting enough.

HELPER: One way of doing this is by taking a look at what a better future would look like.

CLIENT: That sounds interesting, even hopeful. How would we do that?

The counselor's summary hits home — somewhat painfully — and the client draws his own conclusion. Care should be taken not to overwhelm clients with the contents of the summary. Nor should summaries be used to "build a case" against a client. Helping is not a judicial procedure. Perhaps the foregoing summary would have been more effective if the helper had also summarized some of the client's strengths. That would have provided a more positive context.

Lecture Enhancers

You should be able to find the full text of the following items in your library or by using your web-based library access tool of choice (e.g., PsycINFO, EBCoHOst).

Item One: Troubles in Therapy
Troubles in the therapeutic relationship: A pluralistic perspective.

Omer, Haim. (2000). Troubles in the therapeutic relationship: A pluralistic perspective. In Journal-of-Clinical-Psychology. 2000 Feb; Vol 56(2): 201-210.

Synopsis: Therapeutic troubles may include hopeless narratives, failing strategies and ineffective interactions, for which there are no immediate and absolute cures. With the goal of developing a means of restoring the troubled therapeutic relationship, this article provides three separate cases, which highlight possible guidelines for critical intervention: empathic characterization, positive reframing, and proposing a new therapeutic contract.

Item Two: Hope and Depression
Hope and depression: Light through the shadows.

Cheavens, Jen. (2000) Hope and depression: Light through the shadows.
In Snyder, C. R. (Ed); et-al. (2000). Handbook of hope: Theory, measures, and applications. (pp. 321-340). San Diego, CA, US: Academic Press, Inc. xxv, 440 pp.

Synopsis: Research provides that people with high levels of hope experience fewer depressive symptoms than people with lower levels of hope. From this, the author contends that hope theory can be used both to understand the onset and experience of depression and to intervene with applications of hope so as to deal with depressive symptoms.

Item Three: Critiques of Psychotherapy
Facing, understanding and learning from critiques of psychotherapy and counselling.

Feltham,-Colin. (1999). Facing, understanding and learning from critiques of psychotherapy and counselling. In British-Journal-of-Guidance-and-Counselling. 1999 Aug; Vol 27(3):301-311.

Synopsis: This article addresses the difficult issue that therapists must manage when faced with criticism directed at psychotherapy and counselling. The author presents the valuable aspects of valid criticism that could transfer to a proactive examination of therapy's shadow side, an exploration that may well be work to the advantage of the field in terms of social, ethical and clinical effectiveness. In addition, Feltham recommends the self-critique of therapy by those in the field, a skill that could be learned while a student of psychotherapy.

Class Activities

In addition to the exercises in the Workbook that accompanies this text, you may find the following in-class activities to be of value:

Activity #1: The Interrogator!

Interrogation is not probing and probing is not interrogating. In this group activity, have the students form triads and then have them take turns in the roles of helper, client, and observer. In this case the helper plays the role of the interrogator asking numerous questions and pursuing the answer with more interrogation requesting more detail and more information. The helper is to do all he can to play the role of an interrogator and be insensitive to the needs of the client. The client is then asked to share how it felt to be interrogated. The helper should disclose how she felt playing the role of an interrogator and not the role of a helper. The observer also shares her feelings about observing the interrogation.

At the conclusion of the activity, have students share as a class what learned about playing the role of interrogator versus helper.

Activity #2: The Gentle Probe

In this activity have students practice the gentle art of probing with special emphasis on the being sensitive to the needs of the client. Have the helper, the client, and the observer all rotate roles and as the conclusion of each rotation, have the group members share with each other how gentle, sensitive probing is so much more helpful to the client than interrogation.

After the triads have concluded their discussions, have each group report to the full class their experiences and their conclusions about probing versus interrogating. As the instructor, facilitate a discussion of the similarities and differences in the reports from the groups: Are there differences? Why or Why not are there differences.

Activity #3: I Think What You Said Was ....??

In this brief activity, have students work individually to create a list of ten to fifteen items about themselves (e.g., career interests, travels, life experiences, etc.) and then have the students form triads with one student the helper, one the client, and one the observer. Have the client quickly spew out the ten to fifteen items on his or her list as quickly as possible. The challenge for the helper is to try to remember as many of the items as possible and then summarize them back to the client. The client should put a check mark next to each item on his or her list that the helper was able to remember and summarize correctly. Have each triad rotate roles and determine which member of the triad was most successful in summarizing the list items spewed out by his or her client.

Finally, discuss as a class how a helper can use summarizing techniques to enhance the helping relationship.

Videos

Demonstration of the Cognitive Therapy of Depression (40 min, IM). Using role play scenarios, Aaron Beck displays his approaches to therapy.

The Inner World of Counselling with Carl Rodgers (1980, 80 min, IM).
After completing a session, both Rodgers and the client critique the session.

Behavioral Principles for Parents: A Discrimination Program (Research Press, 13 min, colour) Using over 30 scenarios, this video covers the concepts of positive reinforcement, punishment, and extinction in parent-child relationships.

Websites

1. http://psychologyinspain.com/content/full/1197/13bis.htm
   School counselling, helping clients explore problem situations.

2. http://www.behavior.net/column/meichenbaun/
   How people tell their stories (how they change over time).

3. http://faculty-staff.edu/M/Lawerence.J.Marshall-1/notes.html
   All kinds of things about helping people tell their stories.

4. http://calib.com/nccanch/pubs/usermanuals/treatment/assess.htm
   Assessment of child maltreatment (assessing the severity).

Overhead Transparencies

Starting on the next page are copies of recommended overhead transparencies. Please feel free to convert the following pages to overheads as this will enhance the lecture portion of your class presentation.

VERBAL AND NONVERBAL PROMPTS

NONVERBAL PROMPTS:

bodily movements, gestures, nods, and eye movements.

VOCAL AND VERBAL PROMPTS:

"um," "uh-huh," "sure," "yes," "I see," "ah," "okay,"and "oh"

OH 7.1

DIFFERENT FORMS OF PROBES

1. **Statements:**

2. **Requests:**

3. **Questions:**

4. **Single words or phrases that are in effect questions or requests:**

OH 7.2

PRINCIPLES IN THE USE OF PROBES

1. **Help Clients Engage as Fully as Possible in the Therapeutic Dialogue.**

2. **Help Clients Achieve Concreteness and Clarity.**

3. **Help Clients Fill in Missing Pieces of the Picture.**

4. **Help Clients Get a Balanced View of Problem Situations and Opportunities.**

OH 7.3A

PRINCIPLES IN THE USE OF PROBES cont'd.

5. Help Clients Move Into More Beneficial Stages and Steps of the Helping Process.

6. Help Clients Move Forward within Some Step of the Helping Process.

7. Explore and Clarify Clients' Points of View, Decisions, and Proposals.

8. Challenge clients and help them challenge themselves

OH 7.3B

PROVIDING FOCUS AND DIRECTION

1. At the beginning of a new session.

2. During a session that is going nowhere.

3. When the client gets stuck.

4. When the client needs a new perspective.

OH 7.4

Chapter Eight:

Step I-A
Helping Clients Tell Their Stories:
"What Are My Concerns"

	Pages
Chapter Outline	**228**
Detailed Lecture Notes	**229-243**
Lecture Enhancers	**244-245**
Class Activities	**246-247**
Videos	**248**
Websites	**249**
Transparencies	**250-259**

CHAPTER EIGHT OUTLINE

AN INTRODUCTION TO STAGE I: IDENTIFYING AND EXPLORING PROBLEMS AND OPPORTUNITIES

STEP I-A: "WHAT ARE MY KEY CONCERNS?"

HELPING CLIENTS EXPLORE PROBLEM SITUATIONS AND UNEXPLOITED OPPORTUNITIES

➢ Learn to Work with All Styles of Storytelling
➢ Start Where the Client Starts
➢ Help Clients Clarify Key Issues
➢ Assess the Severity of the Client's Problems
➢ Help Clients Talk Productively about the Past

- Help clients talk about the past to make sense of the present.
- Help clients talk about the past to be liberated from it.
- Help clients talk about the past in order to prepare for action in the future.

➢ As Clients Tell Their Stories, Search for Resources, Especially Unused Resources
➢ Help Clients Spot and Explore Unused Opportunities
➢ See Every Problem As an Opportunity

STEP I-A AND ACTION

THE SHADOW SIDE OF STEP I-A

➢ Clients as Storytellers
➢ The Nature of Discretionary Change

EVALUATION QUESTIONS FOR STEP I-A

Detailed Lecture Notes

(Please note: The designation OH in the detailed lecture notes indicates an overhead transparency is available. Please locate the overhead transparencies in the final section of each chapter in this Instructors' Manual.)

Section One: AN INTRODUCTION TO STAGE I: IDENTIFYING AND EXPLORING PROBLEMS AND OPPORTUNITIES

A. Stage I illustrates three ways in which counselors can help clients understand themselves, their problem situations, and their unused opportunities with a view to managing them more effectively. There are three principles.

> **Step I-A: Stories**. Help clients tell their stories in terms of problem situations and unused opportunities.

> **Step I-B: Blind Spots**. Help clients identify and move beyond blind spots to new perspectives on their problem situations and opportunities.

> **Step I-C: Leverage**. Help clients choose to work on issues that will make a difference in their lives.

B. These principles are not restricted to Stage I for these reasons.

1. Clients don't tell all of their stories at the beginning of the helping process. Often the full story "leaks out" over time.

2. Blind spots can appear at any stage or step of the helping process. Blind spots affect choosing goals, setting strategies, and implementing programs.

3. Leverage deals with the "economics" of helping. Choosing the right problem or opportunity to work on is just the beginning. Figure 1 highlights the three steps of Stage I.

C. Stage I of the helping process can be seen as the assessment stage —

1. Finding out what's going wrong, what opportunities lie fallow, what resources are not being used.

2. Helping clients understand themselves, find out "what's going on" with their lives, see what they have been ignoring, and make sense out of the messiness of their lives.

3. It is a kind of learning in which, ideally, both client and helper participate through their ongoing dialogue.

D. In helping, there is an interplay between assessment and intervention. Helpers who continually listen to clients in context are engaging in ongoing assessment. In this sense assessment is part and parcel of all stages and steps of the helping model. As in medicine, though, some initial assessment of the seriousness of the client's concerns is called for.

E. Members of the helping profession use many different procedures to assess clients; however, the "clinical interview," the dialogue between client and helper, is the most common assessment procedure. Other forms of assessment such as psychological testing and applying psychiatric diagnostic categories (American Psychiatric Association, 1994) are beyond the scope of this book.

Section Two: STEP I-A: "WHAT ARE MY KEY CONCERNS?" (OH-8.1)

A. The importance of helping clients tell their stories well should not be underestimated. As Pennebaker (1995b) has noted, "An important... feature of therapy is that it allows individuals to translate their experiences into words. The disclosure process itself, then, may be as important as any feedback the client receives from the therapist" (p. 3). Self-disclosure provides the grist for the mill of problem solving and opportunity development. Here, then, are four goals for Step I-A:

1. **Initial stress reduction**. Help clients "get things out on the table." This can and often does have a cathartic effect that leads to stress reduction. Some clients carry their secrets around for years. Helping them unburden themselves is part of the social-emotional reeducation process alluded to earlier.

2. **Clarity.** Help clients spell out their problem situations and unexploited opportunities with the kind of concrete detail — specific experiences, behaviors, and emotions — that enables them to do something about them. Clarity opens the door to more creative options in living. Vague stories lead to vague options and actions.

3. **Relationship building.** Help clients tell their stories in such a way that the helping relationship develops and strengthens. The communication skills outlined in earlier chapters — suffused, of course, with the values of respect, genuineness, empathy, and empowerment — are basic tools for both clarity and relationship building.

4. **Action.** Right from the beginning help clients act on what they are learning. Clients do not need "grand plans" before they can act on their own behalf. Later in this chapter, more will be said about the "bias toward action" needed in the helping process.

B. Clients differ radically in their ability to talk about themselves and their problem situations.

1. Reluctance to disclose oneself within counseling sessions is often a window into the client's inability to share himself or herself with others and to be reasonably assertive in the social settings of everyday life.

2. One of the goals of the entire counseling process is to help clients develop the skills, confidence, and courage they need to share themselves appropriately.

Section Three: HELPING CLIENTS EXPLORE PROBLEM SITUATIONS AND UNEXPLOITED OPPORTUNITIES (OH-8.2)

As with values and communication skills, there are a number of principles that can guide you as you help clients tell their stories.

A. Learn to Work with All Styles of Storytelling

There are both individual and cultural differences (Wellenkamp, 1995) in clients' willingness to talk about themselves. Both affect storytelling.

1. Your job is to establish a working relationship with your clients and help them tell their stories as a prelude to helping them manage the problems and take advantage of the opportunities buried in those stories.

2. A story that is brought out into the open is the starting point for possible constructive change.

3. Often the very airing of the story is a solid first step toward a better life.

4. If the client tells the "whole" story in a more or less nonstop fashion, it will be impossible for you to share highlights relating to every core issue the client has brought up. But you can then help the client review the most salient points in some orderly way.

5. The highlights you share will let the client know that you have been listening intently and that you are concerned about him or her.

6. Clients who lack the skills needed to tell their stories well or who are reluctant to do so constitute a different kind of challenge. Engaging in dialogue with them can be tough work.

7. Box 8-1 provides questions clients can ask themselves to identify problem situations.

B. Start Where the Client Starts.

1. Clients have different starting points when they launch into their stories.

2. "Story" is used in its widest sense.

3. Your job is to stay with your clients no matter where they are.

4. Helping the client explore the context and background of each of these issues may well bring you to other steps of the helping process.

C. Help Clients Clarify Key Issues.

1. To clarify means to discuss problem situations and unused opportunities — including possibilities for the future, goals, strategies for accomplishing goals, plans, implementation issues, and feelings about all of these — as concretely as possible.

2. Vagueness and ambiguity lead nowhere.

3. A search for some background quickly takes the client's story out of the "routine" category. The right kind and amount of background provides both richness and context.

4. Here are some questions (adapted from a checklist devised by John Scherer as reported in *Training*, January, 1993, p. 14) that you might turn into judicious probes in order to get at background issues relating to the problem or opportunity at being discussed.

   a) What is it about the problem situation that moved the client to seek help in the first place?

   b) Who is being affected, besides the client?

   c) What is the problem or the failure to develop an opportunity costing either the client or others?

    d) To what degree is a larger problem lurking behind the symptoms the client is talking about?

D. Assess the Severity of the Client's Problems.

1. Clients come to helpers with problems of every degree of severity.

2. Objectively, problems run from the inconsequential to the life-threatening.

3. Subjectively, however, even a relatively inconsequential problem can be experienced as severe by a client.

4. One of the tasks of the counselor in this case will be to help the client put the problem in perspective or to teach him or her how to distinguish between degrees of problem severity. Howard (1991, p. 194) put it well.

> "part of the work between client and therapist can be seen as life-story elaboration, adjustment, or repair."

5. Savvy therapists not only gain an understanding of the severity of a client's problem or the extent of the client's unused resources, but also understand the limits of helping.

6. Mehrabian and Reed (1969) suggested the following formula as a way of determining the severity of any given problem situation. It is still useful today.

$$\text{Severity} = \text{Distress} \times \text{Uncontrollability} \times \text{Frequency}$$

> (The multiplication signs in the formula indicate that these factors are not just additive. Even low-level anxiety, if it is uncontrollable or persistent, can constitute a severe problem; that is, it can severely interfere with the quality of a client's life.)

7. The severity of any given problem situation will be reduced if the stress can be reduced, if the frequency of the problem situation can be lessened, or if the client's control over the problem situation can be increased.

E. Help Clients Talk Productively about the Past.

Some schools of psychology suggest that problem situations are not clear and fully understood until they are understood in the context of their historic roots. Therefore, helpers in these schools spend a great deal of time helping clients uncover the past. Others disagree with that point of view.

1. Glasser (2000, p. 23) puts it this way:

> Although many of us have been traumatized in the past, we are not the victims of our past unless we presently choose to be. The solution to our problem is rarely found in explorations of the past unless the focus is on past successes (Glasser, 2000, p. 23)

3. Fish (1995) suggested that attempts to discover the hidden root causes of current problem behavior may be unnecessary, misguided, or even counterproductive. Constructive change does not depend on causal connections in the past. There is evidence to support Fish's contention.

4. Long ago Deutsch (1954) noted that it is often almost impossible, even in carefully controlled laboratory situations, to determine whether event B, which follows event A in time, is actually caused by event A. Therefore, trying to connect present complicated patterns of behavior with past complicated events is an exercise in frustration.

5. Therefore, asking clients to come up with causal connections between current unproductive behavior and past events could be an exercise in futility for a number of reasons.

   a) causal connections cannot be proved; they remain hypothetical.

   b) there is little evidence suggesting that understanding past causes changes present behavior.

   c) talking about the past often focuses mostly on what happened to clients (their experiences) rather than on what they did about what happened to them (their behaviors) and therefore interferes with the "bias toward action" clients need to manage current problems.

6. The fact that past experiences may well *influence* current behavior does not mean that they necessarily *determine* present behavior.

7. Kagan (1996) has challenged what may be called the "scarred for life" assumption: "If orphans who spent their first years in a Nazi concentration camp can become productive adults and if young children made homeless by war can learn adaptive strategies after being adopted by nurturing families" (p. 901), that means that there is hope for us all.

F. **Help clients talk about the past to make sense of the present.**

1. Many clients come expecting to talk about the past or wanting to talk about the past.

2. There are ways of talking about the past that help clients make sense of the present.

3. Making sense of the present needs to remain center stage.

4. *How* the past is discussed is more important than whether it is discussed.

5. If the past can add clarity to current experiences, behaviors, and emotions, then let it be discussed.

6. If it can provide hints as to how self-defeating thinking and behaving can be changed now, let it be discussed.

7. The past, however, should never become the principal focus of the client's self-exploration. When it does, helping tends to slow down needlessly.

G. **Help clients talk about the past to be liberated from it.** A potentially dangerous logic can underlie discussions of the past.

1. Helpers need to understand that clients may see themselves as prisoners of their past, but then, help them move beyond such self-defeating beliefs.

2. When counselors help or encourage clients to talk about the past, they should have a clear idea of what their objective is. Is it to learn from the past? Is it to be liberated from it?

3. To assume that there is some "silver bullet" in the past that will solve today's problem is to search for magic.

H. **Help clients talk about the past in order to prepare for action in the future**.

1. The well-known historian A. J. Toynbee had this to say about history: "History not used is nothing, for all intellectual life is action, like practical life, and if you don't use the stuff — well, it might as well be dead."

2. The insights you help clients get from the past should in some way stir them to action.

3. Help clients invest the past proactively in the future.

I. As Clients Tell Their Stories, Search for Resources, Especially Unused Resources.

1. Incompetent helpers concentrate on clients' deficits.

2. Skilled helpers, as they listen to and observe clients, do not blind themselves to deficits, but they are quick to spot clients' resources, whether used, unused, or even abused.

3. These resources can become the building blocks for the future.

4. Helpers need a resource-oriented mind-set in all their interactions with clients. This is part of positive psychology.

5. The search for resources is especially important when the story being told is bleak.

J. Help Clients Spot and Develop Unused Opportunities.

1. It is probably not an exaggeration to say that unused human potential constitutes a more serious social problem than emotional disorders, since it is more widespread.

2. Maslow (1968) suggests that what is usually called "normal" in psychology "is really a psychopathology of the average, so undramatic and so widely spread that we don't even notice it ordinarily" (p. 16).

3. Many clients you will see, besides having more or less serious problems in living, will also probably be chronic victims of a self-inflicted psychopathology of the average.

4. Clients are much more likely to talk about problem situations than about unused opportunities. That's a pity since clients can manage many problems better by developing unused opportunities instead of dealing directly with their problems.

5. You must become good at spotting opportunities and unused resources in your own life.

K. See Every Problem as an Opportunity.

  1. Clients don't come with just problems *or* opportunities. They come with a mixture of both. Although there is no justification for romanticizing pain, the flip side of human problems is human opportunities.

  2. William Miller (1986) talked about one of the worst days of his life — nothing but failure all around. Later that day, over a cup of coffee, he took some paper, put the title "Lessons Learned and Relearned" at the top, and wrote down as many entries as he could. Some hours and seven pages later, he had listed 27 lessons. The day turned out to be one of the best of his life. So he began to keep a daily "Lessons Learned" journal. It helped him avoid getting caught up in self-blame and defeatism. Subsequently, on days when things were not working out, he would say to himself, "Ah, this will be a day filled with learnings!"

  3. Sometimes helping a client spot a small opportunity, be it the flip side of a problem or a stand alone, provides enough positive-psychology leverage to put him or her on a more constructive tack.

  4. Box 8-2 provides some questions clients can ask themselves in order to identify unused resources and opportunities.

Section Four: STEP I-A AND ACTION (OH-8.3)

One of the principal reasons clients do not manage the problem situations of their lives effectively is their failure to act intelligently, forcefully, and prudently in their own best interests. Covey (1989), in his immensely popular *The Seven Habits of Highly Effective People*, named "proactivity" as the first habit: "It means more than merely taking initiative. It means that as human beings, we are responsible for our own lives. Our behavior is a function of our decisions, not our conditions. We can subordinate feelings to values. We have the... responsibility to make things happen" (p. 71).

A. The Importance of Proactivity

  1. Inactivity can be bad for body, mind, and spirit.

  2. Counselors add value by helping their clients become proactive.

  3. Helping too often entails too much talking and too little action.

B. Using the Time Between Sessions Productively

1. Counselors must help clients use the time between sessions as productively as possible. "How can I leverage what I do within the session to have an impact on what the client does the rest of the week?"

2. Many helpers give their clients homework from time to time as a way of helping them act on what their learning in the sessions (Kazantzis, 2000; Kazantzis & Deane, 1999).

3. Mahrer and his associates (1994) reviewed the methods helpers used to do this. They came up with 16 methods. Among them are:

   a) Mention some homework task and ask the client to carry it out and report back because he or she is now a "new person."

   b) Wait until the client comes up with a post-session task and then help the client clarify and focus it.

   c) Highlight the client's readiness or seeming willingness to carry out some task, but leave the final decision to the client.

   d) Use some contractual agreement to move the client to some appropriate activity.

4. Counselors provide help in defining the activity and custom fitting it to the client's situation.

5. For further suggestions on how to incorporate homework into your helping sessions see Broder (2000).

6. Broder, in conjunction with Albert Ellis, the originator of Rational Emotive Behavior Therapy, has developed a series of audiotapes dealing with many of the problems clients encounter. Clients use these tapes to further their understanding of what they learned in the therapy session and to engage in activities that will help them resolve their conflicts (see www.therapistassistant.com).

7. The principle behind homework is more important than the name, and the principle is clear.

8. Use every stage and every step of the helping process as a stimulus for problem-managing and opportunity-developing action.

9. Have a clear picture of why you are assigning any particular task. Don't routinely assign homework for its own sake

10. Your role demands that you be a catalyst for client action.

C. Appreciating the Self-Healing Nature of Clients

1. Helpers should not underestimate the "agency" of their clients.

2. Bohart and Tallman (1999), in a book on "how clients make therapy work," lay out the principles of client self-healing, principles which, they say, must be respected if therapy is to be a collaborative enterprise.

3. These principles are part of a positive-psychology approach to helping.

4. All the principles support the notion of client agency is a wider sense. Here are the principles in basic form (see pp. 227-235 for a full description of each principle).

Respect Clients' Agency.

Section Four –B: IS STEP I-A ENOUGH?

Some clients seem to need only Step I-A. That is, they spend a relatively limited amount of time with a helper, they tell their story in greater or lesser detail, and then they go off and manage quite well on their own. Here are two ways in which clients may need only the first step of the helping process.

A. A declaration of intent and the mobilization of resources.

1. For some clients, the very fact that they approach someone for help may be sufficient to help them begin to pull together the resources needed to manage their problem situations more effectively.

2. Going to a helper is a declaration, not of helplessness, but of intent: "I'm going to do something about this problem situation."

3. Merely seeking help can trigger a resource-mobilization process in some clients.

4. Once they begin to mobilize their resources, they begin to manage their lives quite well on their own.

B. Coming out from under self-defeating emotions.

239

1. Some clients come to helpers because they are incapacitated, to a greater or lesser degree, by negative feelings and emotions.

2. Often when helpers show such clients respect, listen carefully to them, and understand them in a nonjudgmental way, those self-defeating feelings and emotions subside.

3. The clients benefit from the counseling relationship as a process of social-emotional reeducation and repair.

4. Once that happens, they are able to call on their own inner and environmental resources and begin to manage the problem situation that precipitated the incapacitating feelings and emotions. In short, they move to action. These clients, too, seem to be "cured" merely by telling their story.

5. Many need the kind of help provided by one or more of the other stages and steps of the helping model.

Section Five: THE SHADOW SIDE OF STEP I-A (OH-8.4)

There are a number of shadow-side dimensions to Step I-A. Two are discussed here. The first relates to the ways clients tell their stories. The second deals with the nature of discretionary change.

A. Clients As Storytellers

1. When clients present themselves to helpers, there is no instant or easy way of reading what is in their hearts. This is revealed over the course of helping sessions.

2. And some helpers are much better than others in discovering "what is really going on." As we have seen, clients approach storytelling in quite different ways.

3. Some clients who tell stories that are general, partial, and ambiguous may or may not have ulterior motives. The accountability issue lurks in the background. Another issue is the accuracy of the story.

4. Fudging seems to have something to do with self-image.

5. Kelly (2000a; also see Kelly, Kahn, & Coulter, 1996) sees therapy, at least in part, as a self-presentational process. She suggests that clients benefit by perceiving that their therapists have favorable views of them. Therefore, if therapy contributes to clients' positive identity

development, then we should expect some fudging. Hiding some of the less desirable aspects of themselves, intentionally or otherwise (see Kelly, 2000b), becomes a means to an end.

6. Hill, Gelso, and Mohr (2000) object to this hypothesis, suggesting that research shows that clients don't hide much from their therapists.

7. Arkin and Hermann suggest (2000) that all of this is really more complicated than the others realize.

8. The competent, caring, and savvy helper tackles each project without naivete and without cynicism.

B. The Nature of Discretionary Change

Step I-A is the first, at least logical, step in a process of constructive change. And so the distinction between discretionary and nondiscretionary change is critical for helpers. Nondiscretionary change is mandated change.

1. The shadow-side principle here is quite challenging.

   In both individual and organizational affairs, the track record for discretionary change is quite poor.

2. It's the Okavango/Kalahari phenomenon.

   The Okavango River, which rises in the highlands of Angola, gives way to a beautiful inland delta, a blue-green wilderness of fresh water teeming with life. Where does it go? It never finds the sea. Its water melt, somehow, into the Kalahari desert. It's a metaphor for much of both personal and organizational change. "Whatever happened to that [lush] management development program we started two years ago" The answer. "It's in the Kalahari."

3. Much of counseling is planning. Don't let clients take the [blue-green] planning they do with you and let it melt into the Kalahari.

4. The fact of discretionary change is central to the psychopathology of the average.

5. If we don't *have* to change, very often we don't. We need merely review the track record of our New Year's resolutions.

6. Unfortunately, in helping situations, clients probably see most change as discretionary.

7. A pragmatic bias toward client action on your part — rather than merely talking about action — is a cardinal value.

8. Effective helpers tend to be active with clients and see no particular value in mere listening and nodding.

9. They engage clients in a dialogue. During that dialogue, they constantly ask themselves, "What can I do to raise the probability that this client will act on her own behalf intelligently and prudently?"

10. Savvy helpers know that in some ways or at least in some cases the deck is stacked against them from the start.

Evaluation Questions for Step I-A (OH-8.5)

How effectively am I doing the following?

Establishing a Working Alliance

➢ Developing a collaborative working relationship with the client
➢ Using the relationship as a vehicle for social-emotional reeducation
➢ Not doing for clients what they can do for themselves

Helping Clients Tell Their Stories

➢ Using a mix of tuning in, listening, empathy, probing, and summarizing to help clients tell their stories, share their points, discuss their decisions, and talk through their proposals and concretely as possible
➢ Using probes when clients get stuck, wander about, or lack clarity
➢ Understanding blocks to client self-disclosure and providing support for clients having difficulty talking about themselves
➢ Helping clients talk productively about the past

Building Ongoing Client Assessment into the Helping Process

➢ Getting an initial feel for the severity of a client's problems and his or her ability to handle them
➢ Noting and working with client resources, especially unused resources
➢ Understanding clients' problems and opportunities in the larger context of their lives

Helping Clients Move to Action

➢ Helping clients develop an action orientation
➢ Helping clients spot early opportunities for changing self-defeating behavior or engaging in opportunity-development behavior

Integrating Evaluation into the Helping Process

➢ Keeping an evaluative eye on the entire process with the goal of adding value through each interaction and making each session better

➢ Finding ways of getting clients to participate in and own the evaluation process

BOX 8-1

Problem Finding (OH-8.6)

Here are some questions counselors can help clients ask themselves to "find" and specify problem situations.

➢ What are my concerns?

➢ What's problematic in my life?

➢ What issues do I need to face?

➢ What's troubling me?

➢ What would those who know me best tell me?

➢ What's keeping me back from being what I want to be? from doing what I want to do?

➢ What do I need to resolve?

BOX 8-2

Opportunity Finding (OH-8.7)

Here are some questions counselors can help clients ask themselves to identify unused opportunities.

➢ What are my unused skills/resources?

➢ What are my natural talents?

➢ How could I use some of these?

➢ What opportunities do I let go by?

➢ What ambitions remain unfulfilled?

➢ What could I accomplish if I put my mind to it?

➢ What could I become good at if I tried?

➢ Which opportunities should I be developing?

➢ Which role models could I be emulating?

Lecture Enhancers

You should be able to find the full text of the following items in your library or by using your web-based library access tool of choice (e.g., Psycinfo)

Item One: Health and Communication
Communication: Accurate Communication: Communication takes a Life of its own.

Gerard, Robert V. (1997). Communication: Accurate Communication: Communication takes a Life of its own. (by Robert V. Gerard, Ph.D. Home Page Directory Articles Newsletter)

Synopsis: This article outlines how people's communication styles affects their health and how their interactions with others may influence their general resistance to disease.

Based on over twenty years of study, researchers have concluded that people communicate both internally and externally causing a general chain reaction throughout their bodies. Both the physical characteristics of conversation, such as speaking quickly, loudly, interrupting and/or speaking with animation, and emotions play a role in elevating blood pressure. Conversely, the same research found that when people practice effective listening skills, a relaxing activity, their blood pressure drops and their health and well-being is positively influenced.

Item Two: Effective Communication
Making the Most of Your Communication

Chris Roebuck, Effective Communication, AMACOM; ISBN 0814470203 (1999)

Synopsis: The author stresses how communication affects all aspects of our lives. The resource provides a good discussion of communication skills in the helping relationship as well as in the daily lives of the helper and the client. This resource would be most effective for a discussion of transfer of communication skills in the therapy setting to the client using effective communication in all areas of his or her life. The key is that communication skills quite often lead to the problems that are bringing the client to the therapy session.

Item Three: Accurate Communication
Accurate Communication: Communication takes a Life of its own.

Gerard, Robert V. (1997). Communication: Accurate Communication: Communication takes a Life of its own. (by Robert V. Gerard, Ph.D. Home Page Directory Articles Newsletter)

Synopsis: The author focuses on the importance of finding balance and authenticity in our use of language. Accurate communication is the practice of finding balance with our "mind, intellect, and heart." When we find balance in our conservations through accurate communication, we will find that we are more effective with our clients and model accurate and effective communication for our clients.

Class Activities

In addition to the exercises in the Workbook that accompanies this text, you may find the following in-class activities to be of value:

Activity #1: Story Telling

In this activity your goal is to have students tell their own story. With students in triads, have each student take a turn telling a ten minute story of a significant event in their life. While the one student is telling his or her story, the other students can only listen and not ask questions or share their thoughts.

After each student tells his or her story then allow questions. Ask the students to jot down three to five feelings they had when they could not ask questions. Compare the student responses and look for commonality in their reported feelings.

Activity #2: Tell Me More

Have students in triads tell a story for ten minutes without interruption. Next have the two students in the triad who are listening each ask three questions of the story teller. The questions being asked should range from more details to states of emotion.

The goal of the activity is to help students develop a sense of interest in and wanting to know about others. An important part of being a good helper is wanting to know more about the client before you start to help. Have the students report out to the class the benefits they see of listening to a story before moving on or acting. Also, have the story tellers talk about their feelings as to the different types of questions: detail questions, feelings questions, or clarification questions. Which type of questions did the story tellers find most helpful?

Activity 3: That's Nothing, You Should Hear My Story

Quite often individuals hear a story and immediately think of a similar story about their life. This quick reference to self-story can be very distracting and ineffective in a helping relationship.

Have students form triads and the have one student tell a story, followed by the another student telling, followed by the third student also telling a story. The goal is for each student to attempt to out do the previous student's story. The goal is to see who can tell the most engaging and exciting story.

The final phase of the activity is to have students tell what it felt like to have the next person tell a more engaging story. Have the students reflect on the reported feelings and then ask the students, as a class, to try to come to some conclusions on the inappropriateness of trying to tell "an even better" story than to just listening to the story being told. Ask the students to relate this to the helping situation. (Hint: Inappropriate disclosure by the helper can real devalue the story of the client, especially if the helper has "an even better story.")

Videos

Aspects of Behaviour (1971, 31 min, IM).   An excellent discussions of various focus areas in psychology highlighted by discussions with Stanley Milgram and John Darley.

Attitudes About Attitudes (1975, 27 min, UFC). Attitudes and cognitive dissonance are discussed in this video. Provides helpful insights to counselling practitioners.

Captive Minds: Hypnosis and Beyond (IM, 1985, 55 min, colour). An excellent look at how organizations ranging from cults to military recruit and retain their members.

Conditions for Helping (1973, 27min, TELS). Interesting insights as to when people will and will not offer help.

Discovering Psychology, Part 19: The Power of the Situation (1990, 30 min, ANN/CPB). How different situations affect our beliefs and our actions.

Eye of the Storm (1971, 29 min, CHU). A film that depicts discrimination in a third-grade class where the class is divided by eye color and discrimination is on alternating days. Provides insights as to the affects of discrimination.

Websites

1. www.talkingcure.com

    This is the homepage for the Institute for the Study of Therapeutic Change. This is an excellent site for discussions on the effectiveness of counseling. Make certain you get to "Baloney Watch": go to the website, click on News and Reviews, and then click on "Baloney Watch".

2. www.apa.org

    The homepage of the American Psychological Association.

3. www.cpa.ca

    The homepage of the Canadian Psychological Association.

4. www.counseling.org

    The homepage of the American Counseling Association.

5. www.counselingNetwork.com/

    The homepage for the World Counseling Network.

6. www.Colorado.edu/cspv/blueprints.index.html

    The home page for violence prevention.

7. http://jtc.colstate.edu

    The Journal of Technology in counseling.

Overhead Transparencies

Starting on the next page are copies of recommended overhead transparencies. Please feel free to convert the following pages to overheads as this will enhance the lecture portion of your class presentation.

"WHAT ARE MY KEY CONCERNS?"

1. Initial stress reduction

2. Clarity

3. Relationship building

4. Action

OH 8.1

HELPING CLIENTS EXPLORE

1. Learn to Work with All Styles of Storytelling

2. Start Where the Client Starts

3. Help Clients Clarify Key Issues

4. Assess the Severity of the Client's Problems

5. Help Clients Talk Productively about the Past

6. Help clients talk about the past to make sense of the present

OH 8.2A

HELPING CLIENTS EXPLORE
Cont'd.

7. Help clients talk about the past to be liberated from it

8. Help clients talk about the past in order to prepare for action in the future

9. As Clients Tell Their Stories, Search for Resources, Especially Unused Resources

10. Help Clients Spot and Develop Unused Opportunities

11. See Every Problem as an Opportunity

OH 8.2B

STEP I-A AND ACTION

1. The Importance of Proactivity

2. Using the Time Between Sessions Productively

3. Appreciating the Self-Healing Nature of Clients

4. A declaration of intent and the mobilization of resources

5. Coming out from under self-defeating emotions

OH 8.3

THE SHADOW SIDE OF STEP I-A

1. Clients As Storytellers

2. The Nature of Discretionary Change

In both individual and organizational affairs, the track record for discretionary change is quite poor.

3. Okavango/Kalahari phenomenon

OH 8.4

Evaluation Questions for Step I-A

How effectively am I doing the following?

1. Establishing a Working Alliance

2. Helping Clients Tell Their Stories

3. Building Ongoing Client Assessment into the Helping Process

4. Helping Clients Move to Action

5. Integrating Evaluation into the Heping Process

OH 8.5

BOX 8-1 Problem Finding

1. What are my concerns?

2. What's problematic in my life?

3. What issues do I need to face?

4. What's troubling me?

5. What would those who know me best tell me?

6. What's keeping me back from being what I want to be? from doing what I want to do?

7. What do I need to resolve?

OH 8.6

BOX 8-2 Opportunity Finding

1. What are my unused skills/resources?

2. What are my natural talents?

3. How could I use some of these?

4. What opportunities do I let go by?

5. What ambitions remain unfulfilled?

OH 8.7A

BOX 8-2 Opportunity Finding cont'd.

6. What could I accomplish if I put my mind to it?

7. What could I become good at if I tried?

8. Which opportunities should I be developing?

9. Which role models could I be emulating?

OH 8.7B

Chapter Nine:

Reluctant And Resistant Clients

	Pages
Chapter Outline	**261**
Detailed Lecture Notes	**262-272**
Lecture Enhancers	**273-274**
Class Activities	**275-276**
Videos	**277**
Websites	**278**
Transparencies	**279-284**

CHAPTER NINE OUTLINE

PSYCHOLOGICAL DEFENSES

RELUCTANCE — MISGIVINGS ABOUT CHANGE

RESISTANCE — REACTING TO COERCION

PRINCIPLES FOR MANAGING RELUCTANCE AND RESISTANCE

> Avoid Unhelpful Responses to Reluctance and Resistance
> Develop Productive Approaches to Dealing with Reluctance and Resistance

Detailed Lecture Notes

(Please note: The designation OH in the detailed lecture notes indicates an overhead transparency is available. Please locate the overhead transparencies in the final section of each chapter in this Instructors' Manual.)

Section One: PSYCHOLOGICAL DEFENSES (OH-9.1)

A. It is impossible to be in the business of helping people for long without encountering both reluctance and resistance (Clark, 1991; Ellis, 1985; Fremont & Anderson, 1986; Friedlander & Schwartz, 1985; Harris, 1995; Kottler, 1992; Otani, 1989). Mahalik (1994) developed a Client Resistance Scale to measure clients' opposition to dealing with painful emotions, disclosing intimate or painful material, developing a working alliance with the helper, dealing with blind spots, developing new perspectives, and embracing constructive change. In this book, a distinction is made between reluctance and resistance.

> *Reluctance* refers to clients' hesitancy to engage in the work demanded by the stages and steps of the helping process.

> *Resistance* refers to the push-back by clients when they feel they are being coerced.

B. The seeds of reluctance are in the client, whereas the stimulus for resistance is in the helper (Bischoff & Tracey, 1995) or the social setting surrounding the helping process. In practice, of course, a mixture of reluctance and resistance is often found in the same client. If therapy is to become more efficient, then counselors need to find ways of helping their clients deal with reluctant and resistance as expeditiously as possible.

Section Two: RELUCTANCE — MISGIVINGS ABOUT CHANGE

Reluctance refers to the ambiguity clients feel when they know that managing their lives better is going to exact a price. Clients are not sure whether they want to pay that price. Incentives for not changing often drive out or stand in the way of incentives for changing. This accounts for the sad record for discretionary change.

A. Clients exercise reluctance in many, often covert, ways.

   1. They talk about only safe or low-priority issues, seem unsure of what they want, benignly sabotage the helping process by being overly

262

cooperative, set unrealistic goals and then use them as an excuse for not moving forward, don't work very hard at changing their behavior, and are slow to take responsibility for themselves.

2. They tend to blame others or the social settings and systems of their lives for their troubles and play games with helpers.

3. Clients come "armored" against change to a greater or lesser degree.

B. The reasons for reluctance are many. They are built into the human condition. Here is a sampling. **(OH-9.2)**

1. **Fear of intensity.** Skilled helpers know that counseling is potentially intense. They are prepared for it and know how to support a client who is not used to such intensity.

2. **Lack of trust.** Even when confidentiality is an explicit part of the client-helper contract, some clients are very slow to reveal themselves. A combination of patience, encouraging, and challenging is demanded of the helper.

3. **Fear of disorganization**. Digging into one's inadequacies always leads to a certain amount of disequilibrium, disorganization, and crisis. But growth takes place at crisis points. A high degree of disorganization immobilizes the client, whereas very low disorganization is often indicative of a failure to get at the client's core concerns. A framework for helping provides clients with "channels" that act as safety devices that help them contain their fears. By challenging them to take "baby steps" that don't end in disaster, they help clients build confidence.

4. **Shame.** Shame is a much overlooked variable in human living (Egan, 1970; Kaufman, 1989; Lynd, 1958). Shame is not just being painfully exposed to another; it is primarily an exposure of self to oneself. Shame is often sudden — in a flash, the client sees heretofore unrecognized inadequacies without being ready for such a revelation. Shame is sometimes touched off by external incidents, such as a casual remark someone makes, but it could not be touched off by such insignificant incidents unless, deep down, one was already ashamed. A shame experience might be defined as an acute emotional awareness of a failure to be in some way. Once more, empathy and support help clients deal with whatever shame they might experience.

5. **Fear of change.** Some people are afraid of taking stock of themselves because they know, however subconsciously, that if they do, they will have to change — that is, surrender comfortable but unproductive

263

patterns of living, work more diligently, suffer the pain of loss, acquire skills needed to live more effectively, and so on. The pace and price of change cause problems for some clients. Some clients think that change is impossible, so why try? Others are dissatisfied with the pace of change. For some counseling is too fast, for others too slow. Some clients are looking for short-term relief. Some come with the idea that counseling is magic and are put off when change proves to be hard work. Future rewards are not compelling.

Section Three: RESISTANCE — REACTING TO COERCION

Resistance refers to the reaction of clients who in some way feel coerced. Reluctance is often passive. Resistance can be both active and passive. It is the client's way of fighting back (see Dimond and his associates, 1978, and Driscoll, 1984). Some clients see coercion where it does not exist. But, since people act on their perceptions, the result is still some form of active or passive fighting back.

A. Resistant clients, feeling abused, let everyone know that they have no need for help, show little willingness to establish a working relationship with the helper, and often enough try to con counselors. They are often resentful, make active attempts to sabotage the helping process, or terminate the process prematurely. They can be either testy or actually abusive and belligerent. Resistance to helping is, of course, a matter of degree, and not all these behaviors in their most virulent forms are seen in all resistant clients.

B. Involuntary clients — the term "mandated" clients is sometimes used — are often resisters. Clients like these are found in schools, especially schools below college level, in correctional settings, in marriage counseling, especially if it is court-mandated, in employment agencies, in welfare agencies, in court-related settings, and in other social agencies. But any client who feels that he or she is being coerced or treated unfairly can become a resister.

C. There are all sorts of reasons for resisting, which is to say that clients can experience coercion in a wide variety of ways. The following kinds of clients are likely to be resistant.

1. Clients who see no reason for going to the helper in the first place.
2. Clients who resent third-party referrers (parents, teachers, correctional facilities, social-service agencies) and whose resentment carries over to the helper.
3. Clients in medical settings who are asked to participate in counseling.
4. Clients who feel awkward in participating, who do not know how to be "good" clients.
5. Clients who have a history of being rebels.

6. Clients who see the goals of the helper or the helping system as different from their own. For instance, the goal of counseling in a welfare setting may be to help the clients become financially independent, whereas some clients may be satisfied with financial dependency.

7. Clients who have developed negative attitudes about helping and helping agencies and who harbor suspicions about helping and helpers. Sometimes these clients refer to helpers in derogatory and inexact terms ("shrinks").

8. Clients who believe that going to a helper is the same as admitting weakness, failure, and inadequacy. They feel that they will lose face by going. By resisting the process, they preserve their self-esteem.

9. Clients who feel that counseling is something that is being done to them. They feel that their rights are not being respected.

10. Clients who feel that they have not been invited to participate in the decisions that will affect their lives. This includes decisions about the helping process itself and decisions about their future.

11. Clients who feel a need for personal power and find it through resisting a powerful figure or agency: "I may be relatively powerless, but I still have the power to resist" is the subtext.

12. Clients who dislike their helpers but do not discuss their dislike with them.

13. Clients who differ from their helpers about the degree of change needed.

14. Clients who differ greatly from their helpers — for instance, a poor kid with an older middle-class helper.

D. Many sociocultural variables — gender, prejudice, race, religion, social class, upbringing, cultural and subcultural blueprints, and the like — can play a part in resistance.

Section Four: PRINCIPLES FOR MANAGING RELUCTANCE AND RESISTANCE

Because both reluctance and resistance are such pervasive phenomena, helping clients manage them is part and parcel of all our interactions with clients (Kottler, 1992). Here are some principles that can act as guidelines.

A. Avoid Unhelpful Responses to Reluctance and Resistance.

1. Helpers, especially beginning helpers who are unaware of the pervasiveness of reluctance and resistance, are often disconcerted when they encounter uncooperative clients.

2. Such helpers are prey to a variety of emotions — confusion, panic, irritation, hostility, guilt, hurt, rejection, depression.

3. Distracted by these unexpected feelings, they react in any of several unhelpful ways.

4. When helpers engage "difficult" clients, they experience stress, and some give in to self-defeating "fight or flight" approaches to handling it.

5. The source of this stress is not just the behavior of clients; it also comes from the helper's own self-defeating attitudes and assumptions about the helping process. Here are some of them.

6. Effective helpers neither court reluctance and resistance nor are surprised by them.

B. Develop Productive Approaches to Dealing with Reluctance and Resistance. (OH-9.3)

In a book like this, it is impossible to identify every possible form of reluctance and resistance, much less provide a set of strategies for managing each. Here are some principles and a general approach to managing reluctance and resistance in whatever forms they take.

1. **Explore your own reluctance and resistance.** If you are in touch with the various forms of reluctance and resistance in yourself and are finding ways of overcoming them, you are more likely to help clients deal with theirs.

2. **See some reluctance and resistance as normal.** Help clients see that their reluctance and resistance are not "bad" or odd. Help them see the positive side of resistance.

3. **Accept and work with the client's reluctance and resistance.** This is a central principle. Start with the frame of reference of the client. Accept both the client and his or her reluctance or resistance. Do not ignore it or be intimidated by what you find. Let clients know how you experience it and then explore it with them. Model openness to challenge. Be willing to explore your own negative feelings. The skill of direct, mutual talk (called immediacy, to be discussed later) is extremely important here. Help clients work through the emotions associated with reluctance and resistance. Avoid moralizing. Befriend the reluctance or the resistance instead of reacting to it with hostility or defensiveness.

4. **See reluctance as avoidance.** Reluctance is a form of avoidance that is not necessarily tied to client ill will. Therefore, you need to understand the principles and mechanisms underlying avoidance behavior, which is often discussed in texts dealing with the principles of behavior (see Watson & Tharp, 1993). Constructive change is usually more rewarding than a miserable status quo, but that might not be the perception of the client, especially in the beginning. Find ways of presenting the helping process as rewarding. Talk about outcomes.

5. **Examine the quality of your interventions.** Without setting off on a guilt trip, examine your helping behavior. What are you doing that might seem unfair to the client? In what ways does the client feel coerced? Furthermore, take stock of the emotions that are welling up in you because clients lash back or drag their feet. How are these emotions "leaking out"? No use denying such feelings. Rather, own them and find ways of coming to terms with them. Do not over personalize what the client says and does. If you are allowing a hostile client to get under your skin, you are probably reducing your effectiveness. Of course, the client might be resistant, not because of you, but because he is under pressure from others to deal with his problems. But you take the brunt of it. Find out, if you can.

6. **Be realistic and flexible.** Remember that there are limits to what a helper can do. Know your own personal and professional limits. If your expectations for growth, development, and change exceed the client's, you can end up in an adversarial relationship. Rigid expectations of the client and of yourself become self-defeating.

7. **Establish a "just society" with your client.** Deal with the client's feelings of coercion. Provide what Smaby and Tamminen (1979) called a "two-person just society" (p. 509). A just society is based on mutual respect and shared planning. Therefore, establish as much mutuality as is consonant with helping goals. Invite participation. Help clients participate in every step of the helping process and in all the decision making. Share expectations. Discuss and get reactions to helping procedures. Explore the helping contract with your clients and get them to contribute to it.

8. **Help clients find incentives for participating in the helping process.** Use client self-interest as a way of identifying these. Use brainstorming as a way of discovering possible incentives. For instance, the realization that he or she is going to remain in charge of his or her own life may be an important incentive for a client.

9. **Do not see yourself as the only helper in the lives of your clients.** Engage significant others, such as peers and family members, in

helping clients face their reluctance and resistance. For instance, lawyers who belong to Alcoholics Anonymous may be able to deal with a fellow lawyer's reluctance to join a treatment program more effectively than you can.

10. **Employ clients as helpers.** If possible, find ways to get reluctant and resistant clients into situations where they are helping others. The change of perspective can help clients come to terms with their own unwillingness to work. Group counseling, too, is a forum in which clients become helpers.

C. **Hanna, Hanna, and Keys (2000) have drawn up a list of fifty strategies —** some original, many drawn from the literature — for counseling defiant, aggressive adolescents (also see Sommers-Flanagan & Sommers-Flanagan, 1995). Many of the strategies have wider application to both reluctant and resistant clients of all ages. They divide them into three categories: reaching clients, accepting them, and relating to them. **(OH-9.4)**

1. **Reaching Clients**

   · Avoid desks.
   · Be genuine and unpretentious.
   · Show deep respect.
   · Keep and use your sense of humor.
   · Be able to laugh at yourself.
   · Educate the client about counseling.
   · Avoid being a symbol of authority.
   · Avoid taking an expert stance until the relationship is fairly stable.
   · Avoid asserting your credentials.
   · Avoid thinking in clinical labels.
   · Convey a brief therapy attitude.
   · Let the client "circle in" on more sensitive issues.
   · Balance insight and action.
   · Admire terrific defensive behavior.
   · Address the hurt behind the anger.
   · Encourage resistance.
   · "What percentage of you is made up of that part that is worried about you?"

2. **Accepting Clients**

   · Be clear about the boundaries of acceptable behavior in

counseling sessions.
- Avoid power struggles.
- Deal nondefensively with verbal disrespect: "I wonder who you are really mad at."
- Validate the client's perceptions when they are accurate.
- Deal with issues in the counseling relationship.
- Treat shocking statements with equanimity. Reframe the message embedded in such statements.

3. Relating to Clients

- Admit when you are confused or uninformed.
- Expect crises to happen in clients' lives.
- Tell stories of other clients in similar situations who made changes in their lives.
- Let clients know how much you are learning from your sessions with them
- Stay in touch with similar problems you have had.
- If you think another counselor will be a better fit with a client, think of switching.
- Use sound bytes rather than paragraphs when communicating a point.
- Share only things about yourself that you have worked through and would not mind being repeated.
- Do not allow the depth of caring to interfere with a clear understanding of your client and his or her problem situation.
- Encourage the client to establish a therapeutic peer culture.
- Identify victimization whatever its source.
- If the client is seeking attention, give it: "All right, now that you have my full attention, what do you want to do with it?"
- Make confrontation friendly and empathic.
- Reframe apathy as an attempt to avoid hurt, hassles, and difficulties.

D. **In summary, do not avoid dealing with reluctance and resistance, but do not reinforce these processes either**. Work with your client's unwillingness and become inventive in finding ways of dealing with it. But be realistic.

Section Five: PSYCHOLOGICAL DEFENSES: THE SHADOW SIDE OF RELUCTANCE AND RESISTANCE

It is odd to talk about the shadow side of reluctance and resistance because these realities tend to be part of the shadow side of helping in the first place. Clients don't talk openly about their reluctance and resistance, rather they demonstrate them. In many ways they try to disguise them, call them something else. In some ways psychological defenses are the soil from which reluctance and resistance spring.

A. The very concept of psychological defenses has had a long, somewhat confusing history (Cramer, 2000).

1. Traditionally, they are treated in courses on abnormal psychology. Cramer (1998) differentiates between coping mechanisms and defenses. She sees coping as a conscious and intentional process, while defenses tend to be unconscious and unintentional.

2. Vaillant (2000) talks about defenses as "involuntary coping mechanisms" (p.89).

3. Perhaps we can say that defenses play a role in coping. The "unconscious" part of this with its ties to psychoanalytic theory is a sore point for many.

4. Today, cognitive psychologists generally agree that some mental processes go on outside of awareness. For instance, there is evidence that this is the case with decision making.

5. Using language such as "mental processes outside of awareness" to describe defenses keeps the unconscious from sounding like some kind of black hole inside us.

6. Early psychoanalytic theory saw defenses as ways of managing instinctual drives, but some theoreticians and researchers now see them as playing a role in the maintenance of self-esteem and, generally, keeping ourselves intact (Cooper, 1998).

7. Social psychologists today talk about defenses as processes "by which human deceive themselves, enhance self-esteem, and foster unrealistic self-illusions" (Cramer, 2000, p. 639; see Baumeister, Dales, & Sommer, 1998).

8. "Cognitive dissonance" has been a respected social psychology concept for years. It became almost a brand name and there have been endless studies on it. But some now say that this term itself is just a nicer word for defenses (Paulhus, Fridhandler, & Hayes, 1997).

B. Cramer (2000) places defenses on a maturity continuum.

1. High on the scale are such things as anticipation, altruism, humor, sublimation, and suppression, while delusional projection, psychotic denial, and psychotic distortion sit at the bottom.

2. Going south on the maturity scale we find (without naming them all) intellectualization and isolation, then idealization, then nonpsychotic denial and rationalization, then autistic fantasy, and finally acting out and apathetic withdrawal before hitting the bottom.

3. Vaillant (2000) discusses the positive-psychology role of mature defenses like altruism and anticipation. There is some evidence that as clients get better, the use a immature defenses recedes and the use of mature defenses increases.

4. Cramer (2000) cautions us on this hierarchical ranking of defenses.

C. **While defenses defend people from, let's say, anxiety, they also get people in trouble.**

1. While defenses work to lower anxiety in the short term, they often put such people at risk in the longer term.

2. Defenses, then, can keep us from doing what is in our best interests.

3. In counseling settings, defenses can keep clients from developing insights that would help them admit and deal with their problems more creatively.

4. Some defenses, or "adaptive mental mechanisms," can help get us into and keep us mired in our troubles, while others can help prevent us from getting into trouble and help us cope when trouble strikes. The former need to be challenged and the latter supported.

5. "By thoughtlessly challenging irritating, but partly adaptive, immature defenses, a clinician can evoke enormous anxiety and depression in a patient" (Vaillant, 1994, p. 49) and put the helping relationship itself at risk.

D. **Immature defenses contribute a great deal to both reluctance and resistance.**

1. Clients can arrive on your doorstep with built-in tendencies to reluctance and resistance.

2. This puts a burden on you to listen fully to your clients and to process what they say and do by what you know about human beings.

3. Understanding psychological defenses can help.

4. Understanding personality traits and their implications can help.

5. But in the end, it is you and the client trying to do what is best for the client.

E. Clark (1998) has written a book describing defense mechanisms as they manifest themselves in counseling and suggesting ways of helping clients challenge them. Although he deals with traditional defense mechanisms — denial, displacement, identification, isolation, projection, rationalization, reaction formation, regression, repression, and undoing — he does so with a fresh voice.

Lecture Enhancers

You should be able to find the full text of the following items in your library or by using your web-based library access tool of choice (e.g., Psycinfo)

Item One: Do you listen or hear?
Shhh! Listen, Don't Just Hear

Bjorseth, Lillian D. (1999) Shhh! Listen, Don't Just Hear. Self Improvement Online, Inc. Home PageDirectoryArticlesNewsletter. lillian@duoforce.com or www.duoforce.com

Synopsis: The author does an outstanding job of emphasizing the difference between hearing and listening. Through interesting examples of those who simply hear versus those who really listen, the author nicely emphasizes the importance of developing the skill of listening as opposed to simply hearing. For the skilled helper the implications are obvious; for the client the skill of listening may be a major part of their work-related or relationship related problem. It is important to emphasize communication skills are integral to a successful helping relationship and are just as integral to the client leading a more desirable and effective life: one of the major goals of helping.

Item Two: Social Constructionist Approach to Therapeutic Empathy.
A Narrative Social Constructionist Approach to Therapeutic Empathy.

McLeod, John.; A narrative social constructionist approach to therapeutic empathy. Counselling Psychology Quarterly, Dec99, Vol. 12 Issue 4, p.377

Synopsis: Using a constructionist approach the author provides a context for empathy as a means of adding a level of depth to the helping relationship by viewing empathic listening as a relational process or a means of the client and helper creating of co-construction of the clients life through a narrative process that is greatly fostered by the empathic skills of the helper. With appropriate empathic skills the helper and client can co-create or co-recreate the clients life story in such away that insight and commitment move the relationship forward in a positive and constructive fashion. The author concludes with a discussion of appropriate and training and use by the skilled helper.

Item Three: Reverence and Resistance
Meeting Client Resistance and Reactance With Reverence.

Cowan, Eric W.; Presbury, Jack H., Meeting Client Resistance and Reactance With Reverence. Journal of Counseling & Development, Fall 2000, Vol. 78 Issue 4, p.411, 9p

Synopsis: The authors use a variety of theoretical orientations to explore the function and meaning of resistance in counseling. The authors provide an important insight that client resistance emerges due to the helper interactions with the client. This overlooked cause of resistance can become a major impasse to moving the helping relationship forward to positive and desirable outcomes.

Class Activities

In addition to the exercises in the Workbook that accompanies this text, you may find the following in-class activities to be of value:

Activity #1: The Reluctant Client

In this activity your goal is to have students role play the reluctant client. In triads, have students assume the roles of helper, reluctant client, and observer. Have the reluctant client and the observer meet with the helper outside the room for five minutes. During the time the helper is out of the room the reluctant client will list four "helping skills" the helper can use to breakdown the reluctance. If the helper uses any of the identified "helping skills" the client will be less reluctant

The goal of the activity is to get the helper to use as many helping skills as possible to establish a positive relationship with the client. After the exercise have each individual provide his or her perspective of how difficult it was to break down the reluctance and how effective it is to use a wide range of helping skills when working with a reluctant client.

Activity #2: The Resistant Client

In this activity have students discuss in groups of three or four how they would best help a resistant client. Have the group list up to seven intervention strategies, start with the most effective at the top of their list and the least effective, but still effective, at the bottom of their list. Next have each student group write their group's list on the board.

Do a class discussion of comparing and contrasting the lists of the various groups. Take the time to highlight the similarities and discuss the differences. The final part of the activity is to have students attempt to connect their three most effective interventions to content in Chapter 8. How similar are their responses to the skills identified in the textbook.

Activity #3: Reluctant and Resistant

Have students work individually first and then in pairs to share their responses to the following item: List three times in your life that you have been either reluctant or resistant. Have the students provide the following details:

1. How old was the student at the time of reluctant and/or resistant?

2. What was it that made him or her reluctant and/or resistant?

3. What eventually broke down the reluctance and resistance?

4. What could be taken from each experience that might assist in a helping situation?

After students have worked in pairs, ask for volunteer reports to the entire class. Make the point that some of our own earlier experience in life can help in how we deal with reluctant and resistant clients.

Videos

Emotional Development: Aggression (1923, 20 min, PENN). A discussion of aggression, frustration, and anger. Provides the therapist with insight to some of the most common emotions in a therapeutic relationship.

Gender and Relationships (1990, 30 min, IM). The film discuses attraction, love, and sex. A good review of some of the most basic human feelings.

Helping and Prosocial Behaviour (1989, 30 min, IM). The concept of altruistic behaviour is discussed and issues of social responsibility and reciprocity are explored.

Looks: How they affect your life (1984, 51 min, IM). The concept of beauty is reviewed and the psychological consequences of falling within certain societal standards are presented.

Predicting Our World (1975, 28 min, UFC). Concepts of learned helplessness and the just world phenomenon are presented in this video.

Social Cognitions and Attributions (1989, 30 min, IM). The self-serving bias and self-handicapping are among the attributional concepts discussed in this video.

Social Psychology Series: Communication- Negotiation and Persuasion (1975, 30 min, PENN). Both nonverbal and verbal issues are viewed in the way they affect our behaviours and attitudes.

Social Psychology Series: Conformity (1975, 30 min, PENN). The issue of conformity is presented and discussed. The discussion provides the therapist with insights to what motivates a client.

Websites

1. http://www.salesstar.com/mondaymotivation42400.htm
   Confronting your problems.

2. http://www.positive-way.com/expressi.htm
   Expressing and owning your own problems.

3. http://mentalhelp.net/psyhelp/chap14/chap14t.htm
   Developing attitudes that help you cope.

Overhead Transparencies

Starting on the next page are copies of recommended overhead transparencies. Please feel free to convert the following pages to overheads as this will enhance the lecture portion of your class presentation.

PSYCHOLOGICAL DEFENSES

Reluctance refers to clients' hesitancy to engage in the work demanded by the stages and steps of the helping process.

Resistance refers to the push-back by clients when they feel they are being coerced.

OH 9.1

SAMPLE REASONS FOR RELUCTANCE

1. Fear of intensity

2. Lack of trust

3. Fear of disorganization

4. Shame

5. Fear of change

OH 9.2

PRINCIPLES FOR MANAGING RELUCTANCE AND RESISTANCE

1. Explore your own reluctance and resistance.

2. See some reluctance and resistance as normal.

3. Accept and work with the client's reluctance and resistance.

4. See reluctance as avoidance.

5. Examine the quality of your interventions.

OH 9.3A

PRINCIPLES FOR MANAGING RELUCTANCE AND RESISTANCE
cont'd.

6. Be realistic and flexible.

7. Establish a "just society" with your client.

8. Help clients find incentives for participating in the helping process.

9. Do not see yourself as the only helper in the lives of your clients.

10. Employ clients as helpers.

OH 9.3B

STRAGEGY GROUPINGS FOR COUNSELING DEFIANT, AGGRESSIVE CLIENTS

1. **Reaching Clients**

2. **Accepting Clients**

3. **Relating to Clients**

OH 9.4

Chapter Ten:

Step I-B
I. The Nature Of Challenging

	Pages
Chapter Outline	**286**
Detailed Lecture Notes	**287-299**
Lecture Enhancers	**300**
Class Activities	**301-302**
Videos	**303**
Websites	**304**
Transparencies	**305-313**

CHAPTER TEN OUTLINE

CHALLENGING: THE BASIC CONCEPT

BLIND SPOTS: THE TARGETS OF CHALLENGING

> The Nature of Blind Spots
> Kinds of Blind Spots

NEW PERSPECTIVES LEADING TO NEW PATTERNS OF BEHAVIOR

THE GOALS OF CHALLENGING

CHALLENGING COMMON DYSFUNCTIONAL MINDSETS AND BEHAVIOR
     FOUND IN HELPING SETTINGS

> Invite Clients to Own Their Problems and Unused Opportunities
> Invite Clients to State Their Problems as Solvable
> Invite Clients to Move to a Needed Stage or Step of the Helping Process

THE SHADOW SIDE OF CHALLENGING

> Clients' Shadow-Side Response to Challenge: Dealing with Dissonance
> Challenge and the Shadow Side of Helpers

·   The "MUM Effect"
·   Excuses for Not Challenging
·   Helpers' Blind Spots

Detailed Lecture Notes

(Please note: The designation OH in the detailed lecture notes indicates an overhead transparency is available. Please locate the overhead transparencies in the final section of each chapter in this Instructors' Manual.)

Under the rubric "constructivism," theorists have rediscovered that both cultures and individuals, to a greater or lesser extent, construct the realities that guide their actions (see Borgen, 1992, pp. 120-121; Mahoney, 1991; Mahoney & Patterson, 1992, pp. 671-674; Neimeyer, 1993, 2000; Neimeyer & Mahoney, 1995). Within all cultures, individuals over time create subsets of these world views — that is, their own personal world views. These personal cultures drive behavior.

The tendency to construct reality or perceive the world in an individualist way produces a great deal of diversity among individuals and constitutes a key challenge for helpers. The construction of reality can contribute both to cultural and individual richness and to the creation of social and individual problems. Some mental constructions are self-limiting. Challenging means, in part, helping clients explore their constructions and the actions that follow from them. Then counselors can help them reconstruct their views of themselves and their worlds in more self-enhancing, other-enhancing, and community-enhancing ways. "Community" here means the groups in which clients have membership — family, friends, teams, work groups, church, neighborhood, and so forth.

Section One: CHALLENGE: THE BASIC CONCEPT (OH-10.1)

Effective helpers are not only understanders (listening, processing, sharing empathic highlights) and clarifiers (probing, summarizing), but are also reality testers (challenge).

A. Writers who have emphasized helping as a social-influence process (see Chapter 3) have always seen some form of challenge as central to helping (Bernard, 1991; Dorn, 1984, 1986; Strong & Claiborn, 1982).

B. Helpers as sowers of discord.

    1. Martin (1994) put it well when he suggested that the helping dialogue may add the most value when it is perceived by clients as relevant, helpful, interested, and *"somehow inconsistent (discordant) with their current theories of themselves and their circumstances"* (pp. 53-54, emphasis

added). The same point is made by Trevino (1996, p. 203) in the context of cross-cultural counseling

2. Certain patterns of congruency and discrepancy... between client and counselor facilitate change. There is a significant body of research suggesting that congruency between counselor and client enhances the therapeutic relationship, whereas discrepancy between the two facilitates change.

3. Claiborn (1982, p. 446) concluded that the presentation of discrepant points of view contributes to positive outcomes by changing "the way the client construes problems and considers solutions."

4. Challenge adds that discordant note. Weinrach (1995, 1996), in touting the virtues of Rational Emotive Behavior Therapy (REBT) which incorporates challenge into its core, suggested that some members of the helping profession object to REBT because it is a "tough-minded therapy for a tender-minded profession" (1995, p. 296).

B. Challenge versus confrontation.

1. Note that the word challenge is used here rather than the more hard-hitting term confrontation, a term with even more of an edge. Most people see both confronting and being confronted as unpleasant experiences. But, at least in principle, they more readily buy the softer, gentler option of challenge. This does not completely rule out confrontation, but why bring out the big guns when they are not needed?

D. Stop, start, continue. Challenge is basically simple. It is about stop, start, and keep going. Challenge is an invitation to clients to:

1. **Stop**. Identify and *stop* engaging in activities that keep them mired down in their problem situations or which keep them from identifying and developing resources and opportunities.

2. **Start**. Identify and *start* engaging in activities that would either prevent them from getting into trouble in the first place or in activities that will either get them out of trouble or help them develop resources and opportunities.

3. **Keep going**. Identify and *continue* activities that manage problems or develop opportunities, especially if the client gives signs of flagging.

The basic framework of challenge and the target of challenging is found here in Chapter 10. Methods for helping clients challenge themselves are reviewed in Chapter 11. Finally, how to go about challenging, that is, the wisdom of challenging, is the focus of Chapter 12. As usual, extensive exercises in challenging are found in Chapters 10-12 of *Exercises in Helping Skills*.

Section Two: BLIND SPOTS: THE TARGETS OF CHALLENGING

Just what is it that clients should start, stop, or continue doing? There are five broad targets: mindsets, dysfunctional ways of thinking, self-limiting ways of acting, discrepancies between thinking/saying and doing, and failure to understand and deal with the behavior of others. These targets are called "blind spots." The task of the counselor is twofold. First to help clients identify blind spots. Second, and more important, to helps clients transform blind spots into *new perspectives* that lead to problem-managing and opportunity-developing action.

A. The Nature of Blind Spots (OH-10.2)

Clients fail to see how some of the realities they construct for themselves are self-limiting. Since we are all "constructivist" to one degree or another, our personal "realities" are bound to run up against other realities. And so we live in a conflict-filled world. And we are "blind" in different ways and to different degrees.

1. **Simple unawareness**. There are things that clients are simply not aware of. Becoming aware of them would help them know themselves better and both cope with problems and develop opportunities.

2. **Self-deception**. Clients are like the rest of us. There are things they would rather not know, because, if they knew them, they would be challenged to change their behavior in some way. The defenses mentioned in Chapter 9 offer some degree of explanation. Since there are degrees of defenses, there are degrees of self-deception. Psychotic defenses represent the extreme, but the more moderate defenses such as rationalization are also forms of self-deception.

3. **Choosing to stay in the dark**. Choosing to stay in the dark is a form of evasiveness with oneself. Clients often choose to stay in the dark. When clients are being vague or evasive with their helpers, they may well not want to know. And it is likely that they don't want you to know either.

4. **Knowing, but not caring.** We can use the term blind spot, at least in an extended sense, to describe this kind of behavior because clients don't seem to fully understand or appreciate the degree to which they are choosing their own misery. Or the degree to which they are turning their backs on a better future.

So, as you can see, the term "blind spot," as used here is somewhat elastic. We are unaware, we deceive ourselves, we don't want to know, we ignore, we don't care, or we know, but not fully, that is, we do not fully understand the implications or the consequences of what we know. But it's a good term. It has great face validity. People know what you mean as soon as you use the term.

B. Kinds of Blind Spots or Blind Spot Targets (OH-10.3)

Blind spots are mindsets, internal actions, external actions, or discrepancies that, as we have just seen, clients are unaware of or choose to ignore in one way or another. They are key blind spots if they affect our lives substantially or have the potential to do so.

1. **Mindsets**. Mindsets here refer to more or less permanent states of mind.

   a) They include such things as assumptions, attitudes, beliefs, bias, convictions, inclinations, norms, outlook, unexamined perceptions of self/others/the world, preconceptions, prejudices, reactions, and values.

   b) Mindsets drive external behavior, or at least leak out into external behavior.

   c) Mindsets make a difference. It's just there. It may or may not influence behavior.

   d) Mindsets can decrease or increase options.

   e) Some clients have mindsets that would do them a world of good were they to let these attitudes have some impact on their external behavior.

2. **Internal behavior, ways of thinking**.

   a) Internally we daydream, pray, ruminate on things, believe, make decisions, formulate plans, make judgments, question motives, approve of self and others, disapprove of self and others, wonder, value, imagine, ponder, think through, create standards, fashion norms, mull over, worry, panic, ignore, forgive, rehearse — we *do* all sorts of things.

b) These are behaviors, not just things that happen to us.

c) Since internal behavior, like mindsets, is inside clients' heads that, you can't immediately see it. They have to tell you about it (self-disclosure). Or you have to ask them what's going on inside (probing). Or you may infer what's going on internally from clients' external behavior (making hunches, guessing, interpreting).

d) Clients engage in ways of thinking that do them little good.

3. **External behavior, ways of acting**.

a) This is the stuff people can see or could see if they were looking. For some clients their behavior constitutes trouble.

b) Some clients engage in behaviors that keep them mired in their problems.

c) Clients also fail to make choices and engage in behaviors that would help them cope with problems or develop opportunities.

4. **Discrepancies between thinking/saying and acting**.

Good thinking doesn't always get translated into good behavior. That is, there are often discrepancies between what clients think/say and what they do.

5. **Others' behavior and others' attitude toward and impact on me.**

a) Our blind spots are not limited to our own thinking and acting. We also fail to notice others.

b) Sometimes we are unaware.

c) Sometimes we deceive ourselves.

d) Sometimes we'd rather not know.

e) Sometimes we know and just don't care but are blind to the implications of our not caring.

C. **In practice these five categories are often mixed together**.

1. Helping clients deal with blind spots is one of the most important things you can do as a helper.

2. Helping clients deal with dysfunctional blind spots can prevent damage, limit damage already done, and turn problems into opportunities.

Section Three: NEW PERSPECTIVES LEADING TO NEW PATTERNS OF BEHAVIOR

We do our clients a disservice if all that we do is help them identify and explore self-limiting blind spots. The positive psychology part of challenging is helping clients transform blind spots into new perspectives and helping them translate these new perspectives into more constructive patterns of both internal and external behavior.

A. The Many Names of Developing New Perspectives

1. There are many upbeat names for this process of transforming blind spots into new perspectives.

2. Some terms used to describe this process are framebreaking, framebending, and reframing.

3. All of these imply some kind of cognitive restructuring, developing understanding, or awareness that is needed in order to identify and manage both problems and opportunities.

4. Developing new perspectives, while painful at times, tends to be ultimately prized by clients.

5. Effective helpers assume that clients have the resources to see the world in a less distorted way and to act on what they see.

6. Identifying blind spots is not always the same as developing a new perspective.

B. Linking New Perspectives to Action

1. Overstressing insight and self-understanding — that is, new perspectives — can actually stand in the way of action instead of paving the way for it.

2. Unfortunately, the search for insight can too easily become a goal in itself.

3. Much more attention has been devoted to developing insight than to linking insight to action.

4. Constructive behavioral change leading to valued outcomes is required.

5. Effective counselors, as they help their clients develop insights into themselves and their behavior, maintain a whole-model approach.

6. Insights are not just to be relished. They are to be acted on.

7. Clients should be able to say, "I now see much more clearly how I am putting myself in jeopardy, but *I can do something about it*"

Section Four: THE GOALS OF CHALLENGING (OH-10.4)

A. Goal #1. Invite clients to challenge themselves to change ways of thinking and acting that keep them mired in problem situations and prevent them from identifying and developing opportunities.

B. Goal #2. Become partners with your clients in helping them challenge themselves:

>   to find possibilities in their problems,

>   to discover unused resources, both internal and external,

>   to invest these resources in the problems and opportunities of   their lives,

>   to spell out possibilities for a better future,

>   to find ways of making that future a reality, and

>   to commit themselves to the actions needed to make it all happen.

C. Overriding principle: Help clients replace unproductive thinking and behaving with productive thinking and behaving.

1. This "replacing" can take place at any stage or step of the helping process.

2. Helpers who do no more than listen to clients' stories and help them clarify them are, according to Kiesler (1988), "hooked" by their clients. After all, clients are experts in their own stories.

3. Helpers "unhook" themselves by challenging clients' stories and the quality of their participation in the helping process itself.

4. They unhook themselves further by challenging clients to move from story to possibilities, to goals, and to action.

293

D. Applications: From Blind Spots to New Perspectives to Action

Since challenge does not exist for its own sake, your job is to help clients challenge themselves whenever, in your estimation, it would add value. Once the skill of challenging becomes second-nature to you, you will find yourself routinely inviting clients to take a "second look" at what their mindsets are and what they are thinking, saying, or doing at every stage and step of the helping process. What follows are further examples of some of the common situations calling for challenge. Clients move from blind spots to new perspectives to action.

1. Challenging Mindsets

The principle: Invite clients to transform outmoded, self-limiting mindsets and perspectives into self-liberating and self-enhancing new perspectives that are pregnant with action.

Self-limiting beliefs and assumptions. Albert Ellis has developed a rational-emotional-behavioral approach (REBT) to helping (Dryden, 1995; Dryden, Keenan, Ankara, & Ellis, 1999; Ellis, 1999; Ellis & Harper, 1998; Ellis & MacLaren, 1998). He claims that one of the most useful interventions helpers can make is to challenge clients' irrational beliefs (see also Lazarus, Lazarus, & Fay, 1993). Some of the common beliefs that Ellis believes get in the way of effective living are these: **(OH-10.5)**

> ➤ **Being liked and loved.** I must always be loved and approved by the significant people in my life.
> ➤ **Being competent.** I must always, in all situations, demonstrate competence, and I must be both talented and competent in some important area of life.
> ➤ **Having one's own way.** I must have my way, and my plans must always work out.
> ➤ **Being hurt.** People who do anything wrong, especially those who harm me, are evil and should be blamed and punished.
> ➤ **Being danger-free.** If anything or any situation is dangerous in any way, I must be anxious and upset about it. I should not have to face dangerous situations.
> ➤ **Being problemless.** Things should not go wrong in life, and if by chance they do, there should be quick and easy solutions.
> ➤ **Being a victim.** Other people and outside forces are responsible for any misery I experience. No one should ever take advantage of me.
> ➤ **Avoiding.** It is easier to avoid facing life's difficulties than to develop self-discipline; making demands of myself should not be necessary.
> ➤ **Tyranny of the past.** What I did in the past, and especially what happened to me in the past, determines how I act and feel today.

> **Passivity.** I can be happy by avoiding, by being passive, by being uncommitted, and by just enjoying myself.

2. Challenging Self-Limiting Internal Behavior

The Principle: Invite clients to replace self-limiting and self-defeating internal behaviors with more creative thinking that translate into action.

3. Challenging Self-Limiting External Behavior

The Principle: Invite clients to identify, challenge, and change self-defeating external behaviors. For many clients it is their external behavior that gets them into and keeps them mired down in trouble. The ultimate payoff lies in changing external rather than internal behaviors.

4. Challenging the Predictable Dishonesties of Everyday Life

The Principle: Invite clients to challenge substantial distortions. Some clients would rather not see the world as it is — it is too painful or demanding — and therefore distort it in various ways.

5. **Challenge games, tricks, and smoke screens**. If clients are comfortable with their delusions and profit by them, they will obviously try to keep them. If they are rewarded for playing games, inside the counseling sessions or outside, they will continue a game approach to life (see Berne, 1964). The number of games we can play to avoid the work involved in squarely facing the tasks of life is endless. Clients who are fearful of changing will attempt to lay down smoke screens to hide from the helper the ways in which they fail to face up to life. Such clients use communication in order not to communicate (see Beier & Young, 1984; Argyris, 1999). Therefore, helpers do well if they establish an atmosphere that discourages clients from playing games. An attitude of "nonsense is challenged here" should pervade the helping sessions.

6. **Challenge excuses**. Snyder, Higgins, and Stucky (1983) examined excuse-making behavior in depth. Excuse making, of course, is universal, part of the fabric of everyday life (see also Halleck, 1988; Higginson, 1999; Snyder & Higgins, 1988; Yun, 1998). Like games and distortions, it has its positive uses in life. Even if it were possible, there is no real reason for setting up a world without myths. On the other hand, avoidance behavior and excuse making contribute a great deal to the "psychopathology of the average." Clients routinely provide excuses for why they did something "bad," why they didn't do something "good," and why they can't do something they need to do. This is only skimming the surface of the

games, evasions, tricks, distortions, excuses, rationalizations, and subterfuges resorted to by clients (together with the rest of the population). Skilled helpers are caring and empathic, but they do not let themselves be conned. That helps no one.

E. Strengths and Unused Resources

Part of positive psychology is helping clients get in touch with unexploited opportunities and unused or underused resources. Some of these resources are client-based — for instance, talents and abilities not being used — and some are external — failure to identify and use social support. Gerry Sexton (1999), focusing on internal resources, outlines what it means to be a self-directed learner. Clients often have self-healing resources that are unused or underused. Self-directed learners use resources that are available. According to Sexton, self-directed learners do the following:

1. They work with an underlying sense of **purpose**. For clients this means goals: short-term, medium-term, long-term.

2. They have a **dream** which they refuse to surrender.

3. They focus on their **gifts**

4. They see themselves as **volunteers** rather than victims.

5. They act **despite their fears**.

6. They thrive on **interdependence**.

Section Five: CHALLENGING COMMON DYSFUNCTIONAL MINDSETS AND BEHAVIOR FOUND IN HELPING SESSIONS

How clients talk about their problems and unused opportunities has a lot to do with the "feel" of helping sessions. Three sets of behavior are reviewed here. The first set deals with the ownership of problems and unused opportunities. The second with problem or opportunity definition. The third has to do with movement within the helping model.

A. Invite Clients to Own Their Problems and Unused Opportunities.

1. It is all too common for clients to refuse to take responsibility for their problems and unused opportunities. Instead, there is a whole list of outside forces and other people who are to blame.

2. Clients need to challenge themselves or be challenged to own the problem situation.

3. Lack of ownership is a common blind spot.

4. Carkhuff (1987) talked about helping clients own problem situations and unused opportunities in terms of "personalizing."

5. Not only problems but also opportunities need to be seized and owned by clients. As Wheeler and Janis (1980) noted, "Opportunities usually do not knock very loudly, and missing a golden opportunity can be just as unfortunate as missing a red-alert warning." (p. 18)

B. Invite Clients to State Their Problems as Solvable.

Jay Haley (1976, p. 9) said that if "therapy is to end properly, it must begin properly — by negotiating a solvable problem." Or exploring a realistic opportunity, someone might add.

1. It is not uncommon for clients to state problems as unsolvable.

> **UNSOLVABLE PROBLEM**: In sum, my life is miserable now because of my past. My parents were indifferent to me and at times even unjustly hostile. If only they had been more loving, I wouldn't be in this mess. I am the failed product of an unhappy environment.

   a) This justifies a "poor-me" attitude and a failure to act.

   b) The past cannot be changed.

   c) Clients can change their attitudes about the past and deal with the present consequences of the past.

   d) When a client defines the problem exclusively as a result of the past, the problem cannot be solved.

2. A problem can be stated in solvable way

> **SOLVABLE PROBLEM**: Over the years I've been blaming my parents for my misery. I still spend a great deal of time feeling sorry for myself. As a result, I sit around and do nothing. I don't make friends, I don't involve myself in the community, I don't take any constructive steps to get a decent job.

   a) A solvable or manageable problem is one that clients can do something about

b) This does not mean that all problems are solvable by the direct action of the client. A teenager may be miserable because his self-centered parents are constantly squabbling and seem indifferent to him. He certainly can't solve the problem by making them less self-centered, stopping them from fighting, or getting them to care for him more. But he can be helped to find ways to cope with his home situation more effectively by developing fuller social opportunities outside the home.

c) This could mean helping him develop new perspectives on himself and family life and challenging him to act both internally and externally in his own behalf.

C. **Invite Clients to Move on to the Next Needed Stage or Step of the Helping Process**. We have touched on this already in discussing probing. There is no reason to keep going "'round the mulberry bush" with clients. You can help clients challenge themselves to:

1. clarify problem situations by describing specific experiences, behaviors, and feelings when they are being vague or evasive;

2. talk about issues — problems, opportunities, goals, commitment, strategies, plans, actions — when they are reluctant to do so;

3. develop new perspectives on themselves, others, and the world when they prefer to cling to distortions;

4. review possibilities, critique them, develop goals, and commit themselves to reasonable agendas when they would rather continue wallowing in their problems;

5. search for ways of getting what they want, instead of just talking about what they would prefer;

6. spell out specific plans instead of taking a scattered, hit-or-miss approach to change;

7. persevere in the implementation of plans when they are tempted to give up;

8. review what is and what is not working in their pursuit of change "out there."

In sum, counselors can help clients challenge themselves to engage more effectively in all the stages and steps of problem management during the sessions themselves and in the changes they are pursuing in everyday life. Box 10-1 reviews the kinds of questions counselors can help their clients ask themselves to uncover blind spots.

BOX 10-1
Questions to Uncover Blind Spots (OH-10.6)

These are the kinds of questions you can help clients ask themselves in order to develop new perspectives, change internal behavior, and change external behavior.

➤ What problems am I avoiding?
➤ What opportunities am I ignoring?
➤ What's really going on?
➤ What am I overlooking?
➤ What do I refuse to see?
➤ What don't I want to do?
➤ What unverified assumptions am I making?
➤ What am I failing to factor in?
➤ How am I being dishonest with myself?
➤ What's underneath the rocks?
➤ If others were honest with me, what would they tell me?

Lecture Enhancers

You should be able to find the full text of the following items in your library or by using your web-based library access tool of choice (e.g., Psycinfo)

Item One: Art or Science?
The clinician's art, or why science is not enough.

Gaskovski, Peter. (1999). The clinician's art, or why science is not enough. In Canadian-Psychology. 1999 Nov; Vol 40(4): 320-327.

Synopsis: The author presents a provocative analysis of what it means to be a clinical psychologist from both forms of clinical art: empirical construction that explains the causes of clients' struggles; and creative construction that help clients' to construct new meanings about their issues. The interrelationship and importance of these two art forms emphasizes the need for its further study within the clinician's training.

Item Two: Move a Continent?
Why don't continents move? Why don't people change?

Prochaska,-James-O.; Prochaska,-Janice-M. (1999) Why don't continents move? Why don't people change? In Journal-of-Psychotherapy-Integration. 1999 Mar; Vol 9(1): 83-102

Synopsis: This article examines why people don't change and uses the transtheoretical model for understanding reasons for not changing and subsequently, readiness to change. The stages and levels of change presented in the transtheoretical model assist counselors in their work with clients dealing with change.

Item Three: Enhancing Creativity
Enhancing creativity in cognitive therapy.

Kuehlwein,-Kevin-T. (2000). Enhancing creativity in cognitive therapy. In Journal-of-Cognitive-Psychotherapy. 2000 Sum; Vol 14(2): 175-187 Special Issue: Creativity in the context of cognitive therapy

Synopsis: Resources that focus on nurturing and generating creativity supplement the case examples provided in this article that explores the nature of creativity in psychotherapy. Beck's model and Edward deBobo's model, with their respective methods and frameworks, are presented to guide the cognitive therapist wishing to creatively enhance client sessions.

Class Activities

In addition to the exercises in the Workbook that accompanies this text, you may find the following in-class activities to be of value:

Activity #1: I Challenge You

In this activity your goal is to have students role play a scenario where a client is always late for appointments with the helper. Have the students work in triads with one student the client, one the helper, and one the observer. Have the helper challenge the client on the issue of always being late in two very different ways. The first approach is to show anger and frustration. The second approach is to approach the client with a firm and understanding manner. After each rotation of helper, client, and observer, have each triad member talk about their emotional state between the two different approaches. Have each triad record their responses and conclude the activity by groups randomly sharing some of their responses on their lists.

Activity #2: Challenge The Textbook

In this activity have students discuss in groups of three or four points in the textbook that they challenge as being the best way to challenge clients. Have the students make a list of at least five items in Chapter Nine that they challenge. Have them be very specific in what they are challenging and why they are challenging the textbook material. Quite often they enjoy the rich experience of challenging the procedure.

Activity #3: Challenges I Have Survived

Have students work individually first and then in pairs to share their responses to the following item: List three times in your life that you have been challenged by a friend or family member. Have the students provide the following details:

1. How old was the student at the time of being challenged?

2. What was it that he or she was being challenged on?

3. What was the outcome of the challenge?

4. What could be taken from each experience that might assist in effective challenging in a helping relationship?

      After students have worked in pairs, ask for volunteer reports to the entire class. Make the point that some of our own earlier experience in life can help in how we learn to challenge others.

Videos

Conformity and Independence (1975, 23 min, MTROLA). Social influence is the focus of this video. The work of Asch, Sherif, and Milgram is included in the discussion.

Face Value: Perceptions of Beauty (26 min, FHS). A sociobiological discussion of the perception of beauty is discussed.

Group Dynamics: Groupthink (1973, 22 min, MGHT). The symptoms of group think are presented in this video.

Group Dynamics: Why good people make bad decisions (1994, 17min, LS).
Using high school students grouped to complete a class project, the concepts of interpersonal expectations, social roles, and group think are presented.

Helping Others (1973, 28 min, OEB). Why we help others, both intrinsic and extrinsic satisfaction is examined.

Interpersonal Influence and the small Group: (1971, 30 min, NETCHE). The power of group influence is reviewed.

Websites

1.
http://www.iversonsoftware.com/reference/psychology/Advancedaccurateempathy.htm
   Advanced empathy.

2. http://www.ocii.com/~fisher/courses/comm329/empathy.html
   Empathy Concepts

3. http://www.ocii.com/~fisher/courses/comm329/helping.html
   Help through personal problem solving.

4. http://mentalhelp.net/psyhelp/chap14/chap14t.htm
   Thinking beyond the office.

Overhead Transparencies

Starting on the next page are copies of recommended overhead transparencies. Please feel free to convert the following pages to overheads as this will enhance the lecture portion of your class presentation.

CHALLENGE: THE BASIC CONCEPT

1. Challenge as central to helping

2. Helpers as sowers of discord

3. Challenge versus confrontation

4. Stop, start, continue

OH 10.1

THE NATURE OF BLIND SPOTS

1. **Simple Unawareness**

2. **Self Deception**

3. **Choosing To Stay In The Dark**

4. **Knowing But Not Caring**

OH 10.2

KINDS OF BLIND SPOTS

1. Mindsets.

2. Internal behavior, ways of thinking.

3. External behavior, ways of acting.

4. Discrepancies between thinking/saying and acting.

5. Others' behavior and others' attitude toward and impact on me.

6. In practice these five categories are often mixed together.

OH 10.3

THE GOALS OF CHALLENGING

Overriding principle:

Help clients replace unproductive thinking and behaving with productive thinking and behaving.

OH 10.4

SELF-LIMITING BELIEFS AND ASSUMPTIONS

1. **Liked and loved.**

2. **Being competent.**

3. **Having one's own way.**

4. **Being danger-free.**

OH 10.5A

SELF-LIMITING BELIEFS AND ASSUMPTIONS

5. Liked and loved.

6. Being competent.

7. Having one's own way.

8. Being danger-free.

OH 10.5B

QUESTIONS TO UNCOVER BLIND SPOTS

1. What problems am I avoiding?

2. What opportunities am I ignoring?

3. What's really going on?

4. What am I overlooking?

5. What do I refuse to see?

6. What don't I want to do?

OH 10.6A

QUESTIONS TO UNCOVER BLIND SPOTS cont'd.

7. What unverified assumptions am I making?

8. What am I failing to factor in?

9. How am I being dishonest with myself?

10. What's underneath the rocks?

11. If others were honest with me, what would they tell me?

OH 10.6B

Chapter Eleven:

Step I-B:
II. Specific Challenging Skills

	Pages
Chapter Outline	**315**
Detailed Lecture Notes	**316-327**
Lecture Enhancers	**328-329**
Class Activities	**330-331**
Videos	**332**
Websites	**333**
Transparencies	**334-339**

CHAPTER ELEVEN OUTLINE

ADVANCED EMPATHIC HIGHLIGHTS: THE MESSAGE BEHIND THE MESSAGE

➢ Help Clients Make the Implied Explicit
➢ Help Clients Identify Themes in Their Stories
➢ Help Clients Make Connections They May Be Missing
➢ Share Educated Hunches Based on Empathic Listening and Understanding

INFORMATION SHARING: FROM NEW PERSPECTIVES TO ACTION

HELPER SELF-DISCLOSURE

IMMEDIACY: DIRECT, MUTUAL TALK

➢ Types of Immediacy in Helping and Principles for Using Them
➢ Situations Calling for Immediacy

USING SUGGESTIONS AND RECOMMENDATIONS

CONFRONTATION

ENCOURAGEMENT

EVALUATION QUESTIONS FOR STEP I-B

Detailed Lecture Notes

(Please note: The designation OH in the detailed lecture notes indicates an overhead transparency is available. Please locate the overhead transparencies in the final section of each chapter in this Instructors' Manual.)

There are any number of ways in which helpers can challenge clients to develop new perspectives, change their internal behavior, and change their external behavior. The following are discussed and illustrated in this chapter: (1) sharing advanced empathic highlights, (2) sharing information, (3) helper self-disclosure, (4) immediacy, (5) suggestions and recommendations, and (6) confrontation, (7) encouragement. It has already been noted that both probing and summarizing — and even sharing accurate highlights — can challenge clients to rethink their attitudes and behavior.

Section One: ADVANCED EMPATHIC HIGHLIGHTS: THE MESSAGE BEHIND THE MESSAGE

A. As skilled helpers listen intently to clients, they often see clearly what clients only half see and hint at. This deeper kind of empathic listening involves "sensing meanings of which the client is scarcely aware" (Rogers, 1980, p. 142) or, in broader terms, listening to and grasping the "message behind the message."

   1. One way of challenging clients is to share with the client your understanding of the message behind the message.

   2. When you share basic empathic highlights — provided, of course, that you are accurate — clients recognize themselves almost immediately

   3. Since advanced empathic highlights dig a bit deeper, clients might not immediately recognize themselves in the helper's response.

   4. They might experience a bit of disequilibrium. That's what makes sharing advanced empathic highlights a form of challenge.

   5. Here are some questions helpers can ask themselves to probe a bit deeper as they listen to clients.

      a) What is this person only half saying?
      b) What is this person hinting at?
      c) What is this person saying in a confused way?

d) What covert message is behind the explicit message?

6. Note that advanced empathic listening and processing focuses on what the client is actually saying or at least expressing, however tentatively or confusedly. It is not an interpretation of what the client is saying. Sharing advanced empathic highlights is not an attempt to "psych the client out."

7. Advanced empathic listening in the hands of skilled helpers focuses, not just on the problematic dimensions of clients' behavior, but also on unused opportunities and resources.

8. Effective helpers listen for the resources that are buried deeply in clients and often have been forgotten by them.

B. Advanced empathic highlights can take a number of forms. Here are some of them. **(OH-11.1)**

    1. Help Clients Make the Implied Explicit.

        a) The most basic form of an advanced highlight involves helping clients give fuller expression to what they are implying rather than saying directly.

        b) As with basic highlights, there is no such thing as a good advanced highlight in itself.

        c) Does the response help the client clarify the issue more fully so that he or she might begin to see the need to act differently?

    2. Help Clients Identify Themes in Their Stories.

        a) When clients tell their stories, certain themes emerge.

        b) Once you see a self-defeating theme or pattern emerging from your discussions, you can share your perception and help the client check it out.

    3. Help Clients Make Connections They May Be Missing.

        a) Clients often tell their stories in terms of experiences, behaviors, and emotions in a hit-or-miss way.

b) The counselor's job, then, is to help them make the kinds of connections that provide insights or perspectives that enable them to move forward in the helping process.

4. **Share Educated Hunches Based on Empathic Understanding**.

   a) As you listen to clients, thoughtfully process what they say, and put it in context, hunches about the message behind the message or the story behind the story will naturally begin to form.

   b) You can share the hunches that you feel might add value.

   c) The more mature and socially competent you become and the more experience you have helping others, the more "educated" your hunches become.

   d) Hunches can help clients see the bigger picture.

   e) Hunches can help clients see what they are expressing indirectly or merely implying.

   f) Hunches can help clients draw logical conclusions from what they are saying.

   g) Hunches can help clients open up areas they are only hinting at.

   h) Hunches can help clients see things they may be overlooking.

   i) Hunches can help clients identify themes.

   j) Hunches can help clients take fuller ownership of partially owned experiences, behaviors, feelings, points of view, and decisions.

   j) Like all responses, hunches should be based on your understanding of your clients.

   k) Sharing advanced empathic highlights constructively depends on social competence and emotional intelligence.

Section Two: INFORMATION SHARING:
FROM NEW PERSPECTIVES TO ACTION

A. Sometimes clients are unable to explore their problems fully and proceed to action because they lack information of one kind or another.

1. Information can help clients at any stage or step of the helping process. For instance,

   a) In Stage I it helps many clients to know that they are not the first to try to cope with a particular problem.

   b) In Stage II information can help them further clarify identify possibilities and set goals.

   c) In the implementation stage information on commonly-experienced obstacles can help clients cope and persevere.

B. The skill or strategy of information sharing is included under challenging skills because it helps clients develop new perspectives on their problems or shows them how to act.

   1. It includes both giving information and correcting misinformation. In some cases, the information can prove to be quite confirming and supportive

   2. In other cases the information may be painful and challenging.

   3. In some cases, the new perspectives clients gain from information.

   4. Sharing can be both comforting and painful.

   5. Giving information is especially useful when lack of accurate information either is one of the principal causes of a problem situation or is making an existing problem worse or when information is needed to manage the problem.

   6. In some medical settings, doctors team up with counselors to give clients messages that are hard to hear and to provide them with information needed to make difficult decisions.

C. There are some cautions helpers should observe in giving information.

   1. When information is challenging, or even shocking, be tactful and help the client handle the disequilibrium that comes with the news.

   2. Do not overwhelm the client with information.

   3. Make sure that the information you provide is clear and relevant to the client's problem situation.

4. Don't let the client go away with a misunderstanding of the information.

5. Be supportive; help the client process the information.

6. Be sure not to confuse information giving with advice giving; the latter is seldom useful.

7. Professional guidance is not to be confused with telling clients what to do.

Section Three: HELPER SELF-DISCLOSURE

A third skill of challenging involves the ability of helpers to constructively share some of their own experiences, behaviors, and feelings with clients (Edwards & Murdoch, 1994; Handpick, 1990; Knox, Hess, Petersen, & Hill, 1997; Mathews, 1988; Simon, 1988; Sticker & Fisher, 1990; Watkins, 1990; Weiner, 1983). "The counselor communicates his or her characteristics to the client in every look, movement, emotional response, and sound, as well as with every word" (Strong & Claiborne, 1982, p. 173). This is the kind of indirect disclosure that goes on all the time. Effective helpers, as they tune in, listen, process, and respond, try to track and manage the impressions they are making on clients.

A. Research into direct helper self-disclosure has led to mixed and even contradictory conclusions.

1. Some researchers have discovered that helper self-disclosure can frighten clients or make them see helpers as less well adjusted. Or helper self-disclosure, instead of helping, might place another burden on clients.

2. Other studies have suggested that helper self-disclosure is appreciated by clients. Some clients see self-disclosing helpers as "down-to-earth" and "honest."

3. Direct self-disclosure on the part of helpers can serve as a form of modeling. Self-help groups such as Alcoholics Anonymous use such modeling extensively.

4. Other things being equal, ex-addicts often make excellent helpers in programs like this. They know from the inside the games addicts play. Sharing their experience is central to their style of counseling and is accepted by their clients. It helps clients develop both new perspectives and new possibilities for action. Such self-disclosure is challenging.

5. It puts pressure on clients to talk about themselves more openly or in a more focused way.

320

6. Helper self-disclosure is challenging for at least two reasons.

   a) First, it is a form of intimacy and, for some clients, intimacy is not easy to handle. Therefore, helpers need to know precisely why they are divulging information about themselves.

   b) Second, the message to the client is, indirectly, a challenging "You can do it, too," because revelations on the part of helpers, even when they deal with past failures, often center on problem situations they have overcome or opportunities they have seized. However, done well, such disclosures can be very encouraging for clients.

7. Since current research does not give us definitive answers, we need to stick to common sense.

B. Helper self-disclosure is at present not a science but an art. Here are some guidelines for using it. **(OH-11.2)**

1. **Include helper self-disclosure in the contract.** In self-help groups and in the counseling of addicts by ex-addicts, helper self-disclosure is an explicit part of the contract. If you don't want your disclosures to surprise your clients, let them know that you may talk about your own experiences when they seem relevant to the client's concerns.

2. **Make sure that your disclosures are appropriate.** Sharing yourself is appropriate if it helps clients achieve treatment goals. Don't disclose more than is necessary. Helper self-disclosure that is exhibitionistic is obviously inappropriate. Self-disclosure on the part of helpers should be a natural part of the helping process, not a gambit.

3. **Be careful of your timing**. Timing is critical. Common sense tells us that premature helper self-disclosure can turn clients off (Goodyear and Shumate, 1996).

4. **Keep your disclosure selective and focused.** Don't distract clients with rambling stories about yourself.

5. **Don't disclose too frequently**. Helper self-disclosure is inappropriate if it is too frequent. Some research (Murphy & Strong, 1972) suggested that if helpers disclose themselves too frequently, clients tend to see them as phony and suspect that they have hidden motives.

6. **Do not burden the client.** Do not burden an already overburdened client.

7. **Remain flexible.** Take each client separately. Adapt your disclosures to differences in clients and situations. When asked directly, clients say that they want helpers to disclose themselves (see Handpick, 1988), but this does not mean that every client in every situation wants it or would benefit from it.

Section Four: IMMEDIACY: DIRECT, MUTUAL TALK

Many, if not most, clients who seek help have trouble with interpersonal relationships either as a primary or a secondary concern. The client's interpersonal style can be examined, at least in part, through an examination of his or her relationship with the helper. If counseling takes place in a group, then the opportunity is even greater. The package of skills enabling helpers to explore their relationship with their clients or vice versa or enabling clients to do the same with fellow group members and the group leader has been called "immediacy" by Robert Carkhuff (see Carkhuff 1969a, 1969b; Carkhuff & Anthony, 1979; see Hill & O'Brien, 1999, Chapter 16). As you can see, it is an important tool for monitoring and managing the working alliance, a tool or kind of interaction that can be used by either client or helper.

A. Types of Immediacy in Helping and Principles for Using Them (OH-11.3)

Three kinds of immediacy are reviewed here. First, immediacy that focuses on the overall relationship — "How are you and I doing?" Second, immediacy that focuses on some particular event in a session — "What's going on between you and me right now?" Third, self-involving statements. Self-involving statements are present-tense, personal responses to the client (see Robitschek & McCarthy, 1991). "I like it when you challenge me. It shows spunk."

1. **Overall relationship immediacy: Review your overall relationship with the client if this adds value to the helping process.**

   a) General relationship immediacy refers to your ability to discuss with a client where you stand in your overall relationship with him or her and vice versa.

   b) The focus is not on a particular incident but on the way the relationship itself has developed and how it is helping or standing in the way of progress.

   c) The interaction can, of course, be initiated by the client, though many clients for obvious reasons would hesitate to do so.

2. **Event-focused immediacy: Address relationship issues as they come up.**

a) Here-and-now immediacy refers to your ability to discuss with clients what is happening between the two of you in the here and now of any given transaction.

b) It is not the entire relationship that is being considered, but rather the specific interaction or incident.

c) The purpose of event-focused or here-and-now immediacy is to strengthen the working alliance.

d) Research has shown that too much support can actually weaken the working alliance (see Kivlighan, 1990). The relationship needs some fiber.

e) Immediacy is a way of balancing support with challenge on both sides (Kivlighan & Schmitz, 1992; Tryon & Kane, 1993).

3. **Self-involving statements. Use present-tense "I" statements to make a point.**

a) Such statements can be either positive or negative in tone.

b) Clients tend to appreciate positive self-involving statements: "During the initial interview, the support and encouragement offered through the counselor's positive self-involving statements may be especially important because they put clients at ease and allay their anxiety about beginning counseling" (Watkins & Schneider, 1989, p. 345).

c) Negative self-involving statements are much more directly challenging in tone.

B. Situations Calling for Immediacy (OH-11.4)

Part of skilled helping — and, more generally, social intelligence — is knowing when to use any given communication skill. Immediacy can be useful in the following situations:

1. **Lack of direction.** When a session is directionless and it seems that no progress is being made. Either helper of client could initiate this.

2. **Tension.** When there is tension between helper and client:

3. **Trust.** When trust seems to be an issue:

4. **Diversity.** When diversity, some kind of "social distance," or widely

differing interpersonal styles between client and helper seem to be getting in the way:

5. **Dependency.** When dependency seems to be interfering with the helping process:

6. **Counterdependency.** When counterdependency seems to be blocking the helping relationship:

7. **Attraction.** When attraction is sidetracking either helper or client: Care is needed here. Talking about attraction can increase it. Someone once described romantic moments as "when we are alone together and the topic is only us."

Immediacy — both in counseling and in everyday life — is a difficult, demanding skill. It is difficult, first of all, because the helper — or the client — needs to be aware of what is happening in the relationship without becoming preoccupied with it. Second, immediacy demands both social intelligence and social courage. It is not always easy to bring up relationship issues. Helpers need backbone. Clients need backbone. But it's worth the effort. Immediacy can help both counselor and client move beyond a variety of relationship obstacles. It is also a learning opportunity for clients. If helpers use immediacy well, clients can see its value and learn how to apply it to their own sticky relationships.

Section Five: USING SUGGESTIONS AND RECOMMENDATIONS

A. This section begins with a few imperatives.

1. Don't tell clients what to do.

2. Don't try to take over their lives.

3. Let clients make their own decisions.

4. All these imperatives flow from the values of respect and empowerment.

B. There is a natural tension between helpers' desire to have their clients manage their lives better and respecting their freedom. If helpers build strong, respectful relationships with their clients, then "stronger" interventions sometimes make sense.

1. Helpers move from counseling mode to guidance role.

2. Research has shown that clients will generally go along with recommendations from helpers if those recommendations are clearly related to the problem situation, challenge clients' strengths, and are not too difficult (Conoley, Padula, Payton, & Daniels, 1994).

3. Effective helpers can provide suggestions, recommendations, and even directives without robbing clients of their autonomy or their integrity.

4. In the hands of the socially competent helper, the use of suggestions, advice, and directives is an adjunct to the rest of the process.

5. Suggestions, advice, and directives need not always be taken literally.

6. They can act as stimuli to get clients to come up with their own package.

7. In daily human interactions, people feel free to give one another advice. It goes on all the time. But helpers must proceed with caution.

8. Suggestions, advice, and directives are not for novices. It takes a great deal of experience with clients and a great deal of savvy to know when they might work.

Section Six: CONFRONTATION

A. Some clients who don't want to change or don't want to pay the price of changing simply terminate the helping relationship. However, those who stay stretch across a continuum from mildly to extremely reluctant and resistant.

B. Helpers differ, both theoretically and personally, in their willingness to confront. "Traumatic confrontation" (one wonders about the choice of name) is a cognitive behavior modification technique (Lowenstein, 1993) that involves challenging youths to face up to and change dysfunctional behavior.

C. Confrontation, as intimated earlier, means challenging clients to develop new perspectives and to change both internal and external behavior even when they show reluctance and resistance to doing so.

D. When helpers confront, they "make the case" for more effective living.

E. Confrontation does not involve "do this or else" ultimatums. More often it is a way of making sure that clients understand what it means not to change — that is, making sure they understand the consequences of persisting in dysfunctional patterns of behavior or of refusing to adopt new behaviors.

F. Both advice giving and confrontation require high levels of social intelligence and social competence on the part of the helper. They are not for everyone and, as suggested earlier, can go wrong in the hands of novices.

G. In most cases, they should be used sparingly.

Section Seven: ENCOURAGEMENT

A. If the whole purpose of challenging is to help client move forward and if encouragement (sugar) works as well as challenge (vinegar), then why don't we hear more about encouragement. The sugar-vinegar analogy is not exactly right, because many clients find challenge both refreshing and stimulating. Challenge certainly does not preclude encouragement. After all, encouragement is a form of support and research shows that support is one of the main ingredients in successful therapy (Beutler, 2000, p. 1004).

B. Miller and Rollnick (1991; Rollnick & Miller, 1995) introduced an approach to helping called "motivational interviewing."

C. A simple internet search on "motivational interviewing" reveals an extensive literature, including theory, research, and case studies (for instance, Baer, Kivlahan, & Donovan, 1999; Borsari & Carey, 2000; Colby & associates, 1998; Dench & Bennett, 2000) .

D. Clients are encouraged to find the motives, incentives, or levers of change that make sense for themselves clients and use the change options that they find a best fit.

E. Intrinsic motives, that is, motives that clients have internalized for themselves ("I want to be free"), rather than extrinsic motives ("I'll get in trouble if I don't change") are emphasized.

F. Clients are also given help on identifying obstacles to change and ways of overcoming them.

G. Empathy, both as a value and as a form of communication (empathic highlights), is used extensively.

H. Common sense suggests that direct realistic encouragement be included among and set of helping skills.

I. Effective encouragement is not patronizing. It is not sympathy nor does it rob the client of autonomy. It respect the client's self-healing abilities. It is a fully human nudge in the right direction.

Evaluation Questions for Step I-B:
The Use of Specific Challenge Skills (OH-11.5)

How effectively have I developed the communication skills that serve the process of challenging?

➤   **Sharing advanced empathic highlights.** Sharing hunches with clients about their experiences, behaviors, and feelings to help them move beyond blind spots and develop needed new perspectives.

➤   **Information sharing.** Giving clients needed information or helping them search for it to help them see problem situations in a new light and to provide a basis for action.

➤   **Helper self-disclosure.** Sharing your own experience with clients as a way of modeling nondefensive self-disclosure and helping them move beyond blind spots.

➤   **Immediacy.** Discussing aspects of your relationship with your clients to improve the working alliance.

➤   **Suggestions and recommendations.** Pointing out ways in which clients can more effectively manage problems and develop opportunities, or more productively in the stages and steps of the helping process.

➤   **Confrontation.** Using a solid relationship with the clients to challenge them more forcefully when they show signs of reluctance.

➤   **Encouragement**. Encouraging clients, at any step of the helping process, to find within themselves the desire to move forward.

Lecture Enhancers

You should be able to find the full text of the following items in your library or by using your web-based library access tool of choice (e.g., Psycinfo)

Item One: Challenges
Dealing with challenges in psychotherapy and counselling.

Brems, Christiane. (2000) Dealing with challenges in psychotherapy and counselling. In Belmont, CA, US: Wadsworth Publishing Co. (2000). xiv, 321 pp.

Synopsis: This book explores the potential remedies to challenging situations and critical incidents that present during assessment, treatment planning and treatment in psychotherapy and counselling. With a philosophical framework that reflects humanity, thoroughness,sensitivity, and preparedness, the author emphasizes that to be optimally effective, clinicians must be competent in their understanding of challenges and interventions for each individual client.

Item Two: Motive to Learn
Self-efficacy: An essential motive to learn.

Zimmerman, Barry J. (2000) Self-efficacy: An essential motive to learn. In Contemporary-Educational-Psychology. 2000 Jan; Vol 25(1): 82-91
Special Issue: Motivation and the Educational Process. US: Academic Press Inc. URL-Publisher http://www.academicpress.com

Synopsis: Since the 1980s self-efficacy has surfaced as a highly effective predictor of students' motivation and learning. Researchers have verified both its discriminant validity and convergent validity in predicting common motivational outcomes. Self-efficacy beliefs have supported subtle changes in students' performance and academic achievement and thus is considered an essential motive to learn.

Item Three: Hope
Evoking hope.

Yahne,-Carolina-E.; Miller,-William-R. (1999) Evoking hope. In
Miller, William R. (Ed); et-al. (1999). Integrating spirituality into treatment: Resources
for practitioners. (pp. 217-233). Washington, DC, USA: American Psychological
Association. xix, 293 pp. see book

Synopsis: Also known as optimism, the placebo effect, self-efficacy, and
positive expectancies, hope emerges as an important and central element of healing and
as such, is essential to the perspective of the therapist. The author affirms the concept
that the therapist's role is not one of installing hope as much as evoking it, by
collaboratively drawing its emergence from the client.

Class Activities

In addition to the exercises in the Workbook that accompanies this text, you may find the following in-class activities to be of value:

Activity #1: The Real Challenge

In this activity your goal is to have students list as many of the specific challenging skills as they can from Chapter 11 in the text. Next have the students in groups of three or four share compare and contrast their individual list of specific challenging skills. Finally, have the students rate each skill on a scale of 1 to 10 with 10 being the most effective.

The goal of the activity is to have the students identify and rate the various specific challenging skills.

Activity #2: Guess Which Skill I'm Using

In this activity students can have an educational and a fun time identifying specific challenging skills. Prior to coming to class take the time to write each of the specific challenging skills on a separate 3x5 note card. After discussing specific challenging skills, ask for two student volunteers to come to the front of the classroom. Have them randomly select one of the 3x5 note cards with an individual specific challenging skill written on it. Next, have the two students leave the class for five minutes to determine how they want to act out the specific challenging skill that is written on the 3x5 card they selected. Have the students then return to the classroom to role play a helper-client relationship using the specific challenging skill they have been given. Have the remainder of the class attempt to determine which skill is being used in the helper - client role play. This is usually an enjoyable and engaging activity of sleuthing for even the most astute student.

Activity #3: What Is Not In The Book?

Ask students to think of additional challenging skills that are not in the book. This is a great opportunity to empower students to think of additional ways of challenging. After students work individually for ten minutes, have them work in groups of three or four to compile a list of at five additional challenging skills that are not in the text.

The next step in this activity is to have groups swap lists and then critique each other's list of challenging skills. The critique should include the pros and cons of each recommended challenging skill. The final part of the activity is for the students to speculate as to why the author did not include any of their challenging skills in the book.

Videos

Teens: What makes them tick? (43 min, color, Films for the Humanities & Sciences). Physiological reasons for teen behaviour is examined by Harvard Medical School's Brain Imaging Center.

Emotional Intelligence: The key to Social Skills (28min, color, Films for the Humanities & Sciences). Daniel Goleman explores the nature of emotional intelligence and Maurice Elias discusses the concept of emotional literacy in relation to students and their happiness in life.

Dealing with peer pressure: I made my choice (30 min, color, Films for the Humanities & Sciences). Based on testimonials relating to peer pressure, students grasp the importance of positive goal setting, self-decision making and dealing with related consequences.

Corporal Punishment: "Loving Smacks" (52 min, color, Films for the Humanities & Sciences). Examination of the myths, justification, and short and long term effects of physical punishment on children when inflicted by parents. Alternatives to maintaining discipline are also outlined.

Love, Lust, and Marriage: Why We Stay and Why We Stray (46 min, color, Films for the Humanities & Sciences). Discusses research that verifies married couples are actually healthier and, in their opinion, happier than those who have divorced.

Websites

1. http://www.priory.com/psych/familywork.htm
   Mutual talk and family counselling.

2. http://www.enamp.org/ethics.htm
   Ethics.

3. http://portents.ne.mediaone.net/~matt/cct.evaluating.html
   Empathy towards the client perception of therapist intent.

Overhead Transparencies

Starting on the next page are copies of recommended overhead transparencies. Please feel free to convert the following pages to overheads as this will enhance the lecture portion of your class presentation.

ADVANCED EMPATHIC HIGHLIGHTS: THE MESSAGE BEHIND THE MESSAGE

1. Help Clients Make the Implied Explicit.

2. Help Clients Identify Themes in Their Stories.

3. Help Clients Make Connections They May Be Missing.

4. Share Educated Hunches Based on Empathic Listening and Understanding.

OH 11.1

GUIDELINES FOR USING HELPER DISCLOSURE

1. Include helper self-disclosure in the contract.

2. Make sure that your disclosures are appropriate.

3. Be careful of your timing.

4. Keep your disclosure selective and focused.

5. Don't disclose too frequently.

6. Do not burden the client.

7. Remain flexible

OH 11.2

TYPES OF IMMEDIACY

1. Overall Relationship Immediacy

2. Event-focussed Immediacy

3. Self-involving Statements

OH 11.3

SITUATIONS CALLING FOR IMMEDIACY

1. Lack of direction.

2. Tension.

3. Trust.

4. Diversity

5. Dependency.

6. Counterdependency.

OH 11.4

THE USE OF SPECIFIC CHALLENGE SKILLS

1. Sharing advanced empathic highlights.

2. Information sharing.

3. Helper self-disclosure.

4. Immediacy.

5. Suggestions and recommendations.

6. Confrontation.

7. Encouragement.

OH 11.5

Chapter Twelve:

Step I-B:
III. The Wisdom Of Challenging

	Pages
Chapter Outline	**341**
Detailed Lecture Notes	**342-349**
Lecture Enhancers	**350**
Class Activities	**351**
Videos	**352**
Websites	**353**
Transparencies	**354-358**

CHAPTER TWELVE OUTLINE

GUIDELINES FOR EFFECTIVE CHALLENGING

- ➤ Keep the Goals of Challenging in Mind
- ➤ Encourage Self-Challenge
- ➤ Earn the Right to Challenge
- ➤ Be Tentative but Not Apologetic in the Way You Challenge Clients
- ➤ Challenge Unused Strengths More Than Weaknesses
- ➤ Build on the Client's Successes
- ➤ Be Specific in Your Challenges
- ➤ Respect Clients' Values
- ➤ Deal Honestly, Caringly, and Creatively with Client Defensiveness

LINKING CHALLENGE TO ACTION

EVALUATION QUESTIONS FOR STEP I-B

Detailed Lecture Notes

(Please note: The designation OH in the detailed lecture notes indicates an overhead transparency is available. Please locate the overhead transparencies in the final section of each chapter in this Instructors' Manual.)

GUIDELINES FOR EFFECTIVE CHALLENGING (OH-12.1)

All challenges should be permeated by the spirit of the client-helper relationship values discussed in Chapter 3; that is, they should be caring (not power games or put-downs), genuine (not tricks or games), and designed to increase the self-responsibility of the client (not expressions of helper control). They should also serve the stages and steps of the helping process, moving it forward for the purpose of constructive change (not an endless search for insight). Empathy should permeate every kind of challenge. Clearly, challenging well is not a skill that comes automatically. It needs to be learned and practiced. The following principles constitute some basic guidelines.

A. Keep the Goals of Challenging in Mind.

1. Challenge must be integrated into the entire helping process.

2. Keep in mind that the goal is to help clients develop the kinds of alternative perspectives, internal behavior, and external actions needed to get on with the stages and steps of the helping process.

3. To what degree do the new perspectives developed lead to problem-managing and opportunity-developing action?

4. Are the insights relevant to real problems and opportunities rather than merely dramatic?

5. Are the calls to action solution-focused?

B. Encourage Self-Challenge.

1. Invite clients to challenge themselves, and give them ample opportunity to do so.

2. Provide clients with probes and structures that help them engage in self-challenge.

3. Be inventive with the probes and structures you provide clients to help them challenge themselves.

C. Earn the Right to Challenge.

1. Develop a working relationship. Challenge only if you have spent time and effort building a relationship with your client.

2. Make sure you understand the client. Empathy drives everything. Effective challenge flows from accurate understanding. Only when you see the world through the client's eyes can you begin to see what he or she is failing to see.

3. Be open to challenge yourself. Hesitate to challenge unless you are open to being challenged. Model the kind of nondefensive attitudes and behavior that would like to see in your clients.

4. Work on your own life. Berenson and Mitchell claimed that only people who are striving to live fully according to their value system have the right to challenge others, for only such persons are potential sources of human nourishment for others.

D. Be Tentative but Not Apologetic in the Way You Challenge Clients.

1. Tentative challenges are generally viewed more positively than strong, direct challenges (see Jones & Gelso, 1988).

2. Challenge clients in such a way that they are more likely to respond rather than react.

3. Deliver challenges tentatively, as hunches that are open to review and discussion rather than as accusations.

4. Challenging is certainly not an opportunity to browbeat clients or put them in their place.

5. Challenges that are delivered with too many qualifications — either verbally or through the helper's tone of voice — sound apologetic and can be easily dismissed by clients.

E. Challenge Unused Strengths More Than Weaknesses.

1. Berenson and Mitchell (1974), taking a page from positive psychology, found that successful helpers tend to challenge clients' strengths rather than their weaknesses.

2. Clients who dwell too much on their shortcomings tend to belittle their achievements, to withhold rewards from themselves when they do achieve, and to live with anxiety.

3. Challenging strengths is a positive psychology approach. It means pointing out to clients the assets and resources they have but fail to use.

4. Adverse life experiences can be a source of strength.

5. Counselors, can help clients "mine" benefits from adverse experiences, putting to practical use the age-old dictum that "good things can come from evil things."

F. Build on the Client's Successes.

1. Effective helpers help clients place reasonable demands on themselves and in the process help them appreciate and celebrate their successes.

G. Be Specific in Your Challenges.

1. Specific challenges hit the mark.

2. Vague challenges get lost. Clients don't know what to do about them.

3. Some helpers avoid clarity and specificity because they feel that they're being too intrusive.

4. Helping has to be intrusive to make a difference.

H. Respect Clients' Values.

1. Challenge clients to clarify their values and to make reasonable choices based on them.

2. Be wary of using challenging, even indirectly, to force clients to accept your values.

3. Helpers can assist clients to explore the consequences of the values they hold, but that is not the same as questioning them.

I. Deal Honestly, Caringly, and Creatively with Client Defensiveness.

    1. Do not be surprised when clients react strongly to being challenged even when you're trying to help them respond rather than react.

    2. Help them share and work through their emotions.

    3. If they seem to "clam up," try to find out what's going on inside.

The principles outlined above are, of course, guidelines, not absolute prescriptions. In the long run, use your common sense. The more flexible you are, the more likely you are to add value to your clients' search for solutions.

Section Two: LINKING CHALLENGE TO ACTION

 A. More and more theoreticians and practitioners are stressing the need to link insight to problem-managing and opportunity-developing action. Wachtel (1989, p. 18) put it succinctly: "There is good reason to think that the really crucial insights are those closely linked to new actions in daily life and, moreover, that insights are as much a product of new experience as their cause."

 B. A few well-placed challenges might be all that some clients need to move to constructive action. But others may well have the resources to manage their lives better, but not the will. They know what they need to do but are not doing it. A few nudges in the right direction help them overcome their inertia.

Section Three: THE SHADOW SIDE OF CHALLENGING (OH-12.2)

Challenge because of its very nature has a strong shadow side. While we hate being confronted, we often dislike being challenged, even when it is done well. If helpers are very effective in challenge, they might well sense some reluctance in their clients' responses. If they are poor at it, they are more likely to experience resistance. Inviting clients to challenge themselves and helping them do it to themselves is your best bet.

A. Clients' Shadow-Side Responses To Challenge:
Dealing With Dissonance

    1. Even when challenge is a response to a client's plea to be helped to live more effectively, it can precipitate some degree of disorganization in the client. Different writers refer to this experience under different names: "crisis," "disorganization," "a sense of inadequacy," "disequilibrium," and "beneficial uncertainty" (Beier & Young, 1984). Counseling-precipitated crises can be beneficial for the client. Whether they are or not depends, to a great extent, on the skill of the helper.

2. Cognitive-dissonance theory (Festinger, 1957; Draycott & Dabbs, 1998) gives us some insight into the dynamics of this. Since dissonance (discomfort, crisis, disequilibrium) is an uncomfortable state, the client will try to get rid of it (see Adler & Towne, 1999, pp. 400-405). Outlined below are five of the more typical ways clients experiencing dissonance attempt to rid themselves of their discomfort.

a) **Discredit challengers**. The client might confront the helper whose challenges are getting too close for comfort. Some attempt is made to point out that the helper is no better than anyone else. Counterattack is a common strategy for coping with challenge. You may even have to field some sarcastic barbs.

b) **Persuade challengers to change their views**. In this approach clients reason with their helpers. They urge them to see what they have said as misinterpretations and to revise their views.

c) **Devalue the issue.** This is a form of rationalization. A client who is being invited to challenge himself about his sarcasm points out that he is rarely sarcastic, that "poking fun at others" is just that, good-natured fun, that everyone does it, and that it is a very minor part of his life not worth spending time on. The client has a right to devalue a topic if it really isn't important. The counselor has to be sensitive enough to discover which issues are important and which are not.

d) **Seek support elsewhere for the views being challenged**. Some clients, once challenged, go out and gather testimonials supporting their views. In extreme cases clients leave one counselor and go to another because they feel they aren't being understood. They try to find helpers who will agree with them. More commonly, the client remains with the same counselor and offer evidence from others contesting the helper's point of view.

B. Challenge and the Shadow Side of Helpers (OH-12.3)

Helpers have many characteristics and engage in many behaviors that add value to clients' efforts to manage their lives better. Two shadow-side areas are addressed here — the reluctance of some helpers to challenge clients or invite them to challenge themselves and the blind spots helpers themselves have.

1. **The "MUM effect."** Initially, some counselor trainees are quite reluctant to help clients challenge themselves. They become victims of what has been called the "MUM effect," the tendency to withhold bad news even when it is in the other's interest to hear it (Rosen & Messer, 1970, 1971;

Messer & Rosen, 1972; Messer, Rosen, & Bachelor, 1972; Messer, Rosen, & Messer, 1971). If you are comfortable with the supportive dimensions of the helping process but uncomfortable with helping as a social-influence process, you could fall victim to the MUM effect and become less effective than you might otherwise be.

2. Excuses for not challenging.

Reluctance to challenge is not a bad starting position. In my estimation, it is far better than being too eager to challenge. However, all helping, even the most client-centered, involves social influence. It is important for you to understand your reluctance (or eagerness) to challenge — that is, to challenge yourself on the issue of challenging and on the very notion of helping as a social-influence process. When trainees examine how they feel about challenging others, here are some of the things they discover.

a) I am just not used to challenging others. My interpersonal style has had a lot of the live-and-let-live in it. I have misgivings about intruding into other people's lives.

b) If I challenge others, then I open myself to being challenged. I may be hurt, or I may find out things about myself that I would rather not know.

c) I might find out that I like challenging others and that the floodgates will open and my negative feelings about others will flow out. I have some fears that deep down I am a very angry person.

d) I am afraid that I will hurt others, damage them in some way or other. I have been hurt or I have seen others hurt by heavy-handed confrontations.

e) I am afraid that I will delve too deeply into others and find that they have problems that I cannot help them handle. The helping process will get out of hand.

f) If I challenge others, they will no longer like me. I want my clients to like me.

Vestiges of this kind of thinking persist long after trainees move out into the field as helpers. Helpers, cure yourselves!

3. Helpers' Blind Spots.

    a. There is an interesting literature on the humanity and flaws of helpers (Kottler & Beau, 1989; Kottler, 1993; Pope & Tabachnick, 1994; Wood, Klein, Cross, Lammers, & Elliott, 1985; Yalom, 1989) that can be of enormous help to both beginners — since prevention is infinitely better than cure — and to old-timers — since you *can* teach old dogs new tricks.

    b. Kottler (2000) has provided trainees and novices an upbeat view of what passion and commitment in the helping professions look like.

    c. There is some evidence that adopting a resource-collaborator role is difficult for some helpers (see Bohart & Tallman, 1999, pp. 263-266).

    d. Helpers sometimes prevent clients from moving forward by playing the "insight" game, a perverted form of what has been discussed in this chapter. They help clients develop one insight after another without linking those insights to problem-managing action. Many of the insights end up being oriented to the theories of the helper rather than to the problems of the client. There is an unsurfaced assumption that insight will ultimately cure.

    e. One of the critical responsibilities of supervisors is to help counselors identify their blind spots and learn from them.

    f. Once out of training, skilled helpers use different forums or methodologies to continue this process, especially with difficult cases. They take counsel with themselves, throughout their careers they continue to learn about themselves, their clients, and their profession.

Evaluation Questions for Step I-B:
The Process and Wisdom of Challenging

How well do I do each of the following as I try to help my clients?

The Process of Challenging

➢   Help clients become aware of their blind spots in their mindsets, thinking and acting, and help them develop both new perspectives leading to more constructive behaviors

➢   Use challenge seamlessly whenever it is needed in the helping process

➢   Keep in mind the goals of challenging — that is, helping clients move beyond blinds spots to more effective mindsets and change both internal and external patterns of behavior that keep them mired in problems and ineffective in developing unused opportunities

- Help clients participate fully in the helping process
- Help clients own their problems
- Help clients state problems as solvable and opportunities as doable
- Help clients correct faulty interpretations of their experiences, actions, and feelings
- Help clients identify and move beyond the predictable dishonesties of life
- Help clients spot opportunities
- Help clients get in touch with unused resources
- Help clients link new insights to problem-managing action
- Help clients develop a sense of self-efficacy
- Help clients generally move beyond discussion and inertia to action

The Wisdom of Challenging

- Invite clients to challenge themselves
- Earn the right to challenge by

  - ✓ developing an effective working alliance with my client
  - ✓ working at seeing the client's point of view
  - ✓ being open to challenge myself
  - ✓ managing problems and developing opportunities in my own life

- Be tactful and tentative in challenging without being insipid or apologetic
- Be specific, developing challenges that hit the mark
- Challenge clients' strengths rather than their weaknesses
- Don't ask clients to do too much too quickly
- Invite clients to clarify and act on their own values

The Shadow Side of Challenging

- Identify the games my clients attempt to play with me without becoming cynical in the process
- Become comfortable with the social-influence dimension of the helping role, with the kind of "intrusiveness" that goes with helping
- Incorporate challenge into my counseling style without becoming a confrontation specialist
- Develop the assertiveness needed to overcome the MUM effect
- Challenge the excuses I give myself for failing to challenge clients
- Come to grips with my own imperfections and blind spots both as a helper and as a "private citizen"

Lecture Enhancers

You should be able to find the full text of the following items in your library or by using your web-based library access tool of choice (e.g., Psycinfo)

Item One: Impasses
Impasses in the psychoanalytic relationship.

Newirth, Joseph. (2000). Impasses in the psychoanalytic relationship. In Journal-of-Clinical-Psychology. 2000 Feb; Vol 56(2): 225-231. Special Issue: Millenium issue: The therapeutic alliance.

Synopsis: The author provides clinic examples that nicely demonstrate the therapist's use of countertransference and transistional experience as a resolution to impasses in psychoanalysis. This will in turn help the client participate in an effective and more meaningful manner.

Item Two: Lifestyles
Metaphoric expressions of lifestyle: Exploring and transforming client-generated metaphors.

Kopp,-Richard-R. (1999) Metaphoric expressions of lifestyle: Exploring and transforming client-generated metaphors. In Journal-of-Individual-Psychology. 1999 Win; Vol 55(4): 466-473

Synopsis: The author provides effective direction in the use of metaphors as a means of creative expression of clients' lifestyles in relation to their issue or difficulty. Through exploration and transformation clients may increase awareness and connect their lifestyle movements to current problems. This strategy may then encourage clients to adapt their metaphoric imagery to constructive problem solving.

Item Three: The Sound of Silence
Listening to silence.

Scott,-Vanda; Lester,-David. (1998) Listening to silence. Source: Crisis. 1998; Vol 19(3): 105-108

Synopsis: The authors provide an excellent overview of the usefulness and function of periods of silence that may occur in counseling or psychotherapy. At times the silences may provoke anxiety for both the client and counselor and create an intolerance. This article underscores the critical need for counselors to listen to the silence as a means of helping the client in moments of crisis. These non-verbal moments may actually speak volumes in terms of revealing the client's inner turmoil.

Class Activities

In addition to the exercises in the Workbook that accompanies this text, you may find the following in-class activities to be of value:

Activity #1: Challenging and Wisdom

In this activity have your students form groups of three or four and then list as many instances where they can think it may not be wise to challenge the client. Ask the students to focus on cultural issues, relationship-power issues, and gender issues in the helper-client relationship and specially in challenging. Have the groups compare their lists and get a sense of when it is wise and not so wise to challenge.

Activity #2: Challenging and Defensiveness

In this activity students will think of times in their lives when they have been challenged by others and the response they had to being challenged. Specially ask if students felt defensive when being challenged by a parent as to why they were so late coming in or being challenged by a spouse as to how money was being spent. Have the students record the emotional feelings that had when being challenged (anger, defensiveness, hurt, etc.).

Next have the students think of how a client will feel when being challenged. Ask students to think of ways they can reduce the defensiveness of the client when challenging the client. Your goal is to have the student connect to the emotions of being challenged.

Activity #3: Wisdom and Shadows

Ask students to think of the shadow side of challenging. In groups of three or four have students make a list of all of the shadow aspects of challenging they can think may arise in a help-client relationship. Once each group has at least five shadow issues, have them select there top three and report them out to the class with a recorder recording the reports on the board.

Next have students look for the most common shadow concerns listed on the board and then back in their groups of three or four, have students think of ways they can overcome the shadow issues that have been identified.

This activity helps remind the students of the shadow side of challenging and what can be done to reduce the shadow issues.

Videos

Managing Stress (19 min, Color, Films for the Humanities & Sciences). The effects of both positive and negative stress and how an individual can reduce stress is revealed.

Running Out of Time: Time Pressure, Overtime, and Overwork (57 min, color, Films for the Humanities & Sciences). Investigates of the impact of time pressure and activity and the resulting minimal leisure time.

Stress: Keeping Your Cool (36 min, color, Films for the Humanities & Sciences). Positive and negative stress, causes of stress, stress control, and strategies to modify a frantic lifestyle are examined with a focus on women and teenagers.

Healing Stress: Today and Tomorrow (30 min, color, Films for the Humanities & Sciences). Provides a means of identifying and coping with stressful situations as a means of developing life long stress management strategies.

Achieving Psychosocial Health (29 min, color, Films for the Humanities & Sciences). Elements of psychosocial health, influencing factors and enhancement strategies are reviewed with an emphasis on personal responsibility for and awareness of one's psychosocial well-being.

The Relaxation Response (30 min, color, Films for the Humanities & Sciences). Explanation of the relaxation response is enhanced with student exercises designed to trigger the response.

Websites

1. http://www.rci.rutgers.edu/~gbc/psycDM/
   The psychology of decision making.

2. http://dieoff.com/page163.htm
   Decision making and problem solving.

3. http://www.snu.edu/syllabi/psych/PSY5234/
   Theory and technique of counseling..

Overhead Transparencies

Starting on the next page are copies of recommended overhead transparencies. Please feel free to convert the following pages to overheads as this will enhance the lecture portion of your class presentation.

GUIDELINES FOR EFFECTIVE CHALLENGING

1. Keep the Goals of Challenging in Mind.

2. Encourage Self-Challenge.

3. Earn the Right to Challenge.

4. Be Tentative but Not Apologetic in the Way You Challenge Clients.

5. Challenge Unused Strengths More Than Weaknesses.

OH 12.1A

GUIDELINES FOR EFFECTIVE CHALLENGING cont'd.

6. Build on the Client's Successes.

7. Be Specific in Your Challenges.

8. Respect Clients' Values.

9. Deal Honestly, Caringly, and Creatively with Client Defensiveness.

OH 12.1B

THE SHADOW SIDE OF CHALLENGING

Clients' Shadow-Side Responses To Challenge: Dealing With Dissonance

1. Discredit challengers

2. Persuade challengers to change their views

3. Devalue the issue.

4. Seek support elsewhere for the views being challenged.

OH 12.2

THE SHADOW SIDE OF CHALLENGING

Challenge and the Shadow Side of Helpers:

1. The "MUM effect."

2. Excuses for not challenging.

3. Helpers' Blind Spots.

OH 12.3

Chapter Thirteen:

Step I-C:
Leverage:
Helping Clients Work On The Right Things

	Pages
Chapter Outline	**360**
Detailed Lecture Notes	**361-367**
Lecture Enhancers	**368-369**
Class Activities	**370-371**
Videos	**372**
Websites	**373**
Transparencies	**374-382**

CHAPTER THIRTEEN OUTLINE

THE ECONOMICS OF HELPING

SCREENING: THE INITIAL SEARCH FOR LEVERAGE

LEVERAGE: WORKING ON ISSUES THAT MAKE A DIFFERENCE

SOME PRINCIPLES OF LEVERAGE

FOCUS AND LEVERAGE: THE LAZARUS TECHNIQUE

STEP I-C AND ACTION

EVALUATION QUESTIONS FOR STEP I-C

Detailed Lecture Notes

(Please note: The designation OH in the detailed lecture notes indicates an overhead transparency is available. Please locate the overhead transparencies in the final section of each chapter in this Instructors' Manual.)

Section One: THE ECONOMICS OF HELPING

A. Helping is expensive both financially and psychologically. The issue is raised here because Step I-C introduces the notion of "leverage." The leverage question is — how can we help our clients get the most out of the helping process?

    1. Helpers need to ask themselves,

        a) "Am I adding value through each of my interactions with this client?"

    2. Clients need to be helped to ask themselves,

        a) "Am I spending my time well?"

        b) "Do the decisions I am making have the potential of adding value to my life?"

        c) "Is helping working in this situation?

        d) "Is it worth it?"

B. It's important that helpers determine whether the client is ready to invest in constructive change or not. And to what degree.

    1. Change requires work on the part of clients. If they do not have the incentives to do the work, they might begin and then trail off. If this happens, it's a waste of resources.

    2. Leverage comes from having a good client-helper relationship, working on the right problems and opportunities, choosing the right goals, and pursuing these goals through the right strategies — all ending up in constructive change.

Section Two: SCREENING — THE INITIAL SEARCH FOR LEVERAGE (OH-13.1)

A. Relatively little is said in the literature about screening — that is, about deciding whether any given problem situation or opportunity deserves attention. The reasons are obvious.

   1. Helpers-to-be are rightly urged to take their clients and their clients' concerns seriously.

   2. They are also urged to adopt an optimistic attitude, an attitude of hope, about their clients.

   3. Finally, they are schooled to take their profession seriously and are convinced that their services can make a difference in the lives of clients.

B. The first impulse of the average counselor is to try to help clients no matter what the problem situation might be. However, like other professions, helping can suffer from the "law of the instrument." A child, given a hammer, soon discovers that almost everything needs hammering.

   1. Helpers, once equipped with the models, methods, and skills of the helping process, can see all human problems as needing their attention.

   2. In many cases counseling may be a useful intervention and yet be a luxury whose expense cannot be justified.

   3. The problem-severity formula discussed earlier is a useful tool for screening.

C. Under the term differential therapeutics, Frances, Clarkin, and Perry (1984) discussed ways of fitting different kinds of treatment to different kinds of clients.

   1. They also discussed the conditions under which "no treatment" is the best option. **(OH-13.2)**

   2. In the no-treatment category they included clients who have a history of treatment failure or who seem to get worse from treatment, such as:

      a) criminals trying to avoid or diminish punishment by claiming to be suffering from psychiatric conditions — "We may do a disservice to society, the legal system, the offenders, and ourselves if we are too willing to treat problems for which no effective treatment is available" (p. 227);

b) patients with malingering or fictitious illness;

c) chronic nonresponders to treatment;

d) clients likely to improve on their own;

e) healthy clients with minor chronic problems;

f) reluctant and resistant clients who refuse treatment.

3. The no-treatment or no-further-treatment option can do a number of useful things:

a) interrupt helping sessions that are going nowhere or are actually destructive;

b) keep both client and helper from wasting time, effort, and money; delay help until the client is ready to do the work required for constructive change;

c) provide a "breather" period that allows clients to consolidate gains from previous treatments;

d) provide clients with an opportunity to discover that they can do without treatment;

e) keep helpers and clients from playing games with themselves and one another

f) provide motivation for the client to find help in his or her own daily life.

4. However, a decision on the part of helping professionals not to treat or to discontinue treatment that is proving fruitless is countercultural and therefore difficult to make.

D. Practitioners in the helping professions are not alone in grappling with the economics of treatment.

1. Effective helpers, because they are empathic, pick of clues relating to a client's commitment but they don't jump to conclusions.

2. They test the waters in various ways. If clients' problems seem inconsequential, they probe for more substantive issues. If clients seem reluctant, resistant, and unwilling to work, they challenge clients' attitudes and help them work through their resistance.

3. They realize that there may come a time, to judge that further effort is uncalled for because of lack of results.

4. It is better, to help clients make such a decision themselves or challenge them to do so. In the end, the helper might have to call a halt, but his or her way of doing so should reflect basic counseling values.

Section Three: LEVERAGE:
WORKING ON ISSUES THAT MAKE A DIFFERENCE

A.   Clients often need help to get a handle on complex problem situations. Priorities need to be set. The blunt questions go something like this.

1.   Where is the biggest payoff?

2.   Where should the limited resources of both client and helper be invested?

3.   Where to start?

Section Four: SOME PRINCIPLES OF LEVERAGE (OH-13.3)

A. The following principles of leverage — a reasonable return on the investment of the client's, the helper's, and third-party resources — serve as guidelines for choosing issues to be worked on. These principles overlap; more than one may apply at the same time. The first three principles focus on client priorities. You can first help the client cope and then help him or her move on. Underlying all these principles is an attempt to make clients' initial experiencing of the helping process rewarding so that they will have the incentives they need to continue to work. The leverage mind set is part of positive psychology. It is second nature in effective helpers. Examples of the use and abuse of these principles follow.

1. **If there is a crisis, first help the client manage the crisis.** Although crisis intervention is sometimes seen as a special form of counseling (Baldwin, 1980; Janosik, 1984), it can also be seen as a rapid application of the three stages of the helping process to the most distressing aspects of a crisis situation.

2. **Begin with the problem that seems to be causing the most pain.** Clients often come for help because they are hurting even though they are not in

crisis. Their hurt, then, becomes a point of leverage. Their pain also makes them vulnerable. If it is evident that they are open to influence because of their pain, seize the opportunity, but move cautiously. Their pain may also make them demanding. They can't understand why you cannot help them get rid of it immediately. This kind of impatience may put you off, but it, too, needs to be understood.

3. **Begin with issues the client sees as important and is willing to work on.** The frame of reference of the client is a point of leverage. Given the client's story, you may think that he or she has not chosen the most important issues for initial consideration. However, helping clients work on issues that are important in their eyes sends an important message: "Your interests are important to me."

4. **Begin with some manageable subproblem of a larger problem situation.** Large, complicated problem situations often remain vague and unmanageable. Dividing a problem into manageable bits can provide leverage. Most larger problems can be broken down into smaller, more manageable subproblems.

5. **Move as quickly as possible to a problem that, if handled, will lead to some kind of general improvement.** Some problems, when addressed, yield results beyond what might be expected (spread effect).

6. **Focus on a problem for which the benefits will outweigh the costs.** This is not an excuse for not tackling difficult problems. If you demand a great deal of work from both yourself and the client, then basic laws of both economics and behavior suggest that there will be some kind of reasonable payoff for both of you.

B. Some counselors misuse these principles or otherwise fail to spot opportunities for leverage. They:

1. Begin with the framework of the client, but never get beyond it;

2. Deal effectively with the issues the client brings up, but fail to challenge clients to consider significant issues they are avoiding;

3. Help clients explore and deal with problems, but never help clients translate them into opportunities or move on to other unused opportunities;

4. Recognize the client's pain as a source of leverage, but then overfocus on the pain or allow it pain to mask other dimensions of the client's problems;

5. Help clients achieve small victories, but fail to help clients build on their

successes;

6. Help clients start with small, manageable problems, but fail to help clients face more demanding problems or to see the larger opportunities embedded in these problems;

7. Help clients deal with a problem or opportunity in one area of life (for instance, self-discipline in an exercise program) but fail to help them generalize what they learn to other, more difficult areas of living (for instance, self-control in interpersonal relationships).

Section Five: FOCUS AND LEVERAGE: THE LAZARUS TECHNIQUE (OH-13.4)

A. Arnold Lazarus (Rogers, Shostrom, & Lazarus, 1977), in a film on his multi modal approach to therapy (Lazarus, 1976, 1981), uses a focusing technique.

   1. The technique highlights how important language is in counseling and how important it is to ask questions that help clients point themselves in the right direction.

      a) He asks the client to use just one word to describe her problem.

      b) Then he asks the client to put the word in a phrase.

      c) The helper then moves from a simple sentence to a more extended description of the issue.

   2. This methodology can be used at any stage or step of the helping process. For instance, clients can be asked to use one word to describe what they want.

B. There are other techniques for helping clients in their search for leverage.

   1. In self-examination therapy (SET) clients are given a 45-page booklet containing all the information needed to use it (Bowman, 1995; Bowman, Ward, Bowman, & Scogin, 1996).

      a) Clients used worksheets, first to record what mattered to them and then problems they were having.

      b) They then compared the two lists.

      c) If a problem that bothered them did not relate to what mattered for them, they crossed that particular problem off the list. The economics of working on it would not be good.

d) Next they went on to look for solutions for the problems that remained and were encouraged to try out the solutions that seemed to have the best chance of working.

2. The therapeutic approach is built on leverage.

Section Six: STEP I-C AND ACTION

A. Like every other step of the helping model, Step I-C should act as a stimulus for client action. Helping clients identify and deal with high-leverage issues should, if done well, help them move toward the little actions that precede the formal plan for constructive change.

B. Discussing issues that make a difference can galvanize some clients into using resources that have lain dormant for years.

BOX 13-1

Leverage Questions for Step I-C (OH-13.5)

Help Clients Ask Themselves Such Questions As:

➢ What problem or opportunity should I really be working on?
➢ Which issue, if faced, would make a substantial difference in my life?
➢ Which problem or opportunity has the greatest payoff value?
➢ Which issue do I have both the will and the courage to work on?
➢ Which problem, if managed, will take care of other problems?
➢ Which opportunity, if developed, will help me deal with critical problems?
➢ What is the best place for me to start?
➢ If I need to start slowly, where should I start?
➢ If I need a boost or a quick win, which problem or opportunity should I work on?

Evaluation Questions for Step I-C (OH-13.6)

How well am I doing the following?

➢ Helping clients focus on issues that have payoff potential for them
➢ Maintaining a sense of movement and direction in the helping process
➢ Avoiding unnecessarily extending the problem identification and exploration stage
➢ Moving to other stages of the helping process as clients' needs dictate
➢ Encouraging clients to act on what they are learning

Lecture Enhancers

You should be able to find the full text of the following items in your library or by using your web-based library access tool of choice (e.g., Psycinfo)

Item One: Vocational Interests

The nature and nurture of vocational interests.

Gottfredson,-Linda-S. (1999) The nature and nurture of vocational interests. Chapter found in Savickas, Mark L. (Ed); Spokane, Arnold R. (Ed); et-al. (1999). Vocational interests: Meaning, measurement, and counseling use.
(pp. 57-85). Palo Alto, CA, USA: Davies-Black Publishing. v, 434, pp. See book.

Synopsis: This chapter discusses vocational interests and how they originate. The author concludes that people become who they are through life experiences that emerge from the complex interaction between genes and environments. Career counselling that considers the origins of vocational interests greatly benefit individuals in the choices they make.

Item Two: The Dodo's Verdict

Hope as a common factor
Across psychotherapy approaches: A lesson from
the dodo's verdict.

Snyder,-C.-R.; Taylor,-Julia-D. (2000) Hope as a common factor
Across psychotherapy approaches: A lesson from the dodo's verdict. Found in Snyder C. R. (Ed); et-al. (2000). Handbook of hope: Theory, measures, and applications. (pp. 89-108). San Diego, CA, US: Academic Press, Inc. xxv, 440 pp. See book

Synopsis: The author examines the mechanism(s) that may underlie the effectiveness of psychological interventions. For example, hope theory is explored in relation to its contribution to diverse therapeutic approaches from cognitive-behavioral to psychoanalytic to Gestalt.

Item Three: Accentuating the Positive

Accentuating the positive a positive path of study:
The popularity of optimism research has sold some scholars
on focusing less on misery, more on joy.

Monmaney, Terence. (2000)Vancouver Sun January 8, 2000, Final Edition, p.A9.
Dateline: Los Angeles. Subjects: Psychology; Research and Development; Lifestyles;
United States. Story Source: Los Angeles Times
Short. Accession Number: VS200001080137

Synopsis: Optimism is finally a major focus of researchers and the results are quite promising. Optimism, the human trait of expecting good things to happen instead of bad things, is proving to be a major factor in job success, relationships, and even health.

During the past three decades there have been over 46,000 papers on depression and only about 400 on joy. With a new commitment to studying optimism, researchers are starting the new millennium off with a major focus on the value of optimism in our every day life. The new field of studying optimism falls into the newly designated discipline of Positive Psychology.

Studies in this new field confirm that those individuals with an optimistic outlook live longer, are in fewer accidents, and even live longer when diagnosed with a terminal illness. Optimism and positive psychology may be of great value in all therapeutic settings.

Class Activities

In addition to the exercises in the Workbook that accompanies this text, you may find the following in-class activities to be of value:

Activity #1: Working on the Wrong Things

In this activity students are encouraged to think of times that they have not completed a major goal (e.g., term paper) because they were distracted by other and often easier and more enjoyable things to do (e.g., watch television, visit with a friend). Have students come up with three or four examples in groups of three or four.

Next, have the students record how they felt when the major goal was not completed and how they would have done things differently next time. Have them list reasons why they worked on the wrong things and not the right things. Finally, have them relate this to clients who have important things to do, but prefer to do the wrong things. Have the groups report their findings to the class. Focus on behaviors, actions, reactions, and transfer of knowledge to the helping relationship.

Activity #2: Do The Right Things First

Give the students a goal to be completed (e.g., write a term paper, find a job, write a letter to a friend) and then ask the students to list all of the possible individual activities they need to do to complete the task. Push the students to list as many individual details as possible.

Next have the students form groups of three and four and integrate their individual lists into one large list. Finally, have the groups prioritize the individual tasks in priority order: list the "right things to do" first.

After groups have constructed their individual group list, have them share their list with another group to see how similar their lists are. Have the students compare, contrast, and discuss their lists. What will become apparent is that not all are in agreement as to what is most important to do first. Have the students then apply this knowledge to the helping relationship.

Activity #3: My Right - Your Right

Ask students to discuss situations where the may be a major difference of opinion as to what is right in the mind of one person and quite different in the mind of another. Engage the students to list situations where what is determined to be the right things may be influenced by:

Age:

Race:

Gender:

Culture:

Political Orientation:

Religious Belief:

The point of the exercise is to help students realize that what is right to one person might not be right in the opinion of another person based on any of the following items. Have the students apply this knowledge to the helping relationship.

Videos

Healthy Relationships (35 min, color, Films for the Humanities & Sciences). Guidelines are provided for teenagers to end unhealthy relationships and establish healthy behavior in themselves and others in relation to dating, friendship, and peer pressure.

Putting Your Self-Esteem in Focus (30 min, color, Films for the Humanities & Sciences). The topic of self-esteem is explored with discussion of the problems associated to low self-esteem and how to develop a more positive self-image.

Self-Harm (15 min, color, Films for the Humanities & Sciences). Self-harm, an anxiety-related disorder, is examined with a focus on how victims experience guilt and shame related to their self-inflicted actions that occur to relieve unresolved anxieties.

Teen Suicide (35 min, color, Films for the Humanities & Sciences). This program discusses why teenagers consider, attempt, or commit suicide and stresses specific preventive measures

Everything to Live For (52 min, color, Films for the Humanities & Sciences). Viewers will hear the testimonials of two families of suicide victims who speak of the causes of the tragedies, the unheard cries for help, and the critical need for awareness of warning signals and intervention.

Websites

1. http://www.snu.edu/syllabi/psych/PSY5234/
   Divergent thinking.

2. http://scholar.lib.vt.edu/ejournals/JDC/Spring-2000/kgibson/gibson.html
   Convergent and divergent thinking.

3. http://www.computerlearning.org/articles/95wins.htm
   Creativity and helping.

4. http://www.mindtools.com/
   Helping you to think your way to a better life.

Overhead Transparencies

Starting on the next page are copies of recommended overhead transparencies. Please feel free to convert the following pages to overheads as this will enhance the lecture portion of your class presentation

WHAT IS LEVERAGE?

— a reasonable return on the investment of the client's, the helper's, and third-party resources.

OH 13.1

TYPICAL NO-TREATMENT CATEGORIES:

1. Criminals trying to avoid or diminish punishment by claiming to be suffering from psychiatric conditions.

2. Patients with malingering or fictitious illness;

3. Chronic nonresponders to treatment;

4. Clients likely to improve on their own;

5. Healthy clients with minor chronic problems;

6. Reluctant and resistant clients who refuse treatment.

7. refuse treatment.

OH 13.2

SOME PRINCIPLES OF LEVERAGE

1. If there is a crisis, first help the client manage the crisis.

2. Begin with the problem that seems to be causing the most pain.

3. Begin with issues the client sees as important and is willing to work on.

OH 13.3A

SOME PRINCIPLES OF LEVERAGE cont'd.

4. Begin with some manageable subproblem of a larger problem situation.

5. Move as quickly as possible to a problem that, if handled, will lead to some kind of general improvement.

6. Focus on a problem for which the benefits will outweigh the costs.

OH 13.3B

THE LAZARUS TECHNIQUE

1. Ask the client to use just one word to describe her problem.

2. Then ask the client to put the word in a phrase.

3. The helper then moves from a simple sentence to a more extended description of the issue.

OH 13.4

Leverage Questions for Step I-C

1. What problem or opportunity should I really be working on?

2. Which issue, if faced, would make a substantial difference in my life?

3. Which problem or opportunity has the greatest payoff value?

4. Which issue do I have both the will and the courage to work on?

OH 13.5A

Leverage Questions for Step I-C
cont'd.

5. Which problem, if managed, will take care of other problems?

6. Which opportunity, if developed, will help me deal with critical problems?

7. What is the best place for me to start?

8. If I need to start slowly, where should I start?

9. If I need a boost or a quick win, which problem or opportunity should I work on?

OH 13.5B

Evaluation Questions for Step I-C

How well am I doing the following?

1. Helping clients focus on issues that have payoff potential for them

2. Maintaining a sense of movement and direction in the helping process

3. Avoiding unnecessarily extending the problem identification and exploration stage

4. Moving to other stages of the helping process as clients' needs dictate

5. Encouraging clients to act on what they are learning

OH 13.6

Chapter Fourteen:

Introduction to Stage II:
Helping Clients Identify, Choose, and Shape Goals: "What Do I Need and Want?"

	Pages
Chapter Outline	384
Detailed Lecture Notes	385-398
Lecture Enhancers	399-400
Class Activities	401-402
Videos	403
Websites	404
Transparencies	405-412

CHAPTER FOURTEEN OUTLINE

THE THREE STEPS OF STAGE II

- ➤ Step II-A: "What Possibilities Do I Have For a Better Future?"
- ➤ Step II-B: "What Do I really Want and Need?"
- ➤ Step II-C: "What Am I willing to Pay for What I Want?"

SOLUTION-FOCUSED HELPING

- ➤ Solution-Focused Therapies, Brief Therapy, and Appreciative Inquiry
- ➤ Solutions Versus Solutions
- ➤ The Beneficial Effects of Brief Therapy

HELPING CLIENTS DISCOVER AND USE THEIR POWER THROUGH GOAL SETTING

- ➤ Goals Focus Attention and Action
- ➤ Goal Mobilize Energy and Effort
- ➤ Goals Provide Incentives to Search for Ways of Accomplishing Them.
- ➤ Clear and Specific Goals Increase Persistence

HELPING CLIENTS BECOME MORE EFFECTIVE DECISION MAKERS

- ➤ Rational Decision Making
- ➤ The Shadow Side of Decision Making: Choices in Everyday Life
- ➤ Making Smarter Decisions

Detailed Lecture Notes

(Please note: The designation OH in the detailed lecture notes indicates an overhead transparency is available. Please locate the overhead transparencies in the final section of each chapter in this Instructors' Manual.)

Section One THE THREE STEPS OF STAGE II (OH-14.1)

In many ways Stages II and III together with the Action Arrow are the most important parts of the helping model because they are about "solutions." In these stages, counselors help clients ask and answer the following two commonsense but critical questions.

What do you want?
and
What do you have to do to get what you want?

The steps of Stage II outline three ways in which helpers can partner with their clients with a view to exploring and developing this better future.

A. **Step II-A: Possibilities**. "What possibilities do I have for a better future?" "What are some of the things I think I want?" "What about my needs?" Counselors, in helping clients ask themselves these question, help them develop a sense of hope.

B. **Step II-B: Choices**. "What do I really want and need?" Here clients craft a viable change agenda from among the possibilities. Helping them shape this agenda is the central task of helping.

C. **Step II-C: Commitment**. "What am I willing to pay for what I want?" Help clients discover incentives for commitment to their change agenda. It is a further look at the economics of personal change.

Section Two: SOLUTION-FOCUSED HELPING

The goal of helping is "problems managed," not just "problems explored and understood" and "opportunities developed," not just "opportunities identified and discussed."

A. Solution-Focused Therapies, Brief Therapy, and Appreciative Inquiry

Solution-focused therapies, brief therapy and an approach to problem-management and opportunity development called "appreciative inquiry" are, each in its own way, problem-management and, especially, opportunity -development approaches. For instance, appreciative inquiry (Zemke, 1999) has four stages or steps: discovery, dreaming, design, and delivery.

1. **Discovery:** What gives life? Help clients identify past and current successes, strengths, and resources.

2. **Dreaming**: What might be? Help client identify possibilities for a better future.

3. **Design:** What's the ideal? Help clients design outcomes, mapping out how the client's life will look in the areas of concern.

4. **Delivery:** How do I move forward? Help clients find and implement the best way to realize the future they have designed. Some now call this stage "destiny," meaning that clients who find their own power are now in charge of their own destiny.

B. Here is a quick overview of what these approaches have in common. **(OH-14.2)**

1. **Philosophy**.

   a) In relating with clients, focus on resources rather than deficits; on success and rather than failure; on credit rather than blame; on solutions rather than problems.

   b) Use common sense.

   c) Don't let theory get in the way of helping clients.

2. **View of Clients**. Clients are people like the rest of us.

   a) See them as people with complaints about life, not symptoms.

   b) Don't assume that they will arrive ambivalent about change and resistant to therapy.

   c) Clients have a reservoir of wisdom, learned and forgotten, but still available.

   d) Clients have resources and strengths to resolve complaints.

   e) Clients will have their own view of life just as everyone else.

    f) Respect the reality they construct, even though they might have to move beyond it.

    g) Help them feel competent to solve their own problems. When helpers see clients as problems to be solved, they impoverish them and take their power away.

3. **Dealing With Past**. There is no escape from past trauma. It did happen.

    a) Focus on client's ability to survive problem situation.

    b) Getting at causes does not usually resolve a complaint. Resolving the complaint resolves it.

    c) The best thing that can reflect on bring forward are past successes, what they have done that works.

4. **Role of Helper**. Helpers are consultants, catalysts, guides, facilitators, assistants.

    a) It is very helpful to adopt, at least temporarily, the client's world view. This helps lessen reluctance and resistance.

    b) Sharing highlights helps demonstrate your understanding of the client's world.

    c) Your job is to notice and amplify life-giving forces within the client and any sign of constructive change.

    d) Become a detective for good things.

    e) Listen to problems, but listen even more to the opportunity buried within the problem.

    f) Use questions that inspire and encourage clients to give positive examples.

    g) Question should stimulate dialogue. Remember that questions are not just questions, they are interventions.

5. **The Discovery Phase: Help clients explore and exploit competencies, successes, and "normal times."**

    a) Help them identify ways of thinking, behaving, and interacting that have worked in past.

b) How can they amplify what has been working?

c) Catch clients being competent and resourceful and help them take a good look at themselves at such times.

d) Notice competencies revealed in a client's story and behavior.

6. **The Nature of Problems and How We Talk About Things**.

a) Clients, like the rest of us, become what they talk about.

b) Help clients see problems as external to themselves, not things that define and control their lives.

c) Rather problems are intruders that get the best of us at times.

d) Problems are complaints that bother us rather than define us.

7. **Insight**.

a) Insight is not necessary for change. Too often insight are about problems, not about solutions.

b) Engage in generating "outcome" scenarios.

8. **Dream: Possibilities for a better future**. The principles is this — the future we anticipate is the future we create.

a) The helper and the client should partner in the systematic search for possibilities and potential.

b) The client's imagination needs to be "provoked" to discover new ways of approaching.

c) Questions should stimulate clients to think as creatively as possible about this better future.

d) Appreciative inquiry aims at engaging client and helper in dialogue that leads to the development of a "textured vocabulary of hope," (Ludema & others, 1997).

9. **Design solutions**. Clients define the goal.

a) Help clients actively design solutions that will turn their possibilities into opportunity-developing realities.

b) Help clients to look for simple solutions to complex problems. Often a small change is all that is necessary.

c) Complex problems do not necessarily require complex solutions. Small changes can make a big difference.

d) Help clients find systemic solutions.

e) Look for interventions that break up patterns of self-limiting behavior.

f) Don't hesitate to design solutions that get rid of symptoms.

g) Getting rid of symptoms is not shallow, useless, or dangerous. Part of the solution should be clients' ability to grapple with future problems on their own. Clients should leave therapy with identified tools to do so.

10. **Deliver**. Implementation is everything.

a) The pace of change will be different for each client.

b) Solutions often require that clients develop new ways of relating to their social environment.

c) Simple internet searches in solution-focused therapies, brief therapy, and appreciative inquiry will reveal a world of insights, frameworks, methods, and skills that you can integrate into the overall problem-management and opportunity-development framework.

11. **Criticisms**.

a) There have been some criticisms of this positive-psychology approach (see Zemke, 1999). For instance, some say that it runs the risk of being a don't-worry-just-be-happy approach.

b) Traditional problem-solving approaches to helping also come in for their knocks (Zemke, 1999). Its critics say that it is painfully slow, asks clients to look back at yesterday's failures, looks for the causes of problems, rarely results in a new vision, assumes that either the helper or the client knows what should be in place and leads therefore to talk about closing gaps, places blame and therefore promotes defensiveness, and uses deficit-focused language.

c) Wedding the positive-psychology approach of solution-focused therapies to a problem-management and opportunity-development approach to problem solving faces down these criticisms. There is no question of either/or. The interplay of the two provides the most robust system. The problem-management and opportunity-development approach provides the backbone of helping. But the use of its stages and steps are dictated by client need.

d) The solution-focused philosophy gives direction to *how* clients and helpers partner in using these stages and steps. Flexibility is the key. The arbiter is common sense and social intelligence. Do what is best for the client.

C. Solutions Versus Solutions

1. This book offers a solution-focused approach to helping.

2. There is, however, a semantic problem with the word "solution." It means two distinct things.

   a) First and foremost it means an end state — results, accomplishments.

   b) Solution also means a strategy a client uses to get to the end state.

3. Stage II of the helping process deals with solutions in the primary sense — end states, accomplishments, goals, outcomes.

4. Stage III focuses on solutions in the secondary sense — means, actions, strategies.

5. Link solutions-as-goals to the problem situation or unused opportunity.

6. Goals, not problems, should drive action.

D. The Beneficial Effects of Brief Therapy

1. Brief therapies are of their very essence solution focused. If there is little time, most of it had better be spent focusing on a better future.

2. Solution-focused therapists like to work with fairly well-defined goals that are realizable within a reasonable amount of time.

3. Brief therapy can be brief but still comprehensive (Lazarus, 1997). Asay and Lambert (1999, p. 42), after reviewing the research on brief therapy, drew the following conclusions:

a) The beneficial effects of therapy can be achieved in short periods (5 to 10 sessions) with at least 50% of clients seen in routine clinical practice. For most clients, therapy will be brief.... In consequence, therapists need to organize their work to optimize outcomes within a few sessions. Therapists also need to develop and practice interventions methods that assume clients will be in therapy for fewer than 10 sessions.

4. They also found that there are three categories of clients who do poorly in brief therapy.

   a) First, clients who are poorly motivated and hostile. Therapists who have the skills of handling resistance and know something about "motivational interviewing" have a better chance of success.

   b) Second, clients who come with a history of poor relationships. Therefore, the helper's ability to establish a collaborative working alliance that is a "just society" is paramount.

   c) Finally, clients who expect to be passive recipients of a medical procedure. Helping such clients quickly find a sense of agency, however deeply buried, is the helper's challenge.

Section Three: HELPING CLIENTS DISCOVER AND USE THEIR POWER THROUGH GOAL SETTING (OH-14.3)

A. Goals at their best mobilize our resources, they get us moving. They are a critical part of the self-regulation system. If they are the right goals for us, they get us headed in the right direction. According to Locke and Latham (1984), helping clients set goals empowers them in four ways.

1. **Goals help clients focus their attention and action**. A counselor at a refugee center in London described Simon, a victim of torture in a Middle Eastern country, to her supervisor as aimless and minimally cooperative in exploring the meaning of his brutal experience. Her supervisor suggested that she help Simon explore possibilities for a better future. The counselor started one session by asking, "Simon, if you could have one thing you don't have, what would it be?" Simon came back immediately, "A friend." During the rest of the session, he was totally focused. What was uppermost in his mind was not the torture but the fact that he was so lonely in a foreign country. When he did talk about the torture, it was to

express his fear that torture had "disfigured" him, if not physically, then psychologically, thus making him unattractive to others.

2. **Goals help clients mobilize their energy and effort**. Clients who seem lethargic during the problem-exploration phase often come to life when asked to discuss possibilities for a better future. Clients with goals are less likely to engage in aimless behavior. Goal setting is not just a "head" exercise. Many clients begin engaging in constructive change after setting even broad or rudimentary goals.

3. **Goals provide incentives for clients to search for strategies to accomplish them**. Setting goals, a Stage-II task, leads naturally into a search for means to accomplish them, a Stage-III task.

4. **Clear and specific goals help clients increase persistence**. Not only are clients with clear and specific goals energized to do something, but they also tend to work harder and longer. Clients with clear and realistic goals don't give up as easily as clients with vague goals or with no goals at all.

B. One study (Payne, Robbins, & Dougherty, 1991) showed that high-goal-directed retirees were more outgoing, involved, resourceful, and persistent in their social settings than low-goal-directed retirees. The latter were more self-critical, dissatisfied, sulky, and self-centered.

1. People with a sense of direction don't waste time in wishful thinking.

2. Setting goals, whether formally or informally, provides clients with a sense of direction.

3. People with a sense of direction:

   a) have a sense of purpose
   b) live lives that are going somewhere
   c) have self-enhancing patterns of behavior in place
   d) focus on results, outcomes, and accomplishments
   e) don't mistake aimless action for accomplishments
   f) have a defined rather than an aimless lifestyle.

C. Locke and Latham (1990) pulled together years of research on the motivational value of setting goals. Although the motivational value of goal setting is incontrovertible, the number of people who disregard problem-managing and opportunity-developing goal setting and its advantages are legion. The challenge for counselors is to help clients do it well.

D. There is a massive amount of sophisticated theory and research on goals and goal setting (Karoly, 1999; Locke& Latham, 1996) and self-help literature dealing with goal setting and implementation in everyday life (for instance, D. Ellis, 1999; K. Ellis, 1998; Secunda, 1999).

Section Four: HELPING CLIENTS BECOME MORE EFFECTIVE DECISION MAKERS

The second overall goal for helping is to help clients, either directly or indirectly, to become better problem solvers and opportunity developers in their everyday lives. Since the encouragement of client self-responsibility is a key helping value, helping clients not only make good decisions but also become better decision makers is not an amenity but a necessity.

A. Rational Decision Making

Decision making pervades problem management and opportunity development. Decision making in its broadest sense is the same as problem solving. The focus is on decision making in a narrower sense — the internal (mental) action of identifying alternatives or options and choosing from among them. Traditionally, decision making has been presented as a rational, linear process involving information gathering, analysis, and choice. Here are the bare essentials of the decision-making process. **(OH-14.4)**

1. **Information gathering.** The first rational task is to gather information related to the particular issue or concern.

2. **Analysis.** The next rational step is processing the information. This includes analyzing, thinking about, working with, discussing, meditating on, and immersing oneself in the information. Just as there are many ways of gathering information, so there are many ways of processing it. Effective information processing leads to a clarification and an understanding of the range of possible choices. Effective analysis assumes that decision makers have criteria, whether objective or subjective, for comparing alternatives.

3. **Making a choice.** Finally, decision makers need to make a choice — that is, commit themselves to some internal or external action that is based on the analysis:

Counselors help clients engage in rational decision making; that is, they help clients gather information, analyze what they find, and then base action decisions on the analysis.

B. The Shadow Side of Decision Making: Choices in Everyday Life

Thinking and reasoning is not always what it is supposed to be or seems to be in everyday life. And, when people get into trouble, thinking and reasoning can go even "further south" (Basic Behavioral Science Task Force of the National Advisory Mental Health Council, 1996). It is an ambiguous, highly complicated process with a deep shadow side (Cosier & Schwenk, 1990; Etzioni, 1989; Gilovich, 1991; Heppner, 1989; Kaye, 1992; March, 1994; Schoemaker & Russo, 1990; Stroh & Miller, 1993; Whyte, 1991). A shadow-side analysis of decision making as it is actually practiced reveals a less-than-rational application of the three dimensions outlined above.

1. **Information gathering.**

   a) Information gathering should lead to a clear definition of the issues to be decided.

   b) Decision makers, for whatever reason, are often complacent and engage in perfunctory searches; they get too much, too little, inaccurate, or misleading information; the search for information is clouded with emotion.

   c) In counseling the client trying to decide whether to proceed with therapy may have already made up his or her mind and therefore may not be open to confirming or disconfirming information.

   d) Since full, unambiguous information is never available, all decisions are at risk. In fact, there is no such thing as completely objective information.

   e) All information, especially in decision making, is received by the decision maker and takes on a subjective cast.

   f) Counselors cannot help clients make information gathering perfect, they can help them make it at least "good enough" for problem management and opportunity development.

2. **Processing the information.**

   a) Since it is impossible to separate the decision from the decision maker, the processing of information is as complex as the person making the decision.

   b) Factors affecting the analyzing of information include clients' feelings and emotions, their values-in-use, which often differ from their espoused values, their assumptions about "the way things work," and their level of motivation.

c) There is no such thing as full, objective processing of gathered information.

d) Poorly gathered information is often subjected to further mistreatment.

e) Clients, because of their biases, focus on bits and pieces of the information they have gathered rather than seeing the full picture.

f) Furthermore, few clients have the time or the patience to spell out all possible choices related to the issue at hand, together with the pros and cons of each.

g) Counselors can help clients overcome inertia and biases and tackle the work of analysis.

3. **Choice and execution.** A host of strange things can happen on the way to executing a decision. Decision makers sometimes:

a) skip the analysis stage and move quickly to choice.

b) ignore the analysis and base the decision on something else entirely; the analysis was nothing but a sham, because the decision criteria, however covert, were already in place.

c) engage in what Janis and Mann (1977) called "defensive avoidance." That is, they procrastinate, attempt to shift responsibility, or rationalize delaying a choice.

d) confuse confidence in decision making with competence

e) panic and seize upon a hastily contrived solution that gives promise of immediate relief. The choice may work in the short term but have negative long-term consequences.

f) are swayed by a course of action that is most salient at the time or by one that comes highly recommended, even though it is not right for them.

g) let enthusiasm and other emotions govern their choices.

h) announce a choice to themselves or to others, but then do nothing about it.

i) translate the decision into action only halfheartedly.

395

j) decide one thing but do another.

Pure-form rational, linear decision making has probably never been the norm in human affairs. Decision making goes on at more than one level. The rational decision-making process in the foreground and an emotional or impulsive decision-making process in the background. Gelatt (1989) called for an approach to decision making that factors in these shadow-side realities: "What is appropriate now is a decision and counseling framework that helps clients deal with change and ambiguity, accept uncertainty and inconsistency, and utilize the nonrational and intuitive side of thinking and choosing" (p. 252). Positive uncertainty means, paradoxically, being positive (comfortable and confident) in the face of uncertainty (ambiguity and doubt) — feeling both uncertain about the future and positive about the uncertainty.

C. Making Smarter Decisions

Hammond, Keeney, and Raiffa (1998, 1999), on the other hand, offer a guide to making better decisions, taking into account, of course, the shadow side of decision making. In their article (1998), they focus on hidden traps in decision making and how to handle them. Here are some of them.

1. **The status-quo bias**. Clients often have a bias toward alternatives that perpetuate the status quo. The helper should:

   a) Help him determine what his real objective is.

   b) Help him review the alternatives in the light of what he wants. He might want a combination of things.

   c) Help him see whether he is choosing the status-quo approach precisely because it is the status quo.

   d) Help him determine whether he wants to avoid the risk, pain, or trouble of choosing a non-status-quo alternative. This is a different problem.

   e) Help him look further into the future.

   f) Help him determine whether he is defaulting to the status-quo option because it is difficult to choose from among the other alternatives. If this is the case, help him cope with the agony of making such a choice.

   g) Aim the challenges at the "self-healing person"

2. **The confirming-evidence trap**.

   a) If I have secretly — hidden more or less even from myself — decided to do or to avoid doing something, I can begin looking for evidence that will confirm my choice or avoid evidence that will challenge it. According to Hammond, Keeney, and Raiffa, what could the counselor do? Here are a few suggestions:

- Help the client examine all the evidence with equal vigor.

- Get someone the client respects to act as devil's advocate. Reverse roles. You be the client. Let the client be the helper.

- Have the client take a closer look at her/his motives. It would be helpful for the client to know what she/he is doing and what is moving her/him to do it.

- If the client seeks advice from others, help her/him frame her/his questions so that don't merely invite confirmation of what she/he has already decided.

   b) In their book, *Smart Choices: A Practical Guide to Making Better Decisions*, Hammond, Keeney, and Raiffa (1999) lay out a *system* for making smart choices. The eight elements of the system highlight the eight most common and most serious errors in decision making (p. 189): **(OH-14.5)**

- Working on the wrong problem

- Failing to identify your key objectives

- Failing to develop a range of good, creative alternatives

- Overlooking crucial consequences of your alternatives

- Giving inadequate thought to tradeoffs

- Disregarding uncertainty

- Failing to account for your risk tolerance

- Failing to plan ahead when decisions are linked over time

Finally, since helpers themselves are human, they do not escape the shadow side of decision making. Helpers, as you can see, make decisions throughout the helping process. Pfeiffer, Whelan, and Martin (2000, p. 429), after reviewing the decision-making research, comment:

> When examined as a whole, this research suggests that people tend to preferentially attend to information, gather information, and interpret information in a manner that supports, rather than tests, their decisions about another person. Therapists may not be exempt from this tendency, particularly given the often complex and ambiguous nature of clients' problems.

No matter how empathic you are, as a helper you will still make hypotheses about your clients throughout the helping process and base some of your decisions on these hypotheses. Your challenge is to continually test these hypotheses against the reality of your clients in the context of their lives. Theories are theories. Clients are clients.

Lecture Enhancers

You should be able to find the full text of the following items in your library or by using your web-based library access tool of choice (e.g., Psycinfo)

Item One: The Value of Psychotherapy Experiments

How valuable are psychotherapy experiments?: The idiographic problem.

Erwin,-Edward. (1999) How valuable are psychotherapy experiments?: The idiographic problem. In Journal-of-Clinical-Psychology. 1999 Dec; Vol 55(12): 1519-1530.

   Synopsis: This article debates the question of the study of groups of subjects in psychotherapy experiments versus the clinicians' need for treatment information that relates to a single client. The author concludes that alternative methods to psychotherapy experiments are defective and the idiographic problem can be approached without sacrificing experimental methods.

Item Two: Intervention

Where Should We Intervene?

Hanson, R. Karl; Harris, Andrew J. R. (2000) Effective intervention with sexual offenders requires the targeting of appropriate risk factors. In Criminal Justice & Behavior, Feb. 2000, Vol. 27 Issue 1, p.6

   Synopsis: This article provides information on data collected through interviews with community supervision officers and file reviews of 208 sexual offense recidivists and 201 nonrecidivists. It is imperative that those who provide treatment, community supervision, or risk assessments for sexual offenders must identify the factors related to sexual offence recidivism. The targeting of appropriate risk factors is necessary for effective intervention.

Item Three: Violent Human Behavior

The Systemic Conditions Leading
to Violent Human Behavior.

Roy, Kenneth G. (2000)The Systemic Conditions Leading to Violent Human Behavior.
In the Journal of Applied Behavioral Science, Dec2000, Vol. 36
Issue 4, p389, 18p.

Synopsis: This study reflects on possible reasons for an elevated interest in violence and risk factors related to people who become violent and kill. The author provides definition of the condition for the four levels of human behavior: intrapsychic, interpersonal, intragroup and intergroup. Also provided is a model to comprehend how the risk factors may encourage the development of violent human behavior .

Class Activities

In addition to the exercises in the Workbook that accompanies this text, you may find the following in-class activities to be of value:

Activity #1: The Monetary Windfall

Start this activity by having students working responding individually to the following question: What would you do if you all of a sudden inherited $5,000 ? Give the students five to ten minutes to list ways they would spend the money.

Next, have students work in groups of three or four to share their lists and see what each would do with the money. Now have students challenge each other as to if it was the wise the ways they spent the money. Was it all spent on frivolous items? Did the expenditures relate to actual needs of the student?

Have students debate the issue of what is needed and what is wanted. Finally, have the students apply this knowledge to the helping relationship.

Activity #2: Goal Shaping

Have students form groups of three or four and ask them to think of a goal (e.g., going to the cafeteria to get a cup of coffee, introducing themselves to a classmate for the first time, or getting a better grade in the class). Next have the students list the sequence of behaviors needed to achieve the goal.

After the students have finished the task, ask them to discuss the following: How and why did they pick the particular goal? How did they determine which steps to achieve the goal? Finally have them apply this discussion to the helping process.

Activity #3: Why Did You Select That One?

Ask students to discuss situations where the may be a major difference of opinion as to what is the correct sequence of actions in the mind of one person may be quite different in the mind of another. Engage the students to list situations where what is determined to be the right things may be influenced by:

Age:

Race:

Gender:

Culture:

Political Orientation:

Religious Belief:

The point of the exercise is to help students realize that what is right actions to one person might not be right in the opinion of another person based on any of the following items. Have the students apply this knowledge to the helping relationship.

Videos

Maintaining Self-Esteem Against All Odds (1993, 41 min, NTSC, Social and Developmental Psychology). This program examines the various methods individuals may employ when facing social discrimination or other difficulties in terms of protecting their self-esteem and maintaining a sense of self-worth.

Helping and Prosocial Behavior (1989, 30 min, NTSC, Social and Developmental Psychology). This video discusses modelling effects, diffusion of responsibility, and the influence of mood in relation to altruistic behavior.

Self-Deception: How People Fool Themselves (1992, 31 min, NTSC, Social and Developmental Psychology). Psychologists Roy F. Baumeister and Daniel A. Weinberger review the psychology of self-deception, with a focus on how and why people fool themselves.

Theories Of Development (1997, 29 min, NTSC, Social and Developmental Psychology). Profiling the theories of Piaget, Freud, Erikson, Gesell, Skinner and Vygotsky, this video contrasts cognitive, psychosexual, psychosocial, behaviorist, social learning and sociocultural theories of child development.

The Promise of Play: A World of Your Own (2000, 59 min, NTSC, Social and Developmental Psychology). Provides an overview of various types of play in activities ranging from playing bridge to celebrating hedonism.

Websites

1. http://www.earthinstitute.columbia.edu/library/earthmatters/march99/Pages/page12.html
   Human decision making.

2. http://www.salesdoctors.com/diagnosis/3ware10.htm
   The importance of setting goals.

3. http://fac.cgu.edu/~scrivenm/lectures/needwant/needs.htm
   Needs vs. wants.

Overhead Transparencies

Starting on the next page are copies of recommended overhead transparencies. Please feel free to convert the following pages to overheads as this will enhance the lecture portion of your class presentations.

THE THREE STEPS OF STAGE II

Step II-A: Possibilities.

Step II-B: Choices.

Step II-C: Commitment.

OH 14.1

COMMON FEATURES

1. **Philosophy**

2. **View of Clients**

3. **Dealing With Past**

4. **Role of Helper**

5. **The Discovery Phase: Help clients explore and exploit competencies, successes, and "normal times."**

OH 14.2A

COMMON FEATURES cont'd.

6. The Nature of Problems and How We Talk About Things.

7. Insight

8. Dream: Possibilities for a better future

9. Design solutions

10. Deliver

11. Criticisms

OH 14.2B

DISCOVER AND USE POWER THROUGH GOAL SETTING

1. Goals help clients focus their attention and action.

2. Goals help clients mobilize their energy and effort.

3. Goals provide incentives for clients to search for strategies to accomplish them.

4. Clear and specific goals help clients increase persistence.

OH 14.3

ESSENTIALS OF THE DECISION MAKING PROCESS

1. Information gathering.

2. Analysis.

3. Making a choice.

OH 14.4

COMMON ERRORS IN DECISION MAKING

1. Working on the wrong problem.

2. Failing to identify your key objectives.

3. Failing to develop a range of good, creative alternatives.

4. Overlooking crucial consequences of your alternatives.

OH 14.5A

COMMON ERRORS IN DECISION MAKING cont'd.

5. Giving inadequate thought to tradeoffs.

6. Disregarding uncertainty.

7. Failing to account for your risk tolerance.

8. Failing to plan ahead when decisions are linked over time.

OH 14.5B

Chapter Fifteen:

Step II-A:
"What Do I Need and Want?"
Possibilities for A Better Future

	Pages
Chapter Outline	414
Detailed Lecture Notes	415-428
Lecture Enhancers	429-430
Class Activities	431-432
Videos	433
Websites	434
Transparencies	435-446

CHAPTER FIFTEEN OUTLINE

POSSIBILITIES FOR A BETTER FUTURE

➢ The Psychology of Hope
➢ Possible Selves

SKILLS FOR IDENTIFYING POSSIBILITIES FOR A BETTER FUTURE

➢ Creativity and Helping
➢ Divergent Thinking
➢ Brainstorming: A Tool for Divergent Thinking
➢ Future-Oriented Probes
➢ Exemplars and Models as a Source of Possibilities

CASES FEATURING POSSIBILITIES FOR A BETTER FUTURE

➢ The Case of Brendan: Dying Well
➢ The Washington Family Case

EVALUATION QUESTIONS FOR STEP II-A

(Please note: The designation OH in the detailed lecture notes indicates an overhead transparency is available. Please locate the overhead transparencies in the final section of each chapter in this Instructors' Manual.)

Section One: POSSIBILITIES FOR A BETTER FUTURE

Too often the exploration and clarification of problem situations are followed, almost immediately, by the search for solutions in the secondary sense — actions that will help deal with the problem or develop the opportunity. But in many ways outcomes are more important than actions. *What will be in place* once those actions are completed? There is great power in visualizing outcomes, just as there is a danger in formulating action strategies before getting a clear idea of desired outcomes. Stage II is about identifying or visualizing desired results, outcomes, or accomplishments. Step I-A is about envisioning possibilities. Stage III is about strategies, actions, and plans for delivering those outcomes. From another point of view, Stages II and III are about hope.

A.   The Psychology of Hope. (OH-15.1)

1. Hope plays a key role in both developing and implementing possibilities for a better future.

   a)   An internet search reveals that scientific psychology is more interested in hope that one might initially believe (Stotland, 1969) .

   b)   Rick Snyder, who, as we have seen earlier, has written extensively about the positive and negative uses of excuses in everyday life (Snyder, 1988; Snyder, Higgins, & Stucky, 1983), has become a kind of champion for hope (1994a, 1994b,1995, 1997, 1998; McDermott & Snyder, 1999; Snyder, McDermott, Cook, & Rapoff, 1997; Snyder, Michael, & Cheavens, 1999).

   c)   Indeed, he linked excuses and hope in an article entitled "Reality negotiation: From excuses to hope and beyond" (1989).

   d)   He has also developed scales for measuring both dispositional hope (Snyder and others, 1991) and state hope (Snyder and others, 1996).

2. The nature of hope. Snyder starts with the premise that human beings are goal directed. Hope, according to Snyder is the process :

a) of thinking about one's goals

b) of having the will, desire, or motivation to move toward these

c) of thinking about the strategies for accomplishing one's goals

Hope has emotional connotations. It is not a free-floating emotional. It is the byproduct or outcome of the work of setting goals, developing a sense of agency, and devising pathways to the goal.

3. **The benefits of hope**. Snyder (1997, pp.357-358) has combed the research literature in order to discover the benefits of hope as he defines it. Here is what he has found. Higher as compared with lower hope people: **(OH-15.2)**

   a) have a greater number of goals.

   b) have more difficult goals.

   c) have success at achieving their goals.

   d) perceive their goals as challenges.

   e) have greater happiness and less distress.

   f) have superior coping skills.

   g) recover better from physical injury.

   h) report less burnout at work.

B. Possible Selves

1. Clients come to helpers, not necessarily because they have congealed into their final selves, but because they are stuck in their current selves.

2. Counseling is a process of helping clients get "unstuck" and develop a sense of direction.

3. Markus and Nurius (1986) used the term possible selves to represent "individuals' ideas of what they might become, what they would like to become, and what they are afraid of becoming" (p. 954).

4. Step II-A is about "possible selves." The notion of possible selves has captured the imagination of many helpers and of those interested in human development such as teachers (Cameron, 1999; Cross & Marcus, 1994; Hooker, Fiese, Jenkins, Morfei, & Schwagler, 1996; Strauss & Goldberg, 1999)

5. In Step II-A your job is to help client discover their possible selves.

Section Two: SKILLS FOR IDENTIFYING POSSIBILITIES FOR A BETTER FUTURE

At its best, counseling helps clients move from problem-centered mode to "discovery" mode. Discovery mode involves creativity and divergent thinking. According to Taylor, Pham, Rivkin, and Armor mental stimulation is help to the degree that it "provides a window on the future by enabling people to envision possibilities and develop plans for bringing those possibilities about. In moving oneself from a current situation toward an envisioned future one, the anticipation and management of emotions and the initiation and maintenance of problem-solving activities are fundamental tasks" (p. 429).

A. Creativity and Helping

1. One of the myths of creativity is that some people are creative and others are not. Clients, like the rest of us, can be more creative than they are. It is a question of finding ways to help them be so.

2. A review of the requirements for creativity (see Cole & Sarnoff, 1980; Robertshaw, Mecca, & Rerick, 1978, pp. 118-120) shows, by implication, that people in trouble often fail to use whatever creative resources they might have. The creative person is characterized by: (OH-15.3)

   a) optimism and confidence, whereas clients are often depressed and feel powerless.

   b) acceptance of ambiguity and uncertainty, whereas clients may feel tortured by ambiguity and uncertainty and want to escape from them as quickly as possible.

   c) a wide range of interests, whereas clients may be people with a narrow range of interests or whose normal interests have been severely narrowed by anxiety and pain.

   d) flexibility, whereas clients may have become rigid in their approach to themselves, others, and the social settings of life.

   e) tolerance of complexity, whereas clients are often confused and looking for simplicity and simple solutions.

      f)   verbal fluency, whereas clients are often unable to articulate their problems, much less their goals and ways of accomplishing them.

      g) curiosity, whereas clients may not have developed a searching approach to life or may have been hurt by being too venturesome.

      h) drive and persistence, whereas clients may be all too ready to give up.

      i)   independence, whereas clients may be quite dependent or counterdependent.

      j)   nonconformity or reasonable risk taking, whereas clients may have a history of being very conservative and conformist or may get into trouble with others and with society precisely because of their particular brand of nonconformity.

3. A review of some of the principal obstacles or barriers to creativity (see Azar, 1995) brings further problems to the surface. Innovation is hindered by: **(OH-15.4)**

      a) fear — clients are often quite fearful and anxious.

      b) fixed habits — clients may have self-defeating habits or patterns of behavior that may be deeply ingrained.

      c) dependence on authority — clients may come to helpers looking for the "right answers" or be quite counterdependent (the other side of the dependence coin) and fight efforts to be helped with a variety of games.

      d) perfectionism — clients may come to helpers precisely because they are hounded by this problem and can accept only ideal or perfect solutions.

      e) social networks — being "different" sets clients apart when they want to belong.

B. Divergent Thinking

1. Divergent thinking — thinking "outside the box" — assumes that there is always more than one answer. De Bono (1992) calls it "lateral thinking." In helping, that means more than one way to manage a problem or develop an opportunity.

2. Divergent thinking, is not always rewarded in our culture and sometimes is even punished.

3. When students who think divergently give answers that are different from the ones expected, even though their responses might be quite useful (perhaps more useful than the expected responses), they may be ignored, corrected, or punished.

4. Students too often learn that divergent thinking is not rewarded, at least not in school, and they may generalize their experience and end up thinking that it is simply not a useful form of behavior.

5. For many, divergent thinking is either uncomfortable or too much work.

C. Brainstorming: A Tool for Divergent Thinking

One excellent way of helping clients think divergently and more creatively is brainstorming. Brainstorming is a simple idea-stimulation technique for exploring the elements of complex situations. Here are the rules.

1. **Suspend your own judgment, and help clients suspend theirs**.

   a) When brainstorming, do not let clients criticize the ideas they are generating and, of course, do not criticize them yourself. There is some evidence that this rule is especially effective when the problem situation has been clarified and defined and goals have not yet been set.

   b) Having clients suspend judgment is one way of handling the tendency on the part of some to play a "Yes, but" game with themselves. That is, they come up with a good idea and then immediately show why it isn't really a good idea, as in the preceding example.

   c) Avoid saying such things as "I like that idea," "This one is useful," "I'm not sure about that idea," or "How would that work?" Premature approval and criticism cut down on creativity.

2. **Encourage clients to come up with as many possibilities as possible**.

   a) The principle is that quantity ultimately breeds quality. Some of the best ideas come along later in the brainstorming process.

   b) Cutting the process short can be self-defeating.

   c) Within reason, the more ideas the better.

d) Helping clients identify many possibilities for a better future increases the quality of the possibilities that are eventually chosen and turned into goals. In the end, however, do not invoke this rule for its own sake.

e) Possibility generation is not an end in itself. Use your clinical judgment, your social intelligence, to determine when enough is enough.

f) If a client wants to stop, often it's best to stop.

3. Help clients use one idea to stimulate others.

a) This is called piggybacking.

b) Without criticizing the client's productivity, encourage him or her both to develop strategies already generated and to combine different ideas to form new possibilities.

4. Help clients let themselves go and develop some "wild" possibilities.

a) When clients seem to be "drying up" or when the possibilities being generated are quite pedestrian, you might say, "Okay, now draw a line under the items on your list and write the word wild under the line. Now let's see if you can come up with some really wild possibilities." Later it is easier to cut suggested possibilities down to size than to expand them.

b) The wildest possibilities often have within them at least a kernel of an idea that will work.

c) Clients often need permission to let themselves go even in harmless ways. They repress good ideas because they might sound foolish.

d) Helpers need to create an atmosphere where such apparently foolish ideas will be not only accepted but also encouraged.

e) Help clients come up with conservative possibilities, liberal possibilities, radical possibilities, and even outrageous possibilities.

f) It's not always necessary to use brainstorming explicitly.

g) You as helper can keep these rules in mind and then by sharing highlights and using probes you can get clients to brainstorm even though they don't know that's what they're doing.

h) A brainstorming mentality is useful throughout the helping process.

D. Future-Oriented Probes

One way of helping clients invent the future is to ask them, or get them to ask themselves, future-oriented questions related to their current unmanaged problems or undeveloped opportunities.

1. The following questions are different ways of helping clients find answers to the questions "What do you want? What do you need?" These questions focus on outcomes, that is, on what will be in place after the clients act.

   a) What would this problem situation look like if you were managing it better?

   b) What changes in your present lifestyle would make sense?

   c) What would you be doing differently with the people in your life?

   d) What patterns of behavior would be in place that are not currently in place?

   e) What current patterns of behavior would be eliminated?

   f) What would you have that you don't have now?

   g) What accomplishments would be in place that are not in place now?

   h) What would this opportunity look like if you developed it?

2. It is a mistake to suppose that clients will automatically gush with answers.

3. Ask the kinds of questions just listed, or encourage them to ask themselves the questions, but then help them answer them.

4. Create the therapeutic dialogue around possibilities for a better future.

5. Many clients don't know how to use their innate creativity. Thinking divergently is not part of their mental lifestyle. You have to work with clients to help them produce some creative output.

6. Some clients are reluctant to name possibilities for a better future because they sense that this will bring more responsibility. They will have to move into action mode.

E. Exemplars and Models as a Source of Possibilities

1. Some clients can see future possibilities better when they see them embodied in others.

2. You can help clients brainstorm possibilities for a better future by helping them identify exemplars or models. By models I don't mean superstars or people who do things perfectly. That would be self-defeating.

3. Models or exemplars can help clients name what they want more specifically.

4. Models can be found anywhere: among the client's relatives, friends, and associates, in books, on television, in history, in movies.

5. Counselors can help clients identify models, choose those dimensions of others that are relevant, and translate what they see into realistic possibilities for themselves.

6. Lockwood and Kunda (1999) have shown that, under normal circumstances, individuals can be inspired by role models so that their motivation and self-evaluations are enhanced.

7. But not always. Bringing up role models with people who have been reviewing "best past selves" has a way of deflating people. Their best can pale in comparison with the model. Their best is none to good.

8. In solution-focused therapies, reviewing past successes is an important part of the process.

9. If people are asked to come up with ideas about their "best possible selves" and then are asked to review what they like about a role model, their ability to draw inspiration from the role model is impaired.

10. Using role models as sources of inspiration certainly works, but it can be tricky.

Section Three: CASES FEATURING POSSIBILITIES FOR A BETTER FUTURE

Here are a couple of cases that illustrate how helping clients develop possibilities for a better future had a substantial impact.

A. The Case of Brendan: Dying Well

1. Brendan, heavy drinker, had extensive and irreversible liver damage and it was clear that he was getting sicker. But he wanted to "get some things done" before he died. Brendan's action orientation helped a great deal. Over the course of a few months, a counselor helped him to name some of the things he wanted before he died or on his journey toward death.

2. Brendan came up with the following possibilities:

   a) "I'd like to have some talks with someone who has a religious orientation, like a minister. I want to discuss some of the "bigger" issues of life and death.

   b) "I don't want to die hopeless. I want to die with a sense of meaning."

   c) "I want to belong. You know, to some kind of community, people who know what I'm going through, but who are not sentimental about it. People not disgusted with me because of the way I've done myself in."

   d) "I'd like to get rid of some of my financial worries."

   e) "I'd like a couple of close friends with whom I could share the ups and downs of daily life. With no apologies."

   f) "As long as possible, I'd like to be doing some kind of productive work, whether paid or not. I've been a flake. I want to contribute even if just an ordinary way."

   g) "I need a decent place to live, maybe with others."

   h) "I need decent medical attention. I'd like a doctor who has some compassion. One who could challenge me to live until I die."

   i) "I need to manage these bouts of anxiety and depression better."
   j) "I want to be get back with my family again. I want to hug my dad. I want him to hug me."

   k) "I'd like to make peace with one or two of my closest friends. They more or less dropped me when I got sick. But at heart, they're good guys."

   l) "I want to die in my home town."

3. Of course, Brendan didn't name all these possibilities at once. Through understanding and probes the counselor helped name what he needed and wanted and then helped him stitch together a set of goals from these possibilities (Stage II) and ways of accomplishing them (Stage III).

4. Box 14-1 outlines the kinds of questions you can help clients ask themselves to discover possibilities for a better future.

B. The Washington Family Case

1. This case is more complex because it involves a family. Not only does the family as a unit have its wants and needs, but also each of the individual members has his or her own. Therefore, it is even more imperative to review possibilities for a better future so that competing needs can be reconciled.

> Lane, the 15-year-old son of Troy and Rhonda Washington, was hospitalized with what was diagnosed as an "acute schizophrenic attack." He had two older brothers, both teenagers, and two younger sisters, one 10 and one 12, all living at home. The Washingtons lived in a large city. Although both parents worked, their combined income still left them pinching pennies. They also ran into a host of problems associated with their son's hospitalization — the need to arrange ongoing help and care for Lane, financial burdens, behavioral problems among the other siblings, marital conflict, and stigma in the community ("They're a funny family with a crazy son"; "What kind of parents are they?"). To make things worse, they did not think the psychiatrist and the psychologist they met at the hospital took the time to understand their concerns. They felt that the helpers were trying to push Lane back out into the community; in their eyes, the hospital was "trying to get rid of him." "They give him some pills and then give him back to you" was their complaint. No one explained to them that short-term hospitalization was meant to guard the civil rights of patients and avoid the negative effects of longer-term institutionalization.
>
> When Lane was discharged, his parents were told that he might have a relapse, but they were not told what to do about it. They faced the prospect of caring for Lane in a climate of stigma without adequate information, services, or relief. Feeling abandoned, they were very angry with the mental-health establishment. They had no idea what they should do to respond to Lane's illness or to the range of

family problems that had been precipitated by the episode. By chance the Washingtons met someone who had worked for the National Alliance for the Mentally Ill (NAMI), an advocacy and education organization. This person referred them to an agency that provided support and help.

2. Social workers at the agency helped the Washingtons identify both needs and wants in seven areas (see Bernheim, 1989).

a) **The home environment.** The Washingtons needed an environment in which the needs of all the family members are balanced. They didn't want their home be an extension of the hospital. They wanted Lane taken care of, but they wanted to attend to the needs of the other children and to their own needs as well.

b) **Care outside the home.** They wanted a comprehensive therapeutic program for Lane. They needed to review possible services, identify relevant services, and arrange access to those services. They needed to find a way of paying for all this.

c) **Care inside the home.** They wanted all family members to know how to cope with Lane's residual symptoms. He might be withdrawn or aggressive, but they needed to know how to relate to him and help him handle behavioral problems.

d) **Prevention.** Family members needed to be able to spot early warning symptoms of impending relapse. They also needed to know what to do when they saw those signs, including such things as contacting the clinic or, in the case of more severe problems, arranging for an ambulance or getting help from the police.

e) **Family stress.** They needed to know how to cope with the increased stress all of this would entail. They needed forums for working out their problems. They wanted to avoid family blowups, and when blowups occurred, they wanted to manage them without damaging the social fabric of the family.

f) **Stigma.** They wanted to understand and be able to cope with whatever stigma might be attached to Lane's illness. For instance, when taunted for having a "crazy brother," the children needed to know what to do and what not to do. Family members needed to know whom to tell, what to say, how to respond to inquiries, and how to deal with blame and insults.

g) **Limitation of grief.** They needed to know how to manage the normal guilt, anger, frustration, fear, and grief that go with problem situations like this.

3. For positive-psychology advances in the treatment of serious mental illness see Coursey, Alford, and Safarjan (1997).

When it comes to serious mental illness in a family, Marsh and Johnson (1997) focus, not just on family burden, but family resilience and the internal and external resources that support such resilience.

This is, of course, a positive psychology approach. They list the ways in which helpers can assist families (p. 233):

a) Understanding and normalizing the family experience of mental illness.

b) Focusing on the strengths and competencies of their family and relatives.

c) Learning about mental illness, the mental health system, and community resources.

d) Developing skills in stress management, problem solving, and communication.

e) Resolving their feelings of grief and loss.

f) Coping with the symptoms of mental illness and its repercussions for their family.

g) Identifying and responding to the signs of impending relapse.

h) Creating a supportive family environment.

i) Developing realistic expectations for all members of the family.

j) Playing a meaningful role in their relative's treatment, rehabilitation, and recovery.

k) Maintaining a balance that meets the needs of all members of the family.

5. They outline a number of interventions strategies that can help families meet these objectives:

    a) **Family interventions** that stress the role of the family as a support system rather than the cause of mental illness.

    b) **Family support and advocacy groups** such as the National Alliance for the Mentally Ill. These groups provide support, education, and encourage advocacy for improved services.

    c) **Family consultation** which can aid in helping families determine their own goals and make informed choices regarding their use of available services.

    d) **Family education** with respect to information about mental illness, caregiving, the mental health system, community resources, and the like.

    e) **Family psychoeducation** which focuses on such things as coping strategies and stress management

BOX 14 -1
Questions for Exploring Possibilities (OH-15.6)

Help clients ask themselves these kinds of questions:

- What are my most critical needs and wants?
- What are some possibilities for a better future?
- What outcomes or accomplishments would take care of my most pressing problems?
- What would my life look like if I were to develop a couple of key opportunities?
- What should my life look like a year from now?
- What should I put in place that is currently not in place?
- What are some wild possibilities for making my life better?

Evaluation Questions for Step II-A (OH-15.7)

- To what degree am I an imaginative person?
- In what ways can I apply the concept of "possible selves" to myself?
- What problems do I experience as I try to help clients use their imaginations?
- Against the background of problem situations and unused opportunities, how well do I help clients focus on what they want?
- To what degree do I prize divergent thinking and creativity in myself and others?
- How effectively do I use empathic highlights, a variety of probes, and challenge

to help clients brainstorm what they want?

➤ Besides direct questions and other probes, what kinds of strategies do I use to help clients brainstorm what they want?

➤ How effectively do I help clients identify models and exemplars that can help them clarify what they want?

➤ How easily do I move back and forth in the helping model, especially in establishing a "dialogue" between Stage I and Stage II?

➤ How well do I help clients act on what they are learning?.

Lecture Enhancers

You should be able to find the full text of the following items in your library or by using your web-based library access tool of choice (e.g., Psycinfo)

Item One: Treatment for Rapists

Cognitive-behavioral treatment for rapists: Can we do better?

Marx,-Brian-P; Miranda,-Robert Jr; Meyerson,-Lori-A. (1999) Cognitive-behavioral treatment for rapists: Can we do better? In Clinical-Psychology-Review. 1999 Nov; Vol 19(7): 875-894

   Synopsis: Based on the limited success that current treatment approaches provide, several treatment options requiring empirical testing to determine effectiveness are presented in this article.

Item Two: Intervention

Where Should We Intervene?

Hanson, R. Karl; Harris, Andrew J. R. (2000) Effective intervention with sexual offenders requires the targeting of appropriate risk factors. In Criminal Justice & Behavior, Feb. 2000, Vol. 27 Issue 1, p.6

   Synopsis: This article provides information on data collected through interviews with community supervision officers and file reviews of 208 sexual offense recidivists and 201 nonrecidivists. It is imperative that those who provide treatment, community supervision, or risk assessments for sexual offenders must identify the factors related to sexual offense recidivism. The targeting of appropriate risk factors is necessary for effective intervention.

Item Three: Humanistic Psychology

The humanistic psychology and positive psychology connection: implications for psychotherapy.

Resnick, Stella; Warmoth, Arthur; Serlin, Ilene A. The humanistic psychology and positive psychology connection: implications for psychotherapy. Journal of Humanistic Psychology, Winter 2001, Vol. 41, Issue I, 29p

Synopsis: This article looks at the commonalities between humanistic psychology and responds to the issues in the field of positive psychology that challenge some of the most basic tenants of humanistic psychology. The issues in the article include social value, research approaches, and what can be gained by positive psychology from the field of humanistic psychology.

The article concludes with a nice review of all of the possible connections to positive psychology and humanistic psychology along with sub-fields of humanistic psychology.

Class Activities

In addition to the exercises in the Workbook that accompanies this text, you may find the following in-class activities to be of value:

Activity #1: A Better Future

In this activity students are encouraged to think of times that they have been quite unhappy with a life situation (loss of a job, the end of a relationship, a disappointing grade in a course) and what they did to improve the situation. Have students complete this assignment individually and then share their results in groups of two or three.

Next, have the students record how they felt when they improved their situation. Have them attempt to capture the feelings of success in improving their situation. Finally, have them relate this experience to clients who may in an unpleasant situation and don't know how to improve their undesirable circumstances. Have the groups report their findings to the class. Focus on behaviors, actions, reactions, and the transfer of knowledge to the helping relationship.

Activity #2: The Future Is Now

Have the students select a goal to be completed (e.g., write a term paper, find a job, write a letter to a friend) and then ask the students list all of the possible individual activities they need to do to complete the task. Push the students to list as many individual details as possible.

Next have the students form groups of three and four and integrate their individual lists into one large list. Finally, have the groups prioritize the individual tasks in priority order: list the "right things to do" first.

After groups have constructed their individual group list, have them share their list with another group to see how similar their lists are. Have the students compare, contrast, and discussion their lists. What will become apparent is that not all are in agreement as to what is most important to do first. Have the students then apply this knowledge to the helping relationship. Ask them to explain how this relates to the concept of "The Future is Now" (Hint: What we do now determines how we live in the future.)

Activity #3: Your Future Isn't My Future

Have each student take fifteen to twenty to list fifteen to twenty goals they would like to achieve over the next ten years. Encourage them to be as specific as they can in identifying the specific goals they desire to achieve.

Next have the students work in triads to share their individual goals. Have students compare and contrast their goals and discussion what they observe when comparing and contrasting their goals.

For the next part of the activity have students indicate the following on the top of their individual papers: male or female and over 35 or under 35 years of age. Then list use the four categories to list all of the goals using the following chart:

Male under 35 Male over 35   Female under 35   Female over 35

Have the students compare the lists to determine if they can notice difference between the four columns. The point is to show students that traits such as gender and age greatly influence future goals. It is important for future helpers to be tolerant of and understand the differences in how individuals can have quite different visions of their respective futures.

Videos

Shyness (1998, 30 min, NTSC, Social and Developmental Psychology).
An overview of Philip Zimbardo's research findings on shyness ranging from why people are shy and common characteristics of shyness to how shyness is misunderstood.

Good and Evil (1994, 45 min, NTSC, Social and Developmental Psychology). This video explores racism, sexism, education, the family and religion in relation to contrasting social perceptions of good and evil in everyday life and in times of war,

Early Relationships: Habits of the Heart (1991, 60 min, NTSC, Social and Developmental Psychology). This video provides an analysis of the effect of early experience on the quality of relationships and distinguishes between bonding and attachment.

The Influence of the Family (1991, 60 min, NTSC, Social and Developmental Psychology). This video examines how various family structures and interactions affect children's development.

The Development of Self (1991, 60 min, NTSC, Social and Developmental Psychology). The Perceived Competence Scale for self-concept assessment of children is examined in relation to scholastic performance, athletic competence, popularity, behavioral conduct, and physical appearance.

Websites

1. http://www.runningtimes.com/issues/99nov/palmer.htm
   How bad do you want it?

2. http://www.aife.org/aife_ec_wm.htm
   Psychology of obesity and helping to change it.

3. http://web.utk.edu/~thompson/ActListen.html
   Reality therapy.

4. http://www.counselingzone.com/workshop/dandrea.html
   Counselingzone.com

Overhead Transparencies

Starting on the next page are copies of recommended overhead transparencies. Please feel free to convert the following pages to overheads as this will enhance the lecture portion of your class presentation

THE PSYCHOLOGY OF HOPE

1. Hope plays a key role in both developing and implementing possibilities for a better future.

2. Hope is the process:

a) of thinking about one's goals.

b) of having the will, desire, or motivation to move toward these goals.

c) of thinking about the strategies for accomplishing one's goals.

OH 15.1

PEOPLE WITH HIGHER HOPE:

1. have a greater number of goals.

2. have more difficult goals.

3. have success at achieving their goals.

4. perceive their goals as challenges.

OH 15.2A

PEOPLE WITH HIGHER HOPE cont'd. :

5. have greater happiness and less distress.

6. have superior coping skills.

7. recover better from physical injury.

8. report less burnout at work.

OH 15.2B

CHARACTERISTICS OF CREATIVE PEOPLE

1. Optimism and confidence

2. Acceptance of ambiguity and uncertainty

3. A wide range of interests

4. Flexibility

5. Tolerance of complexity

OH 15.3A

CHARACTERISTICS OF CREATIVE PEOPLE cont'd.

6. Verbal fluency

7. Curiosity

8. Drive and persistence

9. Independence

10. Nonconformity or reasonable risk taking.

OH 15.3B

INNOVATION IS HINDERED BY:

1. Fear

2. Fixed habits

3. Dependence on authority

4. Perfectionism

5. Social networks

OH 15.4

BRAINSTORMING RULES:

1. Suspend your own judgment, and help clients suspend theirs.

2. Encourage clients to come up with as many possibilities as possible.

3. Help clients use one idea to stimulate others.

4. Help clients let themselves go and develop some "wild" possibilities.

OH 15.5

QUESTIONS FOR EXPLORING POSSIBILITIES

1. What are my most critical needs and wants?
2. What are some possibilities for a better future?
3. What outcomes or accomplishments would take care of my most pressing problems?
4. What would my life look like if I were to develop a couple of key opportunities?
5. What should my life look like a year from now?
6. What should I put in place that is currently not in place?
7. What are some wild possibilities for making my life better?

OH 15.6

EVALUATION QUESTIONS FOR STEP II-A

1. To what degree am I an imaginative person?
2. In what ways can I apply the concept of "possible selves" to myself?
3. What problems do I experience as I try to help clients use their imaginations?
4. Against the background of problem situations and unused opportunities, how well do I help clients focus on what they want?
5. To what degree do I prize divergent thinking and creativity in myself and others?

OH 15.7A

EVALUATION QUESTIONS FOR STEP II-A cont'd.

6. How effectively do I use empathic highlights, a variety of probes, and challenge to help clients brainstorm what they want?

7. Besides direct questions and other probes, what kinds of strategies do I use to help clients brainstorm what they want?

8. How effectively do I help clients identify models and exemplars that can help them clarify what they want?

OH 15.7B

EVALUATION QUESTIONS FOR STEP II-A cont'd.

9. How easily do I move back and forth in the helping model, especially in establishing a "dialogue" between Stage I and Stage II?

10. How well do I help clients act on what they are learning?

OH 15.7C

Chapter Sixteen:

Step II-B:
"What Do I Really Want?"
Moving From Possibilities to Choices

	Pages
Chapter Outline	**448**
Detailed Lecture Notes	**449-460**
Lecture Enhancers	**461-462**
Class Activities	**463-464**
Videos	**465**
Websites	**466**
Transparencies	**467-474**

CHAPTER SIXTEEN OUTLINE

FROM POSSIBILITIES TO CHOICES

HELPING CLIENTS SHAPE THEIR GOALS

- ➢ Help Clients State What They Need and Want as Outcomes or Accomplishments
- ➢ Help Clients Move from Broad Aims to Clear and Specific Goals
- ➢ Help Clients Establish Goals That Make a Difference
- ➢ Help Clients Set Goals That Are Prudent
- ➢ Help Clients Formulate Realistic Goals
- ➢ Help Clients Set Goals That Can Be Sustained
- ➢ Help Clients Choose Goals That Have Some Flexibility
- ➢ Help Clients Choose Goals Consistent with Their Values
- ➢ Help Clients Establish Realistic Time Frames for the Accomplishment of Goals

NEEDS VERSUS WANTS

EMERGING GOALS

ADAPTIVE GOALS

THE "REAL OPTIONS" APPROACH

ACTION BIAS AS A METAGOAL

EVALUATION QUESTIONS FOR STEP II-B

(Please note: The designation OH in the detailed lecture notes indicates an overhead transparency is available. Please locate the overhead transparencies in the final section of each chapter in this Instructors' Manual.)

Section One: FROM POSSIBILITIES TO CHOICES

A. Once possibilities for a better future have been developed, clients need to make some choices; that is, they need to choose one or more of those possibilities and turn them into a program for constructive change.

  1. Step II-A is, in many ways, about **creativity**, getting rid of boundaries, thinking beyond one's limited horizon, moving outside the box.

  2. Step II-B is about **innovation** — that is, turning possibilities into a practical program for change.

  3. If implemented, a goal constitutes the "solution" with a Big S for the client's problem or opportunity.

  4. Since goals can be highly motivational, helping clients set realistic goals is one of the most important steps in the helping process.

Section Two: HELPING CLIENTS SHAPE THEIR GOALS

Practical goals do not usually leap out fully formed. Effective counselors add value by engaging clients in the kind of dialogue that will help them design, choose, craft, shape, and develop their goals. The goals that either emerge through this client-helper dialogue are more likely to be workable if they have certain characteristics. They need to be: **(OH-16.1)**

- stated as **outcomes** rather than activities,
- **specific** enough to be verifiable and to drive action,
- **substantive** and challenging,
- both **venturesome** and **prudent**,
- **realistic** in regard to resources needed to accomplish them,
- **sustainable** over a reasonable time period,
- **flexible** without being wishy-washy,
- **congruent** with the client's **values**, and
- set in a reasonable **time frame**.

These characteristics can be seen as "tools" that counselors can use to help clients design and shape or reshape their goals and take on life through the following flexible principles.

A. **Help Clients State What They Need and Want as Outcomes or Accomplishments**.

1. The goal of counseling, as emphasized again and again, is neither discussing nor planning nor engaging in activities.

2. Helping is about solutions with a big S. "I want to start doing some exercise" is an activity rather than an outcome. "Within six months I will be running three miles in less than thirty minutes at least four times a week" is an outcome.

3. It is a pattern of behavior that will be in place by a certain time.

4. Goals stated as outcomes provide direction for clients.

5. You can help clients describe what they need and want by using this "past-participle" approach — drinking stopped, number of marital fights decreased, anger habitually controlled.

6. Helping clients state goals as accomplishments rather than activities helps them avoid directionless and imprudent action.

7. Goals, at their best, are expressions of what clients need and want.

8. Clients who know what they want are more likely to work not just harder but also smarter.

B. **Help Clients Move from Broad Aims to Clear and Specific Goals.**

1. Specific rather than general goals tend to drive behavior. Therefore, broad goals need to be translated into more specific goals and tailored to the needs and abilities of each client.

2. Skilled helpers use probes to help clients move from the general to the specific.

3. Counselors often add value by helping clients move from good intentions and vague desires to broad aims and then on to quite specific goals.

a) Good intentions. "I need to do something about this" is a statement of intent. However, even though good intentions are a good start, they need to be translated into aims and goals.

b) Broad aims. A broad aim is more than a good intention. It has content; that is, it identifies the area in which the client wants to work and makes some general statement about that area.

c) Specific goals. To help the client move toward greater specificity, the counselor uses such probes as "Tell me what this aim will look like."

4. There is a difference between *instrumental* goals and higher-order or ultimate goals.

   a) Instrumental goals are *strategies* for achieving higher order goals,

   b) It's important to make sure that the client has clarity about the higher-order goal.

   c) When you are helping clients design and shape instrumental goals, make sure the clients can answer the instrumental-for-what? question.

5. Helping clients move from good intentions to more and more specific goals is a shaping process.

   a) It is not always necessary to count things to determine whether a goal has been reached, though sometimes counting is helpful.

   b) Helping is about living more fully, not about accounting activities.

   c) At a minimum, however, desired outcomes need to be capable of being verified in some way.

C. Help Clients Establish Goals With Substance, Goals That Make a Difference.

1. Outcomes and accomplishments are meaningless if they do not have the required impact on the client's life. The goals clients choose should have substance to them, that is, some significant contribution toward managing the original problem situation or developing some opportunity.

2. Goals have substance to the degree that they help clients "stretch" themselves.

3. As Locke and Latham (1984, pp. 21. 26) noted: "Extensive research... has established that, within reasonable limits, the... more challenging the goal,

the better the resulting performance.... People try harder to attain the hard goal. They exert more effort.... people become motivated in proportion to the level of challenge with which they are faced....

4. Even goals that cannot be fully reached will lead to high effort levels, provided that partial success can be achieved and is rewarded.

5. If the goal is too easy, people see it as trivial and ignore it. If the goal is too difficult it is not accepted. However, this difficulty-performance ratio differs from person to person. What is small for some is big for others.

D. Help Clients Set Goals That Are Prudent.

1. Discussing and setting goals should contribute to both direction and wisdom. The following case begins poorly but ends well.

2. There are two kinds of prudence — playing it safe is one, doing the wise thing is the other.

3. Problem management and opportunity development should be venturesome. They are about making wise choices rather than playing it safe.

E. Help Clients Formulate Realistic Goals.

1. Setting stretch goals can help clients energize themselves. They rise to the challenge.

2. Goals set too high can do more harm than good. Locke and Latham (1984, p. 39) put it succinctly:

> Nothing breeds success like success. Conversely, nothing causes feelings of despair like perpetual failure. A primary purpose of goal setting is to increase the motivation level of the individual. But goal setting can have precisely the opposite effect if it produces a yardstick that constantly makes the individual feel inadequate.

3. A goal is realistic if the client has access to the resources needed to accomplish it, the goal is under the client's control, and external circumstances do not prevent its accomplishment.

F. Resources: Help clients choose goals for which the resources are available.

    1. It does little good to help clients develop specific, substantive, and verifiable goals if the resources needed for their accomplishment are not available.

G. Control: Help clients choose goals that are under their control.

    1. Sometimes clients defeat their own purposes by setting goals that are not under their control.

    2. For instance, it is common for people to believe that their problems would be solved if only other people would not act the way they do.

    3. In most cases, however, we do not have any direct control over the ways others act.

    4. Goals are not under clients' control if they are blocked by external forces that they cannot influence.

H. Help Clients Set Goals That Can Be Sustained.

    1. Clients need to commit themselves to goals that have staying power.

I. Help Clients Choose Goals That Have Some Flexibility.

    1. In many cases, goals have to be adapted to changing realities.

    2. There might be some trade-offs between goal specificity and goal flexibility in uncertain situations. Napoleon noted this when he said, "He will not go far who knows from the first where he is going."

    3. Sometimes making goals too specific or too rigid does not allow clients to take advantage of emerging opportunities.

    4. Counseling is a living, organic process. Just as organisms adapt to their changing environments, the choices clients make need to be adapted to their changing circumstances.

J. Help Clients Choose Goals Consistent with Their Values.

    1. Although helping is a process of social influence, it remains ethical only if it respects, within reason, the values of the client.

    2. Values are criteria we use to make decisions.

3. Helpers may challenge clients to reexamine their values but they should not encourage clients to perform actions that are not in keeping with their values.

4. Some problems involve a client's trying to pursue contradictory goals or values. The counselor helps identify and use values to consider some trade-offs.

K. Help Clients Establish Realistic Time Frames for the Accomplishment of Goals.

1. Goals that are to be accomplished "sometime or other" probably won't be accomplished at all. Therefore, helping clients put some time frames in their goals can add value.

2. Greenberg (1986) talked about immediate, intermediate, and final outcomes.

    a) **Immediate outcomes** are changes in attitudes and behaviors evident in the helping sessions themselves.

    b) **Intermediate outcomes** are changes in attitudes and behaviors that lead to further change.

    c) **Final outcomes** refer to the completion of the overall program for constructive change through which problems are managed and opportunities developed.

3. Taussig (1987) talked about the usefulness of setting and executing minigoals early in the helping process.

4. The achievement of sequenced minigoals can go a long way toward making a dent in intractable problems.

5. Some goals need to be accomplished now, some soon; others are short-term goals; still others are long-term.

6. There is no particular formula for helping all clients choose the right mix of goals at the right time and in the right sequence. Although helping is based on problem-management principles, it remains an art.

7. It is not always necessary to make sure that each goal in a client's program for constructive change has all the characteristics outlined in this chapter. For some clients, identifying broad goals is enough to kick start the entire problem-management and opportunity-development process.

8. Help clients develop goals that have some sort of agency — if not urgency — built in. In one case, this may mean helping a client deal with clarity; in another, with substance; in still another, with realism, values, or time frame.

9. Box 16-1 outlines some questions that you can help clients ask themselves to choose goals from among possibilities.

Section Three: NEEDS VERSUS WANTS

A. In some cases, what clients want and what they need coincide. In other cases, clients might not want what they need.

1. Brainstorming possibilities for a better future should focus on the package of needs and wants that makes sense for this particular client.

2. Involuntary clients often need to be challenged to look beyond their wants to their needs.

3. The counselors help explore the consequences of their clients choices and try to help look at other options. Was there some kind of tradeoff between what they wanted and what they needed?

4. In the end the decision is the clients'.

Section Four: EMERGING GOALS

A. It is not always a question of *designing* and *setting* goals in an explicit way.

1. Goals can naturally emerge through the client-helper dialogue. Often when clients talk about problems and unused opportunities, possible goals and action strategies bubble up.

2. Clients, once they are helped to clarify a problem situation through a combination of probing, empathic highlights, and challenge, begin to see more clearly what they want and what they have to do to manage the problem.

3. Some clients must first act in some way before they find out just what they want to do.

4. Once goals begin to emerge, counselors can help clients clarify them and find ways of implementing them.

5. "Emerge" should not mean that clients wait around until "something comes up." Nor should it mean that clients try many different solutions in the hope that one of them will work. These kinds of "emergence" tend to be self-defeating.

B. While goals do often emerge, still explicit goal setting is not to be underrated.

1. Taussig (1987) showed that clients respond positively to goal setting even when goals are set very early in the counseling process.

2. A client-centered, "no one right formula" approach seems to be best.

3. Although all clients need focus and direction in managing problems and developing opportunities, what focus and direction will look like will differ from client to client.

Section Five: ADAPTIVE GOALS

Collins and Porras (1994) coined the term "big, hairy, audacious" goals (BHAGs) for goals for "super-stretch" goals. The term, however, fits better into the hype of business than the practicalities of helping. It is true that some clients are looking for big goals. They believe, and perhaps rightly so, that without big goals their lives will not be substantially different. But even for clients who choose goals that can be called "big" in one way or another, a bit-by-bit approach to achieving these goals. It is usually better to take big goals and divide them up into smaller pieces lest the big goal on its own seem too daunting. The term "within reasonable limits" will differ from client to client.

A. **Adaptive goals**. While difficult or "stretch" goals are often the most motivational, this is not true in every case.

1. Wheeler and Janis (1980, p. 98) cautioned against the search for the "absolute best" goal all the time: "Sometimes it is more reasonable to choose a satisfactory alternative than to continue searching for the absolute best."

2. The time, energy, and expense of finding the best possible choice may outweigh the improvement in the choice.

3. In some cases clients will be satisfied with "surface" solutions such as the elimination of symptoms. Some helpers would be disappointed while others would see them as legitimate examples of adapting to rather than changing reality.

4. Clients who do act to achieve some kind of goal, however minimal, did *something* about the way they thought and behaved, and they felt that their lives were better because of it.

B. Coping. Choosing adaptive rather than a stretch goal has been associated with *coping* (Coyne & Racioppo, 2000; Folkman & Moskowitz, 2000; Lazarus, 2000; Snyder, 1999).

1. All human beings cope rather than conquer at times.

2. Sometimes people have no other choice. It's cope or succumb.

3. For some, coping has a bad reputation because it seems to be associated with mediocrity. But in many difficult situations helping clients cope is one of the best things helpers can do.

4. Coping often has an enormous upside.

5. Folkman and Moskowitz (2000), from a positive psychology point of view, see positive affect as playing an important role in coping. And so they ask how positive affect is generated and sustained in the face of chronic stress. They suggest three ways. **(OH-16.2)**

   a) **Positive reappraisal**. Help clients reframe a situation to see it in a positive light.

   b) **Problem-focused coping**. Help clients deal with problems one at a time as they come up.

   c) **Infusing ordinary events with positive meaning**.

6. Lazarus (2000) adds a note of caution to all of this.

   a) He notes that so-called positively-valenced emotions such as love and hope are often mixed with negative feelings and are therefore experienced as distressing. It is painful for caregivers to see those they love in pain.

   b) So-called negatively-valenced emotions such as anger are not unequivocally negative. Anger can be experienced as positive or is often mixed with positive feelings.

   c) While counselors can help clients under great stress do things that will increase the kind of positive affect that makes their lives more livable, there are limits. In other words, Lazarus is cautioning us to use but be careful with positive-psychology approaches.

C. **Strategic self-limitation**. Robert Leahy (1999) relates the kinds of reluctance and resistance reviewed in Chapter 9 to goal setting under the rubric of "strategic self-limitation."

    1. Reluctant and resistant behaviors serve the purpose of setting limits on change. All change carries some risk and uncertainty and these can be distressing in themselves.

    2. Putting up barriers to change limits both risk and uncertainty.

    3. The strategies such clients use are the ordinary ones — attacking the therapist, failing to do homework assignments, emotional volatility, getting mired down in a "this won't work" mentality, and so forth.

    4. Helpers, even though they may point out to clients the ways they are engaging is what Leahy calls "self-handicapping," don't choose goals for clients.

    5. There is a huge difference between best possible goals and goals that are possible for this client in this set of circumstances.

    6. Helping clients cope with the adversities of life does not mean that you are shortchanging them. When you are helping them adapt rather than conquer, you are not failing. Neither are they.

    7. When it comes to outcomes, there is no one universal rule of success.

Section Six: THE "REAL-OPTIONS" APPROACH

A. How can you help clients set goals if the future is uncertain — as it always is to one degree or another.

1. One way is through the "real-options" approach. Borrowed from business settings (Trigeorgis, 1999), it has applications to personal life.

2. The trick is flexibility. If the future is uncertain, it pays to have a broad range of options open. There is no use investing a great deal of time and energy designing a goal that will have to be changed because the client's world changes.

3. The economics are poor. Therefore, help clients choose one or more back-up goals to take care of such eventualities. So if a client comes up with three viable possibilities, one may be pursued while the other two are held in reserve.

4. In this way clients have direction, but they also have a contingency plan. If the world changes then the client can choose the best goals, that is, the one that best fits the circumstances at the times.

    B. While clients can identify and develop further goal options as the risky and uncertain world changes, doing so upfront has advantages.

        1. Choosing need not be a once-and-forever decision.

        2. Having real options helps you kill an option that is no longer working. Or the one that is not working at this time can be put on the back burner.

        3. The real-options approach provides freedom and flexibility and keeps clients from falling into the status-quo decision-making trap outlined earlier.

Section Seven: A BIAS FOR ACTION AS A METAGOAL

Although clients set goals that are directly related to their problem situations, there are also metagoals or superordinate goals that would make them more effective in pursuing the goals they set and in leading fuller lives.

    A. The overall goal of helping clients become more effective in problem management and opportunity development was mentioned in Chapter 1.

    B. Another metagoal is to help clients become more effective "agents" in life — doers rather than mere reactors, preventers rather than fixers, initiators rather than followers.

        1. The doer is more likely to pursue stretch rather than adaptive goals in managing problems.

        2. The doer is also more likely to move beyond problem management to opportunity development.

BOX 16-1

Questions for Shaping Goals (OH-16.3)

➤ Is the goal stated in outcome or results language?
➤ Is the goal specific enough to drive behavior? How will I know when I have accomplished it?
➤ If I accomplish this goal, will it make a difference? Will it really help manage the problems and opportunities I have identified?
➤ Does this goal have "bite" while remaining prudent?
➤ Is it doable?
➤ Can I sustain this goal over the long haul?
➤ Does this goal have some flexibility?
➤ Is this goal in keeping with my values?
➤ Have I set a realistic time frame for the accomplishment of the goal?

Evaluation Questions for Step II-B (OH-16.4)

➤ To what degree am I helping clients choose specific goals from among a number of possibilities?
➤ How well do I challenge clients to translate good intentions into broad goals and broad goals into specific, actionable goals?
➤ To what extent do I help clients shape their goals so that they have the characteristics outlined in Box 16-1?
➤ How effectively do I help clients establish goals that take into consideration both needs and wants?
➤ To what degree do I help clients become aware of goals that are naturally emerging from the helping process?
➤ How well do I help clients identify "real-option" goals when the future is both risky and uncertain?
➤ How effectively do I help clients choose the right mix of adaptive and stretch goals?
➤ How well do I help clients explore the consequences of the goals they are setting?
➤ How do I help clients make a bias toward action one of their metagoals?

Lecture Enhancers

You should be able to find the full text of the following items in your library or by using your web-based library access tool of choice (e.g., Psycinfo)

Item One: Positive Clinical Psychology

A psychology of human strengths: Perspectives on an emerging field.

Seligman, Martin E. P., Peterson, Christopher. (Draft 2000) Chapter prepared for L. G. Aspinwall & U. M. Staudinger (Eds.). A psychology of human strengths: Perspectives on an emerging field. Found in Washington, DC: American Psychological Association Press, (in press). The content of the prevention and therapy sections uses material from Seligman (2000), by the Positive Psychology Network, and by Values-In-Action of the Mayerson Foundation.

Synopsis: This chapter presents the three constituent components of Positive Psychology (PP) namely: the study of positive subjective experience, the study of positive individual traits, and the study of institutions that enable the first two.   The authors assert that PP will flourish only under social conditions free of turmoil as negative emotions will overtake positive emotions; their opinion is that a society that is occupied with fighting fires has minimal resources for building on the positive.

Item Two: Illusions or Authentic?

Positive Social Science

Seligman, Martin E.P. (1998) Positive Social Science. The President's (APA) Column, VOLUME 29 , NUMBER 4 -April 1998

Synopsis: The author illustrates the dominance of research on negative psychological elements in contrast to the minimal attention paid to positive psychological elements that often develop from devastating life events. The article raises thought provoking questions about illusionary versus authentic viewpoints in relation to human strengths and negative motivations.

Item Three: Empirically Supported Treatments

The science and practice of empirically supported treatments.

Dobson, Keith S.; Johnston, Charlotte; Mikail, Samuel; Hunsley, John . (1999) The science and practice of empirically supported treatments. In Canadian Psychology.v.40(4) N'99 pg 316-319.

Synopsis: The authors discuss the matter of empirically supported treatments (ESTs) and endorse the viewpoint that the debate around ESTs is important. Furthermore, the authors support professional psychology progressing by basing training on the appropriate use of ESTs and ensuring that EST listings are comprehensive and of value to practitioners.

Class Activities

In addition to the exercises in the Workbook that accompanies this text, you may find the following in-class activities to be of value:

Activity #1: Reality Sets In

Start this activity by having students responding individually to the following question: What would you do if you could do anything you want with your life? Give students 10 to 15 minutes to respond to this question.

Next, have students work in groups of three or four to share their lists and see what they would do if they could do anything they want. Have the students work individually to make a list of what they think they will really achieve. Have them reform into their group of three or four and talk about why the difference between the two lists. Do some students have drastic differences between the two lists and others just minor changes? Have students discuss why the changes are major or minor. What does the degree of change reveal about the students?

Finally, have the students apply the knowledge gained from this exercise to the helping relationship.

Activity #2: Possibility Thinking

Have students form groups of three or four and ask them to think of all of the possible ways they could get a grade of "A" in the course. Encourage the students to be creative in their ideas (e.g., studying hard, forming a study group, cheating, meeting with the professor, having another student take the final exam for them, hacking into the college computer database and giving themselves a grade of "A".

Now have the students make choices as to which plan of action would be most appropriate based on their values, their fear of consequences, their desire to learn.

Have the student groups report out to the class their creative thinking to get an "A", how they choose the best possible actions, and what values and decision making process influenced their final choices.

Activity #3: A Book Review?

Divide the class into groups of three or four students in each group and then divide the chapter up such that each group has the approximate same number of pages to read and present to the class. Have the students summarize their assigned pages and present the information to the class. Have students ask each other questions about their section of the chapter and what they found to be the most significant points in their part of the chapter.

A creative addition to this activity is to provide each group with a piece of poster paper and several colored markers and ask them to represent their section of the chapter using pictures and symbols, but no words. This helps the students to really conceptualize the content of the chapter. Have the students present their poster paper work to the rest of the class with first asking the class to attempt to decipher the pictures and symbols and then explaining what the pictures and symbols represent. This activity truly helps the students engage and conceptualize the course content.

Videos

Brief Counseling in Action (1998, 45 min, NTSC, Insight Media). Two integrated videos demonstrate the principles, concept and techniques of brief counseling.

Narrative Therapy (1997, 55 min, NTSC, Insight Media). The major tenets of narrative therapy are examined by Ramon Corrales. The theory is applied in a demonstration of Corrales engaged in a session with a couple who are both entering a second marriage and dealing with the potential related complications.

Brief Counselling: Children and Adolescents (2000, 45 min, NTSC, Insight Media). Viewers of this video will experience two therapists employing brief strategies in relation to patients who act out.

An Introduction to Resiliency (1994, 60 min, NTSC, Insight Media). The seven types of resiliency: insight; independence; initiative; ability to form relationships; creativity; humour; and morality are defined and exemplified in this teaching video of how to recognise and foster resiliency.

Trauma and Meaning (1993, 38 min, NTSC, Insight Media). This video proposes that the real impact of trauma on victims may not be the event itself, but the degree to which a victim's beliefs are challenged by the trauma.

Websites

1. http://www.lankton.com/elements.htm
   Engaging clients.

2. http://www.allexperts.com/getExpert.asp?Category=2007
   How to get what you want in life.

3. http://www.psyc.leeds.ac.uk/staff/kenh/SSAALAY.HTM
   Effect of social support for sobriety(just as an example).

Overhead Transparencies

Starting on the next page are copies of recommended overhead transparencies. Please feel free to convert the following pages to overheads as this will enhance the lecture portion of your class presentation

GOALS NEED TO BE:

1. Stated as **outcomes** rather than activities.
2. **Specific** enough to be verifiable and to drive action.
3. **Substantive** and challenging.
4. Both **venturesome** and **prudent**.
5. **Realistic** in regard to resources needed to accomplish them.
6. **Sustainable** over a reasonable time period.
7. **Flexible** without being wishy-washy.
8. **Congruent** with the client's **values**.
9. Set in a reasonable **time frame**.

OH 16.1

POSITIVE AFFECT IN COPING

1. Positive reappraisal.

2. Problem-facing coping.

3. Infusing ordinary events with positive meaning.

OH 16.2

QUESTIONS FOR SHAPING GOALS

1. Is the goal stated in outcome or results language?

2. Is the goal specific enough to drive behavior? How will I know when I have accomplished it?

3. If I accomplish this goal, will it make a difference? Will it really help manage the problems and opportunities I have identified?

4. Does this goal have "bite" while remaining prudent?

OH 16.3A

QUESTIONS FOR SHAPING GOALS cont'd.

5. Is it doable?

6. Can I sustain this goal over the long haul?

7. Does this goal have some flexibility?

8. Is this goal in keeping with my values?

9. Have I set a realistic time frame for the accomplishment of the goal?

OH 16.3B

EVALUATION QUESTIONS FOR STEP II-B

1. To what degree am I helping clients choose specific goals from among a number of possibilities?

2. How well do I challenge clients to translate good intentions into broad goals and broad goals into specific, actionable goals?

3. To what extent do I help clients shape their goals so that they have the characteristics outlined in Box 16-1?

4. How effectively do I help clients establish goals that consider both needs and wants?

OH 16.4A

EVALUATION QUESTIONS
FOR STEP II-B cont'd.

5. To what degree do I help clients become aware of goals that are naturally emerging from the helping process?

6. How well do I help clients identify "real-option" goals when the future is both risky and uncertain?

7. How effectively do I help clients choose the right mix of adaptive and stretch goals?

8. How well do I help clients explore the consequences of the goals they are setting?

OH 16.4B

EVALUATION QUESTIONS FOR STEP II-B cont'd.

9. How do I help clients make a bias toward action one of their met goals?

OH 16.4C

Chapter Seventeen:

Step II-C:
Commitment - "What Am I Willing To Pay For What I Want?"

	Pages
Chapter Outline	476
Detailed Lecture Notes	477-484
Lecture Enhancers	485-486
Class Activities	487-488
Videos	489
Websites	490
Transparencies	491-501

CHAPTER SEVENTEEN OUTLINE

HELPING CLIENTS COMMIT THEMSELVES

- ➤ Help Clients Set Goals That Don't Cost More Than They Are Worth
- ➤ Help Clients Set Appealing Goals
- ➤ Help Clients Own the Goals They Set
- ➤ Help Clients Deal with Competing Agendas

GREAT EXPECTATIONS: CLIENT SELF-EFFICACY

STAGE II AND ACTION

THE SHADOW SIDE OF GOAL SETTING

EVALUATION QUESTIONS FOR STEP I-C

Detailed Lecture Notes

(Please note: The designation OH in the detailed lecture notes indicates an overhead transparency is available. Please locate the overhead transparencies in the final section of each chapter in this Instructors' Manual.)

Clients may formulate goals, but that does not mean that they are willing to pay for them. Once clients state what they want and set goals, the battle is joined, as it were. It is as if the client's "old self" or old lifestyle begins vying for resources with the client's potential "new self" or new lifestyle. Although the job of counselors is not to encourage clients to heroic efforts, counselors should not undersell clients, either. The job of the counselor is to help clients face up to their commitments.

Section One: HELPING CLIENTS COMMIT THEMSELVES TO A BETTER FUTURE (OH-17.1)

There is a difference between initial commitment to a goal and an ongoing commitment to a strategy or plan to accomplish the goal. The proof of initial commitment lies in goal-accomplishing action. There is a range of things you can do to help clients in their initial commitment to goals and the kind of action that is a sign of that commitment. Counselors can help clients by helping them make goals appealing, by helping them enhance their sense of ownership, and by helping them deal with competing agendas.

A. Help Clients Set Goals That Are Worth More Than They Cost.

1. Some goals that can be accomplished carry too high a cost in relation to their payoff.

2. Skilled counselors help clients budget rather than squander their resources — work, time, emotional energy.

3. Since it is often impossible to determine the cost-benefit ratio of any particular goal, counselors can add value by helping clients understand the consequences of choosing a particular goal.

4. Helping clients foresee the consequences of their choices may not be easy.

5. The balance-sheet methodology outlined in the Appendix is a tool you can use selectively to help clients weigh costs against benefits both in choosing goals and in choosing programs to implement goals. The balance sheet is also used in Chapter 19 to help clients choose best-fit strategies for accomplishing their goals.

B. Help Clients Set Appealing Goals.

1. Just because goals will help in managing a problem situation or develop an opportunity and are cost-effective does not mean that they will automatically appeal to the client.

2. Setting appealing goals is common sense, but it is not always easy to do.

3. An incentive is a promise of a reward. As such, incentives can contribute to developing a climate of hope around problem management and opportunity development.

4. Counselors need to help clients in their search for incentives throughout the helping process.

5. Negative goals — giving up something that is harmful — need to be translated into positive goals — getting something that is helpful.

C. Help Clients Embrace and Own the Goals They Set.

1. It is for clients to "own" the problems and unused opportunities they talk about.

2. It is also important for them to own the goals they set. It is essential that the goals chosen be the client's rather than the helper's goals or someone else's.

3. Various kinds of probes can be used to help clients discover what they want to do to manage some dimension of a problem situation more effectively.

4. Choosing goals suggested by others enables clients to blame others if they fail to reach the goals. Also if they simply follow other people's advice, they often fail to explore the down-the-road consequences.

5. Commitment to goals can take different forms.

   a) The least useful is mere *compliance*.
   b) *Buy-in* is a level up from compliance.
   c) *Ownership* is a higher form of commitment.

6. Self-contracts — that is, contracts that clients make with themselves — can also help clients commit themselves to new courses of action. Although contracts are

promises clients make to themselves to behave in certain ways and to attain certain goals, they are also ways of making goals more focused. It is not only the expressed or implied promise that helps but also the explicitness of the commitment.

7. In counseling, contracts are not legal documents but human instruments to be used if they are helpful. They often provide both the structure and the incentives some clients need.

D. Help Clients Deal with Competing Agendas.

Clients often set goals and formulate programs for constructive change without taking into account competing agendas — other things in their lives that soak up time and energy, such as job, family, and leisure pursuits. The world is filled with distractions.

1. Programs for constructive change often involve a rearrangement of priorities. If a client is to be a full partner in the reinvention of his marriage, then he cannot spend as much time with the boys.

2. Sometimes clients have to choose between right and right.

3. This is a question of balance, not frivolity.

4. There is no such thing as a perfect contract. Most people don't think through the consequences of all the provisions of a contract, whether it be marriage, employment, or self-contracts designed to enhance a client's commitment to goals.

5. Even people of goodwill unknowingly add covert codicils to contracts they make with themselves and others .

6. The codicils are buried deep in the decision-making process and only gradually make their way to the surface.

7. Box 17-1 indicates the kinds of questions you can help clients ask themselves about their commitment to their change agendas.

Section Two: GREAT EXPECTATIONS: CLIENT SELF-EFFICACY: "I CAN, I WILL"

The role of expectations in life is being explored more broadly, more deeply, and more practically (Kirsch, 1999). Clients need to find the motivation to seize their goals and run with them. The more they find their motivation within themselves the better. "Self-regulation" is the ideal. Helping clients choose goals, development commitment to them, and develop a sense of agency and assertiveness (Galassi & Bruch, 1992) are part of the self-regulation picture. Expectations, whether "great" or not, are also part of the self-regulation picture. Here we look at client expectations through the lens of "self-efficacy" (Bandura, 1986, 1989, 1991, 1995; 1997; Cervone, 2000; Cervone & Scott, 1995; Lightsey, Jr., 1996; Locke & Latham, 1990; Maddux, 1995; Schwarzer, 1992). Self-efficacy is an extremely useful concept when it comes to constructive change.

A. The Nature of Self-Efficacy

1. As Bandura (1995, p. 2) notes, "Perceived self-efficacy refers to beliefs in one's capabilities to organize and execute the courses of action required to manage prospective situations.

2. Efficacy beliefs influence how people think, feel, motivate themselves, and act." People's expectations of themselves and can-do beliefs have a great deal to do with their willingness to put forth effort to cope with difficulties, the amount of effort they will expend, and their persistence in the face of obstacles.

3. Clients with higher self-efficacy will make bolder choices, moving from adaptation toward stretch goals.

4. Clients tend to take action if two conditions are fulfilled:

   a) **Outcome Expectations**. Clients tend to act if they see that their actions will most likely lead to certain desirable results or accomplishments.

   b) **Self-Efficacy Beliefs**. People tend to act if they are reasonably sure that they have the wherewithal — for instance, working knowledge, skill, time, stamina, guts and other resources — to successfully engage in the kind of behavior that will lead to the desired outcomes.

5. Outcome expectations and self-efficacy beliefs are factors, not just in helping, but in everyday life.

6. Do an internet search around the term Outcome expectations and you will find a rich literature covering all facets of life, for instance, applications to education (Lopez, Lent, Brown, and Gore, 1997; Multon, Brown, & Lent, 1991; Smith & Nadya, 1999; Zimmerman, 1996) health care (O'Leary, 1985; Schwarzer & Fuchs, 1995), physical rehabilitation (Altmaier, Russell, Kao, Lehmann, & Weinstein, 1993); and work (Donnay & Borgen, 1999).

B. Helping Clients Develop Self-Efficacy (OH-17.2)

People's sense of self-efficacy can be strengthened in a variety of ways (see Mager, 1992).

1. **Skills.** *Make sure that clients have the skills they need to perform desired tasks.* Self-efficacy is based on ability and the conviction that I can use this ability to get a task done.

2. **Corrective feedback.** *Provide feedback that is based on deficiencies in performance, not on deficiencies in the client's personality.* Corrective feedback can help clients develop a sense of self-efficacy because it helps clear away barriers to the use of resources. If corrective feedback sounds like an attack on clients' personalities, they will suffer a drop in their sense of self-efficacy. When you give feedback to clients, you would do well to ask yourself, "In what ways will this feedback help them increase their sense of self-efficacy?"

3. **Positive feedback.** *Provide positive feedback and make it as specific as corrective feedback.* Positive feedback strengthens clients' self-efficacy by emphasizing their strengths and reinforcing what they do well. This is especially true when it is specific. Too often negative feedback is very detailed, while positive feedback is perfunctory — "nice job." This and other throw-away phrases probably sound like cliches. The formula for giving specific positive feedback goes something like this. "Here's what you did. Here's the positive outcome it had. And here's the wider upbeat impact." Clients need to interpret feedback as information they need to accomplish a task.

4. **Using success as a reinforcer.** *Challenge clients to engage in actions that produce positive results.* Even small successes can increase a client's sense of self efficacy. Success is reinforcing. Often success in a small endeavor will give clients the courage to try something more difficult. Make sure, however, that the link between success and increased self-confidence is forged. A series on successes on its own does not necessarily increase the strength of a client's self-efficacy beliefs. Success has to be linked to a sense of increased competence.

5. **Models.** *Help clients increase their own sense of self-efficacy by learning from others.* Learning makes clients more competent and increases their self-efficacy.

6. **Providing encouragement**. *Support clients' self-efficacy beliefs without being patronizing.* However, if your support is to increase clients' sense of self-efficacy, your support must be real and what you support in them must be real. Encouragement and support must be tailored to each client and in each instance. A supportive remark to one client might sound patronizing to another.**Reducing fear and anxiety.** *Help clients overcome their fears.* Fear blocks clients' sense of self-efficacy. If clients fear that they will fail, they will be reluctant to act. Therefore, procedures that reduce fear and anxiety help heighten their sense of self-efficacy.

Section Three: STAGE II AND ACTION

A. The work of Step II-A — developing possibilities for a better future — is just what some clients need. It frees them from thinking solely about problem situations and unused resources and enables them to begin fashioning a better future. Once they identify some of their wants and needs and consider a few possible goals, they move into action.

B. For other clients Step II-B is the trigger for action. Shaping goals helps them see the future in a very different way. Once they have a clear idea of just what they want or need, they go for it.

C. For still other clients, the search for incentives for commitment is the trigger for action. Once they see what's in it "for me" — a kind of upbeat and productive selfishness, if you will — they move into action.

Section Four: THE SHADOW SIDE OF GOAL SETTING

A.   Some helpers and clients seem to conspire to avoid goal setting as an explicit process.

1.   As Bandura (1990, p. xii) put it, "Despite this unprecedented level of empirical support [for the advantages of goal setting], goal theory has not been accorded the prominence it deserves in mainstream psychology."

2.   One of the main reasons that counselors do not help clients develop realistic life-enhancing goals is that they are not trained to do so.

3.   Some clients see goal setting as very rational, perhaps too rational. Their lives are so messy and goal setting seems so sterile. Both helpers and clients object to this overly rational approach. There is a dilemma.

4.   Many clients need or would benefit by a rigorous application of the problem-management process, including goal setting. On the other, they resist its rationality and discipline. They find it alien.

5.   Goal setting means that clients have to move out of the relatively safe harbor of discussing problem situations and of exploring the possible roots of those problems in the past and move into the uncharted waters of the future. This may be uncomfortable for client and helper alike.

6.   Clients who set goals and commit themselves to them move beyond the victim-of-my-problems game. Victimhood and self-responsibility make poor bedfellows.

7.   Goal setting involves clients' placing demands on themselves, making decisions, committing themselves, and moving to action.

8. Goals, though liberating in many respects, also hem clients in.

9. There is some truth in the ironic statement "There is only one thing worse than not getting what you want, and that's getting what you want." The responsibilities accompanying getting what you want — a drug-free life, a renewed marriage, custody of the children, a promotion, the peace and quiet of retirement, freedom from an abusing husband — often open up a new set of problems.

10. Even good solutions create new problems. It is one thing for parents to decide to give their children more freedom; it is another thing for them to watch them use that freedom.

11. Finally, there is a phenomenon called post-decisional depression. Once choices are made, clients begin to have second thoughts that often keep them from acting on their decisions.

As to action, some clients move into action too quickly.

1. The focus on the future liberates them from the past, and the first few possibilities are very attractive.

2. They fail to get the kind of focus and direction provided by Step II-B. Failing to weigh alternatives and shape goals often means that they have to do the process all over again.

B. Effective helpers know what lurks in the shadows of goal setting both for themselves and for their clients and are prepared to manage their own part of it and help clients manage theirs.

1. The answer to all of this lies in helpers' being trained in the entire problem-management process and in their sharing a picture of the entire process with the client.

2. Then goal setting, described in the client's language, will be a natural part of the process.

3. Artful helpers weave goal setting, under whatever name, into the flow of helping.

4. They do so by moving easily back and forth among the stages and steps of the helping process even in brief therapy.

BOX 17-1
Questions on Client Commitment (OH-17.3)

You can help clients ask themselves these kinds of questions as they struggle with committing themselves to a program of constructive change:

➢ What is my state of readiness for change in this area at this time?
➢ How badly do I want what I say I want?
➢ How hard am I willing to work?
➢ To what degree am I choosing this goal freely?
➢ How highly do I rate the personal appeal of this goal?
➢ How do I know I have the courage to work on this?
➢ What's pushing me to choose this goal?
➢ What incentives do I have for pursuing this change agenda?
➢ What rewards can I expect if I work on this agenda?
➢ If this goal is in any way being imposed by others, what am I doing to make it my own?
➢ What difficulties am I experiencing in committing myself to this goal?
➢ In what way is it possible that my commitment is not a true commitment?
➢ What can I do to get rid of the disincentives and overcome the obstacles?
➢ What can I do to increase my commitment?
➢ In what ways can the goal be reformulated to make it more appealing?
➢ To what degree is the timing for pursuing this goal poor?
➢ What do I have to do to stay committed?
➢ What resources can help me?

Evaluation Questions for Step II-C (OH-17.4)

➢ What do I need to do to help clients commit themselves to a better future?
➢ What do I do to make sure that the goals the client is setting are really his or her goals and not mine or those of a third party?
➢ How effectively do I help clients examine the benefits of goals they are choosing as measured against the costs?
➢ In what ways do I help clients focus on the appealing dimensions of the goals being set?
➢ How effectively do I perceive and deal with the misgivings clients have about the goals they are formulating?
➢ To what degree do I help clients enter into self-contracts with respect to the accomplishment of goals?
➢ What am I doing to help clients identify, explore, and manage competing agendas?
➢ What do I do to help clients move to initial goal-accomplishing action?
➢ What do I do to help clients acquire and increase their sense of self-efficacy?

Lecture Enhancers

You should be able to find the full text of the following items in your library or by using your web-based library access tool of choice (e.g., Psycinfo)

Item One: Making Therapy Work

How Clients Make Therapy Work

Strano, Donald A. (2000) How Clients Make Therapy Work (Book Review). Found in Family Journal, Apr. 2000, Vol. 8 Issue 2, p208, 1p
Refers to How Clients Make Therapy Work (1999). A. C. Bohart and K. Tallman, Washington, DC: American Psychological Association.

Synopsis: Strano's review of Bohart and Tallman's, *How Clients Make Therapy Work,* provides a great overview of the client's perspective of therapy, which by definition means two whole persons in a dialogue or sharing a collaborative process.   Four basic tenets based on a problem solving model are outlined: (1) the client is a change agent; (2) client self-healing transcends techniques or approach; (3) clients are generative (4) clients actively participate in therapy--thinking and constructing meaning. The therapist's role in the collaborative process is more pragmatic and provides education, resources, and support.

Item Two: Validate Treatment

Realpolitik and the empirically validated treatment debate.

King, Michael C . (1999) Realpolitik and the empirically validated treatment debate. In Canadian Psychology v.40(4) N'99 pg 306-308.

Synopsis: King's article praises authors who have done an outstanding job of summarizing the contentious debate around the empirically validated treatment initiative and the effect it may have on training, credentialing, practice, and service funding in both the United States and Canada. In his commentary, King expands on the directions for practice in Canada and asserts that these directions are quite similar to several occurring in the U.S. context.

Item Three: Empirically Supported Treatment

Empirically supported psychological treatments: a natural extension of the scientist-practitioner paradigm.

Morin, Charles M. (1999) Empirically supported psychological treatments: a natural extension of the scientist-practitioner paradigm. In Canadian Psychology. V.40(4) N'99 pg.312-315

Synopsis: Morin provides a review of the paper by Hunsley, Dobson, Johnston and Mikail that provides a summary of a recent initiative from Division 12 (Clinical) of the American Psychological Association (APA) to identify and disseminate psychosocial treatments with adequate empirical support. Morin considers the paper an excellent working document that provides a balanced coverage of the for and the against debate on this initiative and considers the recommendations to be reasonable. Morin questions why the initiative is inevitable and necessary and provides his opinion.

Class Activities

In addition to the exercises in the Workbook that accompanies this text, you may find the following in-class activities to be of value:

Activity #1: Commitment

In this activity students are encouraged to think of times in life that they really wanted something (e.g., a car, a vacation, a prize) and what they had to do to get what they wanted. In groups of three or four, have students share what it is they wanted and how they obtained or achieved it. Have them be very specific in what it took to get what they wanted. Have the group list all the specific behaviors and actions it took to obtain what they wanted.

Now ask the students to relate their actions and behaviors to the concept of commitment. Have them relate commitment to achieving goals in their own lives. Finally, have the students relate their personal experiences with commitment to the helping process.

Activity #2: Commitment or Luck

Give the students the stories of three great achievers in our society (e.g., athletes, founders of successful companies, successful counselors).

Next have the students form groups of three and four and have them make a list of what they think make the individuals successful. Encourage them to be as creative in their thinking as to why the people in the examples you provide became successful. Once the students have made a list of at least ten to fifteen items as to why the successful person achieved success, have them go down the list and put a big "C" next to the items that took commitment and a big "L" next to the items that were simply lucky (e.g., hard work takes commitment and opening your store in a section of town that grows rapidly may be luck).

Finally have the students tally the number of "Cs" they have and the number of "Ls" they have. Do a class total. If they "Cs" greatly outnumber the "Ls" you can make the point that commitment is usually what it takes to achieve goals. If the "Ls" are more common, you may want to discuss why students attribute achievement to luck more than commitment and what this may do to their approach to helping clients achieve goals. Usually the "Cs" greatly out number the "Ls" and the latter discussion is not needed.

Activity #3: Sacrifices, Sacrifices, Sacrifices

Ask students to pick a major goal in their life (e.g., become a professional counselor) and then have them list what it will take to achieve their goals.

Next have the students list what they are giving up to achieve their goals (i.e., what economists call "opportunity costs") and have them discuss how they feel about giving up the "opportunity" costs to achieve their goals. Have them report out in groups of three how they can justify the lost opportunities to achieve the goals.

Finally, have them justify the sacrifices they are making to achieve their desired goals. Ask them to identify the values that are reflected in their justification. Ask them to relate this knowledge to the helping relationship.

Videos

Critical Thinking and Human Emotions (1990, 60 min, NTSC, Insight Media). This video explores the cause and effect relationship of poor thinking to negative emotions.

Consciousness and the Brain (1998, 90 min, NTSC, Insight Media). With a foundation in recent neurobiological research, this video illustrates how the human mind learns and understands with a focus on seeing, concentrating, feeling hunger, and processing information. The contrast between scientific and popular definitions of consciousness is also discussed.

Emotions, Health, and Intelligence (1996, 210 min, NTSC, Insight Media). The developing study of emotional intelligence is introduced through definition, explanation of how it is measured, and discussion of its implications for adaptive social functioning.

Motivating People in Today's Workplace (180 min, NTSC, Insight Media). This teaching video explores the use of internal motivators and external rewards to inspire the involvement, enthusiasm, and productivity of individuals. Further, the presentation explains how to develop incentive plans and how to remove "demotivators."

Behavior and Motivation (1992, 21 min, NTSC, Insight Media). This video uses the theories of Maslow and Herzberg to describe the basic nature of human behavior and motivation in relation to the workplace.

Websites

1. http://act.psy.cmu.edu/ACT/abstracts/Lovett_Anderson95-abs.html
   Selecting problem solving strategies.

2. http://www.itp.edu/programs/residential.html
   The residential program.

Overhead Transparencies

Starting on the next page are copies of recommended overhead transparencies. Please feel free to convert the following pages to overheads as this will enhance the lecture portion of your class presentation

HELPING CLIENTS COMMIT THEMSELVES

1. Help Clients Set Goals That Don't Cost More Than They Are Worth

2. Help Clients Set Appealing Goals

3. Help Clients Own the Goals They Set

4. Help Clients Deal with Competing Agendas

OH 17.1

HELPING CLIENTS DEVELOP SELF-EFFICACY

1. Make sure that clients have the skills they need to perform desired tasks.

2. Provide feedback that is based on deficiencies in performance, not on deficiencies in the client's personality.

3. Provide positive feedback and make it as specific as corrective feedback

OH 17.2A

HELPING CLIENTS
DEVELOP SELF-EFFICACY
cont'd.

4. Challenge clients to engage in actions that produce positive results.

5. Help clients increase their own sense of self-efficacy by learning from others.

6. Support clients self-efficacy beliefs without being patronizing.

7. Help clients overcome their fears.

OH 17.2B

QUESTIONS ON CLIENT COMMITMENT

1. What is my state of readiness for change in this area at this time?

2. How badly do I want what I say I want?

3. How hard am I willing to work?

4. To what degree am I choosing this goal freely?

5. How highly do I rate the personal appeal of this goal?

OH 17.3A

QUESTIONS ON CLIENT COMMITMENT cont'd.

6. How do I know I have the courage to work on this?

7. What's pushing me to choose this goal?

8. What incentives do I have for pursuing this change agenda?

9. What rewards can I expect if I work on this agenda?

10. If this goal is in any way being imposed by others, what am I doing to make it my own?

OH 17.3B

QUESTIONS ON CLIENT COMMITMENT cont'd.

11. What difficulties am I experiencing in committing myself to this goal?

12. In what way is it possible that my commitment is not a true commitment?

13. What can I do to get rid of the disincentives and overcome the obstacles?

14. What can I do to increase my commitment?

OH 17.3C

QUESTIONS ON CLIENT COMMITMENT cont'd.

15. In what ways can the goal be reformulated to make it more appealing?

16. To what degree is the timing for pursuing this goal poor?

17. What do I have to do to stay committed?

18. What resources can help me?

OH 17.3D

EVALUATION QUESTIONS FOR STEP II-C

1. **What do I need to do to help clients commit themselves to a better future?**

2. **What do I do to make sure that the goals the client is setting are really his or her goals and not mine or those of a third party?**

3. **How effectively do I help clients examine the benefits of goals they are choosing as measured against the costs?**

4. **In what ways do I help clients focus on the appealing dimensions of the goals being set?**

OH 17.4A

EVALUATION QUESTIONS FOR STEP II-C cont'd.

5. How effectively do I perceive and deal with the misgivings clients have about the goals they are formulating?

6. To what degree do I help clients enter into self-contracts with respect to the accomplishment of goals?

7. What am I doing to help clients identify, explore, and manage competing agendas?

OH 17.4B

EVALUATION QUESTIONS FOR STEP II-C cont'd.

8. What do I do to help clients move to initial goal-accomplishing action?

9. What do I do to help clients acquire and increase their sense of self-efficacy?

OH 17.3C

Chapter Eighteen:

Step III-A:
Action Strategies:
"How Many Ways Are There To Get
What I Need and Want?"

	Pages
Chapter Outline	**503**
Detailed Lecture Notes	**504-511**
Lecture Enhancers	**512**
Class Activities	**513-514**
Videos	**515**
Websites	**516**
Transparencies	**517-523**

CHAPTER EIGHTEEN OUTLINE

INTRODUCTION TO STAGE III

MANY DIFFERENT PATHS TO GOALS

➤ Help Clients Brainstorm Strategies for Accomplishing Goals
➤ Develop Frameworks for Stimulating Clients' Thinking about Strategies

"WHAT SUPPORT DO I NEED TO WORK FOR WHAT I WANT?"

"WHAT WORKING KNOWLEDGE AND SKILLS WILL HELP ME GET WHAT I NEED AND WANT?"

LINKING STRATEGIES TO ACTION

EVALUATION QUESTIONS FOR STEP III-A

Detailed Lecture Notes

(Please note: The designation OH in the detailed lecture notes indicates an overhead transparency is available. Please locate the overhead transparencies in the final section of each chapter in this Instructors' Manual.)

Section One: INTRODUCTION TO STAGE III (OH-18.1)

Planning in its broadest sense includes all the steps of Stages II and III. In a narrower sense, planning deals with identifying, choosing, and organizing the strategies needed to accomplish goals. Whereas Stage II is about outcomes — goals or accomplishments "powerfully imagined" — Stage III is about the activities or the work needed to produce those outcomes.

A. Clients, when helped to explore what is going wrong in their lives, often ask, "Well, what should I do about it?" That is, they focus on actions they need to take in order to "solve" things.

    1. Action, though essential, is valuable only to the degree that it leads to problem-managing and opportunity-developing outcomes.

    2. Accomplishments or outcomes, also essential, are valuable only to the degree that they have a constructive impact on the life of the client.

    3. Stage III has three steps, in our usual definition of step. They are all aimed at action on the part of the client.

        a) **Step III-A: Strategies**. Help clients develop possible strategies for accomplishing their goals. "What kind of actions will help me get what I need and want?"

        b) **Step III-B: Best-Fit Strategies**. Help clients choose strategies tailored to their preferences and resources. "What actions are best for me?"

        c) **Step III-C: Plans**. Help clients formulate actionable plans. "What should my campaign for constructive change look like? What do I need to do first? Second? Third?"

4. Stage III, highlighted in Figure III, adds the final pieces to a client's planning a program for constructive change. Stage III deals with the "game plan." However, these three "steps" constitute *planning* for action and should not be confused with action itself. Without action, a program for constructive change is nothing more than a wish list.

FIGURE III
The Helping Model — Stage III

B. Strategies are actions that help clients accomplish their goals.

1. Clients who feel hemmed in by their problems and unsure of the viability of their goals are liberated through this process.

2. Clients who see clear pathways to their goals have a greater sense of self-efficacy. "I can do this."

3. Strategy is the art of identifying and choosing realistic courses of action for achieving goals and doing so under adverse conditions, such as war.

4. The problem situations in which clients are immersed constitute adverse conditions; clients often are at war with themselves and the world around them.

5. Helping clients develop strategies to achieve goals can be a most thoughtful, humane, and fruitful way of being with them. This step in the counseling process is another that helpers sometimes avoid because it is too "technological." They do their clients a disservice.

6. Clients with goals but no clear idea of how to accomplish them are still at sea.

Section Two: MANY DIFFERENT PATHS TO GOALS

Once more it is a question of helping clients stimulate their imaginations and engage in divergent thinking. Most clients do not instinctively seek different routes to goals and then choose the ones that make most sense.

A. Help Clients Brainstorm Strategies for Accomplishing Goals

1. Brainstorming plays an important part in strategy development. The more routes to the achievement of a goal, the better.

2. One of the reasons that clients are clients is that they are not very creative in looking for ways of getting what they want.

3. Once goals are established, getting them accomplished is not just a matter of hard work. It is also a matter of imagination.

4. If a client is having a difficult time coming up with strategies, the helper can "prime the pump" by offering a few suggestions. Driscoll (1984, p.167) put it well.

> Alternatives are best sought cooperatively, by inviting our clients to puzzle through with us what is or is not a more practical way to do things. But we must be willing to introduce the more practical alternatives ourselves, for clients are often unable to do so on their own. Clients who could see for themselves the more effective alternatives would be well on their way to using them. That clients do not act more expediently already is in itself a good indication that they do not know how to do so.

5. Although the helper may need to suggest alternatives, he or she can do so in such a way that the principal responsibility for evaluating and choosing possible strategies stays with the client. For instance, there is the "prompt and fade" technique.

   a) The counselor can say, "Here are some possibilities.... Let's review them and see whether any of them make sense to you or suggest further possibilities." Or, "Here are some of the things that people with this kind of problem situation have tried.... How do they sound to you?"

   b) The "fade" part of this technique keeps it from being advice giving. It remains clear that the client must think these strategies over, choose the right ones, and commit to them.

B. Develop Frameworks for Stimulating Clients' Thinking about Strategies (OH-18.2)

How can helpers find the right probes to help clients develop a range of strategies? Simple frameworks can help. You can use probes and prompts to help clients discover possible strategies by helping them investigate resources in their lives, including people, models, communities, places, things, organizations, programs, and personal resources.

1. **Individuals.** What individuals might help clients achieve their goals?

2. **Models and exemplars.** Who is presently doing what the client wants to do?

3. **Communities.** What communities of people are there through which clients might identify strategies for implementing their goals?

4. **Places.** Are there particular places that might help?

5. **Things.** What things exist that can help clients achieve their goals?

6. **Organizations.** Are there any organizations that are established to deal with this issue?

7. **Programs.** Are there any ready-made programs for people in the client's position?

C. Box 18-1 outlines some questions that you can help clients ask themselves to develop strategies for accomplishing goals.

Section Three: "WHAT SUPPORT DO I NEED TO WORK FOR WHAT I WANT?"

A Step III-A can also be seen as helping clients get the resources, both internal and environmental, they need to pursue goals. Many clients do not know how to mobilize needed resources.

A. One of the most important resources is social support.

1. A great deal is said in the literature about the kind of support helpers should provide their clients (Alford & Beck, 1997; Arkowitz, 1997; Castonguay, 1997; Yalom & Bugental, 1997).

2. Robert Putnam (2000) provides a great deal of evidence indicating that such support may not always be easy to find. His central thesis is that in North American society the supply of "social capital" — both informal social connectedness and formal civic engagement — has fallen dangerously low.

3. Putnam shows that we belong to fewer organizations that meet, know our neighbors less, meet with friends less frequently, and even socialize with our families less often. This is the environment in which clients must do the work of constructive change.

4. Social support is a key element in change (see Basic Behavioral Science Task Force of the National Advisory Mental Health Council, 1996, p. 628).

> Social support has... been examined as a predictor of the course of mental illness. In about 75% of studies with clinically depressed patients, social-support factors increased the initial success of treatment and helped patients maintain their treatment gains. Similarly, studies of people with schizophrenia or alcoholism revealed that higher levels of social support are correlated with fewer relapses, less frequent hospitalizations, and success and maintenance of treatment gains.

5. In a study on weight loss and maintaining the loss (Wing & Jeffery, 1999) client who enlisted the help of friends were much more successful than clients who took the solo path. This is called "social facilitation" and is quite different from dependence.

6. Social facilitation, a positive psychology approach, is energizing, while dependence is often depressing. Therefore, a culture of social isolation does not bode well for clients.

7. All of this reinforces what we already know through common sense. Which of us has not been helped through difficult times by family and friends?

B. When it comes to social support, there are two categories of clients. There are those who lead an impoverished social life, and those that have a social system.

   1. The objective with this group is to help them find social resources, to get back into community in some productive way.

   2. Putnam points out, even when clients, at least on paper, have a social system, they may not use it very effectively.

   3. This provides counselors with a different challenge, that is, helping clients tap into those human resources in a way that helps them manage problem situations more effectively.

   4. Indeed, the National Advisory Mental Health Council study just mentioned showed that people who are highly distressed and therefore most in need of social support may be the least likely to receive it because their expressions of distress drive away potential supporters.

5. Distressed clients can be helped to learn how to modulate their expressions of distress.

6. Potential supporters can learn how to deal with distressed friends and colleagues, even when they let themselves become whiners.

7. The Task Force study suggested two general strategies for fostering social support:

    a) helping clients mobilize or increase support from existing social networks

    b) "grafting" new ties onto impoverished social networks.

8. It's important not only that people be available to provide support but also that those needing support perceive that it is available.

9. Effective helpers right from the beginning try to help them explore the social-support dimensions of problem situations.

10. At the Action Arrow stage, questions like the following are appropriate: "Who might help you do this? Who's going to challenge you when you want to give up? With whom can you share these kinds of concerns? Who's going to give you a pat on the back when you accomplish your goal?"

11. Effective helpers build some kind of resource census into the helping process.

Section Four: "WHAT WORKING KNOWLEDGE AND SKILLS WILL HELP ME GET WHAT I NEED AND WANT?"

A. It often happens that people get into trouble or fail to get out of it because they lack the needed life skills or coping skills to deal with problem situations.

1. Helping clients find ways of learning the life skills they need to cope more effectively is an important broad strategy.

2. The use of skills training as part of therapy — what Carkhuff years ago (1971) called "training as treatment" — might be essential for some clients.

3. Challenging clients to engage in activities for which they don't have the skills is compounding rather than solving the problem.

4. What kinds of working knowledge and skills does this client need to get where he or she wants to go?

B. The literature is filled with programs designed to equip clients with the working knowledge and skills they need to manage problems and lead a fuller life. Some of them focus on specific problems.

1. Deffenbacher and his associates (Deffenbacher, Thwaites, Wallace, & Oetting, 1994; Deffenbacher, Oetting, Huff, & Thwaites, 1995) have devised and evaluated programs for general anger reduction. Although programs such as these need to be tailored to individual clients, they are often gold mines of strategies for accomplishing goals.

Section Five: LINKING STRATEGIES TO ACTION

A. Although all the steps of the helping process can and should stimulate action on the part of the client, this is especially true of Step III-A, which deals with possible actions.
1. Many clients, once they begin to see what they can do to get what they want, begin acting immediately.

2. They don't need a formal plan.

BOX 18-1
Questions for Developing Strategies (OH-18.3)

➤ Now that I know what I want, what do I need to do?
➤ Now that I know my destination, what are the different routes for getting there?
➤ What actions will get me to where I want to go?
➤ Now that I know the gaps between what I have and what I want and need, what do I need to do to bridge those gaps?
➤ How many ways are there to accomplish my goals?
➤ How do I get started?
➤ What can I do right away?
➤ What do I need to do later?

Evaluation Questions for Step III-A (OH-18.4)

How effectively do I do the following?

- Use probes, prompts, and challenges to help clients identify possible strategies?
- Help clients engage in divergent thinking with respect to strategies?
- Help clients brainstorm as many ways as possible to accomplish their goals?
- Use some kind of framework in helping clients be more creative in identifying strategies?
- Help clients identify and begin to acquire the resources they need to accomplish their goals?
- Help clients identify and develop the skills they need to accomplish their goals?
- Help clients see the action implications of the strategies they identify?

Lecture Enhancers

You should be able to find the full text of the following items in your library or by using your web-based library access tool of choice (e.g., Psycinfo)

Item One: Stalkers, Serial Killers, and Other Sociopaths

Stalkers, Serial Killers, and Other Sociopaths: Dr. Park Dietz Explorers the Dark Side of the Mind.

Frank, Christina. (2000) Stalkers, Serial Killers, and Other Sociopaths: Dr. Park Dietz Explorers the Dark Side of the Mind. In Biography, Jun2000, Vol. 4 Issue 6, p82, 5p, 2c

Synopsis: This article profiles forensic psychiatrist Park Dietz including his career history, eduation, and criminal cases where he testified as an expert witness.

Item Two: Speaking of Education

Teaching Positive Psychology

Seligman, Martin E.P. (1999) Teaching Positive Psychology. In VOLUME 30 , NUMBER 7 July/August 1999. APA Home Page

Synopsis: Seligman shares the experience of his 1998 undergraduate seminar in positive psychology and includes textbook choice, assignments, and outcomes of the course.

Item Three: Existential Philosophy

The Impact of Existential Philosophy on Modern Psychology

Litt, Sheldon. (2000) The Impact of Existential Philosophy on Modern Psychology . Home page.

Synopsis: Litt challenges therapists to consider if their clients ever truly fit into "neat categories" or is the use of a diagnostic labels (that may not be a real match for the client's condition) a mere convenience for institutions, betraying the individuality of the client.

Class Activities

In addition to the exercises in the Workbook that accompanies this text, you may find the following in-class activities to be of value:

Activity #1: All Roads Lead to Rome

In this activity students are encouraged to think of times that they achieved a major goal. Have them share with each other in groups of three of four how they achieved their individual goals. Next, have each group member take the achieved goal of one of the group members and explain how the same goal could have been achieved in another way.

Next, move to a group brainstorm as to how many ways one goal can be achieved. Encourage them to move to the "thinking outside box" thought processes and get very creative in achieving their desired goals. It is helpful for students to realize how many ways there are to achieving the same goal.

Ask students to report to the class their most extreme examples of achieving the same goal in completely different ways. Ask the class to apply this activity to the helping process.

Activity #2: The Quick Way or the Right Way?

Give the students a goal to be completed (e.g., write a term paper, find a job, write a letter to a friend) and then ask the students list the quickest way to achieve the goal and the most appropriate way to achieve the goal. Push the students to list as many individual details to both approaches as possible..

Next have the students form groups of three and four and integrate their individual lists into one large list. Finally, have the groups compare the differences between the quick way and the right way.

After groups have constructed their individual group list, have them share their list with another group to see how similar their lists are. Have the students compare, contrast, and discuss their lists. What will become apparent is that not all are in agreement as to what is the quick way and what is the right way. Have the students then apply this knowledge to the helping relationship.

Activity #3: My Right - Your Right

Ask students to think of ways to end a relationship that is no longer desirable to them. Next, have them identify at least three different ways they would end the relationship based on a change in any or all of the following factors:

Age:

Race:

Gender:

Culture:

Political Orientation:

Religious Belief:

The point of the exercise is to help students realize that based on many factors, different clients will use different approaches to achieve the same goals. Have the students apply this knowledge to the helping relationship.

Videos

Erik Erikson: A Life's Work (1992, 38 min, NTSC, Insight Media). Viewers will experience interviews with Erik Erikson in relation to his theoretical principles and biopsychosocial model. Erikson's introduction of ethical perspectives into psychology is also discussed.

Behaviour Modification (1978, 45 min, NTSC, Insight Media). With a focus on helping people to overcome anxieties, break habits, and improve social skills, the techniques of behaviour modification are discussed in this video.

Cognitive-Behaviour Theory (1998, 100min, NTSC, Insight Media). An actual counselling session sets the stage to demonstrate how cognitive-behaviour theory involves learning to shape an individual's life through the modification of thoughts and behaviours.

A Guide to Rational Living: Albert Ellis (1988, 90 min, NTSC, Insight Media). This Albert Ellis interview examines the interelation of behaviour, emotion, and cognition and explains Ellis' approach to therapy.

Websites

1. http://ahpweb.org/aboutahp/whatis.html
   From Maslow to the 21st century.

2. www.apa.org
   The homepage of the American Psychological Association.

3. www.cpa.ca
   The homepage of the Canadian Psychological Association.

4. www.counseling.org
   The homepage of the American Counseling Association.

Overhead Transparencies

Starting on the next page are copies of recommended overhead transparencies. Please feel free to convert the following pages to overheads as this will enhance the lecture portion of your class presentation

STEPS OF STAGE III

1. Help clients develop possible strategies for accomplishing their goals.

2. Help clients choose strategies tailored to their preferences and resources.

3. Help clients formulate actionable plans.

OH 18.1

FRAMEWORKS FOR DEVELOPING STRATEGIES

1. Individuals.

2. Models and exemplars.

3. Communities.

4. Places.

5. Things.

6. Organizations.

7. Programs.

OH 18.2

QUESTIONS FOR DEVELOPING STRATEGIES

1. Now that I know what I want, what do I need to do?

2. Now that I know my destination, what are the different routes for getting there?

3. What actions will get me to where I want to go?

4. Now that I know the gaps between what I have and what I want and need, what do I need to do to bridge those gaps?

OH 18.3A

QUESTIONS FOR DEVELOPING STRATEGIES cont'd.

5. How many ways are there to accomplish my goals?

6. How do I get started?

7. What can I do right away?

8. What do I need to do later?

OH 18.3B

EVALUATION QUESTIONS FOR STEP III-A

How effectively do I do the following:

1. Use probes, prompts, and challenges to help clients identify possible strategies.

2. Help clients engage in divergent thinking with respect to strategies.

3. Help clients brainstorm as many ways as possible to accomplish their goals.

4. Use some kind of framework in helping clients be more creative in identifying strategies.

OH 18.4A

EVALUATION QUESTIONS FOR STEP III-A cont'd.

5. Help clients identify and begin to acquire the resources they need to accomplish their goals.

6. Help clients identify and develop the skills they need to accomplish their goals.

7. Help clients see the action implications of the strategies they identify.

OH 18.4B

Chapter Nineteen:

Step III-B:
Best-Fit Strategies:
"What Strategies Are Best For Me?"

	Pages
Chapter Outline	**525**
Detailed Lecture Notes	**526-532**
Lecture Enhancers	**533**
Class Activities	**534-535**
Videos	**536**
Websites	**537**
Transparencies	**538-544**

CHAPTER NINETEEN OUTLINE

WHAT'S BEST FOR ME? THE CASE OF BUD

HELPING CLIENTS CHOOSE BEST-FIT STRATEGIES

STRATEGY SAMPLING

A BALANCE-SHEET METHOD FOR CHOOSING STRATEGIES

➢   Benefits of Choosing the Residential Program
➢   Costs of Choosing the Residential Program
➢   Realism in Using the Balance Sheet

LINKING STEP III-B TO ACTION

THE SHADOW SIDE OF SELECTING STRATEGIES

EVALUATION QUESTIONS FOR STEP III-B

<table>
<tr><td>

Detailed Lecture Notes

</td></tr>
</table>

(Please note: The designation OH in the detailed lecture notes indicates an overhead transparency is available. Please locate the overhead transparencies in the final section of each chapter in this Instructors' Manual.)

Section One: "WHAT'S BEST FOR ME?" THE CASE OF BUD

A. In the last two steps of Stage III, clients are in decision-making mode once more. After brainstorming strategies for accomplishing goals, they need to choose one or more strategies (a "package") that best fit their situation and resources and turn them into some kind of plan for constructive change.

   1. Counselors, understanding the "technology" of planning, can add value by helping clients find ways of accomplishing goals (getting what they need and want) in a systematic, flexible, personalized, and cost-effective way.

   2. Step III-B discusses ways of helping clients choose the strategies that are best for them.

   3. Step III-C deals with turning those strategies into some kind of step-by-step plan.

   4. Some clients, once they are helped to develop a range of strategies to implement goals, move forward on their own; that is, they choose the best strategies, put together an action plan, and implement it.

   5. Others, however, need help in choosing strategies that best fit their situation, and so we add Step III-B to the helping process.

   6. It is useless to have clients brainstorm if they don't know what to do with all the action strategies they generate.

B. The case of Bud, a man who was helped to discover two best-fit strategies for achieving emotional stability in his life. With these he achieved outcomes that surpassed anyone's wildest expectations.

>   One morning, Bud, then 18 years old, woke up unable to speak or move. He was taken to a hospital, where catatonic schizophrenia was diagnosed. After repeated admissions to

hospitals, where he underwent both drug and electroconvulsive therapy (ECT), his diagnosis was changed to paranoid schizophrenia. He was considered incurable.

A quick overview of Bud's earlier years suggests that much of his emotional distress was caused by unmanaged life problems and the lack of human support. There was simply too much stress and change in his life. He protected himself by withdrawing. He was flooded with feelings of loss, fear, rage, and abandonment.

In the hospital Bud became convinced that he and many of his fellow patients could do something about their illnesses. Somehow Bud, using his own inner resources, managed to get out of the hospital. Eventually, he got a job, found a partner, and got married.

Bud's broad goal was still emotional stability, and he wanted to do whatever was necessary to achieve it. Finding human support and helping others cope with their problems, instrumental goals, were his best strategies for achieving the stability he wanted.

Outside, Bud started a self-help group for ex-patients like himself. In the group, he was a full-fledged participant. Sandra, a social worker, also coached Bud's wife on how to provide support for him at times of stress. As to helping others, Bud not only founded a self-help group but also turned it into a network of self-help groups for ex-patients.

This is an amazing example of a client who focused on one broad goal, emotional stability; translated it into a number of immediate, practical goals; discovered two broad strategies — finding ongoing emotional support and helping others — for accomplishing those goals; translated the strategies into practical applications; and by doing all that found the emotional stability he was looking for.

Section Two: HELPING CLIENTS CHOOSE BEST-FIT STRATEGIES (OH-19.1)

The criteria for choosing goal-accomplishing strategies are somewhat like the criteria for choosing goals outlined in Step II-B.

A. Strategies to achieve goals should be, like goals themselves, specific, robust, prudent, realistic, sustainable, flexible, cost-effective, and in keeping with the client's values.

1. **Specific strategies.** Strategies for achieving goals should be specific enough to drive behavior.

2. **Substantive strategies.** Strategies are robust to the degree that they challenge the client's resources and, when implemented, actually achieve the goal.

3. **Realistic strategies.** If clients choose strategies that are beyond their resources, they are doing themselves in. Strategies are realistic when they can be carried out with the resources the client has, are under the client's control, and are unencumbered by obstacles. There is, of course, a difference between realism and allowing clients to sell themselves short. Robust strategies that make clients stretch for a valued goal can be most rewarding.

4. **Strategies in keeping with the client's values.** Make sure that the strategies chosen are consistent with the client's values. Counselors help clarify and challenge values but made no attempt to impose their own values on the client.

B. Box 19-1 outlines the kinds of questions you can help clients answer as they choose best-fit strategies.

Section Three: STRATEGY SAMPLING

A. Some clients find it easier to choose strategies if they first sample some of the possibilities.
B. Some clients could use strategy sampling as a way of putting off action.

Section Four: A BALANCE-SHEET METHOD FOR CHOOSING STRATEGIES

Some form of balance sheet can be used to help clients make decisions in general. The methodology could be used for any key decision related to the helping process — whether to get help in the first place, to work on one problem rather than another, or to choose this rather than that goal. Balance sheets deal with the acceptability and unacceptability of both benefits and costs.

A.   Benefits of Choosing the Residential Program.

1. What are the benefits of choosing this strategy? for myself? for significant others?

2. To what degree are these benefits acceptable? to me? to significant others?

3. In what ways are these benefits unacceptable? to me? to significant others?

B.   Costs of Choosing the Residential Program

1. What are the costs of choosing this strategy? for myself? for significant others?

2. To what degree are these costs acceptable? to me? to significant others?

3. In what ways are these costs unacceptable? to me? to significant others?

C. Realism in Using the Balance Sheet

1. The balance sheet is not to be used with every client to work out the pros and cons of every course of action.

2. Tailor the balance sheet to the needs of the client.

3. Choose the parts of the balance sheet that will add most value with *this* client pursuing *this* goal or set of goals.

4. One of the best uses of the balance sheet is not to use it directly at all. Keep it in the back of your mind whenever clients are making decisions. Use it as a filter to listen to clients.

5. Then turn relevant parts of it into probes to help clients focus on issues they may be overlooking. "How will this decision affect the significant people in your life?" is a probe that originates in the balance sheet. "Is there any downside to that strategy?" might help a client who is being a bit too optimistic.

6. No formula.

Section Five: LINKING STEP III-B TO ACTION

A. Some clients are filled with great ideas for getting things done but never seem to do anything.

1. They lack the discipline to evaluate their ideas, choose the best, and turn them into action.

2. Often this kind of work seems too tedious to them, even though it is precisely what they need.

3. Strategies suggested to help people pursue broad goals of reducing mistrust of others' motives, reducing the frequency and intensity of such emotions as rage, anger, and irritation, and learning how to treat others with consideration (see Williams, 1989). included:

   a) Keeping a hostility log to discover the patterns of cynicism and irritation in one's life
   b) Finding someone to talk to about the problem, someone to trust
   c) "Thought stopping," catching oneself in the act of indulging in hostile thoughts or in thoughts that lead to hostile feelings
   d) Talking sense to oneself when tempted to put others down
   e) Developing empathic thought patterns — that is, walking in the other person's shoes
   f) Learning to laugh at one's own silliness

   g) Using a variety of relaxation techniques, especially to counter negative thoughts
   h) Finding ways of practicing trust
   i) Developing active listening skills
   j) Substituting assertive for aggressive behavior
   k) Getting perspective, seeing each day as one's last
   l) Practicing forgiving others without being patronizing or condescending

Section Six: THE SHADOW SIDE OF SELECTING STRATEGIES

A. The shadow side of decision making, discussed in Chapter 14, is certainly at work in clients' choosing strategies to implement goals.

   1. Goslin (1985, pp. 7, 9) put it well:

      > In defining a problem, people dislike thinking about unpleasant eventualities, have difficulty in assigning... values to alternative courses of action, have a tendency toward premature closure, overlook or undervalue long-range consequences, and are unduly influenced by the first formulation of the problem. In evaluating the consequences of alternatives, they attach extra weight to those risks that can be known with certainty. They are more subject to manipulation... when their own values are poorly thought through.... A major problem... for... individuals is knowing

when to search for additional information relevant to decisions.

2. In choosing courses of action, clients often fail to evaluate the risks involved and determine whether the risk is balanced by the probability of success.

3. Gelatt, Varenhorst, and Carey (1972) suggested four ways in which clients may try to deal with the factors of risk and probability: wishful thinking, playing it safe, avoiding the worst outcome, and achieving some kind of balance. The first three are often pursued without reflection and therefore lie in the "shadows." **(OH-19.2)**

   a) **Wishful thinking.** In this case, clients choose a course of action that might (they hope) lead to the accomplishment of a goal regardless of risk, cost, or probability. The wishful-thinking client operates blindly, engaging in some course of action without taking into account its usefulness. At its worst, this is a reckless approach. Clients who "work hard" and still "get nowhere" may be engaged in wishful thinking, persevering in using means they prefer but that are of doubtful efficacy. Effective helpers find ways of challenging wishful thinking.

   b) **Playing it safe.** In this case, the client chooses only safe courses of action, ones that have little risk and a high degree of probability of producing at least limited success.

   c) **Avoiding the worst outcome.** In this case, clients choose means that are likely to help them avoid the worst possible result. They try to minimize the maximum danger, often without identifying what that danger is.

   d) **Striking a balance.** In the ideal case, clients choose strategies for achieving goals that balance risks against the probability of success. This "combination" approach is the most difficult to apply, for it involves the right kind of analysis of problem situations and opportunities, choosing goals with the right edge, being clear about one's values, ranking a variety of strategies according to these values, and estimating how effective any given course of action might be. Even more to the point, it demands challenging the blind spots that might distort these activities. Since some clients have neither the skill nor the will for this combination approach, it is essential that their counselors help them engage in the kind of dialogue that will help them face up to this impasse.

BOX 19-1
Questions on Best-Fit Strategies (OH-19.3)

➢ Which strategies will be most useful in helping me get what I need and want?
➢ Which strategies are best for this situation?
➢ Which strategies best fit my resources?
➢ Which strategies will be most economic in the use of resources?
➢ Which strategies are most powerful?
➢ Which strategies best fit my preferred way of acting?
➢ Which strategies best fit my values?
➢ Which strategies will have the fewest unwanted consequences?

Evaluation Questions for Step III-B (OH-19.4)

How well am I doing the following as I try to help clients choose goal-accomplishing strategies that are best for them? How effective am I in:

➢ Helping clients choose strategies that are clear and specific, that best fit their capabilities, that are linked to goals, that have power, and that are suited to clients' styles and values?
➢ Helping clients engage in and benefit from strategy sampling?
➢ Helping clients in selected cases use the balance sheet as a way of choosing strategies by outlining the principal benefits and costs for self, others, and relevant social settings?
➢ Helping clients manage the shadow side of selecting courses of action — that is, wishful thinking, playing it too safe, focusing on avoiding the worst possible outcome rather than on getting what they want, and wasting time by trying to spell out a perfectly balanced set of strategies?
➢ Helping clients use the act of choosing strategies to stimulate problem-managing action?

Lecture Enhancers

You should be able to find the full text of the following items in your library or by using your web-based library access tool of choice (e.g., Psycinfo)

Item One: Domestic abuse and violence.

Wife rape: Understanding the response of survivors and service providers.

Sage Family Studies Abstracts, Feb.99, Vol. 21 Issue 1, p97, 1/3. Review of Bergen, Raquel Kennedy. (1996) Wife rape: Understanding the response of survivors and service providers. Thousand Oaks, CA: Sage Publications, 1996, 179 pp., tables, appendices.

Synopsis: Sage Family Studies Abstracts provides an abstract of the book "Wife Rape: Understanding the Response of Survivors and Service Providers", by Raquel Kennedy Bergen.

Amongst other important information, Bergen's book examines the definition of sexual violence, how women cope with sexual violence and how they seek help. The analysis is based on interviews with 40 survivors of wife rape and 37 service providers.

Item Two: Shoplifting Behaviours

Comparison of Shoplifting Behaviours in Patients With Eating Disorders, Psychiatric Control Subjects, and Undergraduate Control Subjects.

Goldner, Elliot M.; Geller, Josie; Birmingham, C. Laird; Remick, Ronald A. (2000) Comparison of Shoplifting Behaviours in Patients With Eating Disorders, Psychiatric Control Subjects, and Undergraduate Control Subjects. In Canadian Journal of Psychiatry, Jun2000, Vol. 45 Issue 5, p471, 5p, 2 charts

Synopsis: The connection between shoplifting and eating disorder symptomatology is addressed in this study of shoplifting behaviours wherein an eating disorder group, a psychiatric control group, and an undergraduate control group were examined in relation to self-esteem, depression, and eating disorder symptomatology.

Class Activities

In addition to the exercises in the Workbook that accompanies this text, you may find the following in-class activities to be of value:

Activity #1: Best Fit

Start this activity by having students responding individually to the following question: How did or will you decide your future career? Give students 10 to 15 minutes to respond to this question. Encourage them to provide as much detail in their response as possible.

Next, have students work in groups of three or four to share their lists and see how they have or how they will achieve there career goals. Have students discuss the different strategies used to achieve their goals. What do the different strategies reveal about the students?

Finally, have the students apply the knowledge gained from this exercise to the helping relationship.

Activity #2: Thinking Strategically

Have students form groups of three or four and ask them to think of all of the possible ways they could get a grade of "A" in the course. Encourage the students to be creative in their ideas (e.g., studying hard, forming a study group, cheating, meeting with the professor, having another student take the final exam for them, hacking into the college computer database and giving themselves a grade of "A".

Now have the students make choices as to which plan of action would be most appropriate based on their values, their fear of consequences, their desire to learn.

Have the student groups report out to the class their creative thinking to get an "A", how they choose the best possible actions, and what values and decision making process influenced their final choices.

Activity #3: The Book Strategy?

Divide the class into groups of three or four students in each group and then divide the chapter up such that each group has the approximate same number of pages to read and present to the class. Have the students summarize their assigned pages and present the information to the class. Have students ask each other questions about their section of the chapter and what they found to be the most significant points in their part of the chapter.

A creative addition to this activity is to provide each group with a piece of poster paper and several colored markers and ask them to represent their section of the chapter using pictures and symbols, but no words. This helps the students to really conceptualize the content of the chapter. Have the students present their poster paper work to the rest of the class with first asking the class to attempt to decipher the pictures and symbols and then explaining what the pictures and symbols represent. This activity truly helps the students engage and conceptualize the course content.

Videos

Challenge Cases For Differential Diagnosis (35 min, Color, Films for the Humanities & Sciences). This video offers viewers an interactive approach to diagnosing four individuals after observing their interviews.

Love, Love Me, Do: How sex differences affect relationships (51 min, color, Films for the Humanities & Sciences). This video discusses how sex related differences in the brain architecture may affect love, marriage, reproduction and parenthood.

Understanding Grief (25 min, color, Films for the Humanities & Sciences). Understanding grief and its potential effects is introduced in this video by Gordon Lang who explains his approach to grief counselling.

Loss of Job (25 min, color, Films for the Humanities & Sciences). This video profiles Peter who examines his values and turns his losses to gains after losing a job that has consumed his life and negatively affected his health and relationship to his family and friends.

Accepting Life's Transitions (29 min, color, Films for the Humanities & Sciences). This video portrays the ageing process and illustrates the manner in which people come to terms with each of life's transitions.

Websites

1. http://notes3.nms.unt.edu/infrstrt.nsf/78f3b9853d01594b862566e90078f733/20cc0bd2432aaf338625671300779410?OpenDocument
    Developing contingency plans.

2. http://privatewww.essex.ac.uk/~scottj/socscot7.htm
    Rational choice theory.

3. http://www.devilsadvocate.com/Articles/billrts.html
    The clients bill of rights, this includes some info on reluctance to get started and what to do about this.

Overhead Transparencies

Starting on the next page are copies of recommended overhead transparencies. Please feel free to convert the following pages to overheads as this will enhance the lecture portion of your class presentation

HELPING CLIENTS CHOOSE BEST-FIT STRATEGIES

1. Specific strategies.

2. Substantive strategies.

3. Realistic strategies.

4. Strategies in keeping with the client's values.

OH 19.1

HOW CLIENTS DEAL WITH RISK AND PROBABILITY

1. Wishful thinking.

2. Playing it safe.

3. Avoiding the worst outcome.

4. Striking a balance.

OH 19.2

QUESTIONS FOR BEST-FIT STRATEGIES

1. Which strategies will be most useful in helping me get what I need and want?

2. Which strategies are best for this situation?

3. Which strategies best fit my resources?

4. Which strategies will be most economic in the use of resources?

OH 19.3A

QUESTIONS FOR BEST-FIT STRATEGIES cont'd.

5. Which strategies are most powerful?

6. Which strategies best fit my values?

7. Which strategies will have the fewest unwanted consequences?

OH 19.3B

EVALUATION QUESTIONS FOR STEP III-B

How effective am I in:

1. Helping clients choose strategies that are clear and specific, that best fit their capabilities, that are linked to goals, that have power, and that are suited to clients' styles and values?

2. Helping clients engage in and benefit from strategy sampling?

3. Helping clients in selected cases use the balance sheet as a way of choosing strategies by outlining the principal benefits and costs for self, others, and relevant social settings?

OH 19.4A

EVALUATION QUESTIONS FOR STEP III-B cont'd.

4. Helping clients manage the shadow side of selecting courses of action, that is, wishful thinking, playing it too safe, focusing on avoiding the worst possible outcome rather than on getting what they want, and wasting time by trying to spell out a perfectly balanced set of strategies?

5. Helping clients use the act of choosing strategies to stimulate problem-managing action?

OH 19.4B

Chapter Twenty:

Step III-C:
Helping Clients Make Plans:
"What Kind of Plan Will Help Me Get What I Need and Want?"

	Pages
Chapter Outline	546
Detailed Lecture Notes	547-558
Lecture Enhancers	559-560
Class Activities	561-562
Videos	563
Websites	564
Transparencies	565-575

CHAPTER TWENTY OUTLINE

NO PLAN OF ACTION: THE CASE OF FRANK

HOW PLANS ADD VALUE TO CLIENTS' CHANGE PROGRAMS

SHAPING THE PLAN: THREE CASES

HUMANIZING THE TECHNOLOGY OF CONSTRUCTIVE CHANGE

- ➢ Build a Planning Mentality into the Helping Process Right from the Start
- ➢ Adapt the Constructive-Change Process to the Style of the Client
- ➢ Devise a Plan for the Client and Then Work with the Client on Tailoring It to His or Her Needs

TAILORING READY-MADE PROGRAMS TO CLIENTS' NEEDS

EVALUATION QUESTIONS FOR STEP III-C

Detailed Lecture Notes

(Please note: The designation OH in the detailed lecture notes indicates an overhead transparency is available. Please locate the overhead transparencies in the final section of each chapter in this Instructors' Manual.)

After identifying and choosing strategies to accomplish goals, clients need to organize these strategies into a plan. This is the work of Step III-C. In this step counselors help clients come up with the plan itself, the sequence of actions — what should I do first, second, and third? — that will get them what they want, their goals.

Section One: NO PLAN OF ACTION: THE CASE OF FRANK

The lack of a plan — that is, a clear step-by-step process to accomplish a goal — keeps some clients mired in their problem situations.

A. Consider the case of Frank, a vice president of a large West Coast corporation.

Frank was a go-getter. He was very astute about business and had risen quickly through the ranks. He was a "hands-on" manager, meaning, in his case, that he was slow to delegate tasks to others, however competent they might be. He kept second-guessing others when he did delegate, reversed their decisions in a way that made them feel put down, listened poorly, and took a fairly short-term view of the business — "What were last week's figures like?" He was not a leader but an "operations" man. His direct reports called him a micromanager.

One day Vince sat down with Frank and told him that he was considering him as his successor down the line, but that he had some concerns. "Frank, if it were just a question of business acumen, you could take over today. But my job, at least in my mind, demands a leader." Vince went on to explain what he meant by a leader and to point out the things in Frank's style that had to change.

Frank's ultimate aim was to become president. If getting the job meant that he had to try to become the kind of leader his boss had outlined, so be it. Since he was very bright, he came up with some inventive strategies for moving in that direction. But he could never be pinned down to an overall program with specific milestones by which he could evaluate his progress. Frank was always "too busy" or would say that a formal program was "too stifling." That was odd, since formal planning was one of his strengths in the business world.

Frank remained as astute as ever in his business dealings. But he merely dabbled in the strategies meant to help him become the kind of leader Vince wanted him to be. Frank had the opportunity of, not just correcting some mistakes, but of developing and expanding his managerial style. But he blew it. At the end of two years, Vince appointed someone else president of the company.

1. Frank never got his act together. He never put together the kind of change program needed to become the kind of leader Vince wanted as president.

2. Frank had two significant blind spots that the consultant did not help him overcome.

   a) He never really took Vince's notion of leadership seriously. So he wasn't really ready for a change program. He thought the president's job was his, that business acumen alone would win out in the end.

   b) He thought he could change his management style at the margins, when more substantial changes were called for.

3. Franks coach never challenged him as he kept "trying things" that never led anywhere. In a way she was a co-conspirator because she, too, relished their business discussions.

4. When Frank didn't get the job, he left the company, leaving Roseanne to ponder her success as a consultant but her failure as a coach.

Section Two: HOW PLANS ADD VALUE TO CLIENTS' CHANGE PROGRAMS (OH-20.1)

Some clients, once they know what they want and some of the things they have to do to get what they want, get their act together, develop a plan, and move forward. Other clients need help. Since some clients (and some helpers) fail to appreciate the power of a plan, it is useful to start by reviewing the advantages of planning.

A. Formal planning usually focuses on the sequence of the "big steps" clients must take in order to get what they need or want. Clients are helped answer the question, "What do I need to do first, second, and third?" A formal plan in its most formal version takes strategies for accomplishing goals, divides them into workable steps, puts the steps in order, and assigns a timetable for the accomplishment of each step. Formal planning, provided that it is adapted to the needs of individual clients, has a number of advantages.

1. **Plans help clients develop needed discipline**. Many clients get into trouble in the first place because they lack discipline. Planning places reasonable demands on clients to develop discipline. Ready-made programs such as the Twelve Step Program of Alcoholics Anonymous are in themselves plans that demand or at least encourage self-discipline.

2. **Plans keep clients from being overwhelmed**. Plans help clients see goals as doable. They keep the steps toward the accomplishment of a goal "bite-size." Amazing things can be accomplished by taking bite-size steps toward substantial goals.

3. **Formulating plans helps clients search for more useful ways of accomplishing goals, that is, even better strategies**. Planning helps restore order.

4. **Plans provide an opportunity to evaluate the realism and adequacy of goals**.

5. **Plans make clients aware of the resources they will need to implement their strategies**.

6. **Formulating plans helps clients uncover unanticipated obstacles to the accomplishment of goals**. Many clients engage in aimless activity in their efforts to cope with problem situations. Plans help clients make the best use of their time. Finally, planning itself has a hefty shadow side. For a good review of the shadow side of planning, see Dorner (1996, pp. 153-183).

Section Three: SHAPING THE PLAN: THREE CASES (OH-20.2)

A. Plans need "shape" to drive action. A formal plan identifies the activities or actions needed to accomplish a goal or a subgoal, puts those activities into a logical but flexible order, and sets a time frame for the accomplishment of each key step.

   1. Therefore, there are three simple questions.

      a) What are the concrete things that need to be done to accomplish the goal or the subgoal?

      b) In what sequence should these be done? What should be done first, what second, what third?

      c) What is the time frame? What should be done today, what tomorrow, what next month?

2. If clients choose goals that are complex or difficult, then it is useful to help them establish subgoals as a way of moving step-by-step toward the ultimate goal.

3. In general, the simpler the plan the better. However, simplicity is not an end in itself.

4. The question is not whether a plan or program is complicated but whether it is well shaped and designed to produce results.

5. If complicated plans are broken down into subgoals and the strategies or activities needed to accomplish them, they are as capable of being achieved, if the time frame is realistic, as simpler ones.

6. In schematic form, shaping looks like this:

Subprogram 1 (a set of activities) leads to subgoal 1 (usually an instrumental goal).
Subprogram 2 leads to subgoal 2.
Subprogram 3 (the last in the sequence) leads to the accomplishment of the ultimate goal.

B. **The case of Wanda**. Take the case of Wanda, a client who set a number of goals in order to manage a complex problem situation. One of her goals was finding a job.

1. The plan leading to this goal had a number of steps, each of which led to the accomplishment of a subgoal.

2. The following subgoals were part of Wanda's job-finding program. They are stated as accomplishments (the outcome or results approach).

Subgoal 1: Resume written.
Subgoal 2: Kind of job wanted determined.
Subgoal 3: Job possibilities canvassed.
Subgoal 4: Best job prospects identified.
Subgoal 5: Job interviews arranged.
Subgoal 6: Job interviews completed.
Subgoal 7: Offers evaluated.

3. The accomplishment of these subgoals leads to the accomplishment of the overall goal of Wanda's plan — that is, getting the kind of job she wants.

4. Wanda also had to set up a step-by-step process or program to accomplish each of these subgoals. For instance, the process for accomplishing the subgoal "job possibilities canvassed" included such things as doing an internet search on one or more of the many of the job-search sites, reading the *Help Wanted* sections of the local papers, contacting friends or acquaintances who could provide leads, visiting employment agencies, reading the bulletin boards at school, and talking with someone in the job-placement office.

5. Sometimes the sequencing of activities is important, sometimes not. In Wanda's case, it's important for her to have her resume completed before she begins to canvass job possibilities, but when it came to using different methods for identifying job possibilities, the sequence does not make any difference.

C. **The case of Harriet: The economics of planning**. Harriet, an undergraduate student at a small state college, wants to become a counselor.

1. Although the college offers no formal program in counseling psychology, with the help of an advisor she identifies several undergraduate courses that would provide some of the foundation for a degree in counseling.
2. Too late she realizes that she is taking the courses out of optimal sequence. She would be getting much more from the courses had she taken the communication skills course first.

3. Harriet also volunteers for the dormitory peer-helper program run by the Center for Student Services. Harriet realizes that the developmental psychology course would have helped her enormously in this program. It would have helped her understand both herself and her peers better.

4. She sits down with one of the Center's psychologists, reviews the schools offerings with him, determines which courses will help her most, and determines the proper sequencing of these courses. He also suggests a couple of courses she could take in a local community college.

5. Harriet's opportunity-development program would have been much more efficient had it been better shaped in the first place.

D. **The case of Frank revisited**. Here is what planning might have done for Frank, the vice president who needed leadership skills.

1. What does Frank need to do? To become a leader,

   a) Frank decides to reset his managerial style with his subordinates by involving them more in decision making.

b) He wants to listen more, set work objectives through dialogue, ask subordinates for suggestions, and delegate more.

c) He knows he should coach his direct reports in keeping with their individual needs, give them feedback on the quality of their work, recognize their contributions, and reward them for achieving results beyond their objectives.

2. In what sequence should Frank do these things?

a) Frank decides that the first thing he will do is call in each subordinate and ask, "What do you need from me to get your job done? How can I add value to your work? And what management style on my part would help you most?" Their dialogue around these issues will help him tailor his supervisory interventions to the needs of each team member.

b) The planning cycle for the business year is about to begin, and each team member needs to know what his or her objectives are. It is a perfect time to begin setting objectives through dialogue rather than simply assigning them. Frank therefore sends a memo to each of his direct reports, asking them to review the company's strategy and business plan and the strategy and plan for each of their functions, and to write down what they think their key managerial objectives for the coming year should be.

c) He asks them to include "stretch" goals.

3. What is Frank's time frame?

a) Frank calls in each of his subordinates immediately to discuss what they need from him.

b) He completes his objective-setting sessions with them within three weeks.

c) He puts off further action on delegation until he gets a better reading on their performance.

Box 20-1 is a list of questions you can use to help clients think systematically about crafting a plan to get what they need and want.

Section Four: HUMANIZING THE TECHNOLOGY OF CONSTRUCTIVE CHANGE

Planning in the real world seldom looks like planning in textbooks. Textbooks do provide useful frameworks, principles, and processes, but they are seldom used. Most people are too impatient to do the kind of planning just outlined. One of the reasons for the dismal track record of discretionary change mentioned earlier is that even when clients do set realistic goals, they lack the discipline to develop reasonable plans. The detailed work of planning is too burdensome.

A. If helpers skip the goal-setting and planning steps clients need, they shortchange them. On the other hand, if they are pedantic, mechanistic, or awkward in their attempts to help clients engage in these steps — failing to give these processes a human face — they run the risk of alienating the people they are trying to serve. Here are some principles to guide the constructive-change process from Step II-A through Step III-C. **(OH 20.3)**

1. **Build a Planning Mentality into the Helping Process Right from the Start.**

    a) A constructive-change mindset should permeate the helping process right from the beginning.

    b) Helpers need to see clients as self-healing agents capable of changing their lives, not just as individuals mired in problem situations.

    c) Even while listening to a client's story, the helper needs to begin thinking of how the situation can be remedied and through probes find out what approaches to change clients are thinking about — no matter how tentative these ideas might be.

    d) Helping clients act in their real world right from the beginning of the helping process helps them develop some kind of initial planning mentality.

    e) If helping is to be solution-focused, thinking about strategies and plans must be introduced early. When a client tells of some problem, the helper can ask early on, "What kinds of things have you done so far to try to cope with the problem?"

2. **Adapt the Constructive-Change Process to the Style of the Client.**

    a) Setting goals, devising strategies, and making and implementing plans can be done formally or informally.

b) There is a continuum. Some clients actually like the detailed work of devising plans; it fits their style.

c) Kirschenbaum (1985) challenged the notion that planning should always provide an exact blueprint for specific actions, their sequencing, and the time frame. There are three questions:

    · How specific do the activities have to be?
    · How rigid does the order have to be?
    · How soon does each activity have to be carried out?

d) Kirschenbaum (p. 492) suggested that, at least in some cases, being less specific and rigid about actions, sequencing, and deadlines can "encourage people to pursue their goals by continually and flexibly choosing their activities."

e) Flexibility in planning can help clients become more self-reliant and proactive.

f) Rigid planning strategies can lead to frequent failure to achieve short-term goals.

g) A slipshod approach to planning is also self-defeating.

h) Counselors should help clients embrace the kind of rigor in planning that make sense for them in their situations. There are no formulas; there are only client needs and common sense.

i) Sometimes it helps to spell out the actions that need to be done in quite specific terms; at other times it is necessary only to help clients outline them in broad terms and leave the rest to their own sound judgment.

j) If therapy is to be brief, help clients start doing things that lead to their goals. Then, in a later session, help them review what they have been doing, drop what is not working, continue what is working, add more effective strategies, and put more organization in their programs.

k) If you have a limited number of sessions with a client, you can't engage in extensive goal setting and planning. "What can I do that will add most value?" is the ongoing challenge in brief therapy.

3. Devise a Plan for the Client and Then Work with the Client on Tailoring It to His or Her Needs.

a) The more experienced helpers become, the more they learn about the elements of program development and the more they come to know what kinds of programs work for different clients.

b) They build up a stockpile of useful programs and know how to stitch pieces of different programs together to create new programs. And so they can use their knowledge and experience to fashion a plan for any clients who lack the skills or the temperament to pull together a plan for themselves.

c) Their objective is not to foster dependence but to help clients grow in self-determination. For instance, they can first offer a plan as a sketch or in outline form rather than as a detailed program. Helpers then work with clients to fill out the sketch and adapt it to their needs and style.

d) Counselors are free to make up their own programs based on their expertise and experience.

e) Give clients something to work with, something to get involved in. The elaboration of the plan emerges through dialogue with the client and in the kind of detail the client can handle.

f) The ultimate test of the effectiveness of plans lies in the problem-managing and opportunity-developing action clients engage in to get what they need and want.

g) There is no such thing as a good plan in and of itself. Results, not planning or hard work, are the final arbiter.

Section Five: TAILORING READY-MADE PROGRAMS TO CLIENTS' NEEDS

There are many ready-made programs for clients with particular problems. They are often tried-and-true constructive-change programs. The 12-step approach of Alcoholics Anonymous is one of the most well known. It has been adapted to other forms of substance abuse and addiction. Systematic desensitization, a behavioral approach, has been used to treat clients with PTSD, post-traumatic stress disorder (Frueh, de Arellano, & Turner, 1997). This program included sessions in muscle relaxation, the development of a fear hierarchy, and, finally, weekly sessions in the systematic desensitization of these fears. The program helped alleviate such debilitating symptoms as intrusive thoughts, panic attacks, and episodic depression. The manualized treatment programs outlined in Chapter 1 are also examples of ready-made programs. Donald Meichenbaum (1994) published a comprehensive handbook for dealing with PTSD which includes a practical manual.

Counselors add value by helping clients adapt "set" programs to their particular needs. Consider the following cases.

A. **A prevention program for pedophilia**. While there are many treatment programs for pedophilic clients *after* the fact, prevention programs are much scarcer. Consider this case.

1. After a couple of rather aimless sessions, the helper said to Ahmed, "We've talked about a lot of things, but I'm still not sure why you came in the first place." This challenged Ahmed to reveal the central issue, though he needed a great deal of help to do so. It turned out that Ahmed was sexually attracted to prepubescent children of both sexes. Although he had never engaged in pedophilic behavior, the temptation to do so was growing.

2. The counselor adapted a New Zealand program called Kia Marama (Hudson, Marshall, Ward, Johnston, et al., 1995), a comprehensive cognitive-behavioral program for incarcerated child molesters, to Ahmed's situation. The original program includes intensive work in challenging distorted attitudes, reviewing a wide range of sexual issues, seeing the world from the point of view of the victim, developing problem-solving and interpersonal-relationship skills, stress management, and relapse-prevention training. Counselor and client spent some time assessing which parts of the program might be of most help before embarking on an intensive tailored program.

3. The economics of prevention far outweigh the economics of rehabilitation. Not only did Ahmed stay out of trouble, but much of what he learned from the program — for instance, stress management — applied to other areas of his life.

B. **A program for helping people on welfare be successful at work**.

1. One community-based mental-health center worked extensively with people on welfare. When new legislation was passed forcing welfare recipients to get work, they searched for programs that helped people on welfare get and keep jobs. They learned a great deal from one program sponsored by a major hotel chain (see Milbank, 1996). The hotel targeted welfare recipients because it made both economic and social sense. Because of the problems with this particular population, however, the hotel's recruiters, trainers, and supervisors had to become paraprofessional helpers, though they never used that term. The people they recruited — battered women, ex-convicts, addicts, homeless people, including those

556

who had been thrown out of shelters, and so forth — had all sorts of problems. In the beginning the hotel's staff did many things *for* the trainees.

2. They drive welfare trainees to work, arrange their day care, negotiate with their landlords, bicker with their case workers, buy them clothes, visit them at home, coach them in everything from banking skills to self-respect and promise those who stick with it full-time jobs. (Milbank, 1996, A1).

3. But the trainers also challenged their "clients'" mindset that they were not responsible for what happened to them, enforced the hotel's code of behavior with equity, and persevered. The hotel program was far from perfect, but it did help many of the participants develop much needed self-discipline and find a new life both at work and outside.

4. The counselors from a local mental-health center who acted as consultants to the program learned that some of the new employees benefitted greatly from wholesale upfront involvement of trainers and supervisors in their lives. It kick-started a constructive-change process. They also saw that the recruiters, trainers, and supervisors also benefitted. So they started a volunteer program at the mental-health center, looking for people willing to do the kinds of things that the hotel trainers and supervisors did. They knew that both the clients and the volunteers would benefit.

General well-being programs: Exercise. Some programs that contribute to general well-being can be used as adjuncts to all approaches to helping.

1. Exercise programs are probably one of the most underused adjuncts to helping (Burks & Keeley, 1989). McAuley, Mihalko, and Bane (1997) have explored the multidimensional relationship between exercise to self-efficacy.

2. There is evidence showing that exercise programs can help in the treatment of schizophrenia and alcohol dependence. Such programs also help more directly to reduce depression, manage chronic pain, and control anxiety (Tkachuk & Martin, 1999).

3. The self-discipline developed through exercise programs can be a stimulus to increased self-regulation in other areas of life. Kate Hays (1999) has done a comprehensive review of the positive psychology possibilities of exercise in *Working It Out: Using Exercise in Psychotherapy.*

Finally, not all useful ready-made programs are found in sophisticated manuals. Many are found in the best of the self-help literature. Books like *Thoughts and Feelings* (McKay, Davis, & Fanning, 1997) are filled with systematic strategies for the treatment of a wide variety of psychological problems. The best are realistic, practical, and translations of some of the best thinking in the field.

BOX 20-1
Questions on Planning (OH-20.4)

Here are some questions you can help clients ask themselves in order to come up with a viable plan for constructive change:

- Which sequence of actions will get me to my goal?
- Which actions are most critical?
- How important is the order in which these actions take place?
- What is the best time frame for each action?
- Which step of the program needs substeps?
- How can I build informality and flexibility into my plan?
- How do I gather the resources, including social support, needed to implement the plan?

Evaluation Questions for Step III-C (OH-20.5)

Helpers can ask themselves the following questions as they help clients formulate the kinds of plans that actually drive action.

- To what degree do I prize and practice planning in my own life?
- How effectively have I adopted the hologram mind-set in helping, seeing each session and each intervention in the light of the entire helping process?
- How quickly do I move to planning when I see that it is what the client needs to manage problems and develop opportunities better?
- What do I do to help clients overcome resistance to planning? How effectively do I help them identify the incentives for and the payoff of planning?
- How effectively do I help clients formulate subgoals that lead to the accomplishment of overall preferred-scenario goals?
- How practical am I in helping clients identify the action needed to accomplish subgoals, sequence those actions, and establish realistic time frames for them?
- How well do I adapt the specificity and detail of planning to the needs of each client?
- Even at this planning step, how easily do I move back and forth among the different stages and steps of the helping model as the need arises?
- How readily do clients actually move to action because of my work with them in planning?
- How human is the technology of constructive change in my hands?
- How well do I adapt the constructive-change process to the style of the client?
- How effectively do I help clients tailor generic or ready-made change programs to their specific needs?

Lecture Enhancers

You should be able to find the full text of the following items in your library or by using your web-based library access tool of choice (e.g., Psycinfo)

Item One:

Neuropsychological function, drug abuse, and violence: A conceptual framework.

Fishbein,-Diana. (2000) Neuropsychological function, drug abuse, and violence: A conceptual framework. In Criminal-Justice-and-Behavior. 2000 Apr; Vol 27(2): 139-159 US: Sage Publications Inc.

Synopsis: The author reports that neuropsychological dysfunction consistently characterizes both drug abuse and violence and may contribute to traits often cited as precursors to both, e.g., impulsivity, poor decision-making ability, disinhibition, and inability to assess consequences.

Item Two: Evolution and Adaptability

Evolution and Adaption in the Understanding of Behavior, Culture, and Mind.

Rozin, Paul. (2000) Evolution and Adaption in the Understanding of Behavior,Culture, and Mind. In American Behavioral Scientist, Mar2000, Vol. 43 Issue 6, p970, 17p.

Synopsis: This article outlines the "middle ground" between strong evolutionary-adaptationist and strong environmental-determinist positions. The importance of human evolution in comprehending human functions and activities and the role of culture in shaping humans is acknowledged.
Biological, environmental and cultural forces that lead to specificity in different human groups are summarized.

Item Three: Human Decision Making

Risk-Sensitive Decision Making Examined
Within an Evolutionary Framework.

Rode, Catrin; Wang, XT. (2000) Risk-Sensitive Decision Making Examined Within an Evolutionary Framework. In American Behavioral Scientist, Mar2000, Vol. 43 Issue 6, p926, 14p

Synopsis: The authors reexamine two examples of human decision-making biases from an evolutionary perspective and argue that the human mind is fine-tuned to solve complex decision tasks that had been recurrent in hominid evolution. The authors conclude that an evolutionary approach helps to reveal important features of human choice behavior and provides insights into the nature of human decision rationality.

Class Activities

In addition to the exercises in the Workbook that accompanies this text, you may find the following in-class activities to be of value:

Activity #1: A Plan to Plan

In this activity students are encouraged to think of times life in that they really wanted something (e.g., a car, a vacation, a prize) and what they had to do to get what they wanted. In groups of three or four, have students share what it is they wanted and what planning they undertook to achieve their goals. Have them be very specific in what it took to get what they wanted. Have the group list all the specific planning steps they took to obtain what they wanted.

Now ask the students to relate their actions and behaviors to the concept of planning. Have them relate planning to achieving goals in their own lives. Finally, have the students relate their personal experiences with planning to the helping process.

Activity #2: No Plan Is Still A Plan

Have students explain what it means when we say "No Plan Is Still A Plan." In groups of three or four allow the students ten to fifteen minutes to discuss the concept and its meaning.

Next have the groups report out their group's interpretation of the concept. See how many groups get the idea that by having no plan we are actually adopting a plan of not planning. Engage students in discussion to see if they understand that a client with no plan actually has a plan.

Activity #3: Planning Takes Time

Ask students to pick a major goal in their life (e.g., become a professional counselor) and then have them list what it will take to achieve their goals.

Next have the students list what type of planning process they are using to achieve their goals. Determine how many students have great goals, but no plan. The lack of planning will become a focus of how many individuals want to achieve great things, but they just are not willing to take the time to plan.

Finally, have them justify their lack of planning to achieve their desired goals. Ask them to identify the values that are reflected in their justification. Then ask them to list the pros to have a plan to achieve a goal. Ask them to relate this knowledge to the helping relationship.

Videos

Without Pity (56 min, color, Films for the Humanities & Sciences). Christopher Reeve narrates this HBO documentary that applauds the efforts of people with disabilities as they strive to live full, productive lives.

Finding a Way (28 min, color, Films for the Humanities & Sciences). Integration of people with disabilities into the mainstream of life and the challenges they face is the focus of this video.

Healing the Heart: Forgive and Remember (30 min, color, Films for the Humanities & Sciences). This video profiles amazing individuals who have survived dreadful experiences, conquered hate, and moved from shock and the desire for revenge to an attitude of forgiveness.

Safe: Inside a Battered Women's Shelter (49 min, color, Films for the Humanities & Sciences). Three battered women are profiled in this video with discussion of breaking the cycle of violence and seeking refuge, with their children, at a safe house.

Wired for Speed: Technology and the Accelerating Pace of Life (45 min, color, Films for the Humanities & Sciences). The impact of technological innovations are investigated by ABC news anchor Ted Koppel and correspondent Robert Krulwich.

Websites

1. www.talkingcure.com

    This is the homepage for the Institute for the Study of Therapeutic Change. This is an excellent site for discussions on the effectiveness of counselling. Make certain you get to "Baloney Watch": go to the website, click on News and Reviews, and then click on "Baloney Watch".

2. www.apa.org

    The homepage of the American Psychological Association.

3. www.cpa.ca

    The homepage of the Canadian Psychological Association.

4. www.counseling.org

    The homepage of the American Counseling Association.

Overhead Transparencies

Starting on the next page are copies of recommended overhead transparencies. Please feel free to convert the following pages to overheads as this will enhance the lecture portion of your class presentation

HOW PLANS ADD VALUE TO CLIENTS' CHANGE PROGRAMS

1. Plans help clients develop needed discipline.

2. Plans keep clients from being overwhelmed.

3. Formulating plans helps clients search for more useful ways of accomplishing goals, that is, even better strategies.

4. Plans provide an opportunity to evaluate the realism and adequacy of goals.

OH 20.1A

HOW PLANS ADD VALUE TO CLIENTS' CHANGE PROGRAMS
cont'd.

5. Plans make clients aware of the resources they will need to implement their strategies.

6. Formulating plans helps clients uncover unanticipated obstacles to the accomplishment of goals.

OH 20.1B

SHAPING THE PLAN

1. **What are the concrete things that need to be done to accomplish the goal or the subgoal?**

2. **In what sequence should these be done? What should be done first, what second, what third?**

3. **What is the time frame? What should be done today, what tomorrow, what next month?**

OH 20.2

PRINCIPLES FOR CONSTRUCTIVE-CHANGE PROCESS

1. Build a Planning Mentality into the Helping Process Right from the Start.

2. Adapt the Constructive-Change Process to the Style of the Client.

3. Devise a Plan for the Client and Then Work with the Client on Tailoring It to His or Her Needs.

OH 20.3

QUESTIONS ON PLANNING

1. Which sequence of actions will get me to my goal?

2. Which actions are most critical?

3. How important is the order in which these actions take place?

4. What is the best time frame for each action?

OH 20.4A

QUESTIONS ON PLANNING
cont'd.

5. Which step of the program needs substeps?

6. How can I build informality and flexibility into my plan?

7. How do I gather the resources, including social support, needed to implement the plan?

OH 20.4B

EVALUATION QUESTIONS FOR STEP III-C

1. To what degree do I prize and practice planning in my own life?

2. How effectively have I adopted the hologram mind-set in helping, seeing each session and each intervention in the light of the entire helping process?

3. How quickly do I move to planning when I see that it is what the client needs to manage problems and develop opportunities better?

OH 20.5A

EVALUATION QUESTIONS FOR STEP III-C cont'd.

4. What do I do to help clients overcome resistance to planning? How effectively do I help them identify the incentives for and the payoff of planning?

5. How effectively do I help clients formulate subgoals that lead to the accomplishment of overall preferred-scenario goals?

6. How practical am I in helping clients identify the action needed to accomplish subgoals, sequence those actions, and establish realistic time frames for them?

OH 20.5B

EVALUATION QUESTIONS FOR STEP III-C cont'd.

7. How well do I adapt the specificity and detail of planning to the needs of each client?

8. Even at this planning step, how easily do I move back and forth among the different stages and steps of the helping model as the need arises?

9. How readily do clients actually move to action because of my work with them in planning?

10. How human is the technology of constructive change in my hands?

OH 20.5C

EVALUATION QUESTIONS FOR STEP III-C cont'd.

11. How well do I adapt the constructive-change process to the style of the client?

12. How effectively do I help clients tailor generic or ready-made change programs to their specific needs?

OH 20.5D

Chapter Twenty One:

"How Will I Make It All Happen?" Helping Clients Get What They Want and Need

	Pages
Chapter Outline	577
Detailed Lecture Notes	578-594
Lecture Enhancers	595
Class Activities	596-597
Videos	598
Websites	599
Transparencies	600-611

CHAPTER TWENTY ONE OUTLINE

HELPING CLIENTS BECOME EFFECTIVE TACTICIANS

> Help Clients Develop "Implementation Intentions"
> Help Clients Avoid Imprudent Action
> Help Clients Develop Contingency Plans
> Help Clients Overcome Procrastination
> Help Clients Identify Possible Obstacles to and Resources for Implementing Plans
> Help Clients Find Incentives and the Rewards for Sustained Action
> Help Clients Develop Action-Focused Self-Contracts and Agreements
> Help Clients to Be Resilient After Mistakes and Failures

GETTING ALONG WITHOUT A HELPER: DEVELOPING SOCIAL NETWORKS FOR
    SUPPORTIVE CHALLENGE

THE SHADOW SIDE OF IMPLEMENTING CHANGE

> Helpers as Agents
> Client Inertia: Reluctance to Get Started
> Entropy: The Tendency of Things to Fall Apart
> Choosing Not to Change

EVALUATION QUESTIONS FOR THE ACTION ARROW

Detailed Lecture Notes

(Please note: The designation OH in the detailed lecture notes indicates an overhead transparency is available. Please locate the overhead transparencies in the final section of each chapter in this Instructors' Manual.)

In a book called *True Success,* Tom Morris (1994) lays down the conditions for achieving success. They include:

➢   determining what you want — that is, a goal or a set of goals "powerfully imagined,"
➢   focus and concentration in preparation and planning,
➢   the confidence or belief in oneself to see the goal through, that is, self-efficacy,
➢   a commitment of emotional energy,
➢   being consistent, stubborn, and persistent in the pursuit of the goal,
➢   the kind of integrity that inspires trust and gets people pulling for you,
➢   a capacity to enjoy the process of getting there.

The role of the counselor is to help clients engage in all these internal and external behaviors in the interest of goal accomplishment.

Some clients, once they have a clear idea of what to do to handle a problem situation or develop some opportunity, go ahead and do it, whether they have a formal plan or not. Other clients, while choosing goals and coming up with strategies for implementing them, are, for whatever reason, stymied when it comes to action. Most clients fall between these two extremes.

Discipline and self-control play an important part in implementing change programs. Kirschenbaum (1987) found that many things can contribute to not getting started or giving up: low initial commitment to change, weak self-efficacy, poor outcome expectations, the use of self-punishment rather than self-reward, depressive thinking, failure to cope with emotional stress, lack of consistent self-monitoring, failure to use effective habit-change techniques, giving in to social pressure, failure to cope with initial relapse, and paying attention to the wrong things — for instance, focusing on the difficulty of the problem situation rather than the attractiveness of the opportunity.

Self-determination and self-control are essential for action. Kanfer and Schefft (1988, p. 58) differentiated between two kinds of self-control. In *decisional self-control* a single choice terminates a conflict. In *protracted self-control* continued resistance to temptation is required. This is a positive way of staying on guard.

Most clients need both kinds of self-control to manage their lives better. A client's choice to give up alcohol completely (decisional self-control) needs to be complemented by the ability to handle inevitable longer-term temptations. Protracted self-control calls for a preventive mentality and a certain degree of street smarts. It is easier for the client who has given up alcohol to turn down an invitation to go to a bar in the first place than to sit in a bar all evening with friends and refrain from drinking. Figure 21-1 adds the Action Arrow to the helping model.

FIGURE 21-1

The Helping Model
Complementing Planning With Action

Section One: HELPING CLIENTS BECOME EFFECTIVE TACTICIANS (OH-21.1A)

In the implementation phase, strategies for accomplishing goals need to be complemented by tactics and logistics. A strategy is a practical plan to accomplish some objective. Tactics is the art of adapting a plan to the immediate situation. This includes being able to change the plan on the spot to handle unforeseen complications. Logistics is the art of being able to provide the resources needed for the implementation of a plan in a timely way. Since many well-meaning and motivated clients are simply not good tacticians, counselors can add value by using the following principles to help them engage in focused and sustained goal-accomplishing action.

A. **Help Clients Develop "Implementation Intentions."**

   1. Commitment to goals (see Chapter 17) must be followed by commitment to courses of action.

   2. Gollwitzer (1999) has researched a simple way to help clients cope with the common problems associated with translating goals into action — failing to get started, becoming distracted, reverting to bad habits, and so forth.

   3. Strong commitment to goals is not enough. Equally strong commitment to specific actions to accomplish goals is required.

   4. Good intentions, Gollwitzer points out, don't deserve their poor reputation. Strong intentions — "I strongly intend to study for an hour every weekday before dinner" — are "reliably observed to be realized more often than weak intentions" (p. 493).

      Implementation intentions are subordinate to goal intentions and specify the when, where, and how of responses leading to goal attainment. They have the structure of "When situation x arises, I will perform response y!" and thus link anticipated opportunities with goal-directed responses (p. 494).

5. You can help clients enunciate to themselves strong specific intentions that will help them "automatically" handle many of the obstacles to goal implementation.

B. Help Clients Avoid Imprudent Action.

1. For some clients, the problem is not that they refuse to act but that they act imprudently.

2. Rushing off to try the first "strategy" that comes to mind is often imprudent.

3. Counselors can help clients check the validity of their assumptions and set realistic goals.

C. Help Clients Develop Contingency Plans.

1. If counselors help clients brainstorm both possibilities for a better future (goals) and strategies for achieving those goals (courses of action), then clients will have the raw materials, as it were, for developing contingency plans.

2. Contingency plans answer the question, "What will I do if the plan of action I choose is not working?"

3. Contingency plans help make clients more effective tacticians.

4. The formulation of contingency plans is based on the fact that we live in an imperfect world. Often enough goals have to be fine-tuned or even changed. The same is true for strategies for accomplishing goals.

5. Contingency plans are needed especially when clients choose a high-risk program to achieve a critical goal.

6. Having backup plans also helps clients develop more responsibility. If they see that a plan is not working, then they have to decide whether to try the contingency plan.

7. Backup plans need not be complicated.

8. A counselor might merely ask, "If that doesn't work, then what will you do?"

D. Help Clients Overcome Procrastination.

1. At the other end of the spectrum are clients who keep putting action off.

2. There are many reasons for procrastination and techniques to overcome it.

E. Help Clients Identify Possible Obstacles to and Resources for Implementing Plans.

Years ago Kurt Lewin (1969) codified common sense by developing what he called "force-field analysis." In ordinary language, this is simply a review by the client of the major obstacles to and the major facilitating forces for implementing action plans. The slogan is "forewarned is forearmed."

    1. Obstacles. The identification of possible obstacles to the implementation of a program helps make clients forewarned.

        a) The assumption here is that if clients are aware of some of the "wrinkles" that can accompany any given course of action, they will be less disoriented when they encounter them.

        b) Identifying possible obstacles is, at its best, a straightforward census of likely pitfalls rather than a self-defeating search for every possible thing that could go wrong.

        c) Obstacles can come from within the clients themselves, from others, from the social settings of their lives, and from larger environmental forces.

        d) Once an obstacle is spotted, ways of coping with it need to be identified.

        e) Sometimes simply being aware of a pitfall is enough to help clients mobilize their resources to handle it. At other times a more explicit coping strategy is needed.

    2. Facilitating forces.

        a) Counselors can help their clients identify unused resources that facilitate action can be identified.

        b) Brainstorming resources that can counter obstacles to action can be very helpful for some clients.

        c) Helping clients brainstorm facilitating forces raises the probability that they will act in their own interests. They can be simple things.

F. Help Clients Find Incentives and Rewards for Sustained Action.

    1. Clients avoid engaging in action programs when the incentives and the rewards for not engaging in the program outweigh the incentives and the rewards for doing so.

2. The counselors sometimes need to push hard to find and bring to the surface a different, more constructive set of incentives to guide his dealings with people. The new incentives have to drive out the old.

3. The incentives and the rewards that help a client get going on a program of constructive change in the first place may not be the ones that keep the client going.

4. Constructive-change activities that are not rewarded tend over time to lose their vigor, decrease, and even disappear. This process is called extinction.

5. Incentives cannot be put in place and then be taken for granted. They need tending.

G. Help Clients Develop Action-Focused Self-Contracts and Agreements.

1. Self-contracts help clients commit themselves to what they want, that is, their goals.

2. Self-contracts are also useful in helping them both initiate and sustain problem-managing action and the work involved in developing opportunities.

3. Feller (1984) developed a "job-search agreement" to help job seekers persist in their search. The following agreement — clients were to respond "true" to all the following statements and then act on these "truths" — requires clients to commit themselves not only to job-seeking behavior but also to sound psychological practices that promote the right mentality for such behavior.

    a) I agree that no matter how many times I enter the job market, or the level of skills, experiences, or academic success I have, the following appear TRUE:

        ▪ It takes only one YES to get a job; the number of no's does not affect my next interview.

        ▪ The open market lists about 20% of the jobs presently open to me.

        ▪ About 80% of the job openings are located by talking to people.

        ▪ The more people who know my skills and know that I'm looking for a job, the more I increase the probability that they'll tell me about a job lead.

        ▪ The more specifically I can tell people about the problems I can solve or outcomes I can attain, rather than describe the jobs I've had, the more jobs they may think I qualify for.

b) I agree that regardless of how much I need a job, the following appear TRUE:

- If I cut expenses and do more things for myself, I reduce my money problems.

- The more I remain positive, the more people will be interested in me and my job skills.

- If I relax and exercise daily, my attitude and health will appear attractive to potential employers.

- The more I do positive things and the more I talk with enthusiastic people, the more I will gain the attention of new contacts and potential employers.

- Even if things don't go as I would like them to, I choose my own thoughts, feelings, and behaviors each day.

4. It is easy to see how similar "agreements" could act as drivers of action in many different kinds of problem-managing and opportunity-developing situations.

5. Self-contracts and agreements with others focus clients' energies.

H. Help Clients to Be Resilient After Mistakes and Failures.

1. Clients, like the rest of us, stumble and fall as they try to implement their constructive-change programs. However, everyone has some degree of *resilience* (**OH-21.2**) within that enables them to get up, pull themselves together, and move on once more.

2. The ability to bounce back is an essential life capability.

3. Holaday and McPhearson (1997) have compiled a list of common factors that influence resilience. They distinguish between *outcome* resilience and *process* resilience.

4. Resilience in general is the ability to overcome or adapt to significant stress or adversity.

5. Outcome resilience implies a return to a previous state. This is "bounce back" resilience.

6. Process resilience represents the continuous effort to cope that is a "normal" part of some people's lives.

583

7. You can encourage both kinds of resilience in clients.

8. Holaday and McPhearson suggest that the factors that go into resilience are social support, cognitive skills, and psychological resources.

   a) **Social support.** includes the overall values of a society toward people, especially people in trouble; community support, that is, support in the neighborhood, at work, at church, and so forth; personal support through friends and other special relationships; and familial support, the "affectional ties within a family system."

   b) **Cognitive skills**. It seems that at least average intelligence contributes greatly to resilience.

      - There are different kinds of intelligence — academic intelligence, social intelligence, street smarts, and so forth.

      - Holaday and McPhearson point out (p. 350), "intelligence is also associated with the ability to use fantasy and hope."

      - Cognitive skills also include coping style. For instance, a "belligerent style" (Zimrin, 1986) rather than a passively enduring, accepting, or yielding style often contributes more to resilience. "I don't take what others say, it's *not* over; don't tell me I can't do something."

      - Clients can also cope by discussing feelings.

      - Other useful coping strategies include avoiding self-blame and using the energy of anger to cope with the world rather than damage the self.

      - Other cognitive factors in resilience include the degree and the way clients exercise personal control in their lives and how they interpret their experiences.

   c) **Psychological resources**. Certain personality characteristics or dispositions protect people from stress and contribute to "bounce back." They include an internal locus of control, empathy, curiosity, a tendency to seek novel experiences, a high activity level, flexibility in new situations, a sense of humor, the ability to elicit positive regard from others, accurate and positive self-appraisal, personal integrity, a sense of self-protectiveness, pride in accomplishments, and a capacity for fun.

9. There are a range of "resilience levers" in every client. You job is to help them discover the levers, pull them, and bounce back. Resilience is "deep inside you" and inside your clients. It's part of their self-healing nature.

Section Two: GETTING ALONG WITHOUT A HELPER: DEVELOPING SOCIAL NETWORKS FOR SUPPORTIVE CHALLENGE

In most cases helping is a relatively short-term process. But even in longer-term therapy, clients must eventually get on with life without their helpers. Ideally, the counseling process not only helps clients deal with specific problem situations and unused opportunities, but also, as outlined in Chapter 1, equips them with the working knowledge and skills needed to manage those situations more effectively on their own.

A. Since adherence to constructive-change programs is often difficult, social support and challenge in their everyday lives can help them move to action, persevere in action programs, and both consolidate and maintain gains. When it comes to social support and challenge, there are a number of possible scenarios at the implementation stage and beyond.

    1. Counselors helps clients with their plans for constructive change and then clients, using their own initiative and resources, take responsibility for the plans and pursue them on their own.

    2. Clients continue to see a helper regularly in the implementation phase.

    3. Clients see a helper occasionally either "on demand" or in scheduled stop-and-check sessions.

    4. Clients join some kind of self-help group together with one-to-one counseling sessions, which are eventually eliminated.

    5. Clients develop social relationships that provide both ongoing support and challenge for the changes they are making in their lives.

B. **Challenging relationships**.

    1. Support without challenge can be hollow and that challenge without support can be abrasive.

    2. The people in the lives of clients provide a judicious mixture of support and challenge.

    3. Counselors can help clients, as they attempt to change their behavior, find people willing to provide a judicious mixture of support and challenge.

C. Feedback from significant others.

1. Gilbert (1978, p. 175), in his book on human competence, claimed that "improved information has more potential than anything else I can think of for creating more competence in the day-to-day management of performance."

2. Feedback is certainly one way of providing both support and challenge.

3. If clients are to be successful in implementing their action plans, they need adequate information about how well they are performing.

4. Sometimes they know themselves; other times they need a more objective view.

5. The purpose of feedback is not to pass judgment on the performance of clients but rather to provide guidance, support, and challenge.

6. There are two kinds of feedback.

    a) **Confirmatory feedback**. Through confirmatory feedback, significant others such as helpers, relatives, friends, and colleagues let clients know that they are on course, that is, moving successfully through the steps of an action program toward a goal.

    b) **Corrective feedback**. Through corrective feedback, significant others let clients know that they have wandered off course and what they need to do to get back on.

7. Corrective feedback, whether from helpers or people in the client's everyday life, should incorporate the following principles:

    a) Give feedback in the spirit of caring.

    b) Remember that mistakes are opportunities for growth.

    c) Use a mix of both confirmatory and corrective feedback.

    d) Be concrete, specific, brief, and to the point.

    e) Focus on the client's behaviors rather than on more elusive personality characteristics.

    f) Tie behavior to goals.

    g) Explore the impact and implications of the behavior.

    h) Avoid name-calling.

i) Provide feedback in moderate doses. Overwhelming the client defeats the purpose of the entire exercise.

j) Engage the client in dialogue. Invite the client not only to comment on the feedback but also to expand on it. Lectures don't usually help.

k) Help the client discover alternative ways of doing things. If necessary, prime the pump.

l) Explore the implications of changing over not changing.

8. The spirit of these "rules" should also govern confirmatory feedback.

a) Very often people give very detailed corrective feedback and then just say "nice job" when a person does something well.

b) All feedback provides an opportunity for learning.

9. Of course, one of the main problems with feedback is finding people in the client's day-to-day life who see the client in action enough to make it meaningful, who care enough to give it, and who have the skills to provide it constructively.

D. An amazing case of getting along without a helper. As indicated earlier, many client problems are coped with and managed, not solved. Consider the following very real case of a woman who certainly did not choose not to change. Her case is a good example of a no-formula approach to developing and implementing a program for constructive change.

Vickey readily admits that she has never fully "conquered" her illness. Some 20 years ago, she was diagnosed as manic-depressive. The picture looked something like this: She would spend about six weeks on a high; then the crash would come, and for about six weeks she'd be in the pits. After that she'd be normal for about eight weeks. This cycle meant many trips to the hospital. Some seven years into her illness, during a period in which she was in and out of the hospital, she made a decision. "I'm not going back into the hospital again. I will so manage my life that hospitalization will never be necessary." This nonnegotiable goal was her manifesto.

Starting with this declaration of intent, Vickey moved on, in terms of Step II-B, to spell out what she wanted: (1) She would channel the energy of her "highs"; (2) she would consistently manage or at least endure the depression and agony of her "lows"; (3) she would not disrupt the lives of others by her behavior; (4) she would not make important decisions when either high or low. Vickey, with some help from a rather nontraditional

587

counselor, began to do things to turn those goals into reality. She used her broad goals to provide direction for everything she did.

Vickey learned as much as she could about her illness, including cues about crisis times and how to deal with both highs and lows. To manage her highs, she learned to channel her excess energy into useful — or at least nondestructive — activity. Some of her strategies for controlling her highs centered on the telephone. She knew instinctively that controlling her illness meant not just managing problems but also developing opportunities. During her free time, she would spend long hours on the phone with a host of friends, being careful not to overburden any one person. Phone marathons became part of her lifestyle. She made the point that a big phone bill was infinitely better than a stay in the hospital. She called the telephone her "safety valve." She even set up her own phone-answering business and worked very hard to make it a success.

At the time of her highs, she would do whatever she had to do to tire herself out and get some sleep, for she had learned that sleep was essential if she was to stay out of the hospital. This included working longer shifts at the business. She developed a cadre of supportive people, including her husband. She took special care not to overburden him. She made occasional use of a drop-in crisis center but preferred avoiding any course of action that reminded her of the hospital.

1. The central driving force in this case was Vickey's decision to stay out of the hospital. Her determination drove everything else.

2. This case also exemplifies the spirit of action that ideally characterizes the implementation stage of the helping process. Here is a woman who, with occasional help from a counselor, took charge of her life.

3. She set some simple goals and devised a set of simple strategies for accomplishing them. She never looked back. And she was never hospitalized again.

4. Some will say that she was not "cured" by this process. But her goal was not to be cured but to lead as normal a life as possible in the real world.

5. Some would say that her approach lacked elegance. But it certainly did not lack results.

6. Box 21-1 outlines the kinds of questions you can help clients ask themselves as they implement change programs.

Section Three: THE SHADOW SIDE OF IMPLEMENTING CHANGE

There are many reasons why clients fail to act in their own behalf. Three are discussed here: helpers who do not have an action mentality, client inertia, and client entropy. As you read about these common phenomena, recall what was said about "implementation intentions" earlier. They can play an important role in managing the shadow side obstacles outlined here.

A. Helpers as Agents

1. Driscoll (1984, pp. 91-97) discussed the temptation of helpers to respond to the passivity of their clients with a kind of passivity of their own, a "sorry, it's up to you" stance. This, he claimed, is a mistake.

    > A client who refuses to accept responsibility thereby invites the therapist to take over. In remaining passive, the therapist foils the invitation, thus forcing the client to take some initiative or to endure the silence. A passive stance is therefore a means to avoid accepting the wrong sorts of responsibility. It is generally ineffective, however, as a long-run approach. Passivity by a therapist leaves the client feeling unsupported and thus further impairs the already fragile therapeutic alliance. Troubled clients, furthermore, are not merely unwilling but generally and in important ways unable to take appropriate responsibility. A passive countermove is therefore counterproductive, for neither therapist nor client generates solutions, and both are stranded together in a muddle of entangling inactivity. (p. 91)

2. To help others act, helpers must be agents and doers in the helping process, not mere listeners and responders.

3. The best helpers are active in the helping sessions.

4. They keep looking for ways to enter the worlds of their clients, to get them to become more active in the sessions, to get them to own more of the helping process, to help them see the need for action — action in their heads and action outside their heads in their everyday lives.

5. They do all this while espousing the client-centered values outlined in Chapter 3.

6. Although they don't push reluctant clients too hard, thus turning reluctance into resistance, neither do they sit around waiting for reluctant clients to act.

B. Client Inertia: Reluctance to Get Started

Inertia is the human tendency to put off problem-managing action. The main reason that sound action programs don't work, however, is that they are never tried. The list of ways in which we avoid taking responsibility is endless. We'll examine several of them here: passivity, learned helplessness, disabling self-talk, and getting trapped in vicious circles. **(OH-21.4)**

1. Passivity

   a) One of the most important ingredients in the generation and perpetuation of the "psychopathology of the average" is passivity, the failure of people to take responsibility for themselves in one or more developmental areas of life or in various life situations that call for action.

   b) Passivity takes many forms: doing nothing, that is, not responding to problems and options; uncritically accepting the goals and solutions suggested by others; acting aimlessly; and becoming paralyzed, that is, shutting down or becoming violent, blowing up (see Schiff, 1975).

   c) Passivity in dealing with little things can prove very costly. The little things have a way of turning into big things.

2. Learned helplessness.

   a) Seligman's (1975, 1991) concept of "learned helplessness" and its relationship to depression has received a great deal of attention since he first introduced it (Garber & Seligman, 1980; Peterson, Maier, & Seligman, 1995).

   b) Some clients learn to believe from an early age that there is nothing they can do about certain life situations.

   c) There are degrees in feelings of helplessness — from mild forms of "I'm not up to this" to feelings of total helplessness coupled with deep depression.

   d) Learned helplessness, then, is a step beyond mere passivity.

   e) Bennett and Bennett (1984) saw the positive side of helplessness. If the problems clients face are indeed out of their control, then it is not helpful for them to have an illusory sense of control, unjustly assign themselves responsibility, and indulge in excessive expectations. Somewhat paradoxically, they found that challenging clients' tendency to blame themselves for everything actually fostered realistic hope and change.

   f) The trick is helping clients learn what is and what is not in their control.

   g) A man with a physical disability may not be able to do anything about the disability itself, but he does have some control over how he views his disability and the power to pursue certain life goals despite it.

   h) The opposite of helplessness is "learned optimism" (Seligman, 1998) and resourcefulness. If helplessness can be learned, so can resourcefulness.

Indeed, increased resourcefulness is one of the principal goals of successful helping.

i) Optimism, however, is not an unmixed blessing; nor is pessimism always a disaster (Chang, 2001). While optimists do such things as live longer and enjoy greater success than pessimists, pessimists are better predictors of what is likely to happen.

j) The price of optimism is being wrong a lot of the time. Perhaps we should help our clients be hopeful realists rather than optimists or pessimists.

3. Disabling self-talk.

a) Clients often talk themselves out of things, thus talking themselves into passivity.

b) Such self-defeating conversations with themselves get people into trouble in the first place and then prevent them from getting out.

c) Helpers can add great value by helping clients challenge the kind of self-talk that interferes with action.

4. Vicious circles.

a) Pyszczynski and Greenberg (1987) developed a theory about self-defeating behavior and depression. They said that people whose actions fail to get them what they want can easily lose a sense of self-worth and become mired in a vicious circle of guilt and depression.

> Consequently, the individual falls into a pattern of virtually constant self-focus, resulting in intensified negative affect, self-derogation, further negative outcomes, and a depressive self-focusing style. Eventually, these factors lead to a negative self-image, which may take on value by providing an explanation for the individual's plight and by helping the individual avoid further disappointments. The depressive self-focusing style then maintains and exacerbates the depressive disorder. (p. 122)

b) The counselors should focus on the entire "circle"-low self-esteem producing passivity producing even lower self-esteem-and not just the self-esteem part.

c) Instead of just trying to help change the inner world of disabling self-talk, counselors can help intervene in her/his life to become a better problem solver.

d) Small successes in problem solving led to the start of a "benign" circle-success producing greater self-esteem leading to greater efforts to succeed.

5. Disorganization

a) Ferguson (1987, p. 46) painted a picture that may well remind us of ourselves, at least at times.

> When we saddle ourselves with innumerable little hassles and problems, they distract us from considering the possibility that we may have chosen the wrong job, the wrong profession, or the wrong mate. If we are drowning in unfinished housework, it becomes much easier to ignore the fact that we have become estranged from family life. Putting off an important project-painting a picture, writing a book, drawing up a business plan-is a way of protecting ourselves from the possibility that the result may not be quite as successful as we had hoped. Setting up our lives to insure a significant level of disorganization allows us to continue to think of ourselves as inadequate or partially-adequate people who don't have to take on the real challenges of adult behavior.

b) Many things can be behind this unwillingness to get our lives in order, like defending ourselves against a fear of succeeding.

c) Driscoll (1984, pp. 112-117) has provided us with a great deal of insight into this problem. He described inertia as a form of control. He says that if we tell some clients to jump into the driver's seat, they will compliantly do so — at least, until the journey gets too rough.

d) The most effective strategy, he claimed, is to show clients that they have been in the driver's seat right along: "Our task as therapists is not to talk our clients into taking control of their lives, but to confirm the fact that they already are and always will be."

e) Inertia, in the form of staying disorganized, is itself a form of control.

f) The client is actually successful, sometimes against great odds, at remaining disorganized and thus preserving inertia. Once clients recognize their power, then we can help them redirect it.

C. Entropy: The Tendency of Things to Fall Apart

1. Entropy is the tendency to give up action that has been initiated.

2. Kirschenbaum (1987), in a review of the research literature, uses the term "self-regulatory failure."

3. Programs for constructive change, even those that start strong, often dwindle and disappear.

4. Phillips (1987, p. 650) identified what he called the "ubiquitous decay curve" in both helping and in medical-delivery situations. Attrition, noncompliance, and relapse are the name of the game.

5. Wise helpers know that the decay curve is part of life and help clients deal with it.

6. With respect to entropy, a helper might say, "Even sound action programs begun with the best of intentions tend to fall apart over time, so don't be surprised when your initial enthusiasm seems to wane a bit. That's only natural. Rather, ask yourself what you need to do to keep yourself at the task."

7. Brownell and her associates (1986) provided a useful caution. They drew a fine line between preparing clients for mistakes and giving them "permission" to make mistakes by implying that they are inevitable.

8. They also made a distinction between "lapse" and "relapse." A slip or a mistake in an action program (a lapse) need not lead to a relapse-that is, giving up the program entirely.

D. CHOOSING NOT TO CHANGE

Some clients who seem to do well in analyzing problems, developing goals, and even identifying reasonable strategies and plans end up by saying — in effect, if not directly — something like this: "Even though I've explored my problems and understand why things are going wrong — that is, I understand myself and my behavior better, and I realize what I need to do to change — right now I don't want to pay the price called for by action. The price of more effective living is too high."

1. So often we seem to choose our own misery. Worse, we choose to stew in it rather than endure the relatively short-lived pain of behavioral change.

2. Helpers can and should challenge clients to search for incentives and rewards for managing their lives more effectively.

3. They should also help clients understand the consequences of not changing. But in the end it is the client's choice.

4. Savvy helpers are not magicians, but they do understand the shadow side of change, learn to see signs of it in each individual case, and, in keeping with the values outlined in Chapter 3, do whatever they can to challenge clients to deal with the shadow side of themselves and the world around them.

BOX 21-1
Questions on Implementing Plans (OH-21.5)

➤ Now that I have a plan, how do I move into action?
➤ What kind of self-starter am I? How can I improve?
➤ What obstacles lie in my way? Which are critical?
➤ How can I manage these obstacles?
➤ How do I keep my efforts from flagging?
➤ What do I do when I feel like giving up?
➤ What kind of support will help me to keep going?

Evaluation Questions for the Action Arrow (OH-21.6)

How well do I do the following as I try to help this client make the transition to action?

➤ Understand how widespread both inertia and entropy are and how they are affecting this client
➤ Help clients become effective tacticians
➤ Help clients form "implementation intentions" especially when obstacles to goal attainment are foreseen
➤ Help clients avoid both procrastination and imprudent action
➤ Help clients develop contingency plans
➤ Help clients discover and manage obstacles to action
➤ Help clients discover resources that will enable them to begin acting, to persist, and to accomplish their goals
➤ Help clients find the incentives and the rewards they need to persevere in action
➤ Help clients acquire the skills they need to act and to sustain goal-accomplishing action
➤ Help clients develop a social support and challenge system in their day-to-day lives
➤ Prepare clients to get along without a helper
➤ Come to grips with what kind of agent of change I am in my own life.
➤ Face up to the fact that not every client wants to change.

Lecture Enhancers

You should be able to find the full text of the following items in your library or by using your web-based library access tool of choice (e.g., Psycinfo)

Item One: Self-deception

The Evolutionary Psychology of Deception and Self-Deception.
Moomal, Zubair; Henzi, Stephanus Petrus. (2000) The Evolutionary Psychology of Deception and Self-Deception. In South African Journal of Psychology, Sept2000, Vol. 30 Issue 3, p45, 7p, 6 charts

Synopsis: This study examines the testing of evolutionary hypotheses and adaptive advantages of deception and explores the relationship between deception and self-deception. The authors report their findings to show a significantly positive relationship between deception and self-deception and report the relationship between deception and evolutionary fitness promoting factors, derived by factor analysis, as being inconclusive.

Item Two: Evolution and Freedom

Nature, Freedom, and Responsibility:
Ernst Mayr and Isaiah Berlin.
Donnelley, Strachan. (2000) Nature, Freedom, and Responsibility: Ernst Mayr and Issiah Berlin. In Social Research, Winter2000, Vol. 67 Issue 4, p1117, 19p

Synopsis: The author presents the topic of human affairs from the perspective of evolutionary biologist Ernst Mayr and political philosopher Isaiah Berlin. Mayr's views on Darwin's theory of evolution are converged with Berlin's opinion on freedom and human responsibility.

Item Three: Human Motivation

Evolutionary Perspectives on Human Motivation.
Heckhausen, Jutta. (2000) Evolutionary Perspectives on Human Motivation. In American Behavioral Scientist, Mar2000, Vol. 43 Issue 6, p1015, 15p

Synopsis: The author discusses the manner in which evolutionary perspectives are influential in the history and the current state of motivational psychology. Motivational and emotional mechanisms that could provide the missing link to the environment-need fit in the activation and deactivation of behavioral and cognitive modules are also examined.

Activity #1: Making It All Happen

Ask students to think of how the following factors will influence how one decides to achieve a goal:

Age:

Race:

Gender:

Culture:

Political Orientation:

Religious Belief:

The point of the exercise is to help students realize that based on many factors, different clients will use different approaches to achieve the same goals. This is important to appreciate and value as we learn to respect diversity. They students need to understand that there are many ways to achieve goals. Have the students apply this knowledge to the helping relationship.

Activity #3: The Book Strategy?

Divide the class into groups of three or four students in each group and then divide the chapter up such that each group has the approximate same number of pages to read and present to the class. Have the students summarize their assigned pages and present the information to the class. Have students ask each other questions about their section of the chapter and what they found to be the most significant points in their part of the chapter.

A creative addition to this activity is to provide each group with a piece of poster paper and several colored markers and ask them to represent their section of the chapter using pictures and symbols, but no words. This helps the students to really conceptualize the content of the chapter. Have the students present their poster paper work to the rest of the class with first asking the class to attempt to decipher the pictures and symbols and then explaining what the pictures and symbols represent. This activity truly helps the students engage and conceptualize the course content.

Activity #3: Most Important Lessons Learned

Have each student take fifteen to twenty minutes to reflect on the entire course and then list the ten most important concepts they learned in the course.

Next have students form groups of three or four and share their individual lists. For the next part of the activity have the students consolidate their individual lists to one group list of ten items.

Have each group write their list of ten items on the board. Look for similarities in the lists and the differences. If there are some very unique items, ask the groups to explain why they selected the particular unique items.

Close the final activity by having students write a statement of what they plan to take from the course and how they plan to apply what they take from the course to their personal lives and their current or future role as a helper.

Videos

Pleasure Power (53 min, Color, Films for the Humanities & Sciences). In a scientific quest to fully comprehend the power of pleasure, Milhaly Csikszentmilhalyi- author of *Flow: The psychology of Optimal Experience-* and a focus group of psychologists, physiologists, and neuroscientists are interviewed.

Caught in the Speed Trap: Information Age Overload (43 min, color, Films for the Humanities & Sciences). This video investigates the effect of this high-speed, high-tech world, where an increasing number of people are overstressed, becoming ill and even dying.

Focusing the Mind (30 min, color, Films for the Humanities & Sciences). A busy student and a tai chi professional are profiled in this teaching video designed to guide the viewers through relaxation exercises to clear and focus the mind.

Maximizing Performance (30 min , color, Films for the Humanities & Sciences). This video explores the use of relaxation exercises, called affirmations and visualisations, to achieve the full potential of our minds. A student and a psychotherapist provide valuable insights to the relaxation response.

Websites

1. www.socioweb.com/~markbl/socioweb/
    The Socio Web.

2. www.gwu.edu/~tip/festinge.html
    Cognitive Dissonance

3. http://samiam.Colorado.edu/~mcclella/expersim/introsocial.html
    Social Facilitation

4. http://sputnik.ethz.ch/~miguel/humor/funnies/Rejection_lines.html
    Rejection Lines. A humorous and painful look at rejection lines used by men and women.

5. www.public.asu.edu/~kelton/
    The Science of Persuasion and Compliance

Overhead Transparencies

Starting on the next page are copies of recommended overhead transparencies. Please feel free to convert the following pages to overheads as this will enhance the lecture portion of your class presentation

HELPING CLIENTS BECOME EFFECTIVE TACTICIANS

1. Help Clients Develop "Implementation Intentions"

2. Help Clients Avoid Imprudent Action

3. Help Clients Develop Contingency Plans.

4. Help Clients Overcome Procrastination.

5. Help Clients Identify Possible Obstacles to and Resources for Implementing Plans.

OH 21.1A

HELPING CLIENTS BECOME EFFECTIVE TACTICIANS
cont'd.

6. Help Clients Find Incentives and the Rewards for Sustained Action.

7. Help Clients Develop Action-Focused Self-Contracts and Agreements.

8. Help Clients to Be Resilient After Mistakes and Failures.

OH 21.1B

RESILIENCE

1. *Resilience* in general is the ability to overcome or adapt to significant stress or adversity.

2. *Outcome resilience* implies a return to a previous state. This is "bounce back" resilience.

3. *Process resilience* represents the continuous effort to cope that is a "normal" part of some people's lives.

OH 21.2

FACTORS IN RESILIENCE

1. Social support

2. Cognitive skills

3. Psychological resources

OH 21.3

AVOIDING RESPONSIBILITY

1. **Passivity**

2. **Learned helplessness**

3. **Disabling self-talk**

4. **Vicious circles**

5. **Disorganization**

OH 21.4

QUESTIONS ON IMPLEMENTING PLANS

1. Now that I have a plan, how do I move into action?

2. What kind of self-starter am I? How can I improve?

3. What obstacles lie in my way? Which are critical?

4. How can I manage these obstacles?

OH 21.5A

QUESTIONS ON IMPLEMENTING PLANS cont'd.

5. How do I keep my efforts from flagging?

6. What do I do when I feel like giving up?

7. What kind of support will help me to keep going?

OH 21.5B

EVALUATION QUESTIONS FOR THE ACTION ARROW

How well do I do the following as I try to help this client make the transition to action?

1. Understand how widespread both inertia and entropy are and how they are affecting this client.

2. Help clients become effective tacticians.

3. Help clients form "implementation intentions" especially when obstacles to goal attainment are foreseen.

OH 21.6A

EVALUATION QUESTIONS FOR THE ACTION ARROW cont'd.

4. Help clients avoid both procrastination and imprudent action.

5. Help clients develop contingency plans.

6. Help clients discover and manage obstacles to action.

7. Help clients discover resources that will enable them to begin acting, to persist, and to accomplish their goals.

OH 21.6B

EVALUATION QUESTIONS FOR THE ACTION ARROW cont'd.

8. Help clients find the incentives and the rewards they need to persevere in action.

9. Help clients acquire the skills they need to act and to sustain goal-accomplishing action.

10. Help clients develop a social support and challenge system in their day-to-day lives.

OH 21.6C

EVALUATION QUESTIONS FOR THE ACTION ARROW cont'd.

11. Prepare clients to get along without a helper.

12. Come to grips with what kind of agent of change I am in my own life.

13. Face up to the fact that not every client wants to change.

OH 21.6D

TESTBANK

PREFACE

This test bank contains multiple-choice items for each chapter in Gerard Egan's **THE SKILLED HELPER**, seventh edition. Correct answers are indicated by an asterisk (*) at the left of the response options. Additionally, the page numbers for the answers in the text are provided as well as the items being either factual, conceptual, or analytical at the end of each section. Website questions are also provided at the conclusion of each chapter questions.

David E. Reagan

Chapter 1

1. Throughout history there has been a deeply embedded conviction that, under proper conditions,
*   a. some people are capable of helping others
    b. helping only works in certain cultures
    c. people in need of help can be helped
    d. helping works only with trained helpers

2. Clients seek help because they are involved in problem situations they are not handling well or they feel they are not living as fully as they might. Therefore, the starting point of the helping process is quite often
    a. family or friends contacting the helper
*   b. clients' problem situations and unused opportunities
    c. clients' problem situations
    d. clients' not using all opportunities

3. In the helping relationship problems are not mathematical in nature but are instead situations that are
    a. scientific in nature
    b. more complex and challenging than normal problems
*   c. complex and messy problems in living not being well handled
    d. a combination of problems and unused opportunities

4. The goal of helping is not to "solve" problems but to
*   a. help the troubled person manage them more effectively
    b. avoid the problem by taking advantage of new possibilities in life
    c. work with the client until the issue is resolved
    d. help the client learn to live with the problem

5. The case of Carol, the mental health worker suffering from burnout, illustrates the therapeutic effect of
    a. simply providing information
    b. focusing on her developmental history
*   c. creating opportunities
    d. directive approaches in therapy

6. Seligman and Csikszenthihalyi (2000) called for a better balance of perspectives in the helping professions. In their minds, too much attention is foucsed on _____ and too little on what they call _____.
    a. problem situations; unused opportunities
*   b. pathology; "positive psychology"
    c. clients; engaged learning
    d. problems; effective solutions

7. Whether a client lives more effectively or not is a result of
*   a. the client's commitment to change
        b. the helper's skills
        c. the use of problem situations
        d. the dynamic between the helper and the client

8. Goal One of the Helping Relationship is:
        a. Help clients be more positive no matter what challenges they face in life.
*   b. Help clients manage their problems in living more effectively.
        c. Help clients avoid future problems.
        d. Help clients realize what caused their problems in the first place.

9. We know the following about subjective well-being (SWB)
        a. it is another way of saying happiness
        b. scientific knowledge of SWB is both possible and desirable
        c. the psychological community does not take it seriously
*   d. all responses for this item

10. In the Helping Relationship the need for a focus on outcomes is influenced by
        a. the client not wanting to deal with life issues
        b. the inability of the helper to always get results
*   c. third party payments depending on meaningful treatment plans with problem-managing outcomes
        d. the client wanting attention to resolve life problems

11. Goal Two of the Helping Relationship is:
*   a. Help clients become better at helping themselves in their everyday lives
        b. Help clients articulate their needs to the helper and to society
        c. Help clients realize the root of their problem and understand why they need help
        d. Help clients become autonomous within the dynamic of the helping relationship

12. The essence of this book is:
        a. providing helpers with an all inclusive model to help clients
        b. helping clients learn about problem avoidance and opportunity development
*   c. helping clients become better decision makers and more responsible "change agents"
        d. helping clients develop relationships that are positive and helpful.

13. In response to the question: Does Helping Help?, we can respond:
        a. there is full documentation that helping works.
*   b. we have yet to come up with an unqualified yes to this question.
        c. client satisfaction is the basis for knowing that helping models help
        d. manualized treatments provide documentation that helping helps

14. Client satisfaction may be based on:
   - a. the distraction the helping relationship provides from the real problems
   - * b. the client feels less stressed due to the helping relationship
   - c. the client likes his or her counselor
   - d. the hourly rate charged by his or her counselor

15. Because of the controversy surrounding the effectiveness of helping, especially by professional helpers, Egan agrees with Norman Kegan that the basic issue in helping is its
   - a. validity--whether it works or not
   - * b. reliability--whether it works consistency
   - c. norm-base--with whom it works
   - d. utility--whether helping achieves it goals

16. Egan contends that his text is
   - * a. intended to expand a training curriculum but not to substitute for it
   - b. a short-cut though a training curriculum in helping
   - c. unique in that no other training, formal or otherwise, is needed to become an effective helper
   - d. based upon the assumption that the helper-to-be has had a variety of life experiences

17. "All those things that adversely affect the helping relationship, process, outcomes, and impact in substantive ways but that are not identified and explored by helper or client" is Egan's definition of
   - a. client resistance
   - b. therapist counter-transference
   - * c. the "shadow side of helping"
   - d. the "human reality"

18. Managing the shadow side of helping involves understanding what can go wrong with
   - a. helper motives and skills
   - b. client motivations and agendas
   - c. client-helper dynamics
   - * d. all of the responses for this item

19. For Egan, the "wise helper" is one who
   - * a. is idealistic without being naïve.
   - b. possesses multiple therapeutic skills
   - c. is strongly founded in the theory of helping
   - d. widely read in psychology

20. Despite warnings from her supervisor, Jane spent an unusual amount of time in counseling with Dave, an individual convicted of driving under the influence of alcohol several times, only to find that Dave never acknowledged his problem with drinking. Jane certainly

*   a. failed to understand the "shadow side"

      b. didn't possess much social intelligence

      c. should have seen her ineffectiveness

    d. all of the responses for this item

Answer Key: Testbank

1.	A.	Conceptual.	Page 3.
2.	B.	Factual.	Page 4
3.	C.	Conceptual.	Page 4
4.	A.	Factual.	Page 5
5.	C.	Analytical	Page 6
6.	B.	Factual	Page 6
7.	A.	Conceptual	Page 7
8.	B.	Factual	Page 7
9.	D.	Analytical	Page 7
10.	C.	Factual	Page 8
11.	A	Factual	Page 8
12.	C.	Conceptual	Page 9
13.	B	Conceptual	Page 10
14.	B.	Factual	Page 11
15.	B.	Conceptual	Page 13
16.	A.	Conceptual	Page 16
17.	C.	Conceptual	Page 17
18.	D.	Conceptual	Page 18
19.	A.	Conceptual	Page 20
20.	A.	Analytical	Page 18

Website Questions:

1. One clear reality of human problems is that they

      a. may or may not be very manageable

      b. typically do not have a single "correct" solution

      c. can all be reviewed and options developed

*   d. all of the responses for this item.

2. Informal helpers include:

      a. police officers, counsellors, dentists

      b. psychologists, social workers, and nurses

*   c. probation officers, teachers, and supervisors

      d. all of the responses for this item

3. Clients who come to a helper to live more effectively are likely most interested in

*   a. learning to live more fully, to find out what could be better

      b. solve their problem situations without personal change

c. knowing what is wrong

d. being told the right thing to do

4. Ideally, the goals of helping involve both

    a. problem management and development of opportunities

*   b. effective management of current problems or missed opportunities and learning future problem-solving skills

    c. short-term gains and emotional stabilization

    d. finding correct solutions and implementing them

5. The effectiveness debate in helping centers around:

    a. do clients get what they want

    b. the use of manulaized treatments

*   c. does helping help?

    d. does wisdom win out over the shadow side?

6. Egan presents his book as a:

    a. complete curriculum for helping

*   b. a practical model of helping

    c. a theoretical introduction to professional counseling

    d. a model of helping that helps all

7. Egan sees the Shadow Side of helping as:

    a. providing insight for both helper and client

    b. the first step to becoming a wise helper

    c. inevitable in all helping relationships

*   d. an issue to be keenly sensitive to in the helping relationship

Answer Key: Website Quesitons.

1.	D.	Analytical	Page 4
2.	C.	Factual	Page 3
3.	A.	Conceptual	Page 5
4.	B.	Conceptual	Page 7-8
5.	C.	Analytical	Page 9
6.	B	Factual	Page 14
7.	D	Conceptual	Page 18

Chapter 2

1. When faced with a problem situation, most people engage in:

*   a. some version of a natural problem solving process.

    b. an intellectualized, non-emotional, solution-oriented process.

c. an immediate effort to seek help.

d. regression.

2. The "starting point" in Egan's helping model is:

    a. the theoretical orientation of the helper.

*   b. the needs of the client.

    c. the skill level of the helper.

    d. none of these.

3. One of the first things that a helper should do is to:

    a. administer a battery of psychological tests.

    b. determine what the helper has to offer the client.

*   c. examine the client's problems situation and missed
opportunities or unused potentials.

    d. tell the client how to solve the presenting problem.

4. In their correct order, the main "stages" of the skilled-helper model are:

    a. review of the current scenario, planning action to achieve desired goals,
achieving the goals.

    b. review of the current scenario, determining a preferred scenario, waiting for
change.

*   c. review of the current scenario, developing a preferred
scenario, developing action strategies to achieve the goals.

    d. review the skills of the helper, examine the needs of the client, determine if
therapy may be of help.

5. The central feature of the skilled-helper model is that it:

    a. requires clear and logical thinking.

    b. is based upon an emotional understanding of the client.

*   c. is built upon client action throughout each stage.

    d. demands full disclosure from the helper.

6. Elena, a new counselor, meets with Tom and Sarah to discuss a marital problem.
Arguments about money abound in their marriage. After two sessions Julie tells Tom
that Sarah must manage their money; Tom storms out of the session never to return. Julie

    a. did the right thing

    b. probably failed to look at Sarah's needs

*   c. didn't help develop a mutually preferred scenario

    d. empowered Tom to leave

7. Clients must act:

*   a. at every stage in the helping process.

    b. during stage three -- "getting there."

    c. during stage one and stage three.

    d. mostly during stages two and three.

8. Each of the three main stages of the skilled-helper model has three sub-stages. The helper needs to:

    a. help the client move through each in sequence.

    b. be sure not to move to the next stage until the current one is complete.

*   c. be aware that clients are not likely to move through the process sequentially.

    d. orderly progress is the hallmark for success.

9. Step I-A begins with:

    a. an exploration of the early childhood development of the client.

*   b. revelation and clarification of the client's problem situation and any missed opportunities

    c. an analysis of previous efforts at problem-solving

    d. an analysis of previous therapy experiences

10. When challenging a client in Step I-B, the helper should:

    a. continue to demonstrate support for the client.

    b. do so from an understanding of the client's frame of reference.

    c. focus on initiating self-challenge in the client.

*   d. all of these.

11. Jon works with college students. One of his clients, Frank, has spent several sessions discussing how hard he works attending school and holding two 20-hour jobs. He frequently misses his morning classes because he is so tired, but when Jon asks for his analysis of missing classes, Frank continues to talk about all the effort he puts in to be able to go to college. Clearly, Frank

    a. ought to quit school until he can afford it

*   b. has a blind spot about the effects of his work schedule

    c. has missed opportunities

    d. should be told to drop those classes

12. In Step I-C, the helper must:

*   a. help clients deal with issues that made a difference.

    b. deal with the first problem presented.

    c. design a way to deal with all the problems presented.

    d. present solutions that worked for other clients.

13. The best predictor of ultimate success in helping is:

    a. the competence and preparation of the helper.

    b. the amount of self-disclosure during each session.

*   c. what the client does between sessions.

    d. the level of commitment of the client.

14. The basic question of Step II-A is:
*   a. "What does the client want?"
    b. "What is the current problem?"
    c. "Why does the client want that?"
    d. "What is the role of others in the problem?"

15. A "realistic" goal is one that:
    a. is deeply desired by the client.
*   b. is capable of being translated into action.
    c. can be achieved in talk therapy.
    d. involves little self-pain for the client.

16. The principle for Step II-C is:
    a. help clients develop a range of possibilities of a better future
    b. help clients act both within and outside the counseling sessions
    c. help clients identify and work on problems, issues, concerns, or opportunities that will made a difference in their lives
*   d. help clients identify the kinds of incentives that will help them to pursue their chosen goals

17. When clients have a clear idea of what they want and where they would like to go, helping has achieved:
    a. its final goal.
*   b. development of a preferred scenario.
    c. an understanding of the current scenario.
    d. all of the above.

18. In Step III-A, stimulating clients to think of different ways of achieving their goals leads to:
    a. a set of "best fit" strategies for problem solving.
*   b. a wide variety of strategies.
    c. an ordered problem list.
    d. client commitment.

19. Once a plan of action has been developed, the helper needs to:
    a. help clients anticipate difficulties in enacting the plan.
    b. support and challenge the clients to continue with the plan.
    c. let the clients have several weeks to work on their own.
*   d. both a and b.

20. According to Egan, becoming a "skilled helper" requires:
    a. a complete conceptual understanding of the process.
    b. a strong foundation in psychological theories.
*   c. experience and practice.
    d. a fully accredited training program.

21. Pitfalls to the helping model-rigidity, over-control, virtuosity, ineptness-can be overcome if the helper keeps:

        a. the three stages and its nine steps clearly in sequence.

*   b. a clear focus on the abilities and needs of the client.

        c. the initiative in the sessions and minimizes client-generated solutions.

        d. accurate case records.

Answer Key: Testbank

1.	A	Factual	Page 24
2.	B	Factual	Page 25
3.	C	Conceptual	Page 25
4.	C	Factual	Page 26
5.	C	Conceptual	Page 26
6.	C	Analytical	Page 25
7.	A	Conceptual	Page 31
8.	C	Factual	Page 24
9.	B	Conceptual	Page 27
10.	D	Conceptual	Page 27
11.	B	Analytical	Page 27
12.	A	Conceptual	Page 27
13.	C	Conceptual	Page 27
14.	A	Factual	Page 28
15.	B	Conceptual	Page 29
16.	D	Factual	Page 29
17.	B	Conceptual	Page 30
18.	B	Conceptual	Page 30
19.	D	Conceptual	Page 31
20.	C	Conceptual	Page 31
21.	B	Conceptual	Page 39

Website Questions:

1. According to Egan, the helping relationship is:

        a. the essence of psychotherapy.

        b. more important than therapeutic outcomes.

*   c. an alliance between helper and client.

        d. a barometer for mental health.

2. The central feature of the skilled-helper model is that it:

        a. requires clear and logical thinking.

        b. is based upon an emotional understanding of the client.

*   c. is built upon client action throughout each stage.

d. demands full disclosure from the helper.

3. Jon works with college students. One of his clients, Frank, has spent several sessions discussing how hard he works attending school and holding two 20-hour jobs. He frequently misses his morning classes because he is so tired, but when Jon asks for his analysis of missing classes, Frank continues to talk about all the effort he puts in to be able to go to college. Clearly, Frank

   a. ought to quit school until he can afford it
*   b. has a blind spot about the effects of his work schedule
   c. has missed opportunities
   d. should be told to drop those classes

4. When clients have a clear idea of what they want and where they would like to go, helping has achieved:

   a. its final goal.
*   b. development of a preferred scenario.
   c. an understanding of the current scenario.
   d. all of the above.

Answer Key: Testbank

1.	B	Factual	Page 25
2.	C	Conceptual	Page 26
3.	B	Analytical	Page 27
4.	B	Conceptual	Page 30

Chapter 3

1. While the relationship between the client and the helper is very important, Egan takes the position that it is primarily

   a. less important than helping clients manage their lives better
   b. an enabling force in therapy
   c. only a means to an end
*   d. all of the above

2. According to Egan, the helping relationship is:

   a. the essence of psychotherapy.
   b. more important than therapeutic outcomes.
*   c. an alliance between helper and client.
   d. a barometer for mental health.

3. One primary purpose of the therapeutic relationship is to permit
        a. helpers to be consistent
*   b. needed changes in both attitudes and behavior for the client
        c. a humbling experience for the client
        d. learning in only one setting

4. Egan uses the term "values" to indicate:
*   a. a set of criteria for making decisions.
        b. ideals held by the helper.
        c. a set of cognitive beliefs to be avoided in therapy.
        d. the secrets of professional training.

5. Respect for the client means that the helper:
        a. is available to the client whenever needed.
        b. develops attachment feelings for the client
*   c. cherishes the client as an individual with particular needs.
        d. offers services only to those with the same racial, ethnic, and gender
characteristics of the helper.

6. "Tanya, you have failed to work on any of the goals we've worked out during these three sessions. I'm disgusted with you and will no longer see you." This therapist statement to an incarcerated client suggests that the helper
*   a. doesn't assume the client's good will
        b. gave the client an adequate chance
        c. adopted appropriate values
        d. was empathetic not sympathetic

7. Empathy as a value is a commitment on the part of helpers to understand the
        a. client from his or her point of view.
        b. client through the context of their lives.
        c. the dissonance between the client's point of view and reality.
*   d. all of the above

8. It is probably inevitable that diversity issues require that the helper
        a. recognize that a full understanding of every client is
        impossible
        b. must become aware of differences between themselves and their clients
        c. be flexible in applying he Egan model
*   d. all of the above

9. One aspect of being genuine is to act in the role of counselor
*   a. as a part of one's lifestyle
        b. only when professionally compensated
        c. whenever others appear helpless
        d. none of the above

10. Empowerment in the helping process includes all of the following except:
*   a. teaching clients to impose their rights over others' rights.
         b. helping clients gain control over their lives.
         c. helping others gain control of their lives.
         d. creating awareness that control is possible.

11. In regard to self-responsibility in the client, Farrelly and Brandsma (1974) and others have suggested that:
         a. clients are not as fragile than they may seem to the helper.
         b. clients can change if they choose to change.
         c. client self-dissatisfaction can be a motivator for change.
*   d. all of the above.

12. Egan espouses that a "problem-solving mentality"
         a. is rare among most people
         b. is an orientation that can be learned
         c. can be a part of current and future efforts to deal with life
*   d. all of the above

13. Effective helping involves a balance between over-controlling the client and offering no direction at all. A proper balance typically involves:
*   a. being a helper who both empowers the client to act and a consultant to the client one when and how to act.
         b. being consistent about either being directive or non-directive with one's clients.
         c. tending toward being more directive than non-directive.
         d. tending toward being more non-directive than directive.

14. The working charter, the contract, between the client and the helper should:
         a. help both develop mutual expectations about the helping process.
         b. enhance the client's freedom of choice.
         c. provide an overview of the helping process.
*   d. all of the above.

15. The shadow side of the therapeutic relationship involve
         a. ethical flaws
         b. different interpretations of the "working charter"
         c. unprofessional attitudes
*   d. all of the above

Answer Key: Testbank

1.	D	Conceptual	Page 42
2.	C	Conceptual	Page 43
3.	B	Analytical	Page 44

4.	A	Factual	Page 45
5.	C	Analytical	Page 47
6.	A	Analytical	Page 48
7.	D	Conceptual	Page 49
8.	D	Conceptual	Page 50
9.	A	Factual	Page 53
10	A	Conceptual	Page 55
11.	D	Conceptual	Page 56
12.	D	Conceptual	Page 57
13.	A	Conceptual	Page 58
14.	D	Factual	Page 58
15.	D	Conceptual	Page 59

Website Questions:

1. Respect for the client means that the helper:
>   a. is available to the client whenever needed.
>   b. develops attachment feelings for the client
> * c. cherishes the client as an individual with particular needs.
>   d. offers services only to those with the same racial, ethnic, and gender
characteristics of the helper.

2. Empathy as a value is a commitment on the part of helpers to understand the
>   a. client from his or her point of view.
>   b. client through the context of their lives.
>   c. the dissonance between the client's point of view and reality.
> * d. all of the above

3. It is probably inevitable that diversity issues require that the helper
>   a. recognize that a full understanding of every client is
>   impossible
>   b. must become aware of differences between themselves and their clients
>   c. be flexible in applying he Egan model
> * d. all of the above

4. Effective helping involves a balance between over-controlling the client and offering
no direction at all. A proper balance typically involves:
> * a. being a helper who both empowers the client to act and a consultant to the
>   client one when and how to act.
>   b. being consistent about either being directive or non-directive with one's clients.
>   c. tending toward being more directive than non-directive.
>   d. tending toward being more non-directive than directive.

5. The shadow side of the therapeutic relationship involve
        a. ethical flaws
        b. different interpretations of the "working charter"
        c. unprofessional attitudes
*   d. all of the above

Answer Key: Testbank

1.	C	Analytical	Page 47
2.	D	Conceptual	Page 49
3.	D	Conceptual	Page 50
4.	A	Conceptual	Page 58
5.	D	Conceptual	Page 59

Chapter 4

1. Conversations between helpers and their clients should be a therapeutic or helping dialogue. Which of the following is *NOT* a requirement for true dialogue
        a. taking turn
        b. connecting
        c. mutual influencing
*   d. directing outcomes

2. The most basic communication skills a helper needs to master are:
        a. empathy and probing.
*   b. attending and listening.
        c. responding and silence.
        d. challenging and confronting.

3. The ways in which helpers can be with their clients, both physically and psychologically, are:
*   a. called attending skills.
        b. the outcomes of listening.
        c. determined by the surroundings of the sessions.
        d. are sufficient for helping to begin.

4. Basic communication skills and effective helping skills should be:
        a. taught as separate and kept separate in practice.
        b. effectively practiced at different times in client sessions.
*   c. integrated early in a helper training program.
        d. taught with an overemphasis on the communication skills.

5. Which of the following is NOT one of the microskills of attending?
      a. Maintaining strong eye contact.
      b. Facing the client squarely.
*   c. Taking accurate notes in every session.
      d. Being relaxed during the session.

6. The basic microskills of attending, as identified by the acronym SOLER:
*   a. must be practiced with sensitivity to cultural and individual differences.
      b. apply to virtually every human culture.
      c. are an example of what Rogers called the "appalling consequences" of over-emphasizing microskills.
      d. natural skills possessed by most effective helpers.

7. Effective listening involves:
      a. attending to the verbal messages.
      b. understanding the distinction between facial expressions and voice cues.
*   c. hearing the full message-both verbal and non-verbal components.
      d. accurate record keeping or the use of a tape recorder.

8. In reading non-verbal behavior, the goal is to:
*   a. understand the client's message.
      b. analyze the motives of the client.
      c. interpret the client's message.
      d. know what the client is really saying.

9. It is suggested that non-verbal behaviors:
      a. regulate conversations
      b. communicate emotions
      c. modify verbal messages
*   d. all of the above

Answer Key: Testbank

1.	D	Factual Page 65
2.	B	Factual Page 66
3.	A	Factual Page 66
4.	C	Factual Page 66
5.	C	Factual Page 69
6.	A	Factual Page 68
7.	C	Factual Page 68
8.	A	Factual Page 68
9.	D	Factual Page 67

Website Questions:

1. Basic communication skills and effective helping skills should be:
   - a. taught as separate and kept separate in practice.
   - b. effectively practiced at different times in client sessions.
   - *   c. integrated early in a helper training program.
   - d. taught with an overemphasis on the communication skills.

2. Effective listening involves:
   - a. attending to the verbal messages.
   - b. understanding the distinction between facial expressions and voice cues.
   - *   c. hearing the full message-both verbal and non-verbal components.
   - d. accurate record keeping or the use of a tape recorder.

Answer Key: Website Testbank

1.   C   Factual Page 66
2.   C   Factual Page 68

Chapter 5

1. Visibly tuning in is not an end in itself. Full listening means:
   - a. listening actively
   - b. listening accurately
   - c. listening for meaning
   - *   d. all of the above

2. A message is clear if it is understood:
   - a. by the counselor.
   - *   b. in terms of client experiences, behaviors, and affect.
   - c. reflects the counselor's interpretation of the message.
   - d. without referring to non-verbal aspects.

3. Clients experiences differ from their behaviors in the same way that
   - a. emotions differ from affect
   - *   b. what others do differ from what I do
   - c. internal differs from external
   - d. victimization differs from empowerment

4. For Egan's model to work, the counselor must attend to the client's
   - a. experiences
   - b. emotions

c. behaviors

*   d. all of the above

5. Understanding the client's non-verbal behavior requires that the effective helper
     a. dissect the client's behaviors
     b. catalog the meaning of various behaviors

*   c. put these behaviors in context
     d. pay selective attention to it

6. Empathetic listening is
     a. the starting point for empathetic understanding
     b. a key ingredient in empathetic responding
     c. critical to effective helping

*   d. all of the above

7. Counselors engage in "tough-minded" listening when they:
     a. immediately challenge distortion in the client's message.
     b. disclose how their values differ from their clients.

*   c. recognize a client's distortion of reality.
     d. become aware of what the client is going to say before the client actually says it.

8. While most of us evaluate what others say to us, as skilled helpers we must:
     a. evaluate only the pathology of the client's message.

*   b. suspend our evaluative tendency in an effort to understand   the client.
     c. quickly disclose our judgments about the client's actions, thoughts, or emotions.
     d. learn to eliminate this tendency completely.

9. "Filtered listening" is a part of every person's reality. The skilled helper must try to eliminate those filters:
     a. that are a part of our religious heritage.
     b. which arise from our educational experiences.

*   c. that distort listening to the client's message.
     d. which do not have a scientific basis.

10. Which of the following is NOT a barrier to effective listening?
     a. Rehearsing responses to the client's message.
     b. Sympathetic listening.
     c. Interrupting to provide analysis to the client.

*   d. An effective problem-management response.

11. When Egan refers to one's "second channel," he is referring to

*   a. a helper's internal dialogue about themselves, the client or their relationship
     b. a type of ESP that therapists develop
     c. "channeling" the client's emotions

d. thoughts the client is unaware of having

Answer Key: Testbank

1. D   Factual Page 75
2. B   Factual Page 77
3. B   Factual Page 78
4. D   Factual Page 77-81
5. C   Factual Page 86
6. D   Factual Page 77
7. C   Factual Page 87
8. B   Factual Page 91
9. C   Factual Page 90
10. D   Factual Page 90-92
11. A   Factual Page 88

Website Questions:

1. Understanding the client's non-verbal behavior requires that the effective helper
    a. dissect the client's behaviors
    b. catalog the meaning of various behaviors
*   c. put these behaviors in context
    d. pay selective attention to it

2. While most of us evaluate what others say to us, as skilled helpers we must:
    a. evaluate only the pathology of the client's message.
*   b. suspend our evaluative tendency in an effort to understand   the client.
    c. quickly disclose our judgments about the client's actions, thoughts, or emotions.
    d. learn to eliminate this tendency completely.

Answer Key: Testbank

1. C   Factual Page 86
2. B   Factual Page 91

Chapter 6

1. Sharing empathic highlights involves:
    a. understanding the world of the client.
*   b. understanding the world of the client and communicating that understanding.
    c. understanding the world of the client and sharing similar circumstances from your own life.
    d. probing effectively to reveal the unstated causes of the client's behaviors.

2. The three components or dimensions of empathy as a communication skill are:
   a. perceptiveness, compassion for the client, and assertiveness.
   b. assertiveness, technical communication skills, and know-how.
   * c. perceptiveness, know-how, and assertiveness.
   d. compassion for the client, insightful understanding, and affinity for the client.

3. Accurate basic empathy captures:
   * a. the experiences, feelings, and behaviors of the client.
   b. the underlying emotional state of the client.
   c. the hidden agenda of the client for counseling.
   d. the honest reaction of the helper to the client.

4. Effective perceptiveness is built upon common sense, social intelligence and
   a. adequate training
   * b. effective attending and careful listening
   c. proper diagnostic procedures
   d. experience

5. Concerning empathy, Egan highlights the need to differentiate between it's definition a primary orientation value and
   a. a cultural treasure
   b. the felt experience of the helper
   * c. a helpful communication skill
   d. an effective gimmick

6. While "formula responses" may be avoided by experienced helpers, the basic formula Egan prescribes links:
   a. the client's past with the present.
   b. the current scenario with the preferred scenario.
   * c. the client's emotions with the experiences and behaviors that underlie them.
   d. the client's distortions with an accurate representation of reality.

7. The helper needs to identify the _____ of the clients story.
   a. feeling
   * b. key elements
   c. experiential component
   d. behavioral outcomes

8. Accurate basic empathy always responds to the client's:
   a. experiences.
   b. feelings.
   c. behaviors.
   * d. one or more of these.

9. The counselor uses the formula to respond to the client's unwanted pregnancy by saying, "You feel very much alone because you must decide this on your own." This response captures both the client's
*   a. emotion and its intensity
         b. experience and behavior
         c. feelings and behavior
         d. none of the above

10. Client: "You know, I studied for hours for this test and I still got an F. What am I supposed to do?"
     Helper: "Hey, college is tough. You've just got to study harder, spend more time in the library."
In this case, the helper's response:
         a. is an example of basic empathy.
*   b. is a cliché and not a form of empathy.
         c. a probe that will motivate the client.
         d. helps the client focus on the problem.

11. A client's emotion can be expressed best by
         a. single word or phrase
         b. an experiential statement
         c. a behavioral statement
*   d. all of the above

12. To be effective, the empathetic helper uses language that:
         a. mimics the language style of the client.
         b. is close the language style of the client even if it is unnatural for the helper.
*   c. is reflective of the emotional tone of the client's message, but is natural for the helper.
         d. is reflective of the helper's level of education.

13. Empathy will accomplish all of the following except
         a. stimulating client self-exploration.
*   b. immediate sustaining motivation to change.
         c. providing support for the client.
         d. pressure the client to move forward.

14. When a helper is inaccurate in an empathetic response:
         a. the response is typically not noticed by the client.
*   b. the client will usually acknowledge the error providing the helper a chance to correct the message.
         c. the basic trust of the relationship will be eroded and communication from the client will stop.
         d. the helper must trust that the response was really correct and repeat it.

15. Many helper responses, such as questions, interpretations, and advice-giving, do not communicate empathy because:

        a. they are usually not accurate.

*   b. they reflect elements in the helper's agenda.

        c. empathy is a totally intuitive activity.

        d. they are not sympathetic to the client.

16. Which of the following is the best response to this statement from a 12-year-old fifth grader?

   "My teacher is always picking on me. I don't do anything the other kids don't do, but when I do stuff I get caught. Tim does funnier stuff than me and he never gets yelled at!"

        a. "Just what is it that you do?"

        b. "You've got to start following the rules, haven't you."

*   c. "You're mad at your teacher because she picks on you and that's not fair."

        d. "I just hate it when a teacher is unfair like that."

17. Empathetic responding helps build a constructive relationship with the client because it

        a. is more important than attending

*   b. sends a message of being understood

        c. speaks to hidden feelings

        d. is verbal and never action based

Answer Key: Testbank

1.	B	Factual	Page 97
2.	C	Factual	Page 95
3.	A	Conceptual	Page 97
4.	B	Factual	Page 96
5.	C	Factual	Page 97
6.	C	Factual	Page 98
7.	B	Factual	Page 98
8.	D	Factual	Page 99
9.	A	Analytical	Page 99
10.	B	Analytical	Page 99-100
11.	D	Factual	Page 101
12.	C	Conceptual	Page 102
13.	B	Conceptual	Page 97
14.	B	Factual	Page 109
15.	B	Conceptual	Page 115
16.	C	Analytical	Page 113
17.	B	Conceptual	Page 97

Website Questions:

1. The three components or dimensions of empathy as a communication skill are:
   - a. perceptiveness, compassion for the client, and assertiveness.
   - b. assertiveness, technical communication skills, and know-how.
   - *   c. perceptiveness, know-how, and assertiveness.
   - d. compassion for the client, insightful understanding, and affinity for the client.

2. Concerning empathy, Egan highlights the need to differentiate between it's definition a primary orientation value and
   - a. a cultural treasure
   - b. the felt experience of the helper
   - *   c. a helpful communication skill
   - d. an effective gimmick

3. To be effective, the empathetic helper uses language that:
   - a. mimics the language style of the client.
   - b. is close the language style of the client even if it is unnatural for the helper.
   - *   c. is reflective of the emotional tone of the client's message, but is natural for the helper.
   - d. is reflective of the helper's level of education.

4. Empathetic responding helps build a constructive relationship with the client because it
   - a. is more important than attending
   - *   b. sends a message of being understood
   - c. speaks to hidden feelings
   - d. is verbal and never action based

Answer Key: Testbank

1.	C	Factual Page 97
2.	C	Factual Page 97
3.	C	Conceptual	Page 102
4.	B	Conceptual	Page 97

Chapter 7

1. Probes function to achieve all of the following except:
   - *   a. conveying empathy
   - b. filling in missing parts of the client's situation.
   - c. make demands on the client to talk or be more specific.
   - e. influence the client's responses.

2. Statements, interjections, or questions that help clients define and clarify their experiences, emotions, and behaviors are called:

  a. empathetic responses.
  b. parroting responses.
  c. executive functions in counseling.
* d. prompts or probes.

3. Effective use of questions means that the helper:

  a. asks questions that help the client clarify and explain.
  b. uses questions to keep a focus on the client, to provide the client initiative.
  c. moves the client along in problem management.
* d. all of the above.

4. Open-ended questions

  a. help the client talk about specific experiences, feelings, and   behaviors
  b. require more than a simple yes/no response
  c. avoid creating an "interrogation" atmosphere
* d. all of the above

5. Probes, unlike empathic responses, are:

  a. always verbal.
  b. only rarely verbal.
  c. maintain helper control over sessions.
* d. none of the above.

6. John's sister says, "God, I just keep rerunning all that stuff from our childhood. It gets me angry and careless." John responds, "how careless?" John's probe seeks to
* a. specify her careless behaviors
  b. probe other feelings she's having
  c. produce a balanced picture for her
  d. move her ahead in the helping process

7. Summarizing is especially useful when

  a. starting a new session with a client
  b. the current session gets bogged down
  c. the client seems not able to clarify further
* d. all of the above

8. Summaries serve all these purposes except

  a. preventing random talking
* b. insuring attending in the client
  c. applying pressure for more focus from the client
  d. inviting movement to more substantive issues

9. Empathetic responses and probes

    a. are generally incompatible with one another

*   b. can compliment one another

    c. are separate parts of the therapeutic communication system

    d. occur at different times in the helping process

10. Communication skills are:

    a. the most important part of helping.

*   b. effective if they help the outcomes of the helping process.

    c. not as important as attending, listening, empathetic responding, probing, and challenging.

    d. critical because they establish the real goal of helping, the formation of a relationship.

Answer Key: Testbank

1.	A	Factual	Page 122+
2.	D	Conceptual	Page 120
3.	D	Analytical	Page 121
4.	D	Factual	Page 121
5.	D	Conceptual	Page 122
6.	A	Analytical	Page 121-122
7.	D	Factual	Page 131-133
8.	B	Factual	Page 132
9.	B	Conceptual	Page 129-130
10.	B	Conceptual	Page 134

Website Questions:

1. Probes function to achieve all of the following except:

*   a. conveying empathy

    b. filling in missing parts of the client's situation.

    c. make demands on the client to talk or be more specific.

    f. influence the client's responses.

2. Open-ended questions

    a. help the client talk about specific experiences, feelings, and behaviors

    b. require more than a simple yes/no response

    c. avoid creating an "interrogation" atmosphere

*   d. all of the above

3. Summarizing is especially useful when
        a. starting a new session with a client
        b. the current session gets bogged down
        c. the client seems not able to clarify further
*   d. all of the above

Answer Key: Testbank

1.   A   FactualPage 122+
2.   D   FactualPage 121
3.   D   FactualPage 131-133

Chapter 8

1.Assessment serves all of the following except
*   a. providing a basis for fixing the client
        b. reality testing
        c. determining the seriousness of the client's concerns
        d. providing the basis for information and understanding that facilitates helping

2. The goals of Step I-A are:
        a. helping clients tell their story, set action plans, and initiate the plan.
*   b. clarify the clients' story, instill learning about themselves, build a working relationship, and focus on client action.
        c. allay the clients' fears about counseling, model empathy, and induce positive transference.
        d. identify the defenses of the client, challenge distortions, and require action.

3. Helping clients tell their story means:
        a. challenging each distortion of reality as it is presented.
*   b. letting clients explain their concerns about problems or missed opportunities.
        c. demonstrating empathetic responding at every opportunity.
        d. the helper must avoid probes for the first two sessions.

4. When clients tells their story in a nonstop fashion, the helper should:
        a. always interrupt them so that the helper can understand the parts of the story.
        b. insist on a dialogue rather than a monologue.
        c. let the clients tell their story in their own way.
*   d. both b and c.

5. Encouraging clarity in the client's story means that the helper:
*   a. helps the client discuss the specifics of their problem situation or missed opportunities.

b. reflects frequently on the helper's understanding of the problem.

c. avoids probes until the story has been told.

d. uses phrases like "tell me more" or "say that again."

6. Client-centered assessment is best recognized as:

    a. a testing period like Rogers Q-sort assessment.

    b. a diagnostic process enacted by the helper.

*   c. a learning process where client and helper are participants.

    d. primarily the responsibility of the helper.

7. Mehrabian and Reed (1969) have suggested that one can distinguish the degrees of clients problem severity by assessing:

    a. the amount of distress the problem causes.

    b. the felt distress added to the frequency of its occurrence.

    c. how agitated clients are when talking about the problem.

*   d. the product of perceived distress, degree of control over the stressor, and its frequency.

8. Client learning is especially aided by:

    a. recognizing and listing their weaknesses.

*   b. discerning that they possess a variety of resources.

    c. telling the client what to do.

    d. support from the helper.

9. Talking about the client's past is useful if it:

    a. leads to making sense of the present.

    b. liberates the clients from their pasts.

*   c. both of the above.

    d. none of the above.

10. Jim had lived a life full of set-backs, abandoned by his parents, a verbal learning disability, poor grades in school and he just flunked out of college. At the end of his story he jokes, "I'm such a loser, but I keep plugging away."

    A helper might help the search for resources by saying:

    a. "Tell me more about your learning problem."

*   b. "That's your real talent isn't it-you don't quit."

    c. "Have you asked the government for aid money?"

    d. "You feel badly because your life has been a series of failures."

11. Effective helping implies action by the client which requires
   a. a declaration of intent to act
   b. utilization of the client's resources
   c. the conquest of self defeating emotions
* d. all of the above

12. The reason why there must be an emphasis on client action is that
   a. the dialogue of helping substitutes for meaningful change
   b. clients tend to resist non-discretionary change
   c. helpers can't impose discretionary change
* d. all of the above

13. Giving home work to clients between sessions
   a. admits that good things are not happening in the sessions
* b. capitilizes on whatever learning or change takes place
   c. discourages clients from acting on what their learning in sessions
   d. slows down the therapy process

All of the items in this section were factual (4, 7, 9, 11, 13) or conceptual (3, 5, 6, 8, 12) except items 1, 2, and 10, which were analytical. Items 1, 4, 6, & 12, 13may appear in an internet version of this manual.

Answer Key: Testbank

1.   A   Analytical   Page 139
2.   B   Analytical   Page 140
3.   B   Conceptual   Page 140
4.   D   Factual Page 142
5.   A   Conceptual   Page 144
6.   C   Conceptual   Page 39
7.   D   Factual Page 146
8.   B   Conceptual   Page 147
9.   C   Factual Page 148-149
10.   B   Analytical   Page 151-152
11.   D   Factual Page 157
12.   D   Conceptual   Page 154
13.   B   Factual Page 155

Website Questions:

1. Assessment serves all of the following except
* a. providing a basis for fixing the client
   b. reality testing
   c. determining the seriousness of the client's concerns
   d. providing the basis for information and understanding that facilitates helping

2. When clients tells their story in a nonstop fashion, the helper should:

    a. always interrupt them so that the helper can understand the parts of the story.

    b. insist on a dialogue rather than a monologue.

    c. let the clients tell their story in their own way.

*   d. both b and c.

3. Client-centered assessment is best recognized as:

    a. a testing period like Rogers Q-sort assessment.

    b. a diagnostic process enacted by the helper.

*   c. a learning process where client and helper are participants.

    d. primarily the responsibility of the helper.

4. The reason why there must be an emphasis on client action is that

    a. the dialogue of helping substitutes for meaningful change

    b. clients tend to resist non-discretionary change

    c. helpers can't impose discretionary change

*   d. all of the above

5. Giving home work to clients between sessions

    b. admits that good things are not happening in the sessions

*   b. capitilizes on whatever learning or change takes place

    c. discourages clients from acting on what their learning in sessions

    d. slows down the therapy process

Answer Key: Testbank

1.	A	Analytical	Page 139
2.	D	Factual	Page 142
3.	C	Conceptual	Page 39
4.	D	Conceptual	Page 154
5.	B	Factual	Page 155

Chapter 9

1. Reluctance refers to the hesitancy of the client to

    a. engage in coerced therapeutic change

*   b. engage in the work demanded by the various stages and steps in the helping process

    c. form extrinsic counter-transference

    d. benefit from the "good faith" attitude of the helper

2. Resistance refers to the client's
    a. transference to the "rebellious teen" role
*   b. reactance in the face of perceived coercion
    c. inability to self-generate change
    d. none of the above

3. Because change, even therapeutic change, requires a self-generated or discretionary change by the client, clients often exhibit:
*   a. reluctance.
    b. resistance.
    c. rebellion.
    d. defiance.

4. Which of the following is NOT a source of client reluctance?
    a. Fear of change.
    b. Lack of trust in the helper.
*   c. Frequent probes by the helper.
    d. Shame-fear of being exposed to oneself.

5. Client resistance:
    a. is a way of fighting against perceived coercion.
    b. can arise from one's life experiences.
    c. often typifies involuntary clients.
*   d. all of the above.

6. Helpers may be blind to resistance from the client because
    a. clients are rarely overtly coerced
    b. clients are more likely to be reluctant than resistant
*   c. resistance typically arises from variables the helper controls
    d. their training programs insulate them from resistant clients

7. Raul was into the often observed "victim's role"-life was stacked against him: poor parents, absent father, bilingual home, poor grades, trouble with the law. He blamed everyone for his troubles and failed to take responsibility for changing his life. Clearly Raul is exhibiting
*   a. reluctance
    b. resistance
    c. malingering
    d. munchausinism

8. Typical ineffective reactions to client reluctance and resistance include
    a. increasing pressure on the client to change
    b. lowering expectations for change
    c. acceptance of them as normal in the helping process
*   d. both a and b

9. One effective way to manage client reluctance and resistance is to:
   a. challenge the reluctance and resistance directly.
*   b. accept that these phenomena are ones to be dealt with during therapy.
   c. dismiss clients until they want to change.
   d. none of the above.

10 What kind of defences contribute a great deal to both reluctance and resistance
   a. anticipation
   b. humor
* c. immature
   d. mature

Answer Key: Testbank

1.	B	Factual Page 163
2.	B	Factual Page 163&165
3.	A	Conceptual Page 163
4.	C	Conceptual Page 164
5.	D	Conceptual Page 165
6.	C	Factual Page 167
7.	A	Analytical Page
8.	D	Analytical Page 168
9.	B	Factual Page
10.	C	Factual Page 172

Website Questions:

1. Because change, even therapeutic change, requires a self-generated or discretionary change by the client, clients often exhibit:
*   a. reluctance.
   b. resistance.
   c. rebellion.
   d. defiance.

2. Client resistance:
   a. is a way of fighting against perceived coercion.
   b. can arise from one's life experiences.
   c. often typifies involuntary clients.
*   d. all of the above.

3. Typical ineffective reactions to client reluctance and resistance include
   a. increasing pressure on the client to change

b. lowering expectations for change

c. acceptance of them as normal in the helping process

*   d. both a and b

4. What kind of defences contribute a great deal to both reluctance and resistance

        c. anticipation

        d. humor

*   c. immature

        d. mature

Answer Key: Testbank

1.	A	Factual	Page 163
2.	D	Conceptual	Page 163
3.	D	Analytical	Page 168
4.	C	Factual	Page 172

Chapter 10

1. Generative learning and movement to action can be aided by the effective use of:

        a. confrontation.

        b. affronting.

*   c. challenge.

        d. ridicule.

2. Challenge differs from confrontation in that challenge

*   a. dares the client to face a true mirror reflection of themselves and/or their actions

        b. uses power to force action from the client

        c. emphatically demands acceptance of the helper's reality

        d. all of the above

3. The three general goals of challenge are:

*   a. to develop new perspectives about a client's problem, change self-limiting internal actions, and to generate an action potential.

        b. to produce change by means of ridicule and activation of shame motivations.

        c. to empathetically understand the client, to eliminate resistance, and to support the client's situation.

        d. to alter the client's emotional complacency, to alter self-limiting behaviors and thoughts, and to demonstrate the power of the therapist.

4. Developing new perspectives means that the client

        a. begins to mimic the helper's world view

        b. alters his/her mind-set in a more culturally diverse way

* c. engages in cognitive restructuring that leads to more effective problem management

  d. trusts the wisdom of the helper and follows the directives for change that are given

5. Believing that one must always have one's own way is an example of
  a. a controlling action
* b. a self-limiting belief
  c. an existential transference
  d. liberating self-talk

6. Albert Ellis has proposed that the person develops a number of common beliefs which ultimately lead to self-defeating internal dialogue. Which of the following is NOT one of those beliefs?
* a. being sociable with others
  b. avoiding
  c. being hurt by others
  d. having one's own way

7. When clients change and develop new and potentially effective perspectives
  a. positive change will innovatively follow
  b. the new mind-set begins to transform their lives
* c. there is no guarantee that external behaviors will change
  d. their problems situations will disappear

8. Helping clients explore their limiting perspectives, self defeating internal and external behaviors may not lead to changes in those areas but may redefine them as
  a. dysfunctions that can be tolerated
* b. resources that can become life-enhancing
  c. reasons for terminating therapy
  d. none of the above

9. As Carkhuff (1987) uses the term "personalizing" means to:
  a. use confrontation to attack the personality of the client.
  b. employ helper self-disclosure when talking to a client.
* c. help clients learn that they are in some way responsible for their problems.
  d. avoiding cliches in therapy.

10. Since action is a part of the entire helping model, one essential feature of problem presentation is that it must:
  a. have considerable diversity.
* b. be stated in manageable terms.
  c. lead to helper empathy.
  d. generate emotional release for the client.

11. When properly enacted, challenge can help clients to:
    a. express better their emotional status.
    b. feel prime motivators like guilt and shame.
    c. maintain their interpretations of the world and themselves.
  * d. reconstruct their views of themselves and their worlds in self-enhancing ways.

12. Discrepancies can exist between:
    a. what a client says and what the client does.
    b. how clients see themselves and how others see them.
    c. what clients are and what they wish to be.
  * d. all of the above.

13. Distortions arise in clients because:
    a. they are unaware of the opinions that others have of them.
  * b. they cannot face their world as it is.
    c. disabling self-talk prevents action for change.
    d. distortions are in the unconscious and, thus, are uncontrollable.

14. Games, smoke screens, tricks, and excuses are examples of the ways that clients try to:
    a. manipulate others.
    b. avoid change.
    c. appear not to be responsible for events in their lives.
  * d. all of the above.

15. Eric, a young gay male who is very fearful about contracting AIDS, blames his problems on an older brother who seduced him during the early years of high school. When confronted about this distortion, Eric insists that his problems began with his brother's seduction and that he just wants everyone to leave him alone.
    Which of the following is an appropriate follow up confrontation to his distortion?
    a. "I see. Well, I guess that you are destined to be lonely."
  * b. "It's hard for me to believe that you want to be left alone. What do you really want?"
    c. "Well, it is tough being gay. Are you sure that you are?"
    d. "Does that include me?"

16. One of drawbacks to the counselor's use of challenge is:
    a. the acceptance of the reality and congruity of the challenge.
    b. a transformation of a client's new self-perception into positive action.
  * c. increased client resistance.
    d. increased liking of the counselor by the client.

17. Self directed learners use resources available to them by
    a. working with an underlying sense of purpose
    b. having a dream they refuse to surrender
    c. focusing on their gifts
*   d. all of the above

Answer Key: Testbank

1.	C	Conceptual	Page 176
2.	A	Conceptual	Page 177
3.	A	Factual	Page 184
4.	C	Conceptual	Page 181
5.	B	Factual	Page 185
6.	A	Factual	Page 185
7.	C	Analytical	Page 188
8.	B	Conceptual	Page 191
9.	C	Factual	Page 196
10.	B	Conceptual	Page 197
11.	D	Analytical	Page 188&195
12.	D	Factual	Page 190
13.	B	Factual	Page 192
14.	D	Factual	Page 193
15.	B	Analytical	Page 192
16.	C	Conceptual	Page 190
17.	D	Factual	Page 194

Website Questions:

1. Challenge differs from confrontation in that challenge
*   a. dares the client to face a true mirror reflection of themselves and/or their actions
    b. uses power to force action from the client
    c. emphatically demands acceptance of the helper's reality
    d. all of the above

2. When clients change and develop new and potentially effective perspectives
    a. positive change will innovatively follow
    b. the new mind-set begins to transform their lives
*   c. there is no guarantee that external behaviors will change
    d. their problems situations will disappear

3. Helping clients explore their limiting perspectives, self defeating internal and external behaviors may not lead to changes in those areas but may redefine them as

a. dysfunctions that can be tolerated
* b. resources that can become life-enhancing
c. reasons for terminating therapy
d. none of the above

4. One of drawbacks to the counselor's use of challenge is:
a. the acceptance of the reality and congruity of the challenge.
b. a transformation of a client's new self-perception into positive action.
* c. increased client resistance.
d. increased liking of the counselor by the client.

5. Self directed learners use resources available to them by
d. working with an underlying sense of purpose
e. having a dream they refuse to surrender
f. focusing on their gifts
* d. all of the above

Answer Key: Testbank

1.   A   Conceptual   Page 177
2.   C   Analytical   Page 188
3.   B   Conceptual   Page 191
4.   C   Conceptual   Page 190
5.   D   Factual Page 194

Chapter 11

1. A helper response that deals with both the overlooked positive side and the overlooked shadow side of the client's experience and behavior is called:
a. the "MUM effect."
b. a basic empathic response.
* c. advanced empathy.
d. a "forking" response.

2. Advanced empathy is a form of:
a. deep client support response.
* b. challenge.
c. helper self-disclosure.
d. nurturance.

3. An advanced empathy response involves:
* a. making explicit the implicit message from the client.
b. interpreting the client's message.

c. telling the client the insight of the helper.

d. none of the above.

4. The question the helper needs to keep in mind when making an advanced empathy response is,

        a. "Will my response anger this client?"

        b. "What stage of the model are we at right now?"

*   c. "Will this response help clarify and alter the client's perspective and need to act?"

        d. "How can I say this without making demands on this client?"

5. Advanced empathy involves the helper's _____ about the client based upon the helpers experience of the client.

        a. predictions

*   b. hunches

        c. diagnosis

        d. assessment

6. Information sharing, as a challenging skill, includes:

        a. correcting client misinformation.

        b. giving new information to the client.

        c. therapist self-disclosure.

*   d. both a and b.

7. In order to be effective, challenging or shocking information needs to be delivered:

        a. straight without watering it down.

*   b. in a tactful supportive fashion.

        c. with advice-giving to direct the client properly.

        d. based upon the values of the helper.

8. Counselor self-disclosure is a form of:

        a. support for the client that should be used frequently.

        b. both motivational and supportive of the client.

*   c. is a form of challenge that should be used selectively.

        d. narcissism.

9. Helper self-disclosure should

        a. Aid the progress toward therapeutic goals

        b. not be an excuse for nostalgia

        c. quite selective and focused

*   d. all of the above

10. The ability of the helper to discuss with the client where they are in their overall relationship is called:
*   a. general relationship immediacy.
         b. here-and-now immediacy.
         c. self-involving immediacy.
         d. none of the above.

11. The ability of the helper to discuss with the client what is happening within a particular session is called:
         a. general relationship immediacy.
*   b. here-and-now immediacy.
         c. self-involving immediacy.
         d. none of the above.

12. Present-tense, personal responses to the client are called:
         a. general relationship immediacy.
         b. here-and-now immediacy.
*   c. self-involving immediacy.
         d. confrontation.

13. The skill of intimacy is called for in each of the following situations except when:
         a. there is tension between client and helper.
         b. the session appears directionless.
*   c. the client is acting on his or her own initiative.
         d. attraction is sidetracking the client or the helper.

14. When the helper becomes directive, offering suggestions and recommendations, the helper is
         a. engaging in unethical behavior
         b. taking away the client's autonomy
         c. acting as teacher and not as counselor
*   d. being effective in moving the client toward agreed upon goals

15. For confrontation to be effective, the helper must:
         a. make sure the client is understood accurately.
         b. be focusing on the consequences of persisting in dysfunction.
         c. have strong rapport with the client.
*   d. all of the above.

Answer Key: Testbank

1.	C	Factual	Page 200
2.	B	Conceptual	Page 200
3.	A	Conceptual	Page 201
4.	C	Conceptual	Page 202

5.	B	Factual	Page 204
6.	D	Factual	Page 206
7.	B	Factual	Page 206
8.	C	Factual	Page 208
9.	D	Analytical	Page 208
10.	A	Factual	Page 210
11.	B	Factual	Page 211
12.	C	Factual	Page 212
13.	C	Factual	Page 212-213
14.	D	Conceptual	Page 214
15.	D	Conceptual	Page 215

Website Questions:

3. An advanced empathy response involves:
*   a. making explicit the implicit message from the client.
    b. interpreting the client's message.
    c. telling the client the insight of the helper.
    d. none of the above.

5. Advanced empathy involves the helper's _____ about the client based upon the helpers experience of the client.
    a. predictions
*   b. hunches
    c. diagnosis
    d. assessment

9. Helper self-disclosure should
    a. Aid the progress toward therapeutic goals
    b. not be an excuse for nostalgia
    c. quite selective and focused
*   d. all of the above

14. When the helper becomes directive, offering suggestions and recommendations, the helper is
    a. engaging in unethical behavior
    b. taking away the client's autonomy
    c. acting as teacher and not as counselor
*   d. being effective in moving the client toward agreed upon goals

Answer Key: Testbank

1.	A	Conceptual	Page 201
2.	B	Factual	Page 204
3.	D	Analytical	Page 208
4.	D	Conceptual	Page 214

Chapter 12

1. Encouraging self-challenge in the client often involves
*   a. establishing a structure for self-challenge with appropriate probes and supportive statements
     b. direct confrontation
     c. manipulation of the client
     d. requiring divergent thinking by the client

2.. Earning the right to challenge a client means that the helper must:
     a. make sure the client is understood accurately.
     b. live a life congruent with the helper's values.
     c. have strong rapport with the client.
*   d. all of the above.

3. "Well, I don't want you to take this wrong, and I surely might be wrong about this, but it seems that maybe, just maybe, you are a little bit too controlling with your wife." This counselor's statement is
     a. underqualifying an opinion
*   b. likely too tentative
     c. too strong for therapy
     d. likely effective

4. Challenging the client's strengths means:
     a. not being afraid to criticize what the client thinks are accomplishments.
*   b. focusing on the client's unused assets and resources.
     c. focusing the the client's failures.
     d. not being too eager to praise the client for taking action.

5. Effective challenges are
     a. vague so the client can interpret them creatively
     b. specific because clients have tunnel vision
     c. vague so the counselor is not manipulative
*   d. specific in order to make concerns tangible

6. The "MUM effect" is:
  a. the client's unwillingness to be honest.
  b. the counselor's hesitance to offer self-disclosure.
*   c. the counselor's reluctance to use challenge.
  e. the silence of the client after a challenge.

7. Summarizing serves the function of providing:
*   a. focus and challenge to the client.
  b. an opportunity to give direction to the client.
  c. the opening for helper self-disclosure.
  d. an important occasion for interpretation.

Answer Key: Testbank

1.	A	Conceptual	Page 219
2.	D	Conceptual	Page 220
3.	B	Analytical	Page 220
4.	B	Factual Page 221	
5.	D	Factual Page 222	
6.	C	Factual Page	
7.	A	Conceptual	Page

Website Questions:

1. Encouraging self-challenge in the client often involves
*   a. establishing a structure for self-challenge with appropriate probes and supportive statements
  b. direct confrontation
  c. manipulation of the client
  d. requiring divergent thinking by the client

2. The "MUM effect" is:
  a. the client's unwillingness to be honest.
  b. the counselor's hesitance to offer self-disclosure.
*   c. the counselor's reluctance to use challenge.
  the silence of the client after a challenge.

3. Summarizing serves the function of providing:
*   a. focus and challenge to the client.
  b. an opportunity to give direction to the client.
  c. the opening for helper self-disclosure.
  d. an important occasion for interpretation.

Answer Key: Testbank

Chapter 13

1. In Step I-C, "screening" refers to:

    a. identifying all the client's problems without prioritizing them.

    b. concurrent efforts to identify the problems and the preferred outcomes.

*   c. helping the client decide whether counseling is what the client needs.

    d. prioritizing options as "do-able" or not.

2. When a client presents with multiple problems, the helper should:

    a. work with the first problem presented.

    b. identify that core problem which, if resolved, will solve all other problems.

    c. begin with the problem that most theories would agree is most critical.

*   d. attempt to make the initial therapeutic experience rewarding for the client.

3. Zheng was destroyed when she failed her fist test in a graduate computer programming class. She sat silent in her room for five hours just staring at a wall. Her roommate, knowing that this was highly unusual, asked her what was wrong and let her tell her story and verbalize her fears that she would be deported. In this case the roommate

    a. should have just let her be alone

*   b. gained leverage by helping Zheng manage the crisis

    c. lost the chance to joke about the test and put it in proper perspective

    d. all of the above

4. When a client presents with a large, complicated problem, a helper should try to:

    a. precipitate a crisis in order to motivate the client.

*   b. divide the problem into several smaller, more manageable problems.

    c. refer the client to a more intensive setting.

    d. be as supportive as possible for the client's pain.

5. In finding leverage, a "cost-benefits" analysis can lead to:

    a. a screening decision not to enter counseling.

    b. a rejection of a problem as too difficult to resolve.

*   c. identification of problems where the returns outweigh the cost of change.

    d. a reduction of the fees charged to a client who is likely to need long-term therapy.

6. When using leverage, the helper will need to:
*   a. be willing to make demands on clients.
      b. avoid going beyond the client's framework.
      c. deal only with manageable sub-problems.
      d. all of the above.

7. The technique which requests the client to describe the problem in one word is a(n):
      a. challenge technique.
*   b. focusing technique.
      c. "stage" trick.
      d. elaboration-added procedure.

8. Finding leverage with clients is aimed at achieving:
      a. client commitment to therapy.
*   b. the discovery of incentives for action.
      c. mutual self disclosure.
      d. a reconstruction of basic personality features.

Answer Key: Testbank

1.	C	Factual	Page 231
2.	D	Analytical	Page 234
3.	B	Conceptual	Page na
4.	B	Factual	Page 233
5.	C	Factual	Page 236
6.	A	Conceptual	Page 235&237
7.	B	Factual	Page 238
8.	B	Factual	Page 239

Website Questions:

1. Zheng was destroyed when she failed her fist test in a graduate computer programming class. She sat silent in her room for five hours just staring at a wall. Her roommate, knowing that this was highly unusual, asked her what was wrong and let her tell her story and verbalize her fears that she would be deported. In this case the roommate
      a. should have just let her be alone
*   b. gained leverage by helping Zheng manage the crisis
      c. lost the chance to joke about the test and put it in proper perspective
      d. all of the above

2. When using leverage, the helper will need to:
*   a. be willing to make demands on clients.
       b. avoid going beyond the client's framework.
       c. deal only with manageable sub-problems.
       d. all of the above.

Answer Key: Testbank

1.   A   Conceptual   Page 235&237
2.   A   Conceptual   Page 235&237

Chapter 14

1. When moving clients toward change (Stage II), the counselor should be asking the question:
       a. "What is the core of the problem?"
*   b. "What do you want?"
       c. "What can I do to help?"
       d. "What type of challenge will produce leverage?"

2. When the client has determined a preferred scenario, the next issue (Stage III) is:
       a. What is the core problem?
       b. What do you want?
*   c. What do you have to do to get what you want?
       d. How many more sessions can you afford?

3. Clearly, Egan believes that the most important goal of helping is
       a. understanding the problem (or problem situation)
*   b. managing the problem (or problem situation)
       c. generating insight into the core issues of the problem
       d. effective and empowering self disclosure and direction

4. Which of the following is NOT a purpose for goal-setting?
*   a. To encourage self-generated random action.
       b. To motivate the client.
       c. To activate the search for solution strategies.
       d. To encourage goal directed persistence.

5. When a goal does not produce persistent efforts from the client the problem is probably that the goal:
       a. lacks specificity.
       b. isn't clearly stated.
       c. isn't perceived as realistic.
*   d. all of the above.

6. One important reason that helpers fail to help clients develop viable goals is that:
    a. goal-setting is too difficult.
*   b. they aren't trained to do so.
    c. clients drop-out before telling their story.
    d. they fear being too directive.

7. Rational decision making is a process that involves:
    a. making a choice.
    b. gathering information.
    c. analysis of information.
*   d. all of the above.

8. Because humans seldom engage in pure rational decision making, the counselors and clients must proceed with an attitude of:
    a. resignation to the temporal nature of counseling.
*   b. positive acceptance that the future is uncertain.
    c. marginal pessimism about change.
    d. grim determination to succeed.

9. In the "choice and execution" stage of decision-making, clients sometimes just procrastinate because
    a. they fear they have made the wrong choice
    b. may be subject to magical thinking
    c. choices don't always make life easier
*   d. all of the above are possible explanations

10. The focus of Stage II is
*   a. outcomes
    b. activities
    c. exploration
    c. clarification

Answer Key: Testbank

1.	B	Factual	Page 243
2.	C	Factual	Page 244
3.	B	Conceptual	Page na
4.	A	Conceptual	Page 250
5.	D	Conceptual	Page 250
6.	B	Analytical	Page na
7.	D	Factual	Page 252
8.	B	Conceptual	Page 259
9.	D	Conceptual	Page 256
10.	A	Factual	Page 241

Website Questions:

1. Because humans seldom engage in pure rational decision making, the counselors and clients must proceed with an attitude of:

      a. resignation to the temporal nature of counseling.

*   b. positive acceptance that the future is uncertain.

      c. marginal pessimism about change.

      d. grim determination to succeed.

2. Clearly, Egan believes that the most important goal of helping is

      a. understanding the problem (or problem situation)

*   b. managing the problem (or problem situation)

      c. generating insight into the core issues of the problem

      d. effective and empowering self disclosure and direction

3. The focus of Stage II is

*   a. outcomes

      b. activities

      c. exploration

      d. clarification

Answer Key: Testbank

1.	B	Conceptual	Page 259
2.	B	Conceptual	Page na
3.	A	Factual	Page 241

Chapter 15

1. for researchers Markus and Nurius (1986) the concept of "possible selves" refers to

      a. what one might become

      b. what one fears becoming

      c. what one would like to become

*   d. all of the above

2. Which of the following is NOT a reason that creative problem solving often eludes clients:

      a. They possess life histories and personal characteristics that are antagonistic to creativity.

      b. They possess emotional, behavioral, and cognitive inhibitions to innovative thinking.

      c. They have a counselor who doesn't stimulate them to use their creative potential.

*   d. They are typically people who possess little or no creative talent.

3. Which of the following are inhibitors to creative problem solving?
      a. nonconformity
      b. deeply ingrained self-defeating habits
      c. dependence on authority
*   d. both b and c

4. Divergent thinking:
      a. seeks to find the one "correct" answer.
*   b. seeks to find a variety of useful solutions.
      c. is not helpful in dealing with complex problems.
      d. is the easiest course for the helper to encourage.

5. When using a brainstorming technique, the helper must:
      a. encourage a variety of client ideas, even unrealistic ones.
      b. avoid premature criticism of any of the ideas.
      c. request clarification of the items on the list.
*   d. all of the above.

6. The story of Quentin's and Caroline's searches for career fulfillment illustrate
*   a. differences between outcomes for convergent versus
divergent problem solving
      b. that career fulfillment can be achieved by all
      c. the importance of finding the "one right career"
      d. none of the above

7. Future oriented probes are often most useful in the context of:
      a. problem clarification activities.
*   b. a brainstorming strategy.
      c. benevolent challenge
      d. group therapy.

8. "Future-oriented questions"
      a. deal with client needs and wants that will be real after action   is taken to change
      b. must be managed to avoid convergent thinking
      c. emphasize the positive effects of change
*   d. all of the above

9. Encouraging clients to look toward a better future:
   - a. is useful even when in Stage I.
   - b. can offer a client a sense of hope.
   - c. alter the perspective the client has on the problem.
   - * d. all of the above.

10. A future orientation in counseling can be achieved by:
   - a. encouraging a full and complete discussion of the past.
   - * b. encouraging clients to engage in a dialogue between a better future and the unacceptable present.
   - c. focusing on the most outlandish options from a brainstorming session.
   - d. reminding clients that it is their responsibility to change.

11. When helping clients identify models of their wants and needs, the skilled helper:
   - a. should recommend reading books on successful people.
   - b. ought to be able to be the clients' model.
   - * c. knows that models can be found almost anywhere.
   - d. must find the right model for each client.

12. An effective model (or exemplar)
   - a. should not possess any of problems the client has
   - * b. can help clients be more specific about what they want
   - c. is a symbol for the ideal solution
   - d. represents a "fantasy-inducing" thinking strategy

Answer Key: Testbank

1.	D	Factual	Page 263
2.	D	Analytical	Page 263
3.	D	Factual	Page 264
4.	B	Factual	Page 264-265
5.	D	Conceptual	Page 266-267
6.	A	Analytical	Page na
7.	B	Conceptual	Page 268
8.	D	Conceptual	Page 268
9.	D	Conceptual	Page 268-269
10.	B	Conceptual	Page 269
11.	C	Conceptual	Page 270
12.	B	Factual	Page 270

Website Questions:

7. for researchers Markus and Nurius (1986) the concept of "possible selves" refers to
      a. what one might become
      b. what one fears becoming
      c. what one would like to become
*   d. all of the above

9. Which of the following are inhibitors to creative problem solving?
      a. nonconformity
      b. deeply ingrained self-defeating habits
      c. dependence on authority
*   d. both b and c

14. Future oriented probes are often most useful in the context of:
      a. problem clarification activities.
*   b. a brainstorming strategy.
      c. benevolent challenge
      d. group therapy.

Answer Key: Testbank

1.	D	Factual	Page 263
2.	D	Factual	Page 264
3.	B	Conceptual	Page 268

Chapter 16

1. Simple answers to the question, "What do you want?" may not take into account:
      a. the variety of possible futures available.
*   b. what the client needs.
      c. what the helper wants for the client.
      d. none of the above.

2. When identifying client needs (as opposed to client wants), one helpful strategy is to explore:
      a. how much hurt the client is experiencing.
      b. the financial resources of the client.
*   c. the consequences of a client's wants.
      d. when the wants emerged.

3. Clients who are likely to have difficulties in stating their wants and needs:
      a. need more work in Stage I.
      b. aren't future-oriented or lack conceptual skills.

c. may lack imagination or be rooted in past problems.
*   d. both b and c.

4. "I want to start doing some exercise" is an example of a(n):
    a. outcome.
*   b. activity.
    c. need.
    d. interest.

5. "Well, it is clear to me that I have to change" is an example of a(n):
*   a. intention.
    b. broad goal.
    c. specific goal.
    d. verifiable outcome.

6. An optimal outcome is one that:
    a. reflects a client's needs and wants.
    b. has an element of intent-to-act.
    c. is specific and verifiable.
*   d. all of the above.

7. An optimal outcome is one that:
    a. related to better management of the original problem situation.
    b. challenges a client to reach for higher levels of performance.
*   c. both of the above.
    d. none of the above.

8. Lon, a graduate student who lived with his parents, wanted more autonomy. In order to help Lon understand the social implications of his wants, which of the following questions would most helpful for the helper to ask Lon?
    a. "How can you get what you want?"
    b. "Can you afford to live alone?"
*   c. "What would you be doing differently with the people in your life?"
    d. "What accomplishments would be in place that are not in place now?"

9. Joni, although a "straight-A" student, knew that she would have to do very well in her last two years of pre-med studies to be considered for a good medical school. Which of the following goals for hcr study-time management would be "best" for her?
    a. Study as much as last year
*   b. Study more than last year
    c. Study twice as much as last year
    d. Study with others

10. Helping involves taking risks; proper goals should be:
    a. the "safe" choice-minimizing the risk.
*   b. the "wise" choice-leading to positive outcomes.
    c. an "economical" choice-least costly.
    d. a theoretically "correct" choice.

11. Which if the following is NOT one of the criteria for deciding if a goal is realistic?
    a. The client has access to the resources needed.
    b. The goal is under the client's control.
*   c. The goal is one of the client's wants.
    d. Accomplishment of the goal outweighs costs.

12. "I want my children to tell me that they love me at least once a day" is a goal statement this is very likely to be:
    a. motivating to the client.
    b. a source of strength for the family.
*   c. outside of the control of the client.
    d. unachievable because it lacks clarity.

13. Realistic goals must be accomplished in a reasonable time frame. A "reasonable time frame" involves selecting:
    a. goals that part of a larger goal.
    b. immediate and longer-term goals.
    c. goals that lead to substantive solutions.
*   d. all of the above.

14. When a potentially optimal goal is likely to conflict with a client's value system, the counselor should
    a. spend time encouraging the client to do the action in violation of the value system-which would likely change with the success
    b. reconsider the positive effect of therapy for the client
*   c. avoid encouraging the client to engage in the value-conflicting action
    d. none of the above

15. When facing a choice between a challenging goal and an adaptive goal, the counselor should
    a. usually encourage adopting the challenging goal
    b. usually encourage adopting the adaptive goal
*   c. encourage clients to act within their limitations
    d. encourage clients to push beyond their limitations

Answer Key: Testbank

1.   B   Conceptual   Page 286
2.   C   Conceptual   Page 287
3.   D   Conceptual   Page na
4.   B   Factual Page 277
5.   A   Factual Page 278
6.   D   Conceptual   Page na
7.   C   Conceptual   Page na
8.   C   Analytical   Page na
9.   B   Analytical   Page na
10. B   Conceptual   Page 285
11. C   Factual Page 282&283
12. C   Factual Page 283
13. D   Factual Page 285
14. C   Analytical   Page na
15. C   Analytical   Page 289

Website Questions:

1. "I want to start doing some exercise" is an example of a(n):
    a. outcome.
*   b. activity.
    c. need.
    d. interest.

2. Helping involves taking risks; proper goals should be:
    a. the "safe" choice-minimizing the risk.
*   b. the "wise" choice-leading to positive outcomes.
    c. an "economical" choice-least costly.
    d. a theoretically "correct" choice.

3. "I want my children to tell me that they love me at least once a day" is a goal statement this is very likely to be:
    a. motivating to the client.
    b. a source of strength for the family.
*   c. outside of the control of the client.
    d. unachievable because it lacks clarity.

4. When facing a choice between a challenging goal and an adaptive goal, the counselor should
    a. usually encourage adopting the challenging goal
    b. usually encourage adopting the adaptive goal

*   c. encourage clients to act within their limitations

          d. encourage clients to push beyond their limitations

Answer Key: Testbank

1.   B   Factual Page 277
2.   B   Conceptual   Page 285
3.   C   Factual Page 283
4.   C   Analytical   Page 289

Chapter 17

1. Initial commitment to a goal is demonstrated by:
      a. establishing a realistic goal.
      b. finding a goal that reflects client wants.
*   c. movement to action by the client.
      d. the client's level of emotional responsibility.

2. Costs and payoffs are relative. One thing that a skilled helper can help a client do when the cost-benefit ratio is unclear is to:
*   a. examine the consequences of various actions.
      b. impose the helper's values on the action decision.
      c. tell the client to have trust that things will work out.
      d. re-specify the action goal.

3. Goals such as, "I'm going to give up smoking," often fail because:
      a. smoking is a very addictive behavior.
*   b. negative goals seldom provide incentives.
      c. addictions are not under the client's control.
      d. counselors aren't needed for their accomplishment.

4. Goal ownership by the client is important because:
*   a. it makes the client responsible for outcomes.
      b. therapists more readily approval of such goals.
      c. it provides inertia to the process of action.
      d. none of the above.

5. Julius said to his counselor, "I see now that if I'm to find some happiness, I have start to do something about it." This is an example of which level of ownership?
      a. Compliance
*   b. Buy-in
      c. Ownership
      d. Emancipation

6. Contracting with a client to initiate action on a goal;
    a. is useful to provide initial commitment.
    b. provides a structure for action.
    c. can lead to helper ownership of the goal.
*   d. both a and b.

7. Examining "competing agendas" in a program of change:
    a. is the same thing as examining the consequences of action choices.
    b. can lead to better prioritizing a client's behaviors.
    c. produces better balanced decisions.
*   d. all of the above.

8. Helping a client develop a sense of self-efficacy involves
*   a. training in the skills needed to succeed
    b. clarifying how their personal deficiencies affect their actions
    c. not letting the client back-slide with training gets tougher
    d. all of the above

9. A "codicil" in reference to the shadow side of choice and helping is:
*   a. a condition or limitation one one's goal.
    b. the reality that decisions in counseling are co-decisions.
    c. the social influence of the helper in altering client values.
    d. none of the above.

10. According to Albert Bandura, people tend to take action if they know that a particular behavior will lead to a desired outcome and if they
    a. have adequate outcome expectancies
*   b. reasonably sure that they can engage in the behavior
    c. are guided or directed
    d. are reinforced for starting

11. The "shadow side" of goal setting essentially revolves around:
    a. fears that the helper has about taking action.
    b. the fact that goals are themselves limiting.
    c. client resistance to taking self-responsibility.
*   d. all of the above.

12. Since "goal setting" is a rational process that can be alien to the client, Egan suggests that the helper should:
*   a. focus on helping clients explore what they want.
    b. provide formally written goals for the client.
    c. be rather rigid and follow a formal plan.
    d. not be concerned about goals.

Answer Key: Testbank

1. C Factual Page 295
2. A Factual Page 296
3. B Conceptual   Page 297
4. A Conceptual   Page 297
5. B Analytical   Page 298
6. D Conceptual   Page 298
7. D Conceptual   Page 299
8. A Factual Page 302&303
9. A Factual Page na
10. B Factual Page 301
11. D Analytical   Page 305&306
12. A Conceptual   Page 295-300

Website Questions:

1. Costs and payoffs are relative. One thing that a skilled helper can help a client do when the cost-benefit ratio is unclear is to:
*   a. examine the consequences of various actions.
       b. impose the helper's values on the action decision.
       c. tell the client to have trust that things will work out.
       d. re-specify the action goal.

2. Goals such as, "I'm going to give up smoking," often fail because:
       a. smoking is a very addictive behavior.
*   b. negative goals seldom provide incentives.
       c. addictions are not under the client's control.
       d. counselors aren't needed for their accomplishment.

3. Contracting with a client to initiate action on a goal;
       a. is useful to provide initial commitment.
       b. provides a structure for action.
       c. can lead to helper ownership of the goal.
*   d. both a and b.

4. According to Albert Bandura, people tend to take action if they know that a particular behavior will lead to a desired outcome and if they
       a. have adequate outcome expectancies
*   b. reasonably sure that they can engage in the behavior
       c. are guided or directed
       d. are reinforced for starting

Answer Key: Testbank

1.   A   Factual Page 296
2.   B   Conceptual   Page 297
3.   D   Conceptual   Page 298
4.   B   Factual Page 301

Chapter 18

1. In Step III-A, the question to be asked is:
    a. "What do I want?"
*   b. "What do I need to do to get what I want?"
    c. "What resources do I have to use?"
    d. "What are my weaknesses?"

2. Step III-B is intended to be used when the client:
*   a. needs help in choosing strategies that best fit their situation.
    b. is resistant to the idea of action.
    c. needs help in generating a range of possible goals.
    d. is unable to identify "blind spots" in problem discussion.

3. Step III-C is aimed at
    a. selecting "best-fit" strategies
*   b. turning "best-fit" strategies into action
    c. brainstorming action possibilities
    d. none of the above

4. An activity is to an outcome as an outcome is to _____.
*   a. positive impact
    b. negative impact
    c. need fulfillment
    d. need identification

5. The art of identifying and choosing realistic courses of action for achieving goals is called a(n):
    a. agenda.
    b. scheme.
*   c. strategy.
    d. maneuver.

6. In order to avoid problems of ownership. when a helper must offer action suggestions to a client, the helper should:
    a. prompt a variety of possible actions and "fade."
    b. make the client principally responsible for evaluation the suggested actions.

  c. let the client choose which action to take.

*   d. all of the above.

7. Other people, models, formal programs, community assets, are all examples of:
  a. ways a helper can suggest for a client to dilute action
  responsibilities.

*   b. parts of action strategies reflecting resources in the client's life.
  c. excuses that clients commonly use for their inaction.
  d. none of the above.

8. Jules, lives on a farm in Montana miles from the nearest neighbor and has been married for eleven months, she come to a clinic seeking help for depression. Regarding developing her social support resources, a helper should
  a. encourage her to move closer to the town
  b. suggest that she join the church sodality

*   c. help her find ways to use her spouse to help her manage her problem situation
  d. help her understand that isolation, in and of itself, is not the source of her depression

9. When training a shy client in assertiveness skills, the helper is:
  a. not allowing clients to discover solutions on their own.

*   b. following Carkhuff's notion of "training as treatment."
  c. seeking a speedier end to the helping process.
  d. implementing a strategy without seeking client assent.

10. Action strategies are motivating because they:
  a. open the possibility of successful change.
  b. can be developed with a variety of sub-action steps linked to the achievement of a desired outcome.
  c. are perceived as doable by clients.

*   d. all of the above.

11. Which of the following is an inhibition to effective problem manage-ment action?

*   a. Not knowing what to do.
  b. Failure to fully explore one's childhood development.
  c. Inability to attach emotion-based motivators to action.
  d. All of the above.

Answer Key: Testbank

1.	B	Conceptual	Page 311
2.	A	Conceptual	Page 311
3.	B	Conceptual	Page 312
4.	A	Analytical	Page na
5.	C	Factual	Page 315

6.	D	Conceptual	Page na
7.	B	Factual	Page 316
8.	C	Analytical	Page na
9.	B	Factual	Page 319
10.	D	Factual	Page na
11.	A	Analytical	Page 317

Website Questions:

1. An activity is to an outcome as an outcome is to _____.
*   a. positive impact
       b. negative impact
       c. need fulfillment
       d. need identification

2. In order to avoid problems of ownership. when a helper must offer action suggestions to a client, the helper should:
       a.prompt a variety of possible actions and "fade."
       b. make the client principally responsible for evaluation the suggested actions.
       c. let the client choose which action to take.
*   d. all of the above.

3. Which of the following is an inhibition to effective problem manage-ment action?
*   a. Not knowing what to do.
       b. Failure to fully explore one's childhood development.
       c. Inability to attach emotion-based motivators to action.
       d. All of the above.

Answer Key: Testbank

1.	A	Analytical	Page na
2.	D	Conceptual	Page na
3.	A	Analytical	Page 317

Chapter 19

1. That they must be specific, substantive, realistic, and in concert with the client's values are characteristic of:
       a. therapeutic goals.
       b. goal-accomplishing strategies.
       c. problem-management investigations.
*   d. both a and b.

2. One dilemma faced by skilled helpers in devising strategies with their clients is that:
      a. helpers typically under-challenge their clients.
      b. helpers typically over-challenge their clients.
*   c. they must not over- or under-challenge clients.
      d. none of the above.

3. One technique that may be helpful with clients who are reluctant to choose a strategy even after a proper analysis of them is to:
      a. start the helping process again at Step I-B.
*   b. let them sample several of the action options.
      c. "broaden" the action strategy.
      d. increase client anxiety to precipitate a crisis.

4. To help clients assess the viability of a particular action strategy, a skilled helper would employ:
      a. the "cataclysm hypothesis"-examine the worst case scenario.
      b. a variant of the "MUM effect"-avoid being overly directive.
*   c. the "balance sheet method"-look at all sides of a strategy.
      d. "dream analysis"-cross-examine the client's hidden desires.

5. The "balance sheet" method should be utilized:
      a. with virtually every client.
      b. focuses on gains for self without considering others.
*   c. whenever it adds value to the goal-setting process.
      e. as a whole process and not used partially.

6. Like all of the strategies suggested by the skilled helper model, the balance sheet method should be used:
      a. in a rigorous and formal fashion.
      b. with virtually every client the helper sees.
      c. as one important formula in this cookbook approach to helping.
*   d. none of the above.

7. Helping is not a theoretical process, but a real life one. The skilled helper must recognize that:
      a. ideal goals and actions may not be realistic.
      b. action strategies require they be enacted by the clients in their own way.
      c. the client owns both the problem and its solutions.
*   d. all of the above.

8. When a client chooses an action strategy without considering its risk cost or chances for success, the client is:

          a. typically playing it safe.

*   b. engaging in wishful thinking.

          c. trying to avoid the worst case outcome.

          d. trading risks for chances of success.

9. When a client dilutes a well designed action strategy in the face of stress from self-challenge, the client is:

*   a. typically playing it safe.

          b. engaging in wishful thinking.

          c. trying to avoid the worst case outcome.

          d. trading risks for chances of success.

Answer Key: Testbank

1.	D	Conceptual	Page 326
2.	C	Conceptual	Page 330
3.	B	Conceptual	Page 327
4.	C	Factual	Page 328
5.	C	Conceptual	Page 328
6.	D	Analytical	Page 333
7.	D	Analytical	Page 330
8.	B	Conceptual	Page 332
9.	A	Conceptual	Page 332

Website Questions:

1. That they must be specific, substantive, realistic, and in concert with the client's values are characteristic of:

          a. therapeutic goals.

          b. goal-accomplishing strategies.

          c. problem-management investigations.

*   d. both a and b.

2. One dilemma faced by skilled helpers in devising strategies with their clients is that:

          a. helpers typically under-challenge their clients.

          b. helpers typically over-challenge their clients.

*   c. they must not over- or under-challenge clients.

          d. none of the above.

3. Like all of the strategies suggested by the skilled helper model, the balance sheet method should be used:

        a. in a rigorous and formal fashion.

        b. with virtually every client the helper sees.

        c. as one important formula in this cookbook approach to helping.

*   d. none of the above.

Answer Key: Testbank

1.	D	Conceptual	Page 326
2.	C	Conceptual	Page 330
3.	D	Analytical	Page 333

Chapter 20

1. Figuring out what needs to be done in what sequence is:

        a. Step II-B

        b. Step III-B

        c. Step II-C

*   d. Step III-C

2. A clear, objective plan permits helpers and clients to:

*   a. evaluate progress toward specific goals.

        b. better discuss problem management needs.

        c. look at possible outcomes.

        d. emphasize activities and output.

3. Formal plans offer a variety of benefits; one thing that plans CANNOT DO is:

        a. help clients uncover unanticipated obstacles.

        b. help clients search for more effective strategies.

*   c. provide a substitute for action.

        d. make clients aware of needed resources.

4. Formal action planning can help clients deal with post-decisional depression which arises from:

        a. failing to achieve goals early.

*   b. wondering if they made the right decision.

        c. regression to dependency on the helper.

        d. disabling synergistic factors.

5. An effective action plan builds goal-directed actions in such a way that:

        a. ultimate goals are achieved quickly.

*   b. subgoal achievements build toward achieving ultimate goals.

        c. simplicity is the only criterion.

d. clients expend the least effort on each subgoal action.

6. In general, an action-plan needs to have subgoals when:
* a. the goal is complex or difficult to achieve.
   b. the helper is directing client actions.
   c. the clients are adolescents or young adults.
   d. substantive goals are identified.

7. What the client needs to do, in what sequence, and over what time frame are:
   a. questions the helper and client must answer.
   b. critical issues in formulating an action-plan.
   c. questions that do not necessarily demand overly specific nswers.
* d. all of the above.

8. Exacting plans with considerable specification:
   a. are the only plans that typically work.
* b. remove flexibility and limit client self-reliance.
   c. produce serenity for most clients.
   d. emphasize the role of the helper.

9. The "constructive-change mind set"
   a. should be a part of the helping process right from the start
   b. involves creating self-perpetuating change
   c. may be formal or informal depending one the client
* d. all of the above

10. Taylor, a counselor with many years of experience, was unable to help Janice deal with her presenting problem of sexual attraction toward young children. Neither had many ideas on what to include in a plan. When faced with this type of problem, the skilled helper should
   a. refer the client to some other helper or agency
* b. see if a preexisting plan for treating such a problem could be adapted for the client
   c. use some form of systematic desensitization procedure
   d. become more challenging and confronting to the client

Answer Key: Testbank

1.	D	Factual	Page 335
2.	A	Conceptual	Page 337
3.	C	Conceptual	Page 336
4.	B	Conceptual	Page 337
5.	B	Factual	Page 338
6.	A	Factual	Page 338
7.	D	Conceptual	Page 338

8.   B   Conceptual   Page 338
9.   D   Analytical   Page 341-343
10. B   Analytical   Page 344

Website Questions:

1. A clear, objective plan permits helpers and clients to:
*   a. evaluate progress toward specific goals.
       b. better discuss problem management needs.
       c. look at possible outcomes.
       d. emphasize activities and output.

2. An effective action plan builds goal-directed actions in such a way that:
       a. ultimate goals are achieved quickly.
*   b. subgoal achievements build toward achieving ultimate goals.
       c. simplicity is the only criterion.
       d. clients expend the least effort on each subgoal action.

3. Exacting plans with considerable specification:
       a. are the only plans that typically work.
*   b. remove flexibility and limit client self-reliance.
       c. produce serenity for most clients.
       d. emphasize the role of the helper.

Answer Key: Testbank

1.   A   Conceptual   Page 337
2.   B   Factual Page 338
3.   B   Conceptual   Page 338

Chapter 21

1. Even with a well designed action plan, clients sometimes continue to resist change. In order to counteract this problem, skilled helpers should:
       a. accept that some clients will never change.
       b. employ MUM responses concerning action.
*   c. encourage consistent immediacy of action-steps-what is being done today, tomorrow, etc.
       d. return to Step I-A in order to reenergize clients about their current situation.

2. Actions taken by client early in the helping process:
       a. are usually random and fruitless.
*   b. build a momentum for more formal action later in the process.
       c. must be closely monitored in order to retain clients.

        d. none of the above.

3. Decisional self-control is evidenced by which of the following examples?
        a. Avoiding marital conflict by divorcing.
        b. Maintaining sobriety by not attending functions where alcohol is served.
        c. An overburdened worker refusing to take on a new   assignment.
   *   d. All of the above.

4. Protracted self-control is evidenced by which of the following examples?
   *   a. An alcoholic who sits with friends while they drink but avoids   drinking.
        b. Dealing with poor grades by quitting school.
        c. A chronic gambler who decides not to take a free trip to Las Vegas.
        d. All of the above

5. Protracted self-control is more _____ than decisional self-control.
   *   a. difficult
        b. rewarding
        c. tension-reducing
        d. inevitable

6. _____ is the art of adapting a plan to the immediate situation.
        a. A ratchet
        b. A strategy
        c. Logistics
   *   d. Tactics

7. John wanted to take Suomi, the most popular girl in the senior class, to the annual prom. He decided on a plan to get a car, flowers and money for the prom. He achieved all of these goals but Suomi went to the prom with her boyfriend Jeff. John
        a. acted imprudently.
        b. based his actions on only the assumption that his actions would succeed.
        c. failed to think through the relationship of his actions to the ultimate goal.
   *   d. all of the above.

8. Developing contingency plans is an important tactical move when clients:
        a. embark on any action plan.
        b. are filled with inertia.
   *   c. choose high-risk programs for critical goals.
        d. have difficulty setting goals.

9. A search for possible obstacles to implementing a plan is the essence of:
        a. an examination of facilitating forces.
   *   b. becoming aware of restraining forces.
        c. the overly-cautious approach to helping.
        d. inertia prevention.

10. One basic principle involved in initiating implementation of a plan is that:
      a. inertia overcomes entropy.
      b. entropy overcomes inertia.
*   c. action rewards should outweigh inaction rewards.
      d. apathy is to be accepted as normal.

11. Support after ending formal helping sessions can be provided by:
      a. self-help groups
      b. social support groups
      c. friends, acquaintances, and loved ones.
*   d. all of the above.

12. Clients often benefit from _____ as well as confirmatory feedback.
*   a. corrective and challenging feedback
      b. positive but false feedback
      c. judgmental feedback
      d. arbitrary feedback

13. Better client problem coping and problem management:
      a. may not lead to problem solutions.
      b. may not be sufficient to motivate a client.
      c. are a direct function of client choices.
*   d. all of the above.

14. According to Gerard Egan, inevitably, each client:
      a. must be viewed in terms of the client's needs and capabilities.
      b. calls for an adaptation of Egan's helping model.
      c. must control the outcomes of helping.
*   d. all of the above.

15. Failure to act is _____; failure to sustain action is _____ .
*   a. inertia; entropy
      b. entropy; inertia
      c. apathy; paralysis
      d. specific; non-specific

16. It is beneficial for clients to understand that an occasional slip-up or mistake in an action-plan's implementation:
      a. doesn't inevitably lead to a relapse.
      b. is a probability in every plan.
      c. justifies their relapse.
*   d. both a and b.

Answer Key: Testbank

1.	C	Conceptual	Page 352
2.	B	Conceptual	Page 351
3.	D	Analytical	Page 350
4.	A	Analytical	Page 350
5.	A	Factual	Page 350
6.	D	Factual	Page 351
7.	D	Analytical	Page na
8.	C	Factual	Page 353
9.	B	Conceptual	Page 354
10.	C	Conceptual	Page 355
11.	D	Conceptual	Page 360
12.	A	Factual	Page 360,361
13.	D	Conceptual	Page 363
14.	D	Conceptual	Page 364
15.	A	Analytical	Page 364,366
16.	D	Factual	Page 367

Website Questions:

1. Protracted self-control is more _____ than decisional self-control.
*   a. difficult
      b. rewarding
      c. tension-reducing
      d. inevitable

2. _____ is the art of adapting a plan to the immediate situation.
      a. A ratchet
      b. A strategy
      c. Logistics
*   d. Tactics

3. A search for possible obstacles to implementing a plan is the essence of:
      a. an examination of facilitating forces.
*   b. becoming aware of restraining forces.
      c. the overly-cautious approach to helping.
      d. inertia prevention.

4. According to Gerard Egan, inevitably, each client:
      a. must be viewed in terms of the client's needs and capabilities.
      b. calls for an adaptation of Egan's helping model.
      c. must control the outcomes of helping.
*   d. all of the above.

Answer Key: Testbank

1.	A	Factual	Page 350
2.	D	Factual	Page 351
3.	B	Conceptual	Page 354
4.	D	Conceptual	Page 364